HISTORY MAKERS OF HAWAII

A BIOGRAPHICAL DICTIONARY

HISTORY MAKERS OF HAWAII

· BY A. GROVE DAY ·

MUTUAL PUBLISHING
OF HONOLULU

2055 North King Street
Honolulu, Hawaii 96819

First Printing • March 1984

Library of Congress Catalog Card Number
84-60784
|
ISBN 0-935180-09-5

Design by The Art Directors
Typesetting by Innovative Media Inc.

Mutual Publishing of Honolulu
2055 N. King St.
Honolulu, Hawaii 96819

Photo Credits:
Portraits on pages 3, 10, 20, 27, 53, and 108 are used
courtesy of the Hawaiian Mission Children's Society. Those
on pages 34, 36, 43, 45, 62, 64, 92, 123, and 127 are
used courtesy of the State Archives of Hawaii. All others are
drawn from the Baker-Van Dyke collection.

Printed in Japan

OTHER BOOKS BY A. GROVE DAY

Coronado's Quest: The Discovery of the Southwestern States
The Sky Clears: Poetry of the American Indians
Rascals in Paradise (with James A. Michener)
Hawaii and Its People
Hawaii, Fiftieth Star
Hawaii: A History (with Ralph S. Kuykendall)
The Story of Australia
They Peopled the Pacific
James A. Michener
Louis Becke
Explorers of the Pacific
Coronado and the Discovery of the Southwest
Pirates of the Pacific
Adventurers of the Pacific
Jack London in the South Seas
Pacific Islands Literature: One Hundred Basic Books
V. Blasco Ibanez (with Edgar C. Knowlton)
Robert D. FitzGerald
Eleanor Dark
Books About Hawaii: Fifty Basic Authors

Editor
The Spell of the Pacific (with Carl Stroven)
The Greatest American Short Stories (with William F. Bauer)
A Hawaiian Reader (with Carl Stroven)
Best South Sea Stories (with Carl Stroven)
Jack London's Stories of Hawaii
Mark Twain's Letters from Hawaii
True Tales of the South Seas (with Carl Stroven)
South Sea Supercargo
The Spell of Hawaii (with Carl Stroven)
Melville's South Seas
Robert Louis Stevenson's Travels in Hawaii
Hawaiian Legends in English (with Amos P. Leib)
Modern Australian Prose, 1901–1975

(top) Hawaiian warriors perform a hula dance in honor of the arrival in 1816 of the Russian warship Rurik, *commanded by Otto von Kotzebue.*

(right) Thousands of Hawaiians welcome the two exploring ships of Captain James Cook in 1779 at Kealakekua Bay on the island of Hawaii, where Cook was later to meet his death in an affray on the beach.

CONTENTS

INTRODUCTION

The people of Hawaii, because of the exotic history of their islands, are more cosmopolitan than those of any other American state.

The only state to have previously been a Polynesian kingdom, and the only state completely surrounded by ocean, Hawaii from the first attracted venturesome persons from five continents. Since the earliest canoe voyagers settled in the islands more than a thousand years ago, Hawaii has truly been an international frontier. When the ships of Captain James Cook in 1779 gave to the rest of the world the news of a fascinating culture in this North Pacific archipelago, the islands became a welcome way station for warships and trading vessels, a supply base for wandering whale ships, and a barefoot refuge for escapists from Western routine. The arrival of twelve shiploads of earnest New England missionaries beginning in 1820—only a year after the collapse of the ancient worship of pagan images—brought a puritanical influence to the Polynesian paradise. An even stronger magnet for immigration was the discovery of gold in California in 1848; many an adventurer, disappointed in the diggings, followed the western star to the growing port of Honolulu. The arrival of thousands of workers from Asia began in the latter half of the nineteenth century. The roots of a number of prominent families of today may likewise be traced to that period, when the "manifest destiny" of the United States brought Hawaii more and more into the sphere of influence of that expanding country. Even before America became a nation, men of New England and Virginia were serving on the ships of Cook, and in 1898, the year of the Spanish-American War, Hawaii became an incorporated territory of the United States. The attainment of statehood in 1959 brought an even greater influx of residents from the contiguous forty-eight. The arrival of throngs of visitors—some four million of them in 1983—has increased worldwide interest in the alluring history of America's newest state and in the lives of the people who made this history.

As one who has been publishing volumes on Hawaiian history for the past thirty years, I have had to collect in my files the names and achievements of hundreds of figures from the island story. I am happy that it is now possible to publish a volume of brief biographies of more than half a thousand such personalities who have contributed to the history and lore of Hawaii. Space has also been made available for a dozen appendices of useful facts and for a bibliography of general sources of biographical information. It is true that *History Makers of Hawaii* consists mainly of facts, and that an education consists of more than the knowing of facts. However, valuable concepts and opinions can only be based on solid evidence, and the various entries herein are aimed at supplying facts in many areas.

Selection of names to be included in this volume was based originally upon a comprehensive list prepared by an informal subcommittee under the State Commission to celebrate the bicentennial of the signing of the American Declaration of Independence in 1776. Many chiefs and chiefesses of the olden time appear in these pages, some of whom might well serve as role models for young latter-day Hawaiians. Almost all the American missionaries are covered, as well as a number of missionaries from Asia. Selection of a person to be treated is usually based on his or her contribution to the history and culture of the Hawaiian Islands. Did this person have a notable effect upon the course of events? Would this name be encountered in print or conversation often enough so that the average student or other interested reader might wish to know more about the person's life and achievements?

(left) Kalanimoku and Boki are baptized into the Roman faith in 1819 aboard the visiting ship L'Uranie, *under Captain Louis Freycinet.*

Wearing masking helmets of woven fibers, Hawaiian warriors paddle a canoe in the waters of Kealakekua Bay, site of the death of Captain James Cook.

(above) Downtown Honolulu was "a hard-
looking old camp" in the pioneer days of 1826.

(right) Queen Kinau and her ladies returning
from church in 1837, during the visit of a
French warship.

x

Biographies have been chosen from the general areas of agriculture, architecture, art, business, communication, economy, education, ethnic progress, government, labor, law, language, legend, literature, medicine, military, music, ranching, recreation, religion, science, social movements, and transportation. Contributions of the various ethnic and national groups are given due consideration, and an effort has been made to include outstanding women; but no quotas are possible in selecting names, for one must face the fact that, for example, most movers and shakers in Hawaii during the nineteenth century were Hawaiian or Caucasian males.

History Makers of Hawaii may be used for ready reference and as a companion to the study of the history of Hawaii. It does not include biographies of living persons, since these may readily be found in such volumes as *Who's Who in America*, *Men and Women of Hawaii*, *Leaders of Hawaii*, and other current references. Nor does this book duplicate facts to be found in the *Atlas of Hawaii*, the *Hawaiian Dictionary*, or *Place Names of Hawaii*. It is, however, the first place to look when seeking facts about a person from the past of the islands, and often the entry will suffice for most purposes. Frequently, a volume of biography about a subject is listed at the end of the entry (usually, only the date of the first edition of such a volume is cited). If an entire book is not available, the searcher may check the section on Selected General References for additional sources.

A special feature of this biographical dictionary is the appearance in CAPITAL LETTERS of cross references to other entries. Checking such a reference elsewhere will often lead to much further information on a movement or a family. Browsing in this way is to be encouraged. It is hoped, indeed, that every reader will find something of interest on every page.

Conjectural dates in entries are followed by a question mark. All dates before 1778 in Hawaii are conjectural.

All missionary personnel who arrived in the islands with one or another of the twelve "companies" came under the auspices of the American Board of Commissioners for Foreign Missions. Unless otherwise noted, it should be assumed that these persons came under the authority of this Boston organization, so that its unwieldy name need not be frequently repeated.

Aside from the biographies of persons prominent in the history of Hawaii, this volume also contains nine appendices with much supplementary reference information. First is a collection of more that 160 "Legendary Figures of Hawaii Nei," identifying gods, demigods, heroes, and other figures from folklore. A special feature is the "Chronology of Hawaiian and United States History," which details red-letter events for almost every one of the past two hundred years; persons familiar with headline episodes in the American story can comprehend what might be going on at about the same time in the islands. Other appendices provide quick information on heads of government and names of officials both elected and appointed. In particular, reading through the parallel Chronologies will give an organized, panoramic view of the course of Hawaiian history that could be obtained in no other way, juxtaposing as it does landmark crises with cultural advances, cataclysms with athletic contests, gunfire with merry celebrations in the true spirit of island aloha.

A. G. D.

University of Hawaii, April, 1984

Queen Liliuokalani, at the dedication of Pearl Harbor, Dec. 15, 1911.

Sanford B. Dole (left), Liliuokalani, Lucius E. Pinkham (left) and Henry Berger (standing) at a meeting to elicit public support of American aid to the Allied cause in World War I.

(above) Princess Ruth, the richest woman in the islands, is attended by honored kahili bearers, Sam Parker of Parker Ranch (l.) and John Cummins.

(opposite) Two princes and a doctor: Gerrit P. Judd escorted the future Kamehameha V (l.) and the future Kamehameha IV on a tour of Europe and the United States in 1850.

The American flag asserts sovereignty over Hawaii on August 12, 1898, during annexation ceremonies before Iolani Palace.

ADAMS, ALEXANDER (1780–1870)

Born in Forfarshire, Scotland, Adams went to sea at the age of twelve and served in the Royal Navy until 1810, when he arrived in Hawaii on the American ship *Albatross*. He took up residence ashore and through the good offices of John YOUNG was placed in command of the small collection of vessels owned by Kamehameha I. Adams sailed the king and crew of the brig *Kaahumanu* to Kauai in 1816 to expel the Russian filibusters under Georg Anton SCHEFFER. Adams is supposed to have inspired the design of the present Hawaiian flag, putting the Union Jack in the upper corner. On a voyage to China in 1817 with a cargo of sandalwood, Adams was refused entrance to the harbor of Macao because the colors were not recognized.

Along with Young, Adams advised Kamehameha II to allow the American missionaries to remain in the kingdom. When that monarch left for England in 1823, Adams was asked to act as pilot for the port of Honolulu, a post he held for nearly thirty years. He then retired to his estate of more than two thousand acres granted to him by Kamehameha I in Kalihi, Oahu. Adams married three times, twice to daughters of John Harbottle, harbor pilot; the sisters had been reared at the court by Queen KAAHUMANU.

ADAMS, HENRY (1838–1918)

A member of the famed Adams family of New England, Henry was a historian and traveler. In company with painter John LA FARGE, Adams toured the Pacific in 1890. He rode around Oahu, sailed to the Big Island, visited the volcano district, and had an audience with Kalakaua. See *Letters of Henry Adams, 1858-1891*, ed. W. C. Ford (Boston and New York: Houghton, Mifflin, 1930).

ADAMS, JOHN. See KUAKINI.

ADAMS, ROMANZO (1868–1942)

Born in Bloomingdale, Wisconsin, Adams attended the University of Michigan and Western College, Toledo, Ohio, and obtained a doctorate at the University of Chicago in 1904. He was professor of economics and sociology at the University of Hawaii from 1920 until he retired as head of the Department of Sociology in 1935. Adams was author of several books on social problems in the islands, such as *The Peoples of Hawaii* (Honolulu: Institute of Pacific Relations, 1933).

AFONG, CHUN (1825–1906)

The founder of a large Honolulu family arrived in that city from China in 1849 to work in his uncle's store. He went into business for himself and in spite of adversity set up a shop, Afong & Ahchuck, that sold brocades and fine silks. After being naturalized as a Hawaiian subject he married his Hawaiian-Caucasian wife, Julia Hope Fayerweather, the same year. The house he built for her was a showplace, with a garden that held the first lichee tree planted in the islands.

Afong operated a ship between Hawaii and China and was a partner in sugar and coffee plantations. He helped Kalakaua, his wife's foster brother, to be elected king and encouraged a reciprocity treaty between Hawaii and the United States. He was made a noble of the kingdom in 1879, but resigned in order to serve as commercial agent for Imperial China the following year. After the death of his first-born son in 1889 he sold almost all his wide holdings and sailed for China, leaving his friend Samuel M. DAMON as administrator of his estate for the benefit of his wife and many offspring. Afong remained in China for the rest of his life and handled his extensive business interests without returning to Hawaii.

He fathered more than a dozen children, mainly daughters, for whom he often arranged comfortable marriages. Afong inspired a well-known story, "Chun Ah Chun," by Jack LONDON, and a musical play, "Thirteen Daughters," by Eaton Magoon.

AGEE, HAMILTON POPE (1884–1942)

Born in Memphis, Tennessee, Agee obtained a bachelor's degree from Louisiana State University in 1904. He married Fannie Heaslip Lea, a fiction writer, in New Orleans in 1911. Agee began his career as a sugar technologist in Cuban and Puerto Rican mills before serving as assistant director from 1909 to 1911 at the Louisiana Sugar Experiment Station. He began a career at the Hawaiian Sugar Planters' Association Experiment Station in 1911 and was a director from 1913 to 1935. He was also a consultant for Castle & Cooke and the Hawaiian Pineapple Co. Agee was prominent in promoting the technical training of young men entering the sugar industry.

AI, CHUNG KUN (1865–1961)

Chung Kun Ai was born in Saisan, Kwantung Province, China, and was brought to Hawaii at an early age. He was educated at Iolani College in Honolulu and began a merchandising career in 1883 when he opened a drygoods store and tailoring shop. He became a clerk in 1887 in the store of James Isaac DOWSETT but in 1898 opened an importing business. He also organized a company to bore wells for the irrigation of sugar and pineapple plantations. With his associates he founded City Mill Co. He entered the business of pineapple canning as president of the Honolulu Fruit Co.

Ai was active in a number of other enterprises and was president of the Chinese Hospital and the Chinese United Society. He was founder of

1

the Chung Kun Ai Foundation, organized to promote Christian missions and churches. He was recipient of the Order of the Splintered Paddle from the Honolulu Chamber of Commerce. He married Seu Shee in Honolulu in 1895 and they had ten children. See his *My Seventy-nine Years in Hawaii* (Hong Kong: Cosmorama Pictorial Publishers, 1960).

ALAPAINUI (–1754?)

Son of Kauauanuia Mahi and Kalanikauleleaiwinui, he was called in full ALAPAINUI A KAUAUA to distinguish him from another chief named Alapai. Ruler of the island of Hawaii, he led expeditions to fight against the chief of Maui and Molokai, as well as Oahu (his mother was related to the chief of this island). After his defeat by KALANIOPUU in a last battle, Alapai retired to Kawaihae and there died, leaving the rulership of Hawaii to his son Keaweopala.

ALBERT, PRINCE OF HAWAII (1858–1862)

Albert Edward Kauikeaouli Leiopapa a Kamehameha was born on May 20, 1858, son of KAMEHAMEHA IV and EMMA. The birth of an heir to the throne was an occasion for great celebration. With the approval of the privy council he was granted the title of His Royal Highness the Prince of Hawaii (Ka Haku o Hawaii). He was officially named the heir of his father in 1859.

The little prince lived happily with his parents for four years, but then was stricken by a fatal illness. The

royal pair vainly hoped for the arrival of the Rev. T. N. STALEY from England to christen the child; Queen Victoria had consented to be named as his godmother. Ka Haku died on August 27, 1862. Previously he had been christened under the ritual of the Church of England by the Protestant pastor of Kawaiahao Church.

ALENCASTRE, STEPHEN (1876–1940)

Born in Madeira, Portugal, son of a couple that emigrated to Hawaii in 1882, the future bishop attended St. Louis College in Honolulu and in 1895 continued his studies at the University of Louvain in Belgium. Returning to the islands, to serve a parish in Wailuku, Maui, Alencastre was ordained in 1902 in the Cathedral of Our Lady of Peace in Honolulu. He helped to raise funds to build the Church of the Sacred Heart on Wilder Avenue and served there for a dozen years. In recognition of his contributions to the Catholic Church, at his consecration in 1924 he was named Bishop of the See of Arabissus and Vicar Apostolic of the islands. He was awarded the title of Officer of the Royal Crown of Belgium in 1940.

ALEXANDER LIHOLIHO. See KAMEHAMEHA IV.

ALEXANDER, SAMUEL THOMAS (1836–1904)

Third son of William Patterson ALEXANDER and brother of William De Witt ALEXANDER, Samuel was born at Waioli, Kauai. He was educated at Punahou School, the normal school at Westfield, Massachusetts, and Williams College. He married Martha Eliza Cooke, daughter of Amos Starr COOKE, in 1864; they were to have five children. In 1863 he began his career as a sugar planter by becoming manager of Waihee Plantation, Maui. Then, in partnership with his brother-in-law Henry Perrine BALDWIN—a connection recalled by the international conglomerate of Alexander & Baldwin today— Alexander started the Haiku Sugar Co. on Maui in 1869.

Early Hawaiians had irrigated their fields on a small scale, but sugar cultivation required a large supply of water. The task of constructing the Hamakua-Haiku Ditch began in 1876. It extended seventeen miles through mountainous and heavily wooded country, but was finished at the end of a year.

The associates expanded in 1894 to form a new firm in San Francisco under the name of Alexander & Baldwin, for the purpose of conducting a general commercial business, and in 1897 a branch was established in Honolulu. The firm was incorporated in 1900 as Alexander & Baldwin, Ltd., with Baldwin as president. At that time Alexander was living in Oakland, California, having left Hawaii in 1883 to improve his health. However, in his later years he spent much time in world travel. He died far from his native islands, meeting with a fatal accident at Victoria Falls in East Africa.

2

ALEXANDER, WILLIAM DE WITT (1833–1913)

Born in Honolulu, eldest son of William Patterson ALEXANDER, William graduated from Yale University in 1855 and two years later returned to his birthplace as professor of Greek at Punahou School. He continued as professor for six years, became president for seven years, and then headed the Bureau of Government Survey for almost thirty years. He married Abigail Charlotte Baldwin, daughter of the Reverend Dwight BALDWIN, in 1860; the couple had three sons and three daughters. He was a member of the privy council under Kalakaua and Liliuokalani and a distinguished geographer and historian. As surveyor-general of the Territory of Hawaii, he assisted the geodetic survey made by the United States. His books include an early school text, *A Brief History of the Hawaiian People* (New York: American Book Co., 1891) and *The Later Years of the Hawaiian Monarchy and the Revolution of 1893* (Honolulu: Gazette Co., 1896).

ALEXANDER, WILLIAM PATTERSON (1805–1884)

Born in Paris, Kentucky, Alexander was educated at Centre College of Kentucky and Princeton Theological Seminary, and was ordained a few weeks before leaving with members of the Fifth Company that arrived in Honolulu in May, 1832. A month previous to sailing, he married Mary Ann McKinney; and the couple had nine children.

After an unsuccessful attempt to establish a mission station in the Marquesas group, Alexander was assigned to Waioli, Kauai (1834–1843), and to Lahainaluna Seminary (1843–1856). For health reasons he left to manage Ulupalakua Ranch on Maui but continued unpaid church work and taught at Lahainaluna on Saturdays to educate his children. He also acted as pastor of the church at Wailuku, where in 1863 he founded the Theological School. He continued to be active in church work until his death, long after Hawaii had ceased in 1863 to be a field for American missionary efforts. Alexander was a busy translator of tracts and texts. Mrs. Alexander lived in the islands for fifty-one years and was a devoted teacher and accomplished singer, as well as the mother of a family still flourishing in Hawaii. Among the sons were Samuel Thomas ALEXANDER and William De Witt ALEXANDER. See the biography by Mary C. Alexander, *William Patterson Alexander in Kentucky, the Marquesas, and Hawaii* (Honolulu: privately printed, 1934).

ALLEN, ANTHONY (–1835)

Formerly a black slave in Schenectady, New York, Allen arrived in Hawaii in 1810. He married a Hawaiian girl, acquired land and livestock, and became one of the most prosperous foreign residents on Oahu during the next quarter of a century. When the first American missionaries arrived in 1820 he prepared a feast to welcome them, and continued his aid by supplying vegetables and fruit. He operated a farm on the plain toward Waikiki in association with HEWAHEWA, ran a small boardinghouse for seamen, and sold goat's milk in the town.

ALLEN, ELISHA HUNT (1804–1883)

As American consul in Honolulu, Allen was asked to go to Washington in 1851 to discuss with Secretary of State Daniel Webster the possibility of annexation of Hawaii by the United States. In 1853 he was appointed minister of finance in the king's cabinet, and in January, 1854, he notified David L. GREGG, United States commissioner, that although he was in favor of annexation he feared current efforts might result in revolution. The death of Kamehameha III made the discussion moot for many years. In 1877 Allen became the first Hawaiian minister to the United States.

ALLEN, RILEY HARRIS (1884–1966)

Born in Colorado City, Texas, Allen attended the University of Wisconsin and received a bachelor's degree from the University of Chicago in 1905. He màrried Suzanne McArdle in 1910. Having acted as a reporter for the Honolulu *Evening Bulletin* for a year, he left a Seattle newspaper four years later to become city editor of the *Bulletin* in 1910 and was named editor of the *Star-Bulletin* when the *Hawaiian Star* and *Evening Bulletin* combined in 1912. Allen served with the American Red Cross in Siberia during World War I, and returned to the editorship of the *Star-Bulletin* in 1921. He was active in many community affairs and was a champion of statehood for Hawaii for thirty-five years. For years he was the only non-Chinese active member of the Hawaii Chinese Civic Association. He was given an honorary degree by Chaminade College in 1962, the Korean cultural medal the same year, and the Liberty Bell Award in 1966, the year of his death.

ALLYN, EDNA (1861–1927)

Born in Hiram, Ohio, Edna Allyn attended Hiram College and then taught school for many years. She attended the Western Reserve Library School and took a master's degree at Columbia University. She came to the islands and in 1907 was appointed librarian of the Honolulu Library and Reading Room, as well as of the Hawaiian Historical Society Library housed in the same building. She helped to develop the old system into the Library of Hawaii, dating from 1913. She expanded the city service into a territory-wide organization and held the title of first Librarian of Hawaii. She gave much of her attention to the needs of child readers, and the children's wing of the downtown branch was named for her in 1929.

ANA, KEONI. See YOUNG, JOHN II.

ANDREWS, CLAUDIUS BUCHANAN (1817–1877)

Born in Kinsman, Ohio, Andrews graduated from Western Reserve College in 1840 and Lane Seminary, Ohio, in 1843. He was unmarried when he arrived with the Eleventh Company of American missionaries in 1844 and was stationed first at Kaluaaha from 1844 to 1848; he served at Lahainaluna Seminary from 1848 to 1849. On a visit to the United States in 1849–1851 he married Anne Seward Gilson. The couple were stationed at Kaluaaha from 1852 to 1856 and at Lahainaluna from 1856 to 1860, when Andrews resigned from the mission and moved to Makawao in search of a better climate for his wife's health. In 1861 he purchased a piece of land above the village, where he founded the East Maui Female Seminary, later to become Maunaolu Seminary. Mrs. Andrews died in 1862 and in accordance with her wish he married her sister, Samantha Washburn Gilson, in 1863. Andrews spent the years at Makawao and Lahainaluna until 1876, when the couple made a visit to the United States. He died at sea on his way back to Honolulu. Andrews and his first wife had seven children.

ANDREWS, HARRIET COUSENS (1875–1963)

Born in Chicago, Harriet Cousens grew up in Maine. She attended Emerson College in Boston and then taught at Ithaca High School in New York State. She married Cornell professor Arthur L. Andrews in 1903 and came with him in 1910 when he accepted a post in the Department of English at the College of Hawaii. He later became head of the department and dean of the College of Arts and Sciences at the University, which was organized in 1920. Mrs. Andrews was quite active during World War I in several organizations. Among her many other community services was the first presidency of the League of Women Voters of Hawaii, president of the Women's Society of Central Union Church, president of the University of Hawaii Women's Faculty Club, and president of the YWCA of Honolulu. She also served as a member of the Hawaii Council of the Institute of Pacific Relations and as local acting chairman of the first Pan-Pacific Union Women's Conference.

ANDREWS, LORRIN (1795–1868)

A graduate of Princeton Theological Seminary, Andrews arrived with his wife, Mary Ann Wilson Andrews, in 1827. They were stationed at Lahaina, Maui, where in 1831 he was the first head of Lahainaluna Seminary, set up to train young men to be ministers. He resigned as a missionary in 1842 because he objected that the Boston headquarters received funds from some slave states. To earn a living, he was allowed to take charge of the printing and binding office at Lahainaluna, where he taught the students how to print from copper plates. Andrews compiled a Hawaiian vocabulary in 1836, a grammar of the language in 1854, and a dictionary in 1865. Instruction at the seminary was in Hawaiian, and Andrews translated into that language some fifteen books used as texts.

Andrews was appointed judge of the court of Oahu in 1845 and later served the government as secretary of the privy council and first associate justice of the Supreme Court. He and his wife had seven children.

ANDREWS, SETH LATHROP (1809–1893)

Born in Putney, Vermont, Andrews graduated from Dartmouth College in 1831, received a medical degree from the Fairfield Medical College, practised in New York, and then volunteered for missionary service. He married Parnelly Pierce before sailing for Hawaii with the Eighth Company. Arriving in 1837, the couple were assigned to Kailua, Hawaii. Andrews became superintendent of a Sunday school along with his practice of medicine, while his wife taught a school of some fifty pupils.

By 1846 Andrews was the sole physician on the Big Island and had to attend eleven mission stations and a population of more than sixty thousand Hawaiians. In 1848 he performed one of the first autopsies in the Pacific region. The strain of his work weakened his health and he became bedridden. After the loss of a son as well as his wife, he returned to the United States in 1849. Improved in health, he married again and in later years practised medicine in Romeo, Michigan. By his first wife Andrews had four children.

APAKA, ALFRED AHOLO (1919–1960)

Born in Honolulu, Apaka graduated from Roosevelt High School. He had an untrained but attractive voice and began his career by singing with a band at the Royal Hawaiian Hotel. He popularized Hawaiian songs on the mainland and began recording in 1950. He appeared on the Bob Hope and Bing Crosby shows before opening as a vocalist at the Kaiser Hawaiian Village in 1955. For many adults, a visit to Hawaii included listening to Apaka's romantic ballads. His untimely death was widely mourned and he was buried with a microphone in his hands. Apaka married Edna Blake in 1945 and the couple had one son.

ARAGO, JACQUES (1790–1855)

Artist on the French expedition of Louis FREYCINET, Arago wrote an account of Hawaii described by Ralph S. Kuykendall as "somewhat journalistic and cynical" — *Promenade autour du monde* (Paris: Leblanc, 1822; translated as *Narrative of a Voyage Around the World* (London: Treuttel & Wurtz, 1823; New York: Da Capo, 1971). An untranslated volume by Arago is *Souvenirs d' un aveugle; voyage autour du monde* (Paris: Gayet et Lebrun, 1838, 1840). Both works are illustrated by early drawings of Hawaiian life.

ARMAND, ABRAHAM
See MAIGRET.

ARMSTRONG, RICHARD (1805–1860)

Born in Pennsylvania, after three years at Princeton Theological Seminary Armstrong arrived in Hawaii with the Fifth Company, along with his wife Clarissa Chapman Armstrong, in 1832. He was stationed for a year at the mission in the Marquesas Islands and later built a church on Maui. He was pastor of Kawaiahao Church in Honolulu from 1840 to 1848. In that year he left the mission to become minister of public instruction after the death of William RICHARDS. Armstrong was to serve the government for the remainder of his life. He was a member of the privy council and the House of Nobles, and acted as the royal chaplain. He aided efforts to attain Hawaiian independence. He set up the Board of Education under the kingdom in 1855 and was president until his death. The Armstrongs had ten children. A son, Samuel Chapman Armstrong (1839–1929), became a Union general in the American Civil War and was founder of Hampton Institute in Virginia in 1868.

ARNOLD, CHARLES N. (1880–1929)

Born at Ookala, North Hilo, Hawaii, Arnold was educated at city schools in Honolulu. He held several jobs before joining the Honolulu Plantation Co. at Aiea, where he retired as plantation purchaser and warehouse manager after twenty-seven years with the firm. Except for a two-year period, Arnold was a member of the Honolulu Board of Supervisors from 1911 until he was elected mayor of the city in 1926. He had also served one term in the territorial senate. He was defeated for re-election in 1928, a year before his death, by John H. WILSON.

ARNOLD, HARRY LOREN, Sr. (1887–1971)

Born at Owosso, Michigan, Arnold graduated from the University of Michigan Medical School in 1911 and practised at his native town for five years. He accepted a commission in the Army Medical Corps from 1917 to 1921 but decided not to remain in the service after a visit to Hawaii. In Honolulu he was a founding partner in 1921 of the Straub Clinic, working in internal medicine. He was a leader in medical activities until his retirement in 1967, having served not only at Straub but also at Queen's Hospital, from 1939 to 1957. He published articles on his subject and was also the author of the authoritative *Poisonous Plants of Hawaii* (Honolulu: Tongg, 1944).

ASHFORD, MARGUERITE KAMEHAKALANI (1891–1970)

Born in Honolulu, daughter of jurist Clarence W. Ashford, Marguerite decided to follow the law. She graduated from Punahou School and the University of California and obtained a J. D. degree from the University of Michigan Law School in 1915. She was admitted to the bar the following year. She was deputy attorney general for the Hawaii Legislature, 1934–53, delegate to the Constitutional Convention of 1950, and commissioner of public lands in the cabinet of Governor Samuel Wilder KING from 1952 to 1955. She retired from active practice in 1946 and became a district judge on the island of Molokai.

ATHERTON, JOSEPH BALLARD (1837–1903)

Atherton was born and educated in Boston. One of his schoolmates who became a lifelong friend was Peter Cushman JONES. After leaving high school Atherton worked for a commission house before sailing to Hawaii in search of improved health. He was taken into the family of Samuel Northrup CASTLE and held a position in the general store of Castle & Cooke. In 1865 he became junior partner in the firm and married Juliette Montague COOKE. His father-in-law retired from active business in the late 1860s, leaving his son Joseph P. Cooke, along with Atherton, in charge under the direction of Castle. When Castle died in 1894, Atherton became the senior member of the old firm, which in that year was incorporated as Castle & Cooke, Ltd., and was elected president, a post he held until his death.

Early in the 1860s the firm became active in the development of the sugar industry and Atherton was instrumental in representing such groups as the Paia Plantation and the Haiku Sugar Co., both on the island of Maui. He was one of those incorporating the Ewa Plantation Co. on Oahu and in 1898, in association with B. F. DILLINGHAM and others, he organized the Waialua Agricultural Co. Atherton was director of half a dozen other business enterprises and was a trustee and active member for more than twenty years of the Hawaiian Sugar Planters' Association. He was a leader in church work and was one of the founders of the YMCA in Hawaii. He was also among the first in the territory to purchase an automobile, a small electric car. The Athertons had six children.

ATKINSON, ALATAU TAMCHIBOULAC (1848–1906)

The given names of Atkinson derive from his birth on the Kirgiz steppes of Siberia, when his English parents were making an exploration trip. "Alatau" comes from the mountains of the region and his second name was that of a spring at the base of the Alatau range. Atkinson received his education from Rugby School in England and he became a master at Durham College. He married Annie Elizabeth Humble at Newcastle and the pair arrived in Hawaii in 1868.

Atkinson took charge of St. Alban's College, an Episcopal school under Bishop T. N. STALEY, and later became principal of the old Fort Street School. In 1881 Atkinson became editor of the *Hawaiian Gazette* and helped greatly to shape public opinion. He was made inspector general of public schools in 1887 and helped both under the monarchy and the Republic to fashion a competent school system. When Hawaii was annexed by the United States in 1898, he was put in charge of the census. He also served in the House of Representatives that year. At the time of his death, he was survived by seven children, one of whom married Samuel G. WILDER.

BACHELOT, JOHN ALEXIUS AUGUSTINE. See MAIGRET.

BAILEY, EDWARD (1814–1903)

Born in Holden, Massachusetts, Bailey studied languages at Amherst College and married Caroline Hubbard in 1836 before sailing a month later with the Eighth Company of American missionaries. The couple were stationed at Kohala, 1837; Lahainaluna, 1839; and Wailuku Female Seminary, 1840–1848. Bailey was a man of many talents as healer, architect, sugar planter and miller, bridge builder, musician, poet, and artist, as well as teacher. The Baileys left the mission in 1850 but for many years he aided in creating and maintaining the Maunaolu Girls' School at Makawao. The couple moved to California in 1885, where Bailey died, the last male survivor of the workers sent by the Boston mission between 1820 and 1850. The Baileys had five children.

BAKER, RAY JEROME (1880–1972)
Born in Rockford, Illinois, Baker was educated in St. Paul, Minnesota. He learned the art of photography in Montana and for several years ran a photographic studio at Eureka, California, where he married Edith Frost in 1906. On a delayed honeymoon the couple visited Hawaii in 1908 and returned to live in Honolulu in 1910. Baker not only photographed almost every street, building, and corner in that city but also traveled to some sixty countries to take pictures. He, moreover, purchased many nineteenth-century photographs of the islands to add to his collection. In 1919 and 1920 he gave a slide lecture on Hawaii on the Chautauqua Circuit around the Midwest. Baker also produced the first two-reel feature film for the Hawaii Tourist Bureau. He experimented with timed photographs of the blooming of flowers, recording development over a period of twenty-four hours in thirty seconds on the screen.

Baker was an unashamed liberal and a member of a number of local societies. He gave to the Bernice P. Bishop Museum his own collection of some twenty thousand pictures, as well as his collection of other photographs and his camera equipment. In 1976 the Ray Jerome Baker Room was opened in the Museum with an inventory of some 360,000 images of Hawaii, some of them dating back to 1845. Baker retired from active work in 1959 and died in Honolulu just one month short of his ninety-second birthday. See his *Odyssey of a Cameraman* (N.p., 1956?).

BALDWIN, DWIGHT (1798–1886)
Born in Durham, Connecticut, Baldwin studied for two years at Williams College; he graduated from Yale College in 1821 and from Auburn Theological Seminary in 1829. He attended a course of medical lectures at Harvard University but settled for a master of science degree. He was ordained at Utica, New York, in 1830 and married Charlotte Fowler before sailing with the Fourth Company of American missionaries.

The couple arrived in Honolulu in 1831 and were stationed the following year at Waimea, Hawaii; from 1835 to 1870 they served at Lahaina, Maui. During all these years Baldwin was not only a pastor but a busy physician; he was belatedly granted an honorary medical diploma by Dartmouth College in 1859. He began a seaman's chapel at Lahaina. He also translated into Hawaiian a tract on temperance and the first five books of the Bible for a new edition of the New Testament. The couple had eight children, including Henry Perrine BALDWIN. See Mary Charlotte Alexander, *Dr. Baldwin of Lahaina* (Berkeley, Calif.: privately printed, 1953).

BALDWIN, HARRY ALEXANDER (1871–1946)
Harry, eldest son of Henry Perrine BALDWIN, was born at Paliuli, Maui. He was educated in the grammar schools of San Francisco, at Punahou School in Honolulu, at Phillips Andover Academy in Massachusetts, and at Massachusetts Institute of Technology. He returned to begin work as a timekeeper at the Haiku Sugar Co. in 1896; two years later he was appointed manager and served until 1904, when he became head of several other plantations. He served in the territorial senate for five sessions, and filled the unexpired term of Prince KALANIANAOLE after the death of that delegate to Congress. Baldwin married Ethel Frances Smith, daughter of William Owen Smith, in 1897 and the couple had one daughter.

BALDWIN, HENRY PERRINE (1842–1911)

The most successful sugar planter in the islands was born at Lahaina, Maui, fourth son of the Rev. Dwight BALDWIN. After attending Punahou School, the son hoped to study for a medical degree at Williams College, but began managing a rice plantation in Hawaii and then turned to the cultivation of sugar cane. He worked first for his brother, Dwight Baldwin Jr., at Lahaina, and then became head of Waihee Plantation under the management of Samuel T. ALEXANDER, soon to become his brother-in-law and business partner. Baldwin in 1870 married Emily Whitney Alexander and the couple were to have eight children, including Harry A. BALDWIN.

Alexander and Baldwin began in 1876 the year-long construction of the Hamakua-Haiku irrigation ditch, the first major project of its kind. When putting pipes down across the gorge of Maliko, the workers refused to descend on ropes. Although Baldwin had lost one arm in a mill accident, he daily worked his way down a rope and heartened the men to follow.

The success of this project enabled the founding of the firm of Alexander & Baldwin, still a prominent corporation in the islands. When Alexander and his family moved to California in 1883, Baldwin assumed full direction of affairs in Hawaii and for almost thirty years thereafter was a leading businessman. The firm in 1889 established the Hawaiian Sugar Co. on Kauai, and in 1902 acquired control of the Hawaiian Commercial & Sugar Co. of Puunene, Maui, formerly owned by Claus SPRECKELS. During its early years the firm operated a fleet of sailing vessels between Hawaii and the mainland; these were later replaced by steamers of the American-Hawaiian Line and still later by freighters of the Matson Navigation Co.; Matson is still a subsidiary of A&B.

Business affairs did not keep Baldwin from serving in the legislature from 1887 to 1903, and he also devoted a large share of his income to good works in the communty. The Baldwin family has been especially prominent on the island of Maui up to the present. See Arthur Douglas Baldwin, *A Memoir of Henry Perrine Baldwin, 1842 to 1911* (Cleveland: privately printed, 1915).

BARANOV, ALEKSANDER ANDREYEVICH (1747–1819)

As head of the Russian-American Co., founded at Sitka, Alaska, in 1799, Baranov was virtually head of Russian activities in Northwestern America until 1817. He attempted to trade with Hawaii and was the main supporter of the filibustering efforts of Georg Anton SCHEFFER.

BARBER, HENRY

Barber, one of the first captains to trade between the Northwest Coast of America and other parts of the Pacific, first arrived in Hawaii in 1796. Departing on Hallowe'en with a cargo of sea-otter skins obtained on the Northwest Coast of America, he wrecked his vessel *Arthur* on the peninsula near Honolulu that is still called Barbers Point. Six of the crew were lost. John YOUNG salvaged the cargo, but when, after various adventures in Alaska, Barber returned to Honolulu in December, 1802, to recover his cargo, he heard that Kamehameha had taken the ten cannon from the vessel and mounted them in front of his house. When Barber asked for their return, the ruler refused and instead demanded that Barber hand over two kegs of gunpowder needed in the wars. The captain was outbargained, and he had to comply to provision his ship, *Myrtle*, for the voyage to Sitka.

BARKLEY, CHARLES WILLIAM

Master of *Imperial Eagle*, a fur-trading British ship flying Austrian colors, Barkley arrived in Hawaii in 1787 on the way to Canton. John MACKAY remained in the islands. Mrs. Frances Hornsby Trevor Barkley was probably the first European woman to visit Hawaii. The ship took away the first Hawaiian known to sail for foreign lands—a woman hired to be Mrs. Barkley's maid. Her name was listed as "Wynee"; possibly this was an attempt to spell the Hawaiian word wahine, or woman.

BARTIMEUS (BATIMEA, PUAAIKI) (1785–1843)

First named Puaaiki or "little pig," this Hawaiian was blinded at an early age, but became a dancer at the court of Kamehameha I. Because of his piety, he was the second Hawaiian to receive baptism by the American missionaries (the first was the queen mother, KEOPUOLANI). Given the biblical name of Bartimeus, the eloquent blind man was baptized on July 10, 1825, at Lahaina, Maui, having studied with the Rev. William RICHARDS and the Rev. Charles S. STEWART. Bartimeus moved to Hilo in 1829 and then to Wailuku, Maui, where he remained from 1834 until his death. He became a deacon in 1839 and in 1842 the first formally licensed native preacher. In spite of his blindness and ungainly figure he was able to attract many converts. See Hiram Bingham, *Bartimeus, of the Sandwich Islands* (New York: American Tract Society, 1851).

BARTLETT, CHARLES WILLIAM (1860–1940)

The future artist was born in Bridport, Dorsetshire, England. He found his love of art was so strong that he became a student at the Royal Academy in London, and continued for three years in Paris. He developed a special watercolor method that brought him wide recognition in Europe. He went to India in 1913 and spent several years there and in China and Japan. During 1916 he learned the process of Japanese printing by wood blocks; creating Oriental scenes by this method, along with etchings made after he took up residence in Hawaii in 1917, made him one of the best known artists in the islands.

BATES, GEORGE WASHINGTON

Bates spent many months touring the Hawaiian Islands in 1853, when it seemed possible that Hawaii would be annexed by the United States. A proud American expansionist, he traveled around most of the settled regions and his book, *Sandwich Island Notes* (New York: Harper, 1854), published under the pen name of "A Häolé," gives a good account of the life of this time.

BEAUMONT, JOHN HERBERT (1894–1957)

Born in Wheeling, West Virginia, Beaumont obtained a bachelor's degree at the University of West Virginia in 1917. He came to Hawaii in 1936 after teaching at the University of Maryland. He was director of the Hawaii Agricultural Experiment Station from 1939 to 1950 and senior horticulturist from 1950 until his death. He was a leader in the development of such crops as coffee, passion fruit, and papaya, and helped devise means to control the oriental fruit fly. During a Fulbright year at the University of Queensland, Australia, in 1952, he obtained valuable information about the macadamia tree, native to that region, which became an important crop in Hawaii. Beaumont was a member of a number of scientific societies.

BECKLEY, EMMA K. METCALF (Mrs. MOSES NAKUINA) (1847–1929)

The future first woman judge of the Territory of Hawaii was the daughter of Theophilus Metcalf, a sugar planter and government surveyor, and the chiefess Kaili Kapuolono. Emma was educated at Sacred Hearts Academy, Punahou School, and Mills Seminary in Oakland, California. She first married Frederick William K. Beckley, descended from George Beckley, an Englishman who was commandant of the fort begun by the Russians in Honolulu in 1816. Emma's husband was chamberlain under King Kalakaua and was later governor of the island of Kauai. She had intimate friends among royalty, and under the monarchy became judge of the Court of Records and commissioner of private ways and water rights. She served in this post for eighteen years, continuing after annexation. During the 1880s and 1890s she was in charge of the government library and was the first curator of the Hawaiian National Museum, later incorporated within the Bernice P. Bishop Museum. Emma's second husband was the Rev. Moses Nakuina, a deputy registrar of conveyances. Emma published a number of articles on Hawaiiana both as Emma Beckley and as Emma Nakuina. Her son Frederick William Beckley, born in 1874, became an educator and historian.

BECKWITH, MARTHA WARREN (1871–1959)

Martha Beckwith, who spent her childhood in Hawaii with her parents, was born in Massachusetts. She was the grandniece of Lucy Goodale THURSTON. For many years she was a professor of folklore at Vassar College. She worked with Mary Kawena Pukui and others, and became a leading authority on the oral Polynesian narratives of the islands. Beckwith edited *The Kumulipo: A Hawaiian Creation Chant* (Chicago: University of Chicago Press, 1951) and wrote a lengthy study of *Hawaiian Mythology* (New Haven: Yale University Press, 1940). She translated the Laieikawai novel of S. N. HALEOLE (Washington: Bureau of American Ethnology, 1919) and *Traditions of Hawaii* by KEPELINO (Honolulu: Bernice P. Bishop Museum, 1932).

BERGER, HENRY (1844–1929)

The future leader of the Royal Hawaiian Band was born in Berlin. He joined the Prussian Army as an assistant musician in 1861, saw service in several wars, and in 1867 attended the Conservatory of Music in Berlin to study for bandmaster. At the request of Kamehameha V, Berger was selected by Wilhelm I of Germany to be sent to Hawaii to serve as bandmaster for Kamehameha V.

Berger gave his first public concert in Honolulu on June 11, 1872, and thereafter led the band for forty-three years. He took the group on several mainland tours and did much to popularize Hawaiian music. Between 1872 and 1900 the band led by Berger gave almost ten thousand concerts. Berger helped LILIUOKALANI to compose "Aloha Oe" and himself wrote the national anthem, "Hawaii Ponoi." He also acted as organist at Kawaiahao Church. In 1899 Berger married Rose Clarke of New Zealand and they had one daughter. Berger retired in 1916, having served as band leader under Kalakaua, Liliuokalani, the Republic, and the Territory. The Royal Hawaiian Band that Berger founded still performs for the public today.

BERNICE. See BISHOP, BERNICE PAUAHI.

BIGGERS, EARL DERR (1884–1933)

Biggers graduated from Harvard in 1907, worked in newspaper and advertising offices, and wrote plays and novels as well. He visited Hawaii in 1919, and six years later the first of his mystery novels appeared dealing with the deductions of Charlie Chan, supposed to be modeled on Chang Apana, a celebrated and picturesque member of the Honolulu Police Department. It was entitled *The House without a Key* (Indianapolis: Bobbs-Merrill, 1925). In the book, the "house" is the beach residence of the murderee, where people could come and go in the days when burglary was uncommon in Waikiki. The name was later attached to a portion of an inn which became part of the Halekulani Hotel. Biggers went on to publish five more volumes in which Charlie Chan was the detective hero. Films based on this character still appear on late night television shows.

BILGER, LEONORA NEUFFER (1893–1975)

Born in Cincinnati, Leonora Neuffer received three degrees, including the Ph. D. in 1916, from the University of Cincinnati, and also studied at Cambridge University in England. After teaching at Sweet Briar College, Virginia, and at her alma mater, she arrived at the University of Hawaii in 1929, where her future husband, Earl M. Bilger (1898–1964), was also a professor of chemistry. Leonora Bilger acted as chairman of the Department of Chemistry and dean of women. She was the first woman to be elected as chairman of the Hawaii section of the American Chemical Society. For her work in Hawaii she received the Francis P. Garvin Medal of that society in 1953 and the William H. Taft Medal from the University of Cincinnati in 1966. She retired in 1958. Bilger Hall at the Manoa campus of the University of Hawaii is named jointly for Leonora and Earl Bilger.

BINGHAM, HIRAM (BINAMU) (1789–1869)

Born in Bennington, Vermont, Hiram worked his father's farm until he came of age. He belatedly attended Middlebury College and graduated at the age of twenty-six. He spent three years more at Andover Theological Seminary before being accepted for the first American mission to Hawaii under the American Board of Commissioners for Foreign Missions centered in Boston. Since the men of the First Company had to be married, he proposed to Sybil Moseley, who happened to attend his ordination; they were married a fortnight later. Sybil (1792–1848) had been born in Westfield, Massachusetts, and orphaned at the age of nineteen.

The couple were the foremost members of the group that arrived on the brig *Thaddeus* in Hawaii in 1820. Bingham was destined to spend two decades in active mission work. He was a popular preacher and teacher and was especially influential among the ruling chiefs of the time. He helped to devise the seventeen-letter alphabet (later reduced to twelve) used to translate the Bible and many other works into printed Hawaiian, and assisted Elisha LOOMIS in developing the printing trade, even himself carving crude woodcuts to illustrate tracts. A month after the press provided reading matter for scholars, Bingham estimated that he had more than five hundred students chosen from the upper class of Hawaii (children were not schooled until much later). The first edition of the New Testament was completed in 1832, and the complete Bible was first available in 1839.

Bingham was pastor of the first church, Kawaiahao, in Honolulu. His severe upholding of the laws of Jehovah put him in the bad graces of whaling captains and other foreigners. He was attacked when sailors from the U.S.S. *Dolphin* under John PERCIVAL broke into the house of KALANIMOKU on February 26, 1826. The Binghams reared seven children, including Hiram BINGHAM II. Mrs. Bingham, who had been a teacher and a midwife as well, began failing in health and the family left for New England in 1840. She died in 1848 and Hiram married Naomi E. Morse in 1852. The history of the islands from the point of view of a pioneer missionary is told in Bingham's classic book, *A Residence of Twenty-One Years in the Sandwich Islands* (New York: Sherman Converse, 1847).

BINGHAM, HIRAM II (1831–1908)
Born in Honolulu, son of the first Rev. Hiram BINGHAM, the young man graduated from Yale College in 1853 and Andover Theological Seminary in 1856. He married Minerva Clarissa Brewster in the same year and sailed to Honolulu on the brig *Morning Star*, first of a series of vessels of that name that served the mission stations in the South Pacific, financed by Sunday school students in Hawaii and the United States. In 1863 Hawaii became a "home mission" and workers were sent to other parts of the Pacific under the auspices of the Hawaiian Evangelical Association.

Hiram II was the first captain of the second *Morning Star* during 1867, when the couple were doing mission work in the Gilbert Islands. He later served the "home mission" in Honolulu and finished translating the complete Bible into the Gilbertese language in 1893. These Binghams had two sons, including Hiram Bingham III (1875–1956), who had a distinguished political career in the United States and as an archeologist discovered the Machu Picchu ruins in Peru.

BIRD, ISABELLA. See BISHOP, ISABELLA BIRD.

BISHOP, ARTEMAS (1795–1872)
Born in Pompey, New York, Bishop graduated from Union College, New York, in 1819 and from Princeton Theological Seminary in 1822. He married Elizabeth Edwards in November of that year and the couple sailed the same month with the Second Company of American missionaries. They were stationed at Waimea, Kauai, from 1823 to 1824 and at Kailua, Hawaii, from 1824 to 1836. For the next twenty years they lived at Ewa, Oahu, and even after moving to Honolulu, Bishop frequently preached at Ewa. At his request, however, he was released from the American Board in 1848. During his stay at Kailua, he translated into Hawaiian a dozen books of the Bible and eight textbooks. When his wife died at Kailua in 1828 he married Delia Stone. By his first wife Bishop had two children, including Sereno Edwards BISHOP.

BISHOP, BERNICE PAUAHI (1831–1884)
Princess Pauahi was born in Honolulu, a great-granddaughter of Kamehameha I. Her parents were PAKI and KONIA. She was named Pauahi after an aunt whose daughter was Princess RUTH. At the age of eight Bernice began attending Royal School along with other young people of the ruling group. She was married at the school in 1850 to Charles Reed BISHOP.

On the deathbed of Kamehameha V in 1872, he offered to name Bernice his successor to the throne, but she declined. She received in 1875 the Grand Cross of the Order of Kamehameha from King Kalakaua. At the death of Ruth in 1883, Bernice inherited the bulk of her estate and thus became heiress to most of the Kamehameha lands, totalling close to nine per cent of the area of the Hawaiian Islands. Her will established the endowed Kamehameha Schools, to educate young people of Hawaiian blood, which opened the boys' division in 1887 and the girls' division in 1894. See Mary H. Krout, *The Memoirs of the Honorable Bernice Pauahi Bishop* (New York: Knickerbocker Press, 1908).

11

BISHOP, CHARLES REED
(1822 – 1915)

Born at Glens Falls, New York, of New England stock, Bishop was orphaned in early childhood and reared by grandparents. He left home at the age of fifteen, and after holding several small jobs sailed in 1846 for Oregon to seek fortune in the West. He stopped off at Honolulu, obtained his first position in the islands, and began to contribute to the economic history of Hawaii. His first task was posting government books. He became a naturalized subject in 1849. Soon Bishop became collector general of customs at Honolulu and then opened a mercantile business in partnership with W. A. Aldrich.

The firm of Aldrich & Bishop was formed in 1858. Through Bishop's insight into the need for a bank in the city, the company later became the Bank of Bishop and then was incorporated as the Bank of Bishop & Co., Ltd. Today it has the name of First Hawaiian Bank. Bishop gave strong financial support to the growing sugar industry and his influence grew. It was augmented by his marriage in 1850 to Princess Bernice Pauahi BISHOP, who in 1883 inherited from Princess RUTH the bulk of the Kamehameha landed property.

In 1860 Bishop was made a noble of the kingdom and life member of the upper house of the Legislature. He was a member of the privy council during the reigns of four kings and one queen, and was throughout his life an adviser to royalty. He and his princess traveled abroad in 1876; they were presented at the court of Queen Victoria and received by Pope Pius IX. Widely known for his philanthropy, Bishop built as a memorial to his wife the world-renowned Bernice P. Bishop Museum in Honolulu and in his will left funds for its support through the Bishop Trust Co. After the death of his wife in 1884, he made frequent trips to the mainland and in 1894 he moved to San Francisco, where he died in 1915. His body was returned to Honolulu and he was given an impressive state funeral. See Harold W. Kent, *Charles Reed Bishop, Man of Hawaii* (Palo Alto, Calif.: Pacific Books, 1965).

BISHOP, ISABELLA BIRD
(1832 – 1904)

A Scottish traveler who became the first woman fellow of the Royal Geographical Society, Mrs. Bishop arrived in Honolulu in January, 1873, and spent nearly seven months in the islands during that critical year of the reign of LUNALILO. She visited the town of Hilo, described the Kilauea district during a volcanic outburst, and rode astride to such almost inaccessible valleys as Waipio and Waimanu on the Hamakua Coast. In March she explored the crater of Haleakala on Maui and later spent a month in the valleys of Kauai. Her illustrated book, *The Hawaiian Archipelago: Six Months among the Palm Groves, Coral Reefs, and Volcanoes of the Sandwich Islands* (London: John Murray, 1875), has been frequently reprinted.

BISHOP, SERENO EDWARDS
(1827–1909)

Bishop was born at Kaawaloa, Hawaii, son of the Rev. Artemas BISHOP. Sereno was sent to the United States at the age of twelve and graduated from Amherst College in 1846 and Auburn Theological Seminary in 1851. Shortly after his marriage to Cornelia Ann Sessions and after serving as chaplain to seamen in New York City, he returned with his wife to Hawaii and was seaman's chaplain at Lahaina, Maui, from 1853 to 1862. After three years at Hana, Maui, he joined the staff of Lahainaluna Seminary, first as teacher, then as principal.

Bishop moved to Honolulu in 1877 and worked as a land surveyor. He compiled the first detailed map of Kauai and mapped the complex water rights and land titles in Oahu's Nuuanu Valley. From 1887 to 1902 he was editor of *The Friend*, a monthly journal, and was a lively correspondent to the Washington, D.C., *Evening Star*. Bishop explained the halolike circles around the sun noted after the Krakatoa eruption of 1883; these are called "Bishop's Rings" in his honor. His recollections of early Hawaii *Reminiscences of Old Hawaii* (Honolulu: Gazette, 1916), are a valuable source of history.

BLAISDELL, NEAL SHAW (1902–1975)

Neal was the son of William Wallace and Malia K. Merseberg Blaisdell. He was born in Honolulu and attended the Kamehameha School for Boys, St. Louis College, the University of Hawaii, and Bucknell University, where he obtained a bachelor's degree in business administration in 1925. He married Lucy Thurston, a teacher, the following year; she was to bear him two daughters and to act as the first lady of Honolulu during the fourteen years when Blaisdell was mayor of the city.

Blaisdell began a career as a teacher and was an admired athletic director, first at McKinley High School and later at Punahou School, Roosevelt High School, and St. Louis College. From 1930 to 1935 he was with the land department of Bishop Trust Co., and was an executive with the Hawaiian Pineapple Co. from 1937 to 1953. He began his political career in 1944, serving in the Territorial House for three years and the Senate for five. He was director of the Department of Public Welfare from 1953 to 1954 and in 1955 became mayor, a post he held until 1969. He was once president of the United States Conference of Mayors, and was director of several business organizations and presidential commissions. The Neal S. Blaisdell Center in Honolulu, consisting of a concert hall and arena, bears his name.

BLATCHLEY, ABRAHAM (1787–1860)

Born in Connecticut, Blatchley received a medical degree from Yale College. He married Jemima Narvin in 1821 and the couple arrived in 1823 with the Second Company of American missionaries in Honolulu, where they were stationed until 1826. Dr. Blatchley traveled among the islands to practice medicine among Hawaiians and others alike. At Lahaina, Maui, he attended the last illness of KEOPUOLANI and was frequently called to treat KALANIMOKU. After four years as the only medical missionary in the islands, his own health failed. The Blatchleys were released from their post and returned to the United States in 1827.

BLIGH, WILLIAM (1754–1817)

As sailing master with James COOK, Bligh made the first maps of any part of the Hawaiian Islands and commanded a party on the shore after Cook's death. Bligh was later famed as the deposed captain during the mutiny of the *Bounty*, and finally became an admiral in the Royal Navy.

BLOUNT, JAMES HENDERSON (1837–1903)

Colonel of a Georgia regiment during the American Civil War, Congressman Blount arrived in Honolulu on March 29, 1893, as special commissioner of incoming President Grover Cleveland, a Democrat, with a letter to Sanford B. DOLE stating that "in all matters affecting relations with the government of the Hawaiian Islands, his authority is *paramount*." Blount ordered Admiral J. S. Skerritt to haul down the American flag in Honolulu and withdraw the protectorate over the islands. "Paramount" Blount collected information on the change of government until he embarked in the autumn to write a report that led Cleveland to denounce the "lawless occupation of Honolulu under false pretexts by United States forces."

BLOXAM, ANDREW (1801–1878)

A British scientist who accompanied Lord BYRON to Hawaii in 1825 on the *Blonde*, Bloxam kept a valuable journal. See *Diary of Andrew Bloxam, the Naturalist of the "Blonde"* (Honolulu: Bishop Museum Special Publication No. 10, 1925).

BOKI (POKI) (–1830?)

Boki was the son Kuamanoha, a chief of Maui, and was a younger brother of KALANIMOKU, but it was rumored that he was a son of KAHEKILI. His original name was Kamauleule; his nickname came from a variation on Boss, the name of the favorite dog of Kamehameha I.

Boki was appointed governor of Oahu and confirmed in his post by Kamehameha II. He married LILIHA and they shared many adventures. Boki agreed to the breaking of the tabus in 1819 and accepted the Protestant missionaries arriving in 1820, although he had been baptized as a Catholic aboard the French vessel of Louis de FREYCINET, along with Kalanimoku, the previous year. Boki and Liliha were leading members of the expedition to Great Britain during which Kamehameha II and KAMAMALU died of the measles. Returning with Lord BYRON on the *Blonde*, Boki brought to Hawaii an English gardener, John WILKINSON, and with him began raising sugar cane and coffee trees in Manoa Valley. Boki also encouraged the Hawaiians to gather sandalwood for trade, ran a mercantile and shipping business, and opened a liquor store called the Blonde Hotel.

Boki became resentful of the power of KAAHUMANU and her missionary advisers, and not surprisingly allied himself with foreigners like Richard CHARLTON and John PERCIVAL, captain of the first visiting American warship. Boki was also a protector of the French missionaries that began arriving in 1827 (see MAIGRET). Kaahumanu and the council in May, 1827, charged Boki and Liliha with misconduct, intemperance, fornication, and adultery, and had them fined. In return Boki and Liliha objected to the laws passed at the end of the year and made no effort to enforce them.

This disturbing element was removed when, heavily in debt, Boki heard toward the end of 1829 from a visiting Australian ship about a South Pacific island covered with valuable sandalwood trees. Boki fitted out two ships, the *Kamehameha* and the *Becket*, put on board some five hundred of his followers, and sailed south. Somewhere in the Fiji group the ships separated. Eight months later the *Becket* limped back to Honolulu with only twenty survivors aboard. A quarrel had arisen with the natives of an island in the New Hebrides group and a disease had broken out that killed almost two hundred of the crew. Boki and two hundred and fifty of his men apparently died at sea when the *Kamehameha* burned in 1830, possibly when gunpowder stored in the hold blew up as the result of careless smoking.

BOND, ELIAS (1813–1896)

Born in Hallowell, Maine, Bond graduated from Bowdoin College in 1838 and Bangor Theological Seminary in 1840. He married Ellen Mariner Howell in September, 1840, and the couple sailed in October with the Ninth Company of American missionaries. The pair were stationed at Kohala, Hawaii, where Bond was to labor unremittingly for fifty-five years. He founded the Select Boys' Boarding School in 1842, which was merged with the first government English school when it opened in 1854. He also founded the Kohala (Mauna Oliva) Girls' School in 1874. In 1861 he started the Kohala Sugar Plantation to provide employment for his congregation; the first sugar was produced in 1865, and when the reciprocity treaty with the United States began to bring dividends, Bond gave his to mission work. He also erected Kahahikiola Church. The Bonds had ten children. See Ethel M. Damon, *Father Bond of Kohala* (Honolulu: The Friend, 1927).

BOUCHARD, HYPÓLITE (1785–1843)

Born in Marseilles, France, Bouchard was the young captain of the *Argentina*, a forty-four-gun frigate from the United Provinces that arrived in Honolulu in September, 1818, to round up a gang of South American pirates that had sought refuge in the islands. He recaptured the corvette *Santa Rosa*, which was put in command of Peter CORNEY when the two vessels sailed for California later in the autumn. In the opinion of some, Bouchard himself was little better than a pirate.

BREWER, CHARLES (1804–1885)

Brewer was born in Boston, the son of a dry-goods merchant. He was apprenticed at the age of fourteen to a shopkeeper, but at seventeen went to sea and made a voyage to Calcutta; he first visited Hawaii on the return passage in 1823. By the age of twenty-five Brewer was first officer on the brig *Chinchilla*, based in Honolulu. He returned to Boston in 1829 but in October sailed as mate of the brig *Ivanhoe*, plying between Canton and Mexico, via Honolulu, until 1831. He then became captain of a small schooner sailing between Hawaii and the West Coast from Alaska to Mexico. Captain Brewer in 1835 became a partner in the prosperous Honolulu company, owned by Henry A. PEIRCE, which had its origin in the efforts of James HUNNEWELL going back to 1817. Peirce & Brewer traded in cotton goods, rum, and Yankee notions in return for sandalwood and furs. Brewer was the largest contributor in July, 1839, to the sum of $20,000 raised to ransom Honolulu from the cannon of Captain C. P. T. LAPLACE.

In the same year, while visiting Boston, Brewer married Martha Turner. In 1843, when Peirce returned to New England, Brewer took full control and continued the island enterprises under his own name. The firm merged in 1845 with the company established in 1841 by J. F. B. MARSHALL and Francis Johnson. Brewer disposed of most of his Hawaii interests in 1845 and took his family to Boston. His business trip back to Hawaii from 1847 to 1849 ended his years of seafaring, but after the Civil War he established a fleet of barks sailing between Hawaii and the ports of Manila and Hong Kong. He retired from an active career in 1884.

A nephew, Charles Brewer II, had taken over the Honolulu business in 1858 and retired in 1861, but the firm continued under the Brewer name, and contributed greatly to the financing and operation of the sugar industry. The company was rescued from embarrassment in 1879 by Peter Cushman JONES, and a decisive event was the entrance into the firm of Charles R. BISHOP in 1880. The office of C. Brewer & Co., Ltd., are still to be seen on Fort Street, Honolulu, but the company is now part of the I U International Corp. See Brewer's *Reminiscences* (Jamaica Plains, N.Y.: privately printed, 1884).

BRIDGES, HARRY RENTON.
See HALL, JACK.

BRIGHAM, WILLIAM TUFTS (1841–1926)
Born in Boston, Brigham received a bachelor's degree from Harvard University in 1862 and a master's degree in 1865. He first came to Hawaii in 1864 with his companion, Horace Mann, exploring the botany and geology and discovering forty new varieties of plants. He was appointed curator of the Bernice P. Bishop museum in 1890 and served until his retirement in 1920, at the age of seventy-nine. He published works on Hawaiian worship, feather work, stone implements, ancient houses, kapa, and volcanoes; for the latter work he made an extensive survey of Kilauea. Brigham was a member of several international anthropological societies, and was awarded an honorary doctorate by Columbia University in 1905.

BRINSMADE, PETER ALLAN (1804–1859)
Born in Connecticut, Brinsmade studied at Andover Theological Seminary and at Yale Divinity School, and hence was closer to the missionary group than were most island merchants. He arrived in 1833 with his wife and partners, William Ladd and William Northey HOOPER. The

missionaries, in turn, helped the firm, founded as Ladd & Co. in 1835, to obtain from the crown a fifty-year lease on lands of their choice. The three partners started in 1836 the Koloa Plantation on the island of Kauai, the first extensive sugar-growing company to survive. Brinsmade was also principal editor from 1838 to 1840 of a quarterly literary journal, the *Hawaiian Spectator*, one of the first periodicals published in the Pacific region. He was appointed by President Martin Van Buren as United States commercial agent in Hawaii from 1838 to 1846, replacing John Coffin JONES. By 1840, Ladd & Co. added to their growing of sugar the production of silk and of kukui and castor oils.

The failure of world powers to recognize Hawaiian independence imperiled the leasing of lands by foreigners, and Brinsmade agreed to go abroad to lobby for such recognition and to enlist foreign capital for the commercial development of the islands. He bore letters, written by himself and signed by Kamehameha III, to the president of the United States, the queen of Great Britain, and the king of France. With the aid of William RICHARDS and Timothy HAALILIO, a tripartite agreement was signed in Brussels in 1843, called the "Belgian Contract," among Kamehameha III, Ladd & Co., and the Belgian Company of Colonization, which exchanged holdings in Ladd & Co. for shares in a Belgian corporation. This corporation was never organized and Brinsmade, destitute, returned to the islands in 1846. Lacking finances, the company struggled on for some years without marked success until Dr. R. W. WOOD took over the management in 1848. Koloa Plantation is still in operation today.

BROUGHTON, WILLIAM ROBERT.
See VANCOUVER, GEORGE.

BROWN, LYDIA (1780–1865)
Born in Wilton, New Hampshire, Lydia Brown arrived in Hawaii in 1835 with the Seventh Company of American missionaries. Although she was fifty-five years old in that year and thus was the oldest mission member to begin laboring in the field, she was able to devote herself to the work for thirty more busy years. She was stationed with the Richard ARMSTRONG family at Wailuku, Maui, from 1835 to 1840. She instructed native girls in carding, spinning, weaving, and knitting Hawaii-grown cotton and wool. The governor of the Big Island ordered the building of a cotton factory at Kailua in 1837 to carry on the work. By the spring of 1839 about six hundred yards of cotton cloth had been woven at Wailuku and four hundred yards at Kailua.

Lydia Brown was then sent to Kaluaaha and there she conducted a school for young ladies from 1849 to 1851. She left in 1857 for Lahaina and then for Honolulu, where she died at the end of the Civil War, during which she had cheered the advances of the Union Army.

BROWN, WILLIAM
Brown, an early trading captain, first arrived in command of the British ship *Butterworth* in 1793, in which he entered Honolulu Harbor—probably the first foreigner to do so. For a while this was called "Brown's Harbor." He returned in 1794 as master of the *Jackal*, in company with Captain Gordon of the *Prince Lee Boo*. Brown sold arms to KALANIKAPULE and eight sailors from the two vessels fought on the side of this chief against KAEO. Later both Brown and Gordon were murdered under orders of Kalanikapule in an attempt to steal the ships.

BRYAN, WILLIAM ALANSON (1875–1942)
Born in New Sharon, Iowa, Bryan obtained a bachelor's degree from Iowa State College in 1896. He came to Hawaii in 1899 to investigate Hawaiian fauna for the United States Department of Agriculture, and was curator of the Bernice P. Bishop Museum in Honolulu from 1900 to 1907. He organized and acted as first president of the Pacific Scientific Institution in 1907. From 1909 to 1919 he was professor of zoology and geology at the College of Hawaii. From 1921 until his retirement in 1940 he was director of the Los Angeles Museum of History, Science, and Art. He published a number of works on Hawaiian flora and fauna, especially *The Natural History of Hawaii* (Honolulu: Gazette, 1915).

BUCK, SIR PETER HENRY (TE RANGI HIROA) (1880–1951)
Buck was born in New Plymouth, New Zealand. His father was Irish and his mother was Maori. He obtained a medical degree and served during World War I as a major in the Medical Corps with Maori troops. He found that a knowledge of Polynesian culture was essential in treating his patients and began researches for which he received the Rivers Medal from the Royal Anthropological Society in 1936. In that year he was appointed ethnologist and director of the Bernice P. Bishop Museum in Honolulu and served until 1951. He was made a Knight Commander of St. Michael and St. George in 1936. He published a number of scientific papers as well as such popular works as *Vikings of the Sunrise (Vikings of the Pacific)* (New York: Stokes, 1938) and *Arts and Crafts of Hawaii* (Honolulu: Bishop Museum Special Publication No. 45, 1957).

BURNEY, JAMES (1750–1821)
Burney signed on as an able seaman on the *Resolution* in 1772 and later was transferred to the *Adventure* during the second Pacific voyage of James COOK. He became first lieutenant under Charles CLERKE in the *Discovery* in February, 1776, and survived the third Cook voyage, returning to England in command of that ship. Some years later, having served with the East Indies squadron and reached the rank of admiral, Burney retired from the Navy and devoted his leisure to writing. His most important work was a five-volume chronological history of early European voyages in the Pacific, which reached no further than 1764. Burney was a friend of Dr. Samuel Johnson and Charles Lamb, and his sister, Fanny Burney, was a novelist of note. Burney's private journal gives one of the most graphic accounts of Cook's third Pacific voyage.

BURNS, JOHN ANTHONY (1909–1975)
Born at Fort Assiniboine, Montana, Burns attended St. Louis High School and the University of Hawaii. He married Beatrice Majors Van Fleet in 1931, and they had two sons and a daughter. Burns was a member of the Honolulu Police Department from 1934 to 1945, rising to the rank of captain in 1941. Thereafter he was president and manager of a retail store and administrator of the Oahu Civil Defense Agency from 1951 to 1955. He headed the real-estate firm of Burns & Co. from 1955 to 1962.

Burns began a political career in 1948 as chairman of the Democratic County Committee. From 1957 to 1959 he was delegate from the Territory of Hawaii to the United States Congress. He is credited with devising the strategy by which Hawaii finally achieved statehood; he supported the admission of Alaska and thereafter was sure that the claims of Hawaii could not be denied. Burns ran as a Democrat for the first governorship of the new state in 1959, but was defeated by the appointed Republican incumbent, William Francis Quinn. However,

Burns won in the regular election of 1962 and, with strong support from organized union forces and veterans of the American-Japanese volunteers from Hawaii in World War II, led the movement that switched the island political predominance from Republican to Democrat. Burns belonged to a number of civic groups and received several honorary degrees. He left office in 1974 after a third term and died the following April. The John A. Burns School of Medicine at the Manoa campus of the University of Hawaii bears his name.

BYRON, (GEORGE ANSON) LORD (1789–1858)

Captain the Right Honourable George Anson, R.N., who entered the Royal Navy in 1800, commanded the forty-six-gun frigate *Blonde*, which the London government sent to Hawaii in 1824 to carry back the bodies of KAMEHAMEHA II and his wife KAMAMALU. This Lord Byron, a cousin of the poet, visited Hilo, later often called "Byron's Bay," and the volcano at Kilauea, where "Byron's Ledge" lies below the Volcano House Hotel. In 1825 Byron and his men were the first to study the region scientifically. He held instructions to be friendly with the Hawaiian chiefs but not to interfere with their independence. However, at a meeting of chiefs on June 6, Lord Byron offered suggestions, one of which—trial by jury—was adopted. During his visit he presented the first magic-lantern show in the history of the islands, using a projector and slides brought on the ship for this purpose. See his book, *Voyage of H.M.S. "Blonde" to the Sandwich Islands, 1824–25* (London: John Murray, 1826); see also DAMPIER, Robert.

CAMERON, JOHN (1850–1925)

A Scottish sea captain who had many adventures in the Pacific, Cameron was an officer on the inter-island steamers in the early 1880s and installed machinery at the Mormon plantation at Laie, Oahu. His book, *John Cameron's Odyssey*, compiled by Andrew Farrell (New York, Macmillan, 1928), is also a valuable source for the story of the events that inspired the novel *The Wrecker* by Robert Louis STEVENSON.

CAMPBELL, ARCHIBALD (1787–1821?)

Born near Glasgow, Scotland, Campbell ran away to sea at the age of fourteen. He made various voyages before losing both feet from frostbite while wrecked on the coast of Alaska. He arrived in Hawaii in 1809 on the Russian Imperial ship *Neva*, and was employed as a sailmaker for Kamehameha I. Historians are indebted to Campbell for a number of descriptions of this monarch during the height of his power. Campbell also gives good accounts of native customs, seen from the point of view of a wandering Scotsman. Campbell left after more than a year and finally returned to his native land, where he published a successful book, *Voyage Round the World from 1806 to 1812* (Edinburgh: A. Constable, 1816). With the proceeds he went to New York and started a small business; he was last heard of in that city in 1821. A novel based on his life is *The Restless Voyage* (New York: Prentice-Hall, 1948), by Stanley D. PORTEUS.

CAMPBELL, ALEXANDER JAMES (1856–1941)

Born in Honolulu, the young man attended Punahou School and graduated from the University of California in 1879. Campbell took a leading part in developing the banana industry in the islands, and his poultry ranch at Mokuleia became one of the largest and most modern

on Oahu. He was president of A. J. Campbell, Ltd., a brokerage firm, and helped to organize the Honolulu Stock Exchange; he served as president of the Exchange from 1914 to 1915 and from 1925 to 1926. He was a director of several companies and was territorial treasurer under Governors George Robert CARTER and Walter Francis FREAR.

CAMPBELL, JAMES (1826–1900)

Born in Londonderry, Ireland, of Scottish-Irish parents, Campbell ran away to sea at the age of thirteen and survived various adventures in New England and on a South Sea island, where his whaling vessel was wrecked. He finally landed at Lahaina, Maui, where, having saved some money as a carpenter, he started a sugar plantation in 1861. In the early 1870s, in partnership with Harry Turton, Campbell founded the Pioneer Mill at Lahaina, forerunner of a greater operation later sold to H. Hackfeld & Co. Campbell realized the value of land in the islands and constantly increased his holdings; he once owned much of the area where the town of Lahaina now stands, and gained the nickname of "Kimo-ona-milliona" (James the millionaire). Campbell moved to Honolulu and in 1877 married Abigail Kuaihelani Maipinepine. Among their four daughters: Abigail Wahikiaakuula (Princess David KAWANAKOA).

Campbell next turned his efforts to stock raising and bought two ranches on Oahu—one at Kahuku and one at Honouliuli—where the finest blooded cattle were reared; later these properties were used for cultivating sugar cane. At a time when most of the lands in the Ewa area were considered worthless, Campbell acquired huge tracts that became part of the impressive fortune still administered under the Estate of James Campbell. Two Campbell Blocks in the heart of downtown Honolulu were also part of the estate's holdings. Campbell also supported the first telephone and electric-light companies in the islands.

Campbell is best known, perhaps, for having bored the first flowing well of artesian water in Hawaii. This was done near his ranch house at Honouliuli and made possible the successful cultivation of sugar at Ewa. Campbell retired from active business affairs in 1895 and spent some years in travel. He figured in 1896 in a sensational kidnapping case in San Francisco, escaping from a brutal captor who later was given a life sentence for the crime.

CANNON, GEORGE QUAYLE (1827–1901)

Cannon was born in Liverpool, England, where the family became converts to the Church of the Latter-Day Saints when he was thirteen. He crossed the Atlantic in 1842, heading for Mormon headquarters at Nauvoo, Illinois, where he learned the printing business under his uncle, a newspaper editor. Cannon served as a Mormon missionary to Hawaii from 1850 to 1854, assigned to the island

of Maui, and won many converts. He quickly learned the language and early in 1852 began the translation of the Book of Mormon into Hawaiian; in this work he was assisted by two Hawaiians, J. H. Napela and J. W. H. Kauwahi. The final revision was completed just two years later. Cannon left for the mainland in 1854 and published the volume in San Francisco. He returned to Hawaii in the autumn of 1900 as guest of honor at the jubilee of the opening of the Mormon mission to the islands.

CARLSMITH, CARL (1870–1959)

Carl S. Schmidt was born in Cambridge, Vermont, son of Edward Charles and Marilla (Derby) Smith, and studied at the public schools of San Jose, California. He attended the University of California and Stanford University and gained a law degree from Northwestern University in 1896. He came to Hawaii the following year and opened a practice at Hilo, founding a law firm still flourishing today. His surname was legally changed in 1911 to Carlsmith. He married Nellie Wood in 1897 and the couple had four children.

CARTER, ALFRED WELLINGTON (1867–1949)

Born in Honolulu, a grandson of Joseph Oliver Carter, Alfred attended Punahou School and received a law degree from Yale in 1893. He practised with his cousin, Charles L. Carter, who was the first fatality of the counter-revolution of 1895. Alfred served as deputy attorney general and from 1896 to 1897 was judge of the First Circuit. He helped to organize several companies before beginning a new

career as guardian of the estate of Thelma K. Parker, fourth-generation heiress of the celebrated Parker Ranch. Carter gave up his thriving Honolulu practice to manage the ranch on the Big Island. He made many modern improvements and built the holdings into one of the greatest meat producers under the American flag. The ranch also grazed Merino sheep and reared racehorses and polo ponies. The trusteeship ended in 1943 with the death of Thelma's mother, but Carter continued as agent of the new owner, Thelma Parker's son Richard Palmer Smart. See *Alfred W. Carter, Hawaii's Dean of Cattlemen* (Kamuela, Hawaii: privately printed, 1971).

CARTER, GEORGE ROBERT (1866–1933)

Born in Honolulu, son of Henry A. P. CARTER, George attended Phillips Andover Academy, Massachusetts, and Yale University. He began his business career in Honolulu as cashier for C. Brewer & Co. from 1895 to 1898, and then became manager of the Hawaiian Trust Co., 1898–1902, and managing director of the Hawaiian Fertilizer Co., 1900–1902. He was elected to the Territorial Senate in 1901, was appointed secretary of the Territory in 1902, and was appointed governor, 1903–1907, by Theodore Roosevelt. After retirement from active business he collected a private library of Hawaiiana.

Carter succeeded Sanford B. DOLE as governor of the Territory and continued Dole's efforts to guide the islands through the period of adjustment to the territorial form of government. It was still difficult to persuade legislators that the conduct of public business was a serious responsibility, but Carter got along in this enterprise somewhat better than did his predecessor.

CARTER, HENRY AUGUSTUS PEIRCE (1837–1891)

This future financier and diplomat was born in Honolulu, son of Hannah Lord and Captain Joseph Oliver Carter, a New Englander who had traded in the Pacific since 1825. Captain Carter founded an Island family that continued to be prominent for more than a century. In 1840 the captain took his family to Boston and left his sons there to be educated. By 1847 he had lost his fortune and was obliged to send for them to help him. Henry, then a boy of twelve, returned to his birthplace but, when his father died in 1850, went to California and held several small jobs. Back in Honolulu, at the age of nineteen he was hired as a clerk by Charles Brewer II and began an outstanding business career. It was said that he made more money from private investments than from his salary. He was made a partner in the Brewer firm in 1862 and married Sybil Augusta Judd, a daughter of Dr. Gerrit P. JUDD. The pair had five children, including George R. CARTER and Joseph Oliver CARTER Jr.

Henry soon saw the promise of the sugar industry and C. Brewer became a leading sugar factor. In 1871 Carter showed his acumen by bringing into the firm the talents of Peter Cushman JONES during a period of risk and debt. The need for a reciprocity treaty with the United States resulted in the sending of Carter to Washington in 1874 to aid Judge Elisha H. ALLEN in securing such a treaty. Successful, Carter was then sent by the king to explain to the diplomats of Great Britain, France, and Bismarck's Germany this apparent favoritism by the United States. When Carter returned from his European mission he found that the need for new sources of plantation labor required him to go to Portugal in 1882 and there arrange a treaty regulating immigration of workers from that country. In 1883, upon the sudden death of Judge Allen, Hawaiian minister resident in Washington, Carter was sent to replace him, and remained in this important post until his own death. During these years he became dean of the diplomatic corps in the American capital and repeatedly protected the reciprocity treaty; he saw its renewal in 1887, with a clause allowing the United States to use a naval base at Pearl Harbor.

CARTER, JOSEPH OLIVER Jr. (1835–1909)

Carter was the eldest son of Captain Joseph Oliver Carter and the elder brother of Henry A. P. CARTER. Joseph Jr., born in Honolulu, was to become a journalist, public official, diplomat, financier, and philanthropist. He was schooled in Boston from 1840 to 1847, when he returned to Hawaii. After a sojourn in the California goldfields he returned to Honolulu once more and was on the staff of the *Pacific Commercial Advertiser* from the late 1850s until 1872. For a decade he was also marine correspondent in Hawaii for the New York *Herald*. Elected to the legislature in 1872, Carter advocated reforms in the treatment of indentured laborers on plantations. He was appointed registrar of public accounts in 1874 and served until 1880, when he resigned to become cashier for C. Brewer & Co. He became president of that firm in 1891 upon the resignation of Peter Cushman JONES, but resigned in 1894 because of his political views—he had been a privy councillor under LILIUOKALANI.

After the Revolution of 1893, Carter was put in charge of the business affairs of the former queen and also was a trustee of the estate of James CAMPBELL, the estate of Bernice Pauahi BISHOP, and the Kamehameha Schools. He reconciled his differences with the annexationists and became a member of the Board of Health under the Republic. He was active in religious affairs and was a trustee of Central Union Church.

Carter in 1859 married Mary Elizabeth Ladd and they had six children.

CARTWRIGHT, ALEXANDER JOY (1820–1892)

Cartwright, the acknowledged "father of baseball," was the cashier of the Union Bank of New York City when he laid out the first baseball diamond as it is now known and planned the rules of the new game. He also organized the Knickerbocker Baseball Club, ancestor of the big-league teams of today. In 1842 he married Eliza Ann Gerritse Van Wie of Albany and they had three sons and two daughters.

Cartwright joined the California gold rush but soon embarked on a round-the-world cruise. He landed in Honolulu in August, 1849, and was offered a position in the city. Two years later he went into business for himself and founded a prosperous firm. He sent for his family and lived in Hawaii for forty-five years, becoming a close friend of the royal family, especially Kamehameha IV. He joined in the founding of Queen's Hospital, the American Seamen's Institute, and the Honolulu Library and Reading Room. He was also founder of the Honolulu Fire Department in 1851. At his death the firm was carried on by two sons, Bruce and Alexander Joy Cartwright. Bruce was a leader in many business ventures, such as the First National Bank, the Henry Waterhouse Trust Co., and the Honolulu Rapid Transit Co. For Alexander Cartwright, see Harold Peterson, *The Man Who Invented Baseball* (New York: Scribner, 1973).

CARY, MILES E. (1894–1959)

Cary was born at Orting, Washington, and educated at the grammar school and high school of Edmonds, Washington, and at the University of Washington. He was appointed principal of a school at the age of twenty-two but left to enter the United States Army in 1918 as a sergeant. He arrived in Honolulu in 1921 to teach history at McKinley High School and also to act as athletic director, athletic coach, and adviser to the school paper. He was appointed principal of McKinley in 1924 and devoted his energies to advancing the careers of students and others. He worked for statehood and campaigned to get immigrants to become American citizens. During World War II he volunteered to work at government relocation camps for people of Japanese ancestry and proclaimed the patriotism of such citizens. Cary's main contribution to education was advocating the new concept of the core curriculum. After leaving Hawaii he taught at several universities on the mainland.

CASTLE, MARY TENNEY (1819–1907)

Second wife of Samuel N. CASTLE, Mary Tenney was born in Plainfield, New York, and trained as a teacher. In Honolulu she devoted herself to charitable works and helped to establish the Henry and Dorothy Castle Memorial Kindergarten. She was apparently the first woman in the islands to advocate female suffrage. She worked for prison reform and was a member of the Women's Christian Temperance Union and the Women's Board of Missions. She established in 1898 the Mary Castle Trust for charities and education, later the Samuel N. and Mary Castle Foundation.

CASTLE, SAMUEL NORTHRUP (1808–1894)

Born in Cazenovia, New York, Castle arrived in Honolulu in 1837 with the Eighth Company of American missionaries, to serve as assistant superintendent of secular affairs for the mission. Through his experience as a bank cashier, Castle built up a considerable business in handling supplies for the mission and the financial accounts of its members. In 1851 Castle was released from his duties and with Amos Starr COOKE, a fellow mission worker, the firm of Castle & Cooke was founded. Its early success was due partly to obtaining the mission trade. The firm of Castle & Cooke became one of the Big Five corporations and is still outstanding in island business. Castle was a privy councillor for twenty years and a treasurer and trustee of Punahou School for forty years; he served in the Legislature in 1864–65, and was a member of the House of Nobles for three sessions.

Castle in 1836 married Angeline Loraine Tenney, by whom he had one daughter. After his wife's death in Hawaii he made a trip to Boston and there married her sister, Mary Tenney CASTLE, by whom he had ten children. The Castles and their descendants formed a large family still prominent in island history. See William Richard Castle, *The Life of Samuel Northrup Castle* (Honolulu: Samuel N. and Mary Castle Foundation, in cooperation with the Hawaiian Historical Society: privately printed, 1960); see also Frank J. Taylor, Earl M. Welty, and David W. Eyre, *From Land and Sea: The Story of Castle & Cooke* (San Francisco: Chronicle Books, 1976).

CASTRO, ANTONIO DANIEL (1883 – 1957)

Born in the island of Madeira, Castro was brought to Honolulu at the age of three. He was educated in the public schools and from 1899 to 1902 was a clerk in a store. He married Mary Franca in 1911. In 1909 he was treasurer of the Mutual Building & Loan Society, and thereafter was an officer in a number of companies. He began serving as consul for several South American countries in 1915. In 1924 he organized the Honolulu Finance and Thrift Co., the first institution in the islands to make personal loans to wage earners; he was president for a quarter of a century. The firm became a subsidiary of Seaboard Financial Co. in 1956. Castro founded A. D. Castro & Co. the same year. He was a member of the Territorial Legislature from 1906 to 1910 and served on several government commissions. He was treasurer of the Portuguese Charitable Society, president of the Honolulu Realty Board, and a member of various clubs. The Castros had four children.

CATTON, MARGARET MARY LOUISE (1882 – 1971)

Mary Catton was born in Huelo, Maui, one of seven children of Robert Catton, a Scottish manufacturer of machinery used on plantations. She attended Punahou and other private schools in Honolulu and Scotland. She graduated in 1919 from the New York School of Social Work, the first island-born woman to earn such a degree. She pioneered in programs leading to the establishment of the Court of Domestic Relations, the University of Hawaii Psychological and Psychopathic Clinic, and the Palama Settlement Venereal Disease Clinic. She organized and supervised the social services at Queen's Hospital from 1923, those at Kauikeolani Children's Hospital from 1928, and the Japanese (now Kuakini) Hospital from 1929. She also helped to found the Hawaii Medical Service Association in 1938, the Maunalani Hospital and Convalescent Home in 1950, and the Pohai Nani Retirement Residence in 1964. She received a distinguished service award from the Hawaii Medical Association in 1956.

CENTER, GEORGE DAVID (DAD) (1886 – 1962)

Center was born in Kipahulu, Maui, where his father managed a sugar plantation. In 1920 he started a sporting-goods store in that city and ran it until his retirement in 1950. Center was interested early in water sports, and on a surfboard made by him set an unofficial distance record in 1917 from the site of the present Elks Club to Waikiki Beach. He participated in sailing and canoe racing, and was one of the earliest members of the Outrigger Canoe Club. He coached a team including ten swimmers from Hawaii (one of them Duke KAHANAMOKU) for the 1920 Olympics.

CHAMBERLAIN, DANIEL (1782 – 1860)

Chamberlain was born at Westboro, Massachusetts, and was a captain in the War of 1812. He was a skilled farmer. During the summer previous to leaving with the First Company of American missionaries in 1819, Chamberlain and his two older sons attended the Mission School at Cornwall, Connecticut. He and his wife, Jerusha Burnap Chamberlain, and their five children sailed on the *Thaddeus* and on arrival in Honolulu were stationed in that town from 1820 to 1823. Farming by mainland standards was not feasible, and Chamberlain turned his efforts to building houses and caring for mission property. Because the climate was unsuited to his health and because his large family needed schooling, Chamberlain was released from his duties and the family returned to the United States in 1823.

CHAMBERLAIN, LEVI (1792 – 1849)

Born in Dover, Vermont, Chamberlain was an unmarried member of the Second Company of American missionaries that arrived at Honolulu in 1823. He was made superintendent of secular affairs for the mission, traveled around Oahu on foot, and taught classes attended by apprentice teachers. In 1828 he married Maria Patton, a Lahaina mission teacher, and the couple reared no fewer than eight children. In spite of weak lungs, Levi worked tirelessly and was widely respected and loved. Two trips away from Hawaii in search of improved health were his only respite from his labors, which ended in his death in Honolulu.

CHAMISSO, ADELBERT.
See KOTZEBUE, Otto Von.

CHAPIN, ALONZO (1805–1876)
Born in West Springfield, Massachusetts, Chapin graduated from Amherst College in 1826 and took a medical degree at the University of Pennsylvania in 1831. He married Mary Ann Tenney the same year and a month later the couple sailed for Hawaii with the Fifth Company of American missionaries. On arrival in 1832 they were stationed first at Lahaina, Maui, and then at Waimea, Kauai. Chapin later helped Lorrin ANDREWS at the Lahainaluna Press, teaching youths to engrave on wood for illustrating books, and on copper for printing maps. At Honolulu Dr. Chapin assisted Dr. Gerrit P. JUDD during the last illness of Queen KAAHUMANU in 1832.

Owing to the poor health of Mrs. Chapin, the couple returned to Massachusetts in 1837. She none the less survived her husband by nine years and died at the age of eighty-one. The pair had one daughter.

CHARLOT, JEAN (1898–1979)
Born in Paris, Charlot spent his early years in Mexico, where he became acquainted with members of the school of prominent muralists in that country (see his volume, *Mexican Mural Renaissance* [New Haven: Yale University Press, 1963]). His lifelong style in fresco, oil, and other media was influenced by his studies of Mayan and Aztec sculpture. Charlot's own murals are found in Mexico, mainland United

States, Hawaii, and Fiji. He participated in a number of shows and received various awards.

Charlot came to the Art Department of the University of Hawaii in 1946 and taught until his retirement in 1967. He published other volumes of art criticism, and illustrated many books, especially those for children. Charlot also wrote several plays, published in both English and Hawaiian. He married Dorothy Zohmah Day in 1939 and the couple had three sons and a daughter. See his *An Artist on Art: Collected Essays of Jean Charlot* (Honolulu: University Press of Hawaii, 1972). The Jean Charlot Collection in the Hamilton Library at the University is a major archive of documents and art works relating to the life of the scholarly painter.

CHARLTON, RICHARD (– 1852)
Charlton was British consul in Hawaii from 1825 to 1842, and led the opposition of local traders to the influence of the American mission on the ruling chiefs. During the abortive rebellion of BOKI in 1829, one of Charlton's cows was shot and killed by a Hawaiian, a trifling event that led to the "cow edict" by Kamehameha III that was his first attempt to codify the laws of the kingdom. It offered the same protection to foreigners as that given to natives. Later events caused Charlton to work for British interference in Hawaiian affairs. In 1840 he claimed some land that he said had been given him years before. En route to England in 1842 to present his claims, he apparently complained in Mexico to Lord George PAULET, who was sent to Hawaii in 1843. In 1847 Charlton, still in England, finally got legal title to the land.

CHORIS, LOUIS (LUDWIG) (1795–1828)
Choris, a young Russian of German descent, accompanied Otto von KOTZEBUE on the voyage of the *Rurik* and made many sketches and watercolors of the islands in 1816, during the reign of Kamehameha I (including several portraits from life of this ruler in his later years). On a later round-the-world voyage, this time under French auspices, Choris was murdered by bandits while traveling from Vera Cruz to Mexico City. See his *Voyage pittoresque autour du monde* (Paris: Firmin Didot, 1822).

CLARK, EPHRAIM WESTON (1799–1878)
Born in Haverhill, New Hampshire, Clark graduated from Dartmouth College in 1824 and earned a master's degree in 1827. He graduated from Andover Theological Seminary in the same year and married Mary Kittredge in September. The couple sailed in November with the Third Company of American missionaries and were stationed at Honolulu from 1828 to 1834, laboring among seamen before the establishment of the Seamen's Chapel by the Rev. John DIELL.

Clark was sent to Lahainaluna in 1834 and stayed there until 1843, with a five-month respite in 1839 during which he sailed to China for his health. From 1843 to 1848 he labored at Wailuku, Maui, and then returned to Honolulu to become third pastor of Kawaiahao Church for fifteen years. Clark translated a number of books into Hawaiian. He was appointed chairman of a committee to revise the Hawaiian Scriptures in 1857 and in 1864 went to New York to supervise its publication. He resigned from the American Board in that year and was put in charge of the Hawaiian printing at the Tract House, New York, in 1867, where he translated the Bible dictionary and put it through the press. By his first wife (he was remarried in 1859 to Sarah Helen Richards Hall after Mary Kittredge died in 1857) he had eight children.

CLEGHORN, ARCHIBALD SCOTT (1835 – 1910)

Born in Edinburgh, Scotland, Cleghorn came to Hawaii at the age of sixteen and rose to be a prosperous merchant. He married Princess Miriam LIKELIKE in 1870 and as the brother-in-law of KALAKAUA and LILIUOKALANI was for years a valued adviser to the crown. Moreover, as the father of Princess KAIULANI, he was a prominent figure in the revolutionary period from 1887 to 1895. Cleghorn built the mansion on Emma Street that became the original Pacific Club, of which he was president for forty-six years. He was likewise the first

president of Queen's Hospital, and was a member of the privy council under Kalakaua, the Board of Health, the Board of Prison Inspectors, and the Board of Immigration. He was Honolulu's first park commissioner and has been called "the father of Hawaii's park system," designer of Emma Park, Thomas Square, Kawaiahao Church grounds, Royal Mausoleum grounds, and Kapiolani Park. He built a spacious estate at Ainahau, Waikiki, a showplace where he entertained residents and visitors for many years. He succeeded John Owen DOMINIS in 1891 as governor of the island of Oahu, and in 1907 was considered for the post of governor of the Territory of Hawaii.

CLEMENS, SAMUEL LANGHORNE (MARK TWAIN) (1835–1910)

Clemens, "the Lincoln of our literature," who had only recently begun to use the pen name of "Mark Twain," arrived in Honolulu aboard the steamer *Ajax* on March 18, 1866, and stayed for four months, writing a series of travel letters for a California newspaper. Born in Florida, Missouri, Clemens had been a printer and reporter, riverboat pilot, and Western journalist. This first trip outside his native United States gave him a much-needed period of refreshment as well as material for another profession (that of popular lecturer), and provided amusing articles still worth reading.

A tireless sightseer, he usually rode around Oahu garbed in a starched, brown linen duster reaching to his ankles, talking and gesticulating so much that people who did not know him thought he was drunk. After a tour of Maui, where he climbed to the summit of the crater of Haleakala and then viewed Iao

Valley, he took a schooner to the Kona coast, visited the Kau district, and described eruptions at Kilauea Volcano. Visiting the sugar plantations of the Hamakua region, he then caught a little steamer at Kawaihae to return to Honolulu. His series of twenty-five picturesque letters give the best and most intimate evocation of Island life in the year following the end of the American Civil War. Five chapters of Twain's *Roughing It* (1872) also draw upon his Hawaii adventure.

When Clemens returned to California he was "about the best-known honest man on the Pacific Coast." He began there a series of lectures often billed as "Our Fellow Savages of the Sandwich Islands." The later career of Mark Twain, author of *The Innocents Abroad* and *Huckleberry Finn*, is an outstanding chapter in American literature. See Walter Francis FREAR, *Mark Twain and Hawaii* (Chicago; privately printed, 1947) and *Mark Twain's Letters from Hawaii* (New York: Appleton-Century, 1966; Honolulu: University Press of Hawaii, 1975).

CLERKE, CHARLES (1743–1779)

Clerke, who began a sea career at the age of twelve, had sailed twice previously on Pacific voyages with James COOK before coming to Hawaii. He had been master's mate and third lieutenant of the *Endeavour* and lieutenant on the first voyage of the *Resolution*. He was put in command of the *Discovery* in February, 1776, and fled from the threat of debtor's prison for having signed a promissory note for his brother. Before departing he had caught the dread germs of tuberculosis, and his condition worsened throughout the third voyage. He was in command of the *Discovery*, the ship from which the Hawaiians at Kealakekua Bay stole his best boat, and logically should have been the captain to go ashore and reclaim it. After consultation with Cook, Clerke rowed back to his own ship and ordered a cordon of boats to guard the bay. When he returned to the *Resolution*, Cook had suddenly decided to go ashore, with fatal results.

Clerke immediately assumed command of the flagship, the *Resolution*, on February 14, 1779, and on the return voyage died at sea on August 22.

CLEVELAND, RICHARD JEFFREY (1773–1860)

Born in Salem, Massachusetts, son of a privateer in the Revolutionary War, Cleveland made his first voyage to China in 1792. As a trader on the Northwest Coast he first visited Hawaii in 1799. In 1803, in partnership with William SHALER, he brought the first horses to Hawaii in the *Lelia Byrd*. The animals came from California. A mare and a foal were landed at Kawaiahae Bay for John YOUNG. The ship then proceeded to Lahaina, Maui, where Kamehameha I visited aboard and viewed the horse and mare before they were landed. Kamehameha himself was the first to learn horsemanship; he was followed in later years by thousands of dedicated riders. See Cleveland's book, *A Narrative of Voyages and Commercial Enterprises*, 2nd ed. (Cambridge, Mass.: John Owen, 1843) and H. W. S. Cleveland, *Voyages of a Merchant Navigator* (New York: Harper, 1886).

COAN, TITUS (1801–1882)

Born in Connecticut, Coan was educated at Auburn Theological Seminary, Massachusetts, and was ordained in 1833. After a missionary exploring trip to Patagonia, he married Fidelia Church in 1834 and the couple arrived in Honolulu in 1835 with the Seventh Company of American missionaries. They were stationed at Hilo, Hawaii, where Coan spent most of the remainder of his life. He was a leader in the "great revival" of 1838–1840; on one Sunday in July, 1838, the Hilo missionaries baptized 1,705 converts and gave communion to 2,400 church members. Three years later, seven thousand people belonged to Coan's church, making it the largest Protestant congregation in the world at the time. Important visitors to Hilo usually were invited to stay with the Coans. The minister was an active student of the volcano region, and led many trips to Kilauea. He recorded almost all that is known of volcanic action from 1835 to 1865 in letters to the *Missionary Herald* and *American Journal of Science*.

The first Mrs. Coan died in 1872, leaving four children, and Titus married Lydia Bingham, a daughter of Hiram BINGHAM I. Coan wrote a useful autobiography, *Life in Hawaii* (New York: A. D. F. Randolph, 1882). See also Lydia Bingham Coan, *Titus Coan: A Memorial* (Chicago: Fleming H. Revell, 1884).

COLL, RAY Sr. (1872–1962)

Born in Pittsburgh, Pennsylvania, Coll early became a newspaperman interested in politics. He worked in Arizona and California for several years before returning to Pennsylvania, where he was editor of the Pittsburgh *Dispatch* from 1912 to 1921. On a world cruise he stopped over to visit a sister-in-law in Hawaii. When his wife, Annette Towzey, pointed out that he was without a job, Coll began working for the Honolulu *Advertiser*, and became editor in 1922; he was active in that post until

1959. He was the first person to broadcast an account of the Pearl Harbor attack of December 7, 1941. For many years he conducted a weekly news program on KGU radio. He received an honorary doctorate from the University of Hawaii in 1958 and the Order of the Splintered Paddle from the Honolulu Chamber of Commerce in the same year.

COLNETT, JAMES (1755?–1806)

An early trader to the Northwest Coast and Hawaii, Colnett was master of the *Prince of Wales*, 1787–1788, and of the *Argonaut*, 1791. The *Princess Royal*, captained by Charles Duncan, and the *Prince of Wales*, under Colnett, were in Hawaiian waters from January 2 to March 18, 1788. Archibald MENZIES was among the crew of the latter ship. The *Argonaut* and the *Prince of Wales* were captured by the Spanish during the Nootka Sound controversy in 1789. The *Argonaut* was soon returned to Colnett and came to Hawaii in April, 1791. The *Princess Royal*, under Spanish colors and commanded by Manuel QUIMPER, was in the islands at this time. The two ships met off the coast of the Big Island and Colnett, fearing that the Spanish were trying to take over Hawaii and seeing his captured ship under the Spanish ensign, almost came to the point of firing a broadside at the *Princess Royal*. See "The Journal of James Colnett aboard the *Prince of Wales* and *Princess Royal* from 16 Oct. 1786 to 7 Nov. 1788," original manuscript in the British Record Office, London; typed copy, University of Hawaii Library. See also "Journal of Capt. James Colnett aboard the *Argonaut* from April 26, 1789, to November 3, 1791," edited by F. W. Howay (Toronto: Champlain Society, 1940; Westport, Conn. Greenwood, 1968).

COOK, JAMES (1728–1779)

The leader of the expedition that first revealed the existence of the Hawaiian Islands to the rest of the world was born in a farm cottage in Yorkshire in northern England. He sailed the North Sea before rising to the rank of master's mate in the Royal Navy, and then served during the battle for Quebec in the French and Indian War. He learned to be an expert navigator and for four years mapped the coast of Newfoundland. With the rank of lieutenant, Cook was chosen to command the *Endeavour* during his first Pacific voyage.

On June 3, 1768, he observed at Tahiti the passage of the planet Venus across the face of the sun. During the next six months, Cook and his men mapped the coasts of New Zealand and the eastern coast of Australia. The small vessel went home to England around the world and Cook was soon asked to head a second Pacific expedition. On this voyage, during which he commanded the *Resolution* and *Adventure*, Cook was the first to sail south of the Antarctic Circle and discovered or rediscovered many Pacific islands. The *Resolution* returned to England in July, 1775, having sailed more than sixty thousand miles in a voyage lasting more than three years—the longest then on record. Thanks to Cook's experiments in the need for vitamins in diet, not one of his crew died of the dread disease of scurvy.

On his famed third voyage, which completed a career of ten years as the foremost figure in Pacific exploration, Cook commanded the *Resolution*; his consort ship was the *Discovery* under Captain Charles CLERKE. After revisiting islands in the South Pacific and discovering Christmas Island, the ships headed northward. On January 18, 1778, Cook sighted an island to the northeast and, soon after, another to the north. Next day, another was seen to the northwest. These were Oahu, Kauai, and Niihau, westernmost of the main islands of the Hawaiian group. Cook christened them the Sandwich Islands in honor of his patron in the British Admiralty, the Earl of Sandwich.

Many canoes came off from the coast of Kauai to the ships, which the Hawaiians called "floating islands." Trade began, helped by the fact that

(above) Captain Cook was greeted by the Hawaiians as their ancient god Lono. Unaware of the consequences of his deification, Cook agreed to undergo a ritual on the temple platform at Kealakekua Bay.

the local language was similar to that of Tahiti, and some Tahitians were aboard Cook's ships. The Hawaiians were especially eager to obtain iron nails, which they used for fishhooks. Captain Cook went ashore for the first time at the village of Waimea, Kauai, on January 21. He was greeted everywhere as if he were one of the highest chiefs. Cook also went ashore a few days later at the small island of Niihau. He was given a few yams and salt for curing pork. In return, he gave the people three goats and two English pigs, as well as some seeds to plant—melon, pumpkin, and onion.

The two ships headed north early in February, to seek the legendary Northwest Passage that would enable ships to sail between the Atlantic and Pacific Oceans north of North America. Cook spent many months exploring the coasts from Oregon on the American side across to Kamchatka on the Asian side, and

went north beyond the Arctic Circle without finding the fabled Passage. Cook decided to sail south to spend the coming winter in the warm Sandwich Islands among its friendly people. On November 26, 1778, the ships sighted the north coast of Maui, and next day viewed the mass of Haleakala Volcano. Two chiefs, KAHEKILI and KALANIOPUU, who were fighting against each other, visited the ships separately. A young chief, nephew of Kalaniopuu, spent a night aboard the *Resolution*. His name was KAMEHAMEHA, and he was quick to observe the objects that made the white strangers appear to be powerful.

Instead of running south, where he would have found the shelter of the Kona Coast, Cook began to circle the Big Island for six weeks, by way of the Hamakua Coast, Cape Kumakahi, and Ka Lae, and then went north until a haven was found at Kealakekua Bay. No fewer than ten

thousand Hawaiians, shouting and singing, "swimming about the ships like shoals of fish," or riding on surfboards, surrounded the visitors. During the months since Cook had visited the northwestern islands, the people had decided that he was their god LONO, returning to his people during the makahiki season of peace and games. Cook went through a ceremony at the heiau alongshore, but he thought that the title of "Erono" was merely one of high respect. He did not understand that from now on he was supposed to act like a god.

Kalaniopuu returned to his domain and on January 25, 1779, began visits to the ships with his procession of canoes. Gifts were exchanged and the sailors freely visited with the people ashore. The work of refitting the battered ships and collecting provisions for the voyage to Asia was marred by occasional incidents of theft. After a farewell feast, the

Captain Cook and his marines, moments before he was killed at Kealakekua Bay in 1779.

English ships sailed north on February 4. But on the night of the 7th, strong southerly winds damaged the foremast of the *Resolution* and the ships had to creep back to Kealakekua. Cook feared that he had worn out his welcome, for the makahiki season was over and all the supplies had disappeared from the region. The mast was laid out ashore, but work was interrupted by further stealing, and fights broke out between natives and sailors. When it was found that the largest boat of the *Discovery* had been stolen, Captain Cook decided to teach the Hawaiians a lesson. He went ashore early on the morning of February 14 with a lieutenant and nine marines, and attempted to take Kalaniopuu as a hostage until the boat was returned. After a series of unfortunate events, the shore party was attacked by a howling crowd of two or three hundred angry Hawaiians. They were unaware of the power of the sailors' guns, and showered the party with stones. Cook was hit with a club and then was stabbed in the neck or shoulder with one of the iron daggers made aboard the ships for trade. Cook groaned, and the Hawaiians decided that he was not their god Lono after all. Under fire from the boats offshore, the Hawaiians carried inland the bodies of their many dead and wounded, along with the bodies of four marines and the dead captain.

After some further fighting, the mast was brought back on the *Resolution* and a truce was arranged.

Part of the body of Cook was delivered to Captain Clerke, now in command, and was buried on February 21 in the waters of the bay. Other parts had been given to various chiefs ashore who had taken part in the fighting. The ships departed for the second time on the 22nd. They sailed west of Maui and north of Molokai, and skirted the north shore of Oahu before spending a few hours off Waimea, Kauai. On March 15 the ships left the Sandwich Islands and the grave of their captain in their wake. But thereafter Cook's fame spread as the world's greatest explorer by sea, and for some years the Hawaiian group was considered to be under the protection of the spreading British Empire.

Hundreds of books and articles have been published concerning James Cook and his voyages. The official account of the third voyage was published in three volumes in 1784, based on the journal of Cook himself and his successor in command of the *Resolution*, James KING. Books were also published by other members of the crew —Heinrich Zimmermann, John Rickman, William Ellis, John LEDYARD, and David SAMWELL. The best biography is John C. Beaglehole, *The Life of Captain James Cook* (Stanford, Calif.: Stanford University Press, 1974). Beaglehole edited *The Journals of Captain James Cook* (Cambridge, England, 1955–1969), in four volumes.

COOKE, AMOS STARR (1810–1871)

Born in Danbury, Connecticut, Cooke married Juliette Montague in 1836 and the couple arrived in Hawaii with the Eighth Company of American missionaries in 1837; shipmates on the voyage were Samuel Northrup CASTLE and his wife. The Cookes, as early teachers, pioneered the educational system in the islands. They took charge in 1838 of the recently founded Chiefs' Children's School (later called Royal School), attended by prominent young Hawaiians, including all five of the future monarchs of the kingdom. Juliette Cooke (1812–1896) was an especially gifted music teacher; by 1843 the royal students were performing as an orchestra. Instruction was not limited to church hymns, and Mrs. Cooke's efforts blossomed into a form new to the world, Hawaiian music. The Cookes spent a decade in this exhausting work, in addition to rearing their own children, numbering five. Cooke in 1849, at the death of Levi CHAMBERLAIN, became assistant superintendent of secular affairs for the mission. Released from service after fourteen unremitting years, Cooke became Castle's partner and began an association that resulted in the development of Castle & Cooke, a firm still outstanding in Hawaii today. Children of the Cookes, who founded a prominent island family, included

Joseph Platt Cooke, Martha Eliza Cooke, Juliette Montague Cooke ATHERTON, Amos Frank Cooke, and Clarence Warren Cooke. See Mary A. Richards, ed., *The Chiefs' Children's School: A Record Compiled from the Diary and Letters of Amos Starr Cooke and Juliette Montague Cooke* (Honolulu: Star-Bulletin, 1937).

COOKE, ANNA CHARLOTTE (RICE) (1853–1934)

Born at Punahou School, daughter of William Harrison RICE and Mary Sophia Hyde Rice, Anna spent her early years on Kauai. She was educated at Punahou School and Mills College, Oakland, California. She married Charles Montague COOKE Sr. in 1874. With her husband she established the Cooke Library at Punahou and the Aquarium at Waikiki. Mrs. Cooke also founded and endowed the Honolulu Academy of Arts, which opened in 1927 and is still a notable gallery and museum.

COOKE, CHARLES MONTAGUE Sr. (1849–1909)

Second son of Amos Starr COOKE and Juliette Montague Cooke, Charles was born in Honolulu and educated at Punahou School. After attending Amherst Agricultural College he entered the family company of Castle & Cooke. He joined in 1877 the firm of Lewers & Dickson, lumber merchants; when Joshua G. Dickson died in 1880, Cooke bought Dickson's interest and the name was changed to Lewers & Cooke. C. M. Cooke retired to California in 1894 but his talents were needed in Honolulu and he returned in 1898 to become president of the Bank of Hawaii, Ltd., succeeding the retiring Peter Coffin

JONES. In 1899 Cooke was elected president of C. Brewer & Co., an office he held till his death. He was also active in the development of several sugar plantations and was one of the original trustees of the estate of Bernice Pauahi BISHOP. With his wife, Anna Charlotte (Rice) COOKE, he helped to establish the Cooke Library at Punahou and the Aquarium at Waikiki. The couple had six children, including Charles Montague COOKE Jr. and Clarence Hyde Cooke.

COOKE, CHARLES MONTAGUE Jr. (1874–1948)

Son of Charles Montague COOKE Sr. and Anna Charlotte (Rice) COOKE, young Charles was educated at Punahou School and Yale University, where he received the bachelor's degree in 1897 and the doctorate in 1901. He married in that year Eliza Lefferts of Brooklyn, New York, and the couple went to Europe to do scientific research. Cooke returned to Hawaii in 1902 and began a lifelong affiliation with the Bernice P. Bishop Museum as a malacologist. He assembled the largest collection of Polynesian land and sea shells in the world, numbering several million. He led several zoological expeditions to Pacific islands for the Museum and published a number of scientific articles and several books on conchology. He was a regent of the University of Hawaii, president of the board of trustees of Bishop Museum, and president of the Honolulu Academy of Arts, founded by his mother.

COOPER, HENRY ERNEST (1857–1929)

Born in New Albany, Indiana, Cooper studied law in Boston and was admitted to the Massachusetts bar in 1879. He visited Hawaii in 1890 to study opportunities in investment in coffee growing, and returned soon after to organize the Hawaiian Abstract & Title Co. Cooper was a member of the

Committee of Safety in January, 1893, and when the monarchy was overthrown he read the proclamation dissolving that government. He was judge of the First Circuit Court from 1893 to 1895. He served as minister of foreign affairs in 1895 and later held half a dozen posts under the Republic, of which he was acting president for three months in 1898. Cooper was the first secretary of the Territory when that regime was established in 1900.

CORNEY, PETER (–1835)

Corney, a British seaman and adventurer, spent most of the years from 1813 to 1835 in the employ of the North West Company and later the Hudson's Bay Company. He first arrived in the Hawaiian Islands in January, 1815, as chief officer of the trading schooner *Columbia*. When this vessel was sold for twice its bulk in sandalwood, Corney stayed ashore. He became involved in 1818 in the incursion of some South American pirates, and left in command of the insurgent vessel *Santa Rosa* under the leadership of Hypólite BOUCHARD. Under Bouchard, Corney took part in the piratical raid on Monterey, capital of Spanish California.

In 1835 Corney was appointed chief officer of another *Columbia*, a bark built for the Hudson's Bay Company, and sailed from London with his wife and four children. Unfortunately, he died when the ship was in the English Channel. His family continued the voyage and settled in Honolulu, where Corney's eldest daughter, Anna, at the age of fifteen married Jules DUDOIT. Corney's book, *Voyages in the Northern Pacific, 1813–1818* (Honolulu: Thos. G. Thrum, 1896), gives an excellent account of the islands during the sandalwood era.

COX, J. HALLEY (1910–1974)
Born in Des Moines, Iowa, Cox earned degrees at San Jose State College and the University of California. After teaching in California he joined the University of Hawaii in 1948 and taught art there until his death, having served for a time as chairman of the department. He was especially skilled in watercolor and won a number of awards locally and on the mainland. Cox was particularly interested in the prehistoric art of Hawaii and the South Pacific and was co-author, with Edward Stasack, of *Hawaiian Petroglyphs* (Honolulu: Bishop Museum Press, 1970) and, with William H. Davenport, of *Hawaiian Sculpture* (Honolulu: University Press of Hawaii, 1974).

CRACROFT, SOPHIA (1816–1892)
A niece of the renowned Arctic explorer Sir John Franklin and a lifelong companion of his wife, Lady Jane Franklin, Sophia Cracroft accompanied Lady Jane to Hawaii in the summer of 1861. Her letters home, supplemented by extracts from the journals of Lady Franklin, give a lively account of the experiences of the two visitors during more than two months of travel not only on Oahu but also Kauai and the Big Island, where they viewed the volcano of Kilauea. In a second part of *The Victorian Visitors* (Honolulu: University of Hawaii Press, 1958), a collection edited by Alfons L. Korn, the tour of Europe by the widowed Queen EMMA in 1865, during which she visited Lady Franklin and Miss Cracroft in their London home, is narrated.

CRANE, CHARLES SPENCER (1869–1958)
Crane was the son of an early settler in Hawaii who captained interisland sailing ships. After studying at Punahou School, Crane worked for the Mutual Telephone Co. and then joined the Advertiser Publishing Co. in 1897; he retired as executive vice president of the firm. As a Republican he was elected supervisor of the City and County of Honolulu in 1932 and again in 1934. He completed the unexpired term of Mayor George Fred WRIGHT in 1936 and was elected mayor for one term in 1938. Crane worked for the Boy Scouts of America for forty-five years and was a prominent Mason. He lived in California from 1945 to 1953 but returned to Hawaii for his last five years.

CRAWFORD, DAVID LIVINGSTON (1889–1974)
Crawford was born in a Mormon colony in northern Sonora, Mexico, a son of Matthew A. Crawford and Harriet Sturges, a descendant of early American missionaries in the Pacific. Like his brother, Will Crawford, David attended Pomona College and then Stanford University and Cornell University, qualifying as an entomologist. He married Leona Mudgett in 1914. After managing a co-operative fruit-marketing company in eastern Mexico, he taught at Pomona College before coming in 1917 to the College of Hawaii (later the University of Hawaii). He was also athletic coach at the College from 1917 to 1919 and coached the 1919 championship football team of the Territory. He became first head of the University Extension Service and in 1927 was appointed president, serving until 1942.

At the time Crawford took office he was the youngest university president in the United States. He developed a thriving summer-session program, and the regular enrollment grew during his tenure from 236 to 1,500 students. After leaving Hawaii during World War II, he worked for the War Production Board in Puerto Rico and later served with the United States Foreign Economic Administration in Mexico. He and his wife were authors of *Missionary Adventures in the South Pacific* (Rutland, Vt. and Tokyo: Tuttle, 1967), an account of her American grandparents, Albert and Susan Sturges.

CROSBY, WILLIAM (1889–1961)
Born in Nebraska, Crosby obtained a bachelor's degree from Yale School of Forestry in 1911 and a master's degree in 1913. He worked in Cuba and the Philippines before coming to act as head forester on the island of Maui from 1927 to 1939, when he became head of the Territorial Forestry Department, retiring in 1955. In this post Crosby was responsible for one million acres of forest reserve and watershed lands. Millions of trees were planted on these areas under his direction.

CUMMINS, JOHN ADAMS (1835–1913)
Born on Oahu, Cummins was the son of an English settler in Hawaii with wide sugar, cattle, and agricultural holdings, and a Hawaiian mother; through her he was distantly related to Kamehameha I. After attending the Royal School, Cummins worked on his father's ranch, becoming manager in 1855. He married a lady named Kahalewai in 1863, and after her death married Kapeka Mersburg in 1902. He founded the lucrative Waimanalo

Sugar Plantation on the east side of Oahu, where he was often visited by royalty, his close friends. Cummins was appointed minister of foreign affairs by King Kalakaua in 1890. He took part in the counter-revolution of 1895 and was fined for conspiracy to overthrow the Republic. He was a promoter of horse racing and introduced some blooded stock to the islands; he was a charter member of the Hawaiian Jockey Club in 1885. Cummins was given a ten-ton pilot boat by friends in Boston, in which he cruised from his dock at Waimanalo to every port and inlet in the islands. In order to visit the Cummins house, portly King Kamehameha V had a short railway line laid from the boat landing.

CUNHA, ALBERT R. (SONNY) (1879–1933)
Born in Honolulu, Cunha graduated from St. Louis High School and Punahou School (1897) and for a time attended Yale Law School; he is credited with composing Yale's "Boola Boola" song. He went on to a career as composer and arranger, band leader, pianist, singer, businessman, and politician. He was an active performer not only in the islands but also on the mainland. He is considered the chief popularizer of hapa-haole songs, and published the first collection of these (*Famous Hawaiian Songs* [Honolulu: Bergstrom Music Co., 1914]). He influenced such other popularizers as Johnny NOBLE and Henry Kailimai. Later Cunha set up the Cunha Music Co. to publish his work and that of others. He was interested not only in Hawaiian music but also in jazz and ragtime, march, semi-classical works, and opera. Cunha was elected to the Territorial House of Representatives from 1923 to 1924 and was a member of the Honolulu Board of Supervisors from 1924 to 1927. He married May Williams in 1910 and the couple had one son and one daughter.

CURTIS, CAROLINE (1884–1979)
Born in Adrian, Michigan, the future teacher and author graduated from Mount Holyoke College in 1906 and attended several universities. She came to teach at Hanahauoli School in 1928 and spent a dozen years at that school. She was asked to teach the culture of ancient Hawaii and began a lifelong study of the daily life and lore of these people. Later she taught for twenty years in the preparatory department of the Kamehameha Schools before retiring in 1964 at the age of eighty. She was nationally known as a storyteller, and published seven books of Hawaiian tales, three of them in collaboration with Mary Kawena Pukui.

DAMIEN, FATHER (JOSEPH DE VEUSTER) (1840–1889)
Born in Tremeloo, Belgium, Damien came to Hawaii in 1864 as a Picpus father and was ordained in Honolulu. He worked among the Hawaiian people on other islands before being sent, at his request, in 1873 to the leper colony on Molokai. He labored there until his death from the disease, contracted in 1883, and was buried at the church he built there. In 1936 his body was removed in great state to Antwerp. Much notoriety came to Damien from the "open letter" published by Robert Louis STEVENSON to the Rev. Charles McEwen HYDE. A statue of Damien by Marisol Escobar is one of the two representing the State of Hawaii in the national capitol in Washington; the other statue is of KAMEHAMEHA I. See Charles Warren Stoddard, *The Lepers of Molokai* (Notre Dame, Ind.: Ave Maria Press, 1885) and A. Gavin Daws, *Holy Man* (New York: Harper, 1973).

DAMON, ETHEL MOSELEY (1883–1965)
Ethel Damon was born in Honolulu, a descendant of Samuel Chenery DAMON. She was educated at Punahou School and earned a bachelor's degree from Wellesley College in 1909. She taught at Punahou until 1917 and then served for two years with the American Red Cross in France. She was awarded the Belgian Order of Elizabeth for her work with refugees. Returning to Hawaii, she began writing local history. Among her writings are *Koamalu*, a two-volume history of Kauai and especially the family of William Harrison RICE (Honolulu: privately printed, 1931), and a half a dozen other studies.

DAMON, FRANCIS WILLIAMS (1852–1915)
Son of Samuel Chenery DAMON, Francis married Mary R. Happar in 1884 and the couple were prominent in church and school work. They helped to found the First Chinese Church of Christ, and in 1892 opened their home as a school for teaching English to Chinese boys. This later became the Mills School, which was combined with the Kawaiahao Girls' Seminary and the Okamura School to form the present Mid-Pacific Institute. The Damons also inspired the founding of the Free Kindergarten Association in Hawaii, along with Julia Montague Cooke ATHERTON.

DAMON, SAMUEL CHENERY (1815–1885)

Damon, born in Holden, Massachusetts, was educated at Amherst College and Andover Theological Seminary. In 1841 he was ordained and married Julia Sherman Mills. He was sent to Honolulu by the American Seamen's Friend Society to act as chaplain at Honolulu, where the couple arrived in 1842. Damon was pastor of Oahu Bethel Church for forty-two years. He was also editor and publisher of *The Friend*, a periodical established in 1843 that ran well into the twentieth century. Damon traveled widely on church business and served on a number of local boards. The Damons had five children, including Francis Williams and Samuel Mills DAMON. The family is still prominent in Hawaii today. See Ethel M. Damon, *Samuel Chenery Damon* (Honolulu: privately printed, 1966).

DAMON, SAMUEL MILLS (1845–1924)

Born in Honolulu, son of Samuel Chenery DAMON, Samuel was educated at Punahou School. He began his outstanding business career as a clerk in the store of W. N. Ladd & Co. He married Harriet M. Baldwin of Lahaina, Maui, in 1872 and they had no fewer than ten children. In 1871 Damon went to the Bank of Bishop & Co., then the only bank in the islands. He was made a partner in 1881, and when Charles R. BISHOP moved to California in 1894, Damon acquired his interest and headed this institution. Damon realized the promising future of the sugar industry and became a director of a number of large plantations.

Damon was made minister of finance under Kalakaua in 1887 and held that post through the periods of the Provisional Government and the Republic. It was Damon who frankly advised Liliuokalani during the Revolution of 1893 to yield to those who wanted a change of government. However, in 1897 he was sent to London to represent the former queen at the Diamond Jubilee of Queen Victoria. Damon's interest in education was keen and he served as a member of the Bernice P. Bishop Trust, whose income went to the support of the Kamehameha Schools. Perhaps his most memorable contribution was the creation of the lovely Moanalua Gardens on the large estate that he owned to the west of Honolulu, bequeathed to him by Bernice Pauahi BISHOP.

DAMPIER, ROBERT (1800–1874)

Ship's artist under Lord BYRON on H. M. S. *Blonde*, Dampier kept a journal and made a number of drawings of Hawaii in 1824. See *To the Sandwich Islands on H. M. S. "Blonde"* (Honolulu: University Press of Hawaii, 1971), edited by Pauline King Joerger.

DANA, RICHARD HENRY (1815–1882)

Dana, a Boston lawyer and author of *Two Years before the Mast* (1840), came to Hawaii on a round-the-world trip in the autumn of 1859. He presented letters of introduction and soon was a visitor at the homes of a number of prominent residents. He was given a special audience by Kamehameha IV. Dana also visited the prison, various churches, the Royal School, and Punahou School. He took a schooner to the Big Island, crossed the Ka'u Desert and viewed Kilauea Crater, and suffered a riding accident during his stay in Hilo. Remarks on his two-month tour of the islands are to be found in his *Journal* (Cambridge, Mass.: Harvard University Press, 1968), edited by Robert F. Lucid.

DAVIES, THEOPHILUS HARRIS (1833–1898)

Davies was born in England and left Liverpool for Hawaii in 1856. He was under a five-year contract to Robert Janion, who had returned to England after setting up a merchandising business in Honolulu with various partners. Davies became a close friend of Kamehameha V during his five-year term and after a short absence returned to Honolulu. He opened a store under the name of Theo. H. Davies in 1868 with Janion as a silent partner; in 1870, Janion, Green & Co. was merged with Theo. H. Davies, which was incorporated in 1894. The firm acted as financial agent for twenty-two sugar plantations on several islands.

Davies was a prominent member of the Episcopal Church of Honolulu. By 1890 he had accumulated a large fortune and had retired from active management. He returned to England, where he became the guardian of KAIULANI for four years while she studied there. He escorted her to Washington, D.C., in 1893 to help advance her claim to the throne of Hawaii abdicated by her aunt, LILIUOKALANI. Theo. H. Davies & Co. was considered one of the Big Five firms of Hawaii. See *Davies* (Honolulu: Topgallant, 1983), by Edwin P. Hoyt.

DAVIS, ISAAC (AIKAKE) (c. 1758–1810)

Davis, born in Milford, England, was the sole survivor of the massacre in 1790 of the crew of the *Fair American* (see John YOUNG) because he had fought bravely. He was found tied to a canoe, half blind and half dead. He was nursed back to health by an American beachcomber named Isaac Ridler. Like his friend Young, Davis was made a high chief and helped Kamehameha I in his dealings with foreigners and in his wars of conquest.

Davis married a relative of the king and founded a prominent family in the islands. He held estates on Hawaii, Maui, Molokai, and Oahu, and for a time was governor of Oahu. His daughter, Betty, married George P. KAUMUALII, and it is said that Davis was poisoned and died because he warned King KAUMUALII of a plot to kill him when the ruler of Kauai came to Honolulu in 1810 to confirm the cession of his island to Kamehameha. Three children of Davis's second marriage (to Kalukuna, also known as Grace Kamaikui) were adopted by John Young after Davis died. Isaac Young Davis, a grandson and one of nineteen children, was the second husband of Princess RUTH.

DAVIS, WILLIAM HEATH, Sr. (–1822)

Davis, a genial Boston ship captain, arrived in the islands in the *Isabella* in 1812 and is credited, along with Jonathan and Nathan WINSHIP, with setting up the market for sandalwood in that year. Davis

was popular at first with Kamehameha I and his son Liholiho but often neglected business in favor of heavy drinking. In 1817 Davis brought from Boston a ship named *Eagle* and soon afterward the middle-aged captain married seventeen-year-old Hannah Holmes, daughter of Oliver HOLMES. Two sons were born of this union: Robert G. Davis (Lopaka), a member of the Hawaii legislature and justice of the supreme court, and William Heath Davis Jr., a pioneer builder in California.

During 1818 and 1819 Davis in the *Eagle* voyaged to Sitka, California, and Mexico. In 1821 and 1822 John Coffin JONES twice chartered another *Eagle*, a schooner, to Davis. On the second voyage, under a captain named John Rogers, the crew failed to recapture another vessel, the *Cossack*, and was wrecked. Jones accepted the loss for his firm but Davis, broken by the news, literally drank himself to death in November, 1822.

DEAN, ARTHUR LYMAN (1878–1952)

Born in Southwick, Massachusetts, Dean obtained a bachelor's degree from Harvard in 1900 and a doctorate from Yale in 1902. He taught chemistry at Sheffield Scientific School at Yale before coming in 1914 to serve as president of the College of Hawaii, which became the University of Hawaii in 1920; he resigned from the presidency in 1927. Dean was chosen executive director of the Territorial Food Commission in 1917 and director of the Association of Hawaiian Pineapple Canners in 1927. In 1930 he became a vice president of Alexander & Baldwin and head of the pineapple division. Dean was a founder of the Institute of Pacific

Relations and a president of the Honolulu Council of Social Agencies, as well as a member of a number of local and national societies. He solved the problem of refining chaulmoogra oil into specific use as a palliative in the treatment of leprosy. Dean married Leora E. Parmalee and they had three children.

DEBORAH. See KAPULE.

DELANO, AMASA (1763–1823)

Born in Duxbury, Massachusetts, Delano was a sea officer for much of his life. He visited Hawaii in 1801 and again in 1806; Chapter 21 of his book, *A Narrative of Voyages and Travels* (Boston: E. G. House, 1817), describes his later visit.

DESHA, STEPHEN LANGHERNE Sr. (1859–1934)

Desha was born at Lahaina, Maui, son of John Rollin Langherne Desha of a Kentucky family and Eliza (Brewer) Desha. Stephen attended the Royal School and North Pacific Institute. He married Mary K. Kekumano in 1884 and they had three children, including Stephen L. DESHA Jr. After his first wife's death in 1915 he married Julia Keonaona.

Desha was one of the most eloquent contemporary orators in the Hawaiian language. He began his career as pastor of the Napoopoo Church at Kona in 1884 and served there for five years, when he was called to the pastorate of the Haili Church, Hilo. He was a supervisor of the County of Hawaii when county government was begun in 1905; he was elected to the third Board of Supervisors in 1909. Later he served for three terms in the territorial senate. In 1907 he began acting as editor and business manager of the newspaper *Ka Hoku o Hawaii*, and was known as an authority on Hawaiian legends. He was a member of various Hawaiian civic groups.

DESHA, STEPHEN LANGHERNE Jr. (1885–1957)
Born at Napoopoo, Hawaii, son of Stephen L. DESHA Sr., Stephen Jr. was educated at the Kamehameha School for Boys and Punahou School. He taught in the public schools and became a clerk of the District Court of South Hilo from 1910 to 1913. He then attended George Washington University and obtained the bachelor degree in law in 1917. He established in 1919 the law firm of Desha & Desha with his brother, Judge John R. Desha. From 1920 to 1934 Stephen served as district judge, South Hilo, as well as United States commissioner for the district. He decided in 1934 to enter the ministry and attended San Francisco Theological Seminary. He served as minister at large for West Hawaii before taking his father's post in 1950 as pastor of Haili Church in Hilo. Desha was secretary of the Republican Committee for the County of Hawaii and a member of various Hilo organizations.

DE SILVA, ERNEST G. (1873–1955)
Born at Madeira, Portugal, De Silva came to Hawaii at the age of fifteen. He worked as a jeweler with H. S. Wichman & Co. in Honolulu while studying for the ministry with the Hawaiian Board of Missions. He was ordained in 1899 and, except for a few years on the island of Maui, he was associated with the Central Christian Church in Hilo, Hawaii, from 1899 until his death.

DE VEUSTER, JOSEPH. See DAMIEN, FATHER.

DIBBLE, SHELDON (1809–1845)
Born at Skaneateles, New York, Dibble graduated from Hamilton College in 1827 and obtained a master's degree at Auburn Theological Seminary in Massachusetts in 1830. In the same year he married Maria M. Tomlinson and sailed for Hawaii with the Fourth Company of American missionaries. The couple were stationed at Hilo in 1831 and at Lahainaluna Seminary, Maui, in 1834. After the death of his wife in 1837, he traveled to the United States in search of improved health. He married Antoinette Tomlinson in 1839 before returning to Lahaina in 1840.

Dibble taught history at the seminary and introduced the seminar method to the islands by having his students return to their homes and collect oral history from their elders. He assisted in the translation of the Bible and from 1832 to 1840 translated more than a dozen volumes of scholarly and scriptural work for the benefit of Hawaiian readers. He was author of *A History and General Views of the Sandwich Islands Mission* (New York: Taylor & Dodd, 1839) and *History of the Sandwich Islands* (Lahaina, Maui: Press of the Mission Seminary, 1843), as well as a history in Hawaiian, *Ka Moolele Hawaii* (Lahainaluna: Mission Press, 1838); a translation into English by Reuben Tinker was issued serially in 1839 and 1840.

DICKEY, CHARLES WILLIAM (1871–1942)
Born in Alameda, California, Dickey attended public schools in Oakland and obtained a bachelor's degree from Massachusetts Institute of Technology in 1894. He married Frances Greene in 1899. Dickey came to Hawaii and designed business buildings, churches, hotels, schools, public buildings, and private homes. Among these were the Kamehameha School for Boys; Montague Hall at Punahou School; Castle & Cooke Building; Toyo, Varsity, Hilo, and Waikiki Theaters; Halekulani Hotel; Kona Inn; Naniloa Hotel in Hilo; Wilcox Memorial Hospital at Lihue; and Kula Sanatorium on Maui. He was associated with the design of Honolulu's City Hall and central fire station, as well as Mayor Wright Homes and Kamehameha Homes. He was a member of the Honolulu City Planning Commission from 1931 to 1938. In addition to contributing much to architecture in the islands, Dickey was a sailing enthusiast and book collector.

DIELL, JOHN (1808–1841)
Born in Cherry Valley, New York, Diell graduated from Hamilton College in 1827 and Andover Theological Seminary in 1832. He married Caroline A. Platt in July of that year and the couple sailed with the Sixth Company in November. He was the first chaplain of the American Seamen's Friend Society in Honolulu in 1833. He organized the Oahu Bethel Church in 1837, the first church opened for foreigners in the islands. The Bethel Hall could hold five hundred people, and the Diells distributed Bibles, tracts, and even spelling books to help sailors to read. Diell was succeeded by the Rev. Samuel C. DAMON in 1842. The Diells left for the United States in 1840 and he died at sea in the Pacific. The Diells had four children.

DILLINGHAM, BENJAMIN FRANKLIN (1844–1918)

The founder of the Dillingham clan in Hawaii, who stayed in the islands as a result of a broken leg, was born in West Brewster, Massachusetts, of old Puritan stock. He left the public schools of Worcester at the age of fourteen for a voyage around Cape Horn. As an officer on a Northern ship during the Civil War, he was landed in Brazil when the vessel was burned by the raider *Alabama*. As first officer of the bark *Whistler*, which stopped at Honolulu in 1864, Dillingham was thrown by a horse when riding ashore and began a long stay in the hospital. He was befriended by the Rev. Lowell SMITH, whose daughter, Emma Louise, married Dillingham in 1869.

The former sailor began a business career as a clerk in the hardware store of Henry DIMOND on six months' trial. With the financing of his partner Alfred Castle, a son of Samuel Northrop CASTLE, Dillingham bought Dimond's business and changed the name to Dillingham & Co. In 1889 Dillingham gave his full attention to linking Honolulu with the north shore of Oahu by means of a railroad. Part of the plan called for the acquisition of six thousand acres of agricultural land on the arid Ewa plain, to be cultivated by laborers from Portugal. Despite opposition, both parts of the plan were successfully carried out. Dillingham and his associates obtained a franchise for the Oahu Steam Railway in 1888, and its roadbed reached Ewa within a year. "Dillingham's Folly," with 170 miles of track, became the greatest single factor in the agricultural development of the island of Oahu. By 1890, railroads were in operation not only on Oahu but on Maui and Hawaii.

The development of artesian wells at Ewa was a boon to Dillingham. Pumping of underground water made possible the irrigation of spreading canefields on Ewa Plantation. Dillingham turned his energies to furnishing more freight for the railroad by developing other plantations at Kahuku, Honolulu, and Waialua. Later he extended his operations to neighbor islands and promoted McBryde Sugar Co.; Kihei Plantation Co., Ltd.; Puna Sugar Co., Ltd.; and Olaa Sugar Co., Ltd. He also built on Hawaii what was later known as the Hawaii Consolidated Railway. Such operations extended Dillingham's credit to the point where in 1903 his obligations totaled more than the public debt of the Republic at the time of annexation. Fortunately, his son Walter F. DILLINGHAM was able to assume responsibility for the financial direction of the many family enterprises. The father was free to retire and enjoy the realization of his dreams, but remained as president of the Oahu Railway & Land Co. until his death. Other children of the Dillinghams were Harold Garfield Dillingham, Mary Emma Dillingham FREAR, and Marion Dillingham Erdman. See *Millstones and Milestones: The Career of B. F. Dillingham in Hawaii, 1844–1918* (Honolulu: University Press of Hawaii, 1981), by Paul T. Yardley.

DILLINGHAM, WALTER FRANCIS (1875–1963)

Born in Honolulu, son of Benjamin Franklin DILLINGHAM, Walter was educated at Punahou School and Harvard University. He began his business life as a clerk in the offices of the Oahu Railway & Land Co. founded by his father, and in 1900 became manager of Dowsett & Co., Ltd. He organized and was the first manager and treasurer of the Hawaiian Dredging Co., Ltd., and began a lifelong concern for developing harbors at Honolulu, Hilo, Kahului, Ahukini, and Kamelapau, and for improving the Pearl Harbor Naval Base—where his firm as joint contractor built a gigantic drydock completed in 1919. In 1904, when his father became ill, Walter with the help of his brother, Harold Garfield Dillingham, took over the family interests and weathered a financial crisis. The firm also reclaimed land in Waikiki and Ala Moana Park and dredged Kewalo Basin for the fishing boats; later, under the supervision of Walter's eldest son, Lowell Smith Dillingham, the spreading Ala Moana Center shopping complex was constructed. During World War II, Hawaiian Dredging did major contracting work at Kaneohe Bay, Oahu, and at Johnston, Midway, Wake and Guam Islands.

Walter Dillingham was a director of many local firms and promoted the construction of the Dillingham Transportation Building. He also helped to develop the Los Angeles Steamship Co., later merged with

Matson Navigation Co. Despite his many business interests, Dillingham was a sharpshooter and commander of mounted reserves during the counter-revolution of 1895 and was often called upon to head such efforts as the Board of Health campaign during the cholera epidemic of 1899. His favorite recreation was polo; he organized the Hawaii Polo and Racing Association and captained victorious teams in many matches on the mainland.

Walter Dillingham, a confirmed Republican who never sought office, is regarded as the leader of the anti-statehood forces that for many years were able to defer the granting of full citizenship to Hawaii residents. He married Louise Olga Gaylord in Florence, Italy, in 1910. In addition to Lowell, the couple had three other children: Benjamin Franklin Dillingham Jr., Henry Gaylord Dillingham (a flyer killed in World War II), and Elizabeth Louise Dillingham. For years their home, La Pietra, on Diamond Head, was a showplace and the foremost center of hospitality for visiting celebrities.

DILLON, GUILLAUME PATRICE. See Jules DUDOIT and Leogarant de TROMELIN.

DIMOND, HENRY (1808–1895)
Born in Fairfield, Connecticut, Dimond was trained as a bookbinder and studied for almost three years at New York University before marrying Ann Maria Anner in November, 1834, and sailing with the Seventh Company of American Missionaries a month later. The Dimonds were stationed at the Mission Press in Honolulu where, under his charge, hundreds of thousands of church publications were turned out. The first complete edition of the Bible in Hawaiian was finished in May, 1839. After 1850 Dimond was not needed and he was released by the mission to engage in a mercantile business in Honolulu. The Dimonds had seven children.

DIXON, GEORGE
Dixon was armorer on the *Discovery* under James COOK during his third Pacific voyage. As master of the *Queen Charlotte*, Dixon sailed in company with Nathaniel PORTLOCK on trading voyages between the Northwest Coast of America and China that first visited the Hawaiian Islands in 1786. The *Queen Charlotte* arrived May 20 and departed June 13; it returned November 16 and departed March 15, 1787. On a third voyage it arrived September 5, 1787, and departed September 18.

DOI, ISAMI (1903–1965)
Born at Ewa, Oahu, Doi studied art for two years under Professor Chipman at the University of Hawaii and spent five more years at Columbia University. He returned to Oahu in 1928 and held his first one-man show, but maintained a studio in New York City from 1931 to 1937. He moved from Oahu to Kauai in 1938. Doi published two books of wood engravings, including some chosen among the fifty best prints in the United States in several competitions. Best known for his oils, Doi also worked in jewelry, ceramics, and engravings. The Honolulu Academy of Arts possessed two watercolors, six oils, and forty of his prints at the time of his death.

DOLE, DANIEL (1808–1878)
Born in Bloomfield, Maine, Dole graduated from Bowdoin College in 1836 and Bangor Theological Seminary in 1839. He was ordained in 1840 and with his wife, Emily Hoyt Ballard Dole, arrived with the Ninth Company of American Missionaries at Hawaii the following year. In 1841 Dole was the first principal of an academy built on

the outskirts of Honolulu for the education of the children of Protestant missionaries; in 1853 it was granted a government charter under the title of "Punahou School and Oahu College." It is still thriving, known as "the oldest high school west of the Rockies." Dole resigned as principal in 1853 and became pastor of a congregation at Koloa, Kauai, and although released from the mission worked at Koloa until his death. By his first marriage Dole had two children: George Hathaway Dole and Sanford Ballard DOLE, who later headed the government of the islands for a decade. When his first wife died in 1844, Daniel Dole married Mrs. Charlotte Close Knapp, widow of missionary Horton Owen Knapp.

DOLE, JAMES DRUMMOND (1877–1958)
Dole was born in Boston, a relative of Sanford Ballard DOLE. He attended private and public schools in Boston and obtained a bachelor's degree from Harvard University in 1899. In that year he came to Hawaii and pioneered in the pineapple industry, still the second most important source of agricultural income in the islands. A band of farmers from southern California had homesteaded around Wahiawa, Oahu. They had reduced stoop labor by planting the prickly rows of pineapples with lanes between so that they could be cultivated by horse-drawn vehicles. The mechanics of preparing and canning the fruit so that the product would not explode on

docks or grocery shelves was, however, still to be solved. Dole realized that the future lay in developing an export trade in canned fruit of high quality. On December 4, 1901, he organized the Hawaiian Pineapple Co., whose first crop was packed in 1903. The company in 1906 set up a plant in the Iwilei district of Honolulu which was one of the largest fruit canneries in the world.

Dole was president and general manager of the company from 1903 to 1932, when he was made chairman of the board until his retirement in 1948. The company purchased most of the island of Lanai in 1922 for $1,100,000 and developed a harbor, a "city" for workers, and a vast plantation. Marketing a luxury fruit was a problem and the Hawaiian Pineapple Growers Association was formed in 1908 to begin a successful publicity campaign. A publicity effort not so successful was Dole's offer in 1927 of two prizes, amounting to $25,000, for the first civilian aircraft to fly from California to Hawaii. Out of eight planes starting from Oakland, two smashed while taking off, two were forced to turn back, two others disappeared in the Pacific, and only two entries completed this longest overwater race up to that time. Altogether, the "Dole Derby" cost the lives of ten persons.

Eased out of active management of Hawaiian Pineapple Co. in 1932, Dole worked in the Agricultural Adjustment Administration in Washington, D.C., in 1933, and in 1937 moved to San Francisco, where he remained until he returned to Hawaii in 1958. In 1937 he developed a process for canning natural carrot juice, and in 1940, one for canning and bottling apple juice.

He later devised a milk canning process. In 1906 Dole married Belle Dickey of Honolulu and they had five children.

DOLE, SANFORD BALLARD (1844–1926)

The long life of Dole spanned the pre-statehood epochs of modern Hawaiian history, in which he took a leading role. He was born in Honolulu, son of Daniel DOLE, founder of Punahou School. Sanford spent a year at Williams College, Massachusetts, and studied for another year in the office of a Washington, D.C., lawyer before being admitted to the courts of Suffolk County, Massachusetts, in 1867. He returned to Hawaii soon thereafter and set up a practice while engaging in a lifelong concern with politics. He married Anna P. Cate of Castine, Maine, in 1873 (she died childless in 1921).

Dole was elected to the legislature of the kingdom in 1884 and was prominent in the reform movement that led to the "Bayonet Constitution" of 1887. In 1884 he drafted and saw enacted the first Hawaiian homestead law. He was appointed to the Supreme Court in 1886 as an associated justice and served for six years. A leader among those who overturned the monarchy in 1893, Dole was elected president of the Provisional Government and firmly led the islands through the difficult times of the Republic and into annexation by the United States. He diplomatically weathered the counter-revolution led by Robert W. WILCOX to restore Queen LILIUOKALANI, and was appointed by President William McKinley as first governor of the Territory of Hawaii in 1900. He served until 1903 and then was named United States district judge, a post he held until 1916, when he retired to private practice. In 1911 Dole and the former queen were publicly reconciled. For a

number of terms Judge Dole, unmistakable with his long white beard, was president of the Hawaiian Bar Association. Dole was early interested in literature and his *Memoirs of the Hawaiian Revolution* (Honolulu: Advertiser Publishing Co., 1936) appeared after his death. See Ethel M. Damon, *Sanford Ballard Dole and His Hawaii* (Palo Alto, Calif.: Pacific Books, 1957).

DOMINIS, JOHN OWEN (1832–1891)

Born in Schenectady, New York, the future prince consort was the son of a ship captain from the Mediterranean who had prospered in the trade in furs and casks of salmon from Northwestern America. The son arrived with his parents in Hawaii around 1840. The captain was apparently lost at sea in the next decade. Dominis worked for G. B. Post & Co., San Francisco, during the gold rush, and then for several years with R. Cody & Co., ship chandlers in Honolulu.

Dominis became secretary and chamberlain to King Kamehameha IV. On the death of Mataio KEKUANAOA in 1868, Kamehameha V appointed Dominis governor of Oahu, a post he held until 1887. He was also commissioner of crown lands and a lieutenant general in the army of Kalakaua. In 1862 Dominis married Lydia LILIUOKALANI. They lived in the Dominis home, Washington

Place, now the official residence of the governors of Hawaii. Dominis exercised wise restraint over his somewhat headstrong wife, and had he lived during her crisis her abrupt abdication might have been averted; however, he died seven months after her accession to the crown in 1891.

DOUGLAS, DAVID (1798–1834)

Douglas was a Scottish botanist who collected many plants in Oregon and California as well as in Hawaii. The Douglas fir bears his name. He visited Hawaii first in 1832 and returned in 1833. In his last year, he tried to walk across the Big Island. He was found in a pit with a trapped bull and apparently gored to death, but people who knew him claimed that he had been robbed and murdered. A plaque marks the spot, known on maps as Kaluakauka, or "the doctor's pit." See William Frederick Wilson, *David Douglas, Botanist in Hawaii* (Honolulu: privately printed, 1919) and William Morwood, *Traveler in a Vanished Landscape: The Life and Times of David Douglas* (New York: C. N. Potter, 1973).

DOUGLAS, WILLIAM. See John MEARES.

DOWSETT, JAMES ISAAC (1829–1898)

Dowsett, eldest son of Samuel James DOWSETT, was said to have been the first Anglo-Saxon child, not of missionary parentage, born in the islands. Less than five years old when his father sailed away, he was hardly more than twelve when he was hired by the Hudson's Bay Co. but continued his schooling on the side. His mother refused offers of remarriage and remained a widow until her death.

During his youth, Dowsett was a playmate of Kamehameha IV, Kamehameha V, and future king Lunalilo. The young man made small investments and became one of the leaders in developing the whaling trade in the islands. He soon owned a fleet of whaling ships that made annual forays into the Arctic. He also engaged in the lumber business and had a little fleet of schooners and small steamers operating among the islands. He also owned ranches and sugar plantations on Oahu, and later obtained the famous Ulupalakua Ranch on Maui. He developed blooded stock and was the first to import Aberdeen Angus cattle. During the 1880s and 1890s, Dowsett engaged in politics; he was a member of the House of Nobles during the reigns of Kalakaua and Liliuokalani, but was a supporter of the Revolution of 1893.

Dowsett died on June 14, 1898, shortly before the American flag was raised over Hawaii. He had married Annie Green Ragsdale and the couple were parents of thirteen children left to develop his wide holdings. The most successful capitalist in the family was Samuel Henry Dowsett, a grandson of the sea captain, who was manager of the Dowsett Co., Ltd.

DOWSETT, SAMUEL JAMES (1794–1834?)

Dowsett, an early settler in the islands, was born at Rochester, Kent, in England, the eldest of twenty-one brothers and one of twenty-three children. His wife, Mary Bishop, was also of English descent. Dowsett first saw the islands in 1822 as first officer of the cutter *Mermaid*, which accompanied the schooner *Prince Regent*, a six-gun vessel promised to Kamehameha I by George VANCOUVER. Dowsett returned to his station at Sydney, Australia, and there purchased a ship, *Wellington*, which he sailed to Honolulu in 1828, accompanied by his wife and infant daughter. The captain engaged in trade in Hawaii. On June 1, 1834, he sailed from Honolulu in command of the ship *Victoria* on a pearl-fishing expedition to the Pescadores Islands, leaving behind a wife and four children: Deborah Melville (born at Melville Island); James ISAAC; Elizabeth Jane, who later married M. C. MONSARRAT; and Samuel Henry Dowsett. When Captain Dowsett had not returned after a year, the government sent the brig *Waverly* to seek him. The brig was cut off by natives of Strong's Island, captain and crew were murdered, and the ship burned. No trace was ever seen of Captain Dowsett.

DUDOIT, JULES (1803–1866)

Born in Port-Louis, Mauritius, Dudoit went to America at the age of thirteen to become a seaman, and was back in Mauritius in 1826 as captain of a bring, *Le Courrier de Tamatave*. He sailed for Australia in 1832 in command of the brig *Clementine*, named for his wife, who had died less than a year after the wedding. After several years of Pacific trading he first arrived in Hawaii in 1835. He returned to Honolulu and married a fifteen-year-old shipmate, Anna Corney, orphaned daughter of Peter CORNEY. The *Clementine*, which Dudoit had chartered to several local businessmen in 1837, was the prison of the French priests Bachelot and Short (see MAIGRET). Dudoit served as the rather contentious French consul from 1837 to 1848, when he was replaced by Guillaume Patrice Dillon, an even more chauvinistic career diplomat (see TROMELIN). Dudoit became a Hawaiian subject and continued his business affairs in Honolulu until he was murdered by his Chinese cook. The name of Dudoit is not uncommon in Hawaii today.

DUTTON, IRA BARNES (BROTHER JOSEPH) (1843–1931)

Dutton, who became a Catholic lay missionary at the leper colony on the island of Molokai, was born at Stowe, Vermont. He attended the academy at Milton, Wisconsin, where his mother was a teacher. Dutton enlisted in the Union forces as a private and in 1865 was commissioned as a first lieutenant and regimental quartermaster. After ten years of government service, as a Catholic convert he heard of the labors of Father DAMIEN. Dutton went at once to Molokai and began a lifelong devotion to the work of the mission. In more than forty years he did not leave the peninsula for one day, and was untiring in his labors. In 1889 Brother Dutton administered the estate of Damien and later became builder and superintendent of the Baldwin Home for orphan boys and helpless cases at Kalawao, two miles from the settlement at Kalaupapa. Dutton's greatest recognition came when the American Great White Fleet, on a world cruise, saluted him from the Molokai Channel in 1908.

DWIGHT, SAMUEL GELSTON (1815–1880)

Born in Northampton, Massachusetts, Dwight graduated from Union Theological Seminary in New York City in 1847. A single man, he sailed with the Twelfth Company of American missionaries and in 1848 was stationed at Kaluaaha, Molokai. He was released from the service in 1854 and married Anna Mahoe, but remained as scribe at Kaluaaha until 1857 and also operated a dairy farm at Pukoo. The Dwights then moved to Honolulu for the rest of their lives. They had six children.

EDMONDSON, CHARLES HOWARD (1876–1970)

Born in Milton, Iowa, Edmondson obtained a doctorate at Iowa State University. After teaching on the mainland he became a professor of zoology and director of the Marine Laboratory at the University of Hawaii from 1920 until his retirement in 1942. He carried on much research on the growth of corals and life on the coral reef, and published a number of papers. Edmondson Hall on the Manoa campus is named for him.

ELLIS, WILLIAM (1794–1872)

Born in London of a poor family, Ellis was ordained in 1815 as a member of the London Missionary Society. For five years after 1817 he and his wife labored in the Society Islands in the South Pacific, where he was a pioneer printer in the region. He arrived in Hawaii on March 28, 1822, in the *Prince Regent* with a delegation of the Society. His knowledge of the Tahitian language enabled him to learn Hawaiian quickly, and he was the first person to preach a sermon in the latter tongue. His help at the printing press set up by Elisha LOOMIS was so greatly appreciated that he was invited to return to Hawaii and work permanently.

Ellis returned from the South Pacific with his family in 1823. At that time no mission station had been opened on the island of Hawaii, and Ellis was a member of a party sent to look for suitable sites. In June they began a two-month circuit of the Big Island by foot and canoe. Ellis and three other members of the group, including the Rev. Asa THURSTON and the Rev. Artemas BISHOP, were the first foreigners to ascend the active volcano of Kilauea.

After eighteen months the Ellises left for England because of the wife's health. His *Narrative of a Tour through Hawaii* was published in 1825 in Boston by Crocker & Brewster and in New York by J. P. Haven; it appeared in 1826 in London, printed for the author by H. Fisher, Son & Jackson.

EMERSON, JOHN S. (1800–1867)

Born in Chester, New Hampshire, Emerson graduated from Dartmouth College in 1826 and from Andover Theological Seminary in 1830. He married Ursula Sophia Newell in October, 1831, and in November the couple sailed for Hawaii with the Fifth Company of American missionaries. They opened the station at Waialua, Oahu, in 1832 and first served there until 1842; there Emerson translated several books and encouraged reading of the Bible in Hawaiian. He worked at Lahainaluna School from 1842 to 1846 and again at Waialua until 1864, remaining there after he resigned from the mission. Mrs. Emerson walked hundreds of miles to attend the sick and was a skilled teacher. The family reared eight children, including Nathaniel Bright EMERSON. See Oliver P. Emerson, *Pioneer Days in Hawaii* (New York: Doubleday, Doran, 1928).

EMERSON, NATHANIEL BRIGHT (1839–1915)

Emerson was born at Waialua, Oahu, son of the Rev. John S. EMERSON. After attending Punahou School, the son served for two years in the Union Army during the American Civil War. He then completed his course at Williams College in Massachusetts and studied medicine at Harvard University and at the College of Physicians and Surgeons in New York, which granted him an M.D. degree in 1869. He was called back to Hawaii in 1878 as general inspector of lepers and leper stations. He married Dr. Sarah E. Pierce in 1881 and succeeded Dr. George P. TROUSSEAU as president of the Board of Health.

Emerson's knowledge of the Hawaiian language and people enabled him to become a skilled translator and outstanding student of island folklore. His translations include such works as *Unwritten Literature of Hawaii: The Sacred Songs of the Hula* (Washington, D.C.: Bureau of American Ethnology, 1909), the best source of knowledge about the ancient hula, and the expanded legend *Pele and Hiiaka* (Honolulu: Star-Bulletin, 1915).

EMMA (1836–1885)

At birth, the future queen was given the name of KALANIKAUMAKEAMANO; after the death of her husband and son she took the name of KALELEONALANI. She was a granddaughter of John YOUNG and his second wife, the chiefess Kaonaeha (Melie Kuamoo). Emma was also the great-granddaughter of KELIIMAIKAI, full brother of KAMEHAMEHA I. Her parents were George Naea and Fanny Kakelaokalani Young. As a child, Emma was adopted by her maternal aunt, Grace Kamaikui Young Rooke, whose husband was Dr. Thomas Charles Byde Rooke, a member of the Church of England. However, for a time Emma attended the Chiefs' Children's School and later had an English governess, receiving an excellent education in western ways.

Emma was married on June 19, 1856, to KAMEHAMEHA IV and shared the experiences of his reign. She took outstanding roles in the founding of the Queen's Hospital, named for her, and during the short life of ALBERT, the Prince of Hawaii. The couple shared the introduction of the Episcopal Church in Hawaii. Emma also sponsored the founding of St. Andrew's Priory, a school for girls.

After the death of Kamehameha IV, Emma made a trip abroad, during which she became a friend of Queen Victoria of the British Empire. She returned to Hawaii in 1866 and lived quietly until she felt called upon to return to the throne. When King Lunalilo died in 1874 without naming a successor, under the constitution the new king had to be elected by the Legislative Assembly. Both David KALAKAUA and Emma, the dowager queen, announced as candidates. Right after the election of 1874, when only six votes out of thirty-nine were cast for Emma, a mob of her supporters attacked the courthouse. Further riot was prevented only after Kalakaua arranged for American and British marines to be landed from warships in the harbor. Emma acknowledged Kalakaua as king on February 13 and advised her followers to do the same.

During her life, Emma was an active letter writer; for a sample of her interests, see *News from Molokai: Letters between Peter Kaeo and Queen Emma, 1873–1876* (Honolulu: University Press of Hawaii, 1976).

EMMONS, DELOS C. (1889–1965)

Emmons graduated from West Point in 1909, and in 1917 qualified as a pilot when only ten airplanes were in service in the Army Air Corps. Ten days after the attack on Pearl Harbor by the Japanese on December 7, 1941, Emmons replaced Walter C. SHORT as Commander of the Hawaiian Department of the United States Army. Under the succeeding military rule many civil rights were suspended, but criticism of General Emmons is modified by praise for his support of Hawaii's Americans of Japanese ancestry (AJA). He influenced many employers in the islands to retain their AJA workers, and organized the all-AJA battalions that later fought in Europe. When he became Western Defense

Commander in 1943, he released thousands of AJA citizens from West Coast relocation centers. Previous to his retirement in 1948, he also served as head of the Alaska Command and as commandant of the Armed Forces Staff College in Norfolk, Virginia. Emmons received the Distinguished Flying Cross, the Distinguished Service Cross, and the Legion of Honor.

EMORY, WALTER LEAVITTE (1868–1929)

Born in Fitchburg, Massachusetts, Emory married Winifred A. Pike in 1893. The couple came to Hawaii in 1898 to invest in coffee plantations, but instead he became assistant superintendent of construction at the Alexander Young Building. He continued in construction work until 1908, when he formed a partnership with architect Marshal H. Webb, the second such firm formed in Honolulu. This company was responsible for the design of such edifices as the Advertiser Building, the James Campbell Building, the Palama and Hawaii Theaters, the Blaisdell Hotel, the new Central Union Church, Love's Bakery, the Liberty House Annex, and the Castle Hall dormitory and Cooke Art Gallery at Punahou School. Emory was first president of the Hawaii Chapter of the American Institute of Architects, and was also a noted collector of stamps.

ENA, JOHN (1843–1906)

Born at Hilo of Chinese and Hawaiian parentage, Ena worked at various trades until at the age of thirty-four he became a clerk for T. R. Foster & Co. of Honolulu. This firm owned a fleet of seven schooners plying among the islands and soon acquired its first steamer. It was incorporated in 1883 as the Inter-Island Steam Navigation Co., and Ena invested heavily in the stock. He was a member of the House of

Nobles under the monarchy and was decorated in 1888 by King Kalakaua. He served with the Board of Health under the Provisional Government, and was a member of the constitutional convention that set up the Republic of Hawaii. He became president of Inter-Island in 1899 and served until 1902, when he retired to Long Beach, California.

ESCHSCHOLTZ, JOHANN FRIEDRICH. See KOTZEBUE.

FARRINGTON, JOSEPH RIDER (1897–1954)

Born in Washington, D.C., eldest son of Wallace Rider FARRINGTON, Joseph continued the family combination of journalism and politics. He graduated from Punahou School in 1915 and obtained a bachelor's degree from the University of Wisconsin in 1919. He was a reporter in Philadelphia and Washington, D.C. before becoming managing editor of the Honolulu *Star-Bulletin* in 1924, when his father was governor of the Territory. Joseph was elected a director of the newspaper in 1926 and vice president in 1929, and succeeded his father as president and general manager after the death of the latter in 1933.

Farrington was elected to the territorial senate in 1934 and sponsored legislation for the creation of an Equal Rights Commission that would guarantee to the residents of Hawaii the same rights as those living on the mainland. He also supported the broadening of support of public schools, modernization of the administration of the Hawaiian Homes Commission and of the City and County of Honolulu, reapportionment of the Legislature, and attainment of statehood. His more active career in politics began in 1937 during the repercussions of the trial of Thalia MASSEY, when he accepted a position as secretary of the legislative commission established to protect territorial government from domination by

non-resident appointees. He was re-elected to the Senate in 1938 and in 1943 he became Hawaii's delegate to Congress.

Farrington held this important office for the rest of his life. He successfully sponsored legislation to grant equal rights for Chinese, Filipino, Korean, Japanese, and Samoan residents, and procured $16,000,000 in cash relief grants to the people of Hilo when they were struck by a tsunami. Other bills led to the funding of research programs on Pacific fishing and control of the oriental fruit fly, the creation of the National Memorial Cemetery in Punchbowl Crater, and increased economic aid to Hawaii in many areas. Farrington fought for many years for statehood for Hawaii, the justice of which was clearly demonstrated at the time of his death in office in June, 1954. His unexpired term was filled by the appointment of his wife, Mary Elizabeth (Betty) Pruett Farrington, whom he had married in 1920. She was later elected for one term as delegate.

FARRINGTON, WALLACE RIDER (1871–1933)

Born in Orono, Maine, Farrington was educated at Bridgton Academy and Brewer High School, and received the bachelor's degree from the University of Maine in 1891. He began an outstanding career in journalism in that year by working as a reporter on the Bangor *Daily News*. He came to Hawaii as managing editor of the *Pacific Commercial Advertiser*, as the daily paper was then called. Farrington became managing editor of the evening *Bulletin*; in 1913 this was merged with the *Hawaiian Star* with him as vice president and general manager of the resulting *Star-Bulletin*, still a daily evening paper.

Farrington resigned these positions when he was first appointed governor of the Territory of Hawaii by President Warren G. Harding in

40

1921. Farrington's acts were approved when he was the first chief executive of the islands to be reappointed to office; he received that distinction from President Calvin Coolidge in 1925. He fostered Hawaii's "Bill of Rights" and the Declaration of Rights ending discrimination against citizens of Chinese and Japanese ancestry. He supported the continuation of land grants to Hawaiians and the work of the Hawaiian Homes Commission, and was a lifelong proponent of statehood for the Territory. Public finance was put on a sounder footing and the government was able to spend large sums for improvements. At the end of his term in 1929 he became publisher of the *Star-Bulletin*.

Farrington was active in various civic groups and a leading spirit in the organization of the Honolulu Ad Club, of which he was honorary president. In 1896 he married Catherine McAlpine Crane of San Francisco and they had three children, of which the eldest was Joseph Rider FARRINGTON. See Thornton Sherburne Hardy, *Wallace Rider Farrington* (Honolulu: Star-Bulletin, 1935) and Riley Harris Allen, *Wallace R. Farrington, Newspaperman: The Story of Thirty-Nine Years in Hawaii* (Honolulu: Star-Bulletin, 1937).

FERN, JOSEPH JAMES (1872–1920)

Born at Kohala, Hawaii, son of James and Kaipo Fern, the young man lived for years in the mountains of that region, hauling firewood on a bullock cart. He went to Honolulu at the age of nineteen and drove a mule car on the street railway. Later he worked on the docks for the Wilder Steamship Co., and retained his position as labor-relations agent when the company consolidated with Inter-Island Steam Navigation Co.; he later held the post of shipping master.

When the City and County of Honolulu held its first elections in 1908, Fern, a Democrat, was chosen mayor by a margin of seven votes, and held this office for most of the rest of his life. He lost the election of 1914, but regained the mayoralty in 1917, and died in office in 1920. Fern was able to converse in five languages and appealed heavily to the strong native Hawaiian vote of the time. He married three times and had numerous children.

FERNANDEZ, EDWARD KANE (1883–1970)

The future showman of Hawaii was born in Honolulu, a descendant on his mother's side of chiefs of Maui. At the age of one year he was given a "baby luau" by King Kalakaua. The young man was a close friend of Prince Kuhio KALANIANAOLE. Fernandez attended Brigham Young University in Utah. He made early films and earned the nickname of "Keiki Kii Oni Oni," or moving-picture kid. He was manager and player on the first foreign baseball team to play Keio and Waseda Universities in Japan. Fernandez was elected to the Territorial House of Representatives in 1911 and remained in office until 1923.

E. K. Fernandez organized his first circus in 1915, with twenty performers and six animals, including a skating bear. He took road shows and carnivals not only around the Hawaiian Islands but also to the Far East, Canada, and the United States mainland; in the 1930s, three million people attended his performances. During World War II he managed the old Aala Park Civic Centre Theatre, which gave shows for war workers. His efforts were honored by the Showmen's League of America and the International Association of Fairs and Expositions. The E. K. Fernandez Shows are still a part of life in the islands, managed by his son Kane S. Fernandez.

FORBES, COCHRAN (1805–1880)

Born in Goshen, Pennsylvania, Forbes graduated from Princeton Theological Seminary in 1831. He married Rebecca Duncan Smith in October of that year, and the couple sailed for Hawaii with the Fifth Company of American missionaries in November. They were stationed at Kaawaloa and Kealakekua, Hawaii, from 1832 to 1845 and at Lahaina, Maui, from 1845 to 1847, where he filled the post of seaman's chaplain at a time when as many as two hundred whale ships visited the port annually. The family returned to the United States in 1847. Among their five children was Anderson Oliver Forbes (1833–1888), who married a daughter of Levi CHAMBERLAIN and was a preacher in Hawaii from 1858 to 1888.

FORD, ALEXANDER HUME (1868–1945)

Ford was born in Charleston, South Carolina, of an old Southern family. He graduated from Porter Military Academy in that city but turned to writing plays and magazine articles, and working on newspapers. On a research trip he visited Hawaii for a week's stay in 1907 and remained for the rest of his life. He decided to revive the old recreations of hiking and water sports; out of these efforts grew the Hawaiian Trail and Mountain Club and the Outrigger

Canoe Club on Waikiki Beach. Ford also supported the establishing of the Boy Scouts of America in the islands. He organized a Hands-Around-the-Pacific Club and called a Pan-Pacific Conference, which was held in Honolulu in 1911, coincident with the birth of *Mid-Pacific Magazine*, a monthly edited by Ford for the Pan-Pacific Union. As director general of the Union, Ford named as honorary officers the heads of every Pacific government of the period. The Pan-Pacific Club of Tokyo was the outstanding luncheon group of the Japanese Empire at the time. The Union sponsored conferences in Honolulu and promoted others elsewhere in the Pacific. Ford retired from active work in 1939. He was well known in Honolulu as a publicist and spent much time at the Outrigger Club, where he was a friend of Jack LONDON. See Valerie Noble, *Hawaiian Prophet: Alexander Hume Ford*, New York: Exposition, 1980.

FORD, SETH PORTER (1818–1866)

Ford was born in Washington, Connecticut. He studied with several physicians and was an associate of Dr. Willard Parker, who spoke highly of Ford's surgical skill. Dr. Ford arrived in Hawaii in 1851 and practised for fifteen years, eventually serving with the United States

Marine Hospital and the Hawaiian Insane Asylum. He had an extremely large practice on the island of Oahu and skillfully attended patients as far away as Laie on the North Shore. Ford Island in Pearl Harbor was named for his son, Seth Porter Ford Jr.

FORNANDER, ABRAHAM (1812–1887)

Fornander spent his early years in a rectory in Sweden as a university student preparing for the ministry. He deserted from a whaling ship in 1844 and passed the rest of his life in Honolulu, except for an interval when he prospected for gold in California. He was successively coffee planter, surveyor, newspaper and magazine editor, first inspector of schools, and judge. He married Alanakapu Kauapinao, daughter of Kaenaku Kalili, a medical kahuna and former governor of Molokai.

Fornander became a champion of the declining Hawaiian community and this sympathy brought him into collision with the "missionary" element in the government. He sent several young Hawaiian men on tours to collect oral tradition in an attempt to piece together a history of the Hawaiian branch of the Polynesian race. He became the foremost collector of Hawaiian lore from native informants like David MALO and S. N. KAMAKAU, and published *An Account of the Polynesian Race* (London: Trübner, 1878–1885). His *Collection of Hawaiian Antiquities and Folklore* was published by Thomas G. THRUM. He was awarded the Linnean Medal by the Royal Swedish Academy of Sciences. See Eleanor Harmon Davis, *Abraham Fornander: A Biography* (Honolulu: University Press of Hawaii, 1979).

FOSTER, MARY E. (1844–1930)

Mary was born in Honolulu, daughter of James ROBINSON, pioneer shipbuilder who came to Hawaii after his whale ship was wrecked on Pearl and Hermes Reef and opened a shipyard on the waterfront. Around 1879 the daughter married Thomas R. Foster, one of the organizers of the Inter-Island Steam Navigation Co. At the end of a long life, Mary's will provided for the conversion of her Nuuanu Street home into a botanical garden, now called Foster Gardens, on the site of the garden of Dr. William HILLEBRAND. She also provided bequests for half a dozen other charitable enterprises, with which she had been connected as a philanthropist.

FRANKLIN, LADY JANE
See CRACROFT.

FRASER, JULIETTE MAY (1887–1983)

A kamaaina artist who rose to be dean of island painters and one of Hawaii's "living treasures," May Fraser was born in Honolulu of schoolteacher parents during the reign of King Kalakaua. After graduation from Punahou School she earned a bachelor's degree in art from Wellesley College and later studied in New York and California and at the University of Hawaii. During World War II she headed a group that painted camouflage nettings. All her life she was a modest but genial personality with an informal manner.

Miss Fraser's inborn versatility enabled her to produce drawings, etchings, paintings in oil and watercolor, linoleum cuts, lithographs, and stitchery. She illustrated such books as *Ke Anuenue* (University of Hawaii Press, 1949). After World War II she met Jean CHARLOT and learned the art of painting murals and frescoes. Some of her works in these media can be found at Bilger Hall on the University campus, the Ala Moana

Hotel, the Board of Water Supply, the Kapiolani branch of American Savings & Loan, the Hawaii State Library, and the Benjamin Parker Elementary School. A giant mural, "Makahiki," was recently retrieved from the Honolulu Academy of Arts basement and adorns a wall in the Hamilton Library on the University campus.

Miss Fraser also excelled in ceramic tile creations, such as that on the façade of Bakken Hall on the Mid-Pacific Institute campus. During the winter of 1962–63 she and her younger associate, David Asherman, painted Hawaiian style frescoes at the Ipapandi Chapel on the Greek island of Chios as a gift to the people. The grateful townsfolk named a street after her. At her death in her ninety-sixth year she was working on a ceramic mural for the new District Court Building in downtown Honolulu.

May Fraser was a founding member and first president of Hawaii Painters and Sculptors League and a past president of the Honolulu Print Makers.

FREAR, MARY EMMA DILLINGHAM (1870–1957)

Born in Honolulu, eldest daughter of Benjamin Franklin DILLINGHAM, Mary graduated from Punahou School in 1888 and from Wellesley College in 1893. She married Walter Francis FREAR in 1893. Mrs. Frear was a founder of the College Club of Honolulu and the local YWCA, of which she was president for five years. She was one of the strong supporters of the University of Hawaii and a member of its Board of Regents from 1920 to 1942; she was granted an honorary degree in 1943, and Frear Hall on the Manoa campus bears her name. Mrs. Frear lectured on literary topics and published half a dozen books of prose and verse; the most memorable is *Lowell and Abigail: A Realistic Idyll* (New Haven, Conn.: privately printed, 1934), a biography of her

missionary grandparents, Lowell and Abigail SMITH. At Mrs. Frear's death, the Frear estate on Punahou Street was left to Punahou School; in 1967 a retirement residence called "Arcadia" opened on the site under the sponsorship of Central Union Church in co-operation with the school and the Dillingham Corporation.

FREAR, WALTER FRANCIS (1863–1948)

Born in Grass Valley, California, of French Huguenot stock on his father's side and Pilgrim ancestry on his mother's, Frear arrived in Hawaii with these parents at the age of seven. He graduated from Punahou School in 1881, received a bachelor's degree from Yale University in 1885, and a law degree from Yale in 1890. Returning to Hawaii, he was a law partner of Lorrin A. THURSTON for two years. Frear was appointed second judge of the First Circuit Court by Queen Liliuokalani in January, 1893, just before the Revolution, and was appointed second associate justice of the Supreme Court by the Provisional Government in March. During the Republic he was made first associate justice of the Supreme Court in 1896. He was appointed chief justice of the Supreme Court of the Territory of Hawaii in 1900 and served until 1907, when he was named third governor of the territory by President Theodore Roosevelt. Frear was thus on the bench during four regimes within eight years. He had also been one of the five commissioners appointed in 1898 to recommend to Congress the future form of government; this group drafted a bill that set up the Territory of Hawaii under American law.

During Frear's term as governor (1907–1913) the territory's fiscal affairs were well managed, and rather

large expenditures were made for harbor improvements, road construction, and other public works. Frear paid special attention to the problem of Hawaiian homesteading and land settlement. He was chairman of the Hawaii delegation to the Republican National Convention in 1912.

Frear left the senior partnership of a law firm to become president of the Bishop Trust Co. in 1924; he retired as chairman of the board in 1934. He took time to engage in various civic and charitable efforts; he was president of the trustees of Central Union Church, a vice president of the Hawaiian Evangelical Association, and a trustee of Punahou School. He was likewise a director of various business and banking concerns. Like his wife, Mary Emma Dillingham FREAR, he was a writer; his best known works are two legal studies, "The Evolution of the Hawaiian Judiciary" and "The Development of Hawaiian Statute Law," and a biographical volume, *Mark Twain and Hawaii* (Chicago: privately printed, 1947). The Frears had two daughters, Virginia and Margaret.

FREYCINET, LOUIS CLAUDE DESAULCES DE (1779–1842)

Freycinet, a French Navy captain, was sent out in 1800 by Napoleon I to explore Australian waters. In 1817 he was in command of another expedition, and his ship *Uranie* was one of the first French vessels to visit the Hawaiian Islands. The party stopped at Oahu and Maui in August, 1819. The captain's wife, Rose de Freycinet, accompanied him on the voyage; see *Realms and Islands: The World Voyage of Rose de Freycinet in the Corvette "Uranie," 1817–1820* (London: Oxford University Press, 1962), by Marnie Bassett. The artist on the expedition was Jacques ARAGO.

FRONK, CLARENCE E. (1883–1968)

Born in Conway, Iowa, Fronk studied medicine at St. Louis University in Missouri and received the M.D. in 1906. He entered the United States Army in 1908 and rose to the rank of colonel in the reserve following his resignation in 1923. He was sent to Hawaii in 1922 with the rank of major, to take charge of the surgical service at Tripler General Hospital. Dr. Fronk was co-founder of the Fronk-Wynn Clinic in 1925 and director of the Fronk Clinic from 1934 to 1956. He was a big-game hunter in various parts of the world and a notable horseman whose hobby was breeding, training, and riding show horses. He was a member of a number of military, professional, and other groups.

FULLARD-LEO, ELLEN BARBER (1884?–1974)

Born in Cape Colony, South Africa, one of thirty natural and adopted children of her parents, Ellen Fullard married Leslie Leo in 1908 and moved to British Columbia. The family came to Hawaii in 1915, where the husband was a contractor and sportsman with wealth from diamond mining. Soon thereafter the couple purchased from Honolulu judge Henry E. Cooper the Palmyra Islands in the Central Pacific for $15,000; Leslie Vincent Fullard-Leo and two other sons inherited this property, which was proposed by the Federal government in 1979 as a storage site for nuclear waste.

The mother became the "grande dame of amateur athletics in Hawaii." She was the first woman to serve on the national executive committee of the American Amateur Athletic Union. She was also a member of the Olympics executive committee, a judge at the 1924 Paris Olympics, and a timer at both the Pan-American Games in Buenos Aires in 1951 and the 1952 Helsinki Olympics. She revived the Hawaiian Trail and Mountain Club in 1920 and was named Mother of the Year in 1972.

FULLAWAY, DAVID TIMMINS (1880–1964)

Born in Philadelphia, Fullaway served in the Army in the Philippines during the Spanish-American War. He graduated from Stanford University in 1908 and was hired by the United States Agricultural Experiment Station in Hawaii. He returned to Stanford for a master's degree in entomology before joining the Territorial Board of Agriculture and Forestry. Fullaway worked from the time of its establishment in 1914 until he retired as chief entomologist in 1948.

FURNEAUX, CHARLES (1838?–1913)

Born in Boston, Furneaux came to Hawaii for a vacation around 1880 and decided to make his home in the islands. For many years previous to annexation he was United States consular agent and shipping commissioner at the port of Hilo. An intimate friend of the local painter Jules TAVERNIER, Furneaux became an artist of distinction. He was famous for his oils of the 1881 and 1887 Mauna Loa eruptions, along with views of Kilauea and other volcanoes. He invested considerable sums in coffee and banana plantations and owned sizeable properties on the Big Island.

GIBSON, WALTER MURRAY (1822–1888)

Son of parents emigrating from Northumberland, England, to the United States, Gibson was orphaned at an early age and grew up in South Carolina. After many adventures in several parts of the world, Gibson became interested in the work of the Church of Latter-Day Saints or Mormons. He went to Salt Lake City and in 1860 became a missionary of the group. With the idea of converting many Pacific islanders to this religion and with the blessing of Brigham Young, Gibson arrived in Honolulu on July 4, 1861, passing himself off as a world traveler. Thereafter he played a dramatic role in Hawaii for twenty-six years. The Mormon convert began his labors among the native church members, whose former leader had returned to Utah three years earlier during the Mormon War. Gibson was especially concerned with the development of the island of Lanai, where a small colony had grown up. An investigating committee of Mormon elders discovered that Gibson had diverted church funds toward the purchase of about half the island and put the property in his own name. Gibson was excommunicated by the Mormons in 1864 and became a naturalized citizen of Hawaii in 1866. After cultivating land on Lanai he moved to Hawaii in 1872 and entered politics.

Under the slogan of "Hawaii for the Hawaiians," he attached himself to the fortunes of King Kalakaua and began a career of corruption. He was a glib publicist in both English and Hawaiian, and acquired control of the leading newspaper, the *Pacific Commercial Advertiser*. He was appointed premier and minister of foreign affairs in 1882 and thereafter was able to have his own way in the operation of the kingdom. Gibson's downfall finally came when he picked up an idea first proposed by an Australian journalist, Charles St. Julian, concerning the "primacy of the Pacific" —the idea that Hawaii would be first among a federation of governments of all the Polynesian island groups that had not yet been made colonies of European powers. Kalakaua would be Emperor of the Pacific. When this "calabash empire" collapsed, leaders of the Revolution of 1887 deposed Gibson and, one day before Kalakaua signed the "Bayonet Constitution," the former premier was allowed to leave the islands to escape lynching.

Gibson spent his remaining years in San Francisco. At his death his body was embalmed and returned to Honolulu, where hordes of mourners came to pay their respects to this adventurer and dreamer.

GILMORE, JOHN WASHINGTON (1872–1942)

Born in White County, Arkansas, son of a farmer, Gilmore attended public schools at Fort Worth, Texas, and obtained a bachelor's degree from Cornell University in 1898 and a master's degree in 1905. He helped in 1898 to establish the first agricultural school in China, at Wuchang. He married Elizabeth May Vetter-Hitchcock at Ithaca, New York, in 1900. Gilmore taught during 1900 at the Honolulu Normal and Training School, and in 1901–1902 helped to establish the school system in the Philippines. He taught at Cornell and Pennsylvania State College before coming back to Hawaii in 1908 to act as first president of the College of Hawaii, retiring in 1913. Thereafter he was a professor at the University of California and the University of Chile. He was known for his efforts to synthesize rubber, especially from the guayule plant.

GOLOVNIN, VASILY MIKHAILOVICH (1776–1831)

As part of Russian expansion after the fall of Napoleon I, Golovnin was sent out as captain of the round-the-world sloop *Kamchatka* to report on Russian activities in the North Pacific. He arrived in the Hawaiian Islands in the fall of 1818 and visited the Big Island and Oahu. His book gives a good account of Kamehameha I in his final year and the political situation after the failure of the filibustering expedition under Georg Anton SCHEFFER. See Golovnin's *Around the World on the Sloop "Kamchatka"* (Honolulu: University Press of Hawaii, 1979), translated by Ella Lury Wiswell.

GOODRICH, JOSEPH
(1794–1852)

Born in Wethersfield, Connecticut, Goodrich was educated at Yale College and was ordained at Kailua, Hawaii, in 1826, after arriving in the islands with the Second Company of American missionaries in 1823. He and his wife, Martha Barnes Goodrich, were parents of seven children. He and Samuel RUGGLES established the station at Hilo, where he served until 1835. Twice Goodrich was called back to Honolulu, each time for a period of two years, to superintend the printing office and book bindery. In addition to being a preacher, teacher, and printer, he was also a good mechanic and agriculturist, showing the people how to grow coffee and food products. He returned with his family to the United States in 1836.

GORDON-CUMMING, CONSTANCE FREDERICA

Born of a prominent Scottish clan, this traveler arrived in Hawaii in 1878. She made an extensive tour of the group, writing about Honolulu, the North Shore, and other parts of Oahu. She sailed to Hilo, met Titus COAN, climbed to Kilauea Volcano, visited sugar plantations, and stopped at Lahaina on her return to Honolulu. She includes in her two-volume book, *Fire-Fountains: The Kingdom of Hawaii, Its Volcanoes and the History of the Missions* (London: Blackwood, 1883), a brief history of the people and a description of the two elected kings, Lunalilo and Kalakaua.

GORE, JOHN (1730?–1790)

Born in Virginia when it was a British colony, Gore had twice circled the globe on the fast ship *Dolphin* before signing on as third lieutenant on James COOK's first Pacific voyage. On the fateful third voyage, Gore was first lieutenant of the flagship and brought the *Resolution* home to England after his captain was killed in Hawaii.

GRAY, ROBERT (1775–1806)

The first American vessel to touch at the Hawaiian Islands was the *Columbia Rediviva*, an armed ship from Boston commanded by Robert Gray, arriving in August, 1789. Gray went on to achieve the distinction of navigating the first American ship to circumnavigate the globe. In May, 1792, he discovered, entered, and named the Columbia River of the American Northwest. The *Columbia* returned to Hawaii under the command of Gray in the autumn of that year.

GREEN, JONATHAN SMITH
(1796–1878)

Born in Lebanon, Connecticut, Green graduated from the Andover Theological Seminary and was ordained in 1827, shortly before sailing with the Third Company of American missionaries to Hawaii. Before leaving he married Theodotia Arnold, by whom he was to have four children. After making an exploring trip along the Pacific Coast, Green was stationed at Lahaina, Maui, for a year, at Hilo for another year, and at Wailuku, Maui, from 1832 to 1836. He was the first principal of the Wailuku Girls' Seminary from 1836 to 1842. In the latter year the Greens left the Boston Mission for reasons of conscience concerning slavery and went to Makawao, Maui, where he was an independent pastor. He translated several books of the Bible into Hawaiian along with half a dozen tracts. After the death of his first wife he married Asenath Cargill Spring at Providence, Rhode Island, in 1861, and brought her with him to Hawaii in 1863. They had two children, one of whom was Laura Capron Spring GREEN.

GREEN, LAURA CAPRON SPRING (1864–1943)

Laura Green was born at Makawao, Maui, daughter of the Rev. Jonathan Smith GREEN. In her early years she had a Hawaiian nurse and "thought, read, and prayed in Hawaiian." She was educated in New England. Laura worked with Mary Kawena Pukui in writing about island folklore, and both collaborated with Martha BECKWITH. Green was author of three volumes of folklore based on stories by Pukui and her husband. Green also was senior collaborator with Beckwith on several articles on Hawaiian customs.

GREGG, DAVID LAWRENCE (1814?–1868)

Gregg emigrated from Albany, New York, to Illinois at an early age, and began a political career which culminated in the post of secretary of state for Illinois from 1850 to 1853. He was United States commissioner in Hawaii from 1853 to 1858, when he was succeeded by James W. Borden. Gregg arrived at a time when annexation by the United States was first being discussed—a proposal cut short by the death of King Kamehameha III in 1854. Later Gregg was minister of finance and adviser to Kamehameha IV, and then practised law in Honolulu. He returned to the United States in 1863 and was appointed to a government post at Carson City, Nevada, where he died. Gregg's dispatches from Hawaii to Washington are a valuable source of diplomatic history. See *The Diaries of David Lawrence Gregg: An American Diplomat in Hawaii, 1853–1856* (Honolulu: Hawaiian Historical Society, 1982), edited by Pauline King.

GREGORY, HERBERT ERNEST (1869–1952)

Born in Middleville, Michigan, Gregory obtained a bachelor's degree from Yale in 1896 and a doctorate in 1899. He was appointed Silliman Professor of Geology at Yale in 1904 and held the post for two decades. He also served with the United States Geological Survey and worked in a number of countries. Gregory visited Honolulu in 1916 and became fascinated by the problem of the origin of the Polynesian race. He arrived once more in May, 1919, to become director of the Bernice P. Bishop Museum, a position he held until 1936. He published a number of papers on geology and geography. Gregory married Edna Hope in 1908 and the couple had one daughter.

GULICK, PETER JOHNSON (1796–1877)

Born in Freehold, New Jersey, Gulick graduated from Princeton College in 1825 and from Princeton Theological Seminary in 1827. He married Fanny Hinckley Thomas in September of that year and the couple sailed in November with the Third Company of American missionaries. They were stationed at Waimea, Kauai, from 1828 to 1835; at Koloa from 1835 to 1843; at Kaluaaha from 1843 to 1846, where Gulick was superintendent of Molokai schools; and at Waialua, Oahu, from 1846 to 1857. In that year the family retired to live in Honolulu. In 1874 the Gulicks could look back on a lifetime of bringing up six sons who were ordained missionaries and a daughter who was also involved in foreign missionary work. Prominent in the second generation in Hawaii were Luther Halsey Gulick (1828–1891), medical missionary in the Caroline and Marquesas Islands, and Orramel Hinckley Gulick (1830–1923), a pioneer Protestant missionary in Japan.

HAALILIO, TIMOTEO (1808–1844)

An early convert to Christianity who studied with the Rev. Hiram BINGHAM, Haalilio learned to read and write in English and Hawaiian and became private secretary to Kamehameha III and a member of his treasury board. In 1842 Haalilio joined the Rev. William RICHARDS as an envoy sent abroad in search of confirmation of the independence of the kingdom. Haalilio studied social conditions and schools during his visits to Washington, London, and Paris, hoping to make use of his knowledge on his return to Hawaii. Unfortunately, he died on shipboard en route home to his native land.

HACKFELD, HEINRICH (HENRY) (1815–1887)

Born near Palmenhorst in Oldenburg, Germany, Hackfeld was captain of his own trading vessel on the China coast before 1848, when he left the port of Hamburg for Hawaii. He opened a shop in Honolulu in 1849 as a ship's chandler and general agent. He moved to a location on Fort Street that today is the site of his company's successor, Amfac's Liberty House. Hackfeld developed a business of importing machinery and supplies for the spreading sugar plantations and exported raw sugar. H. Hackfeld & Co. became prominent factors—agents and shippers—for plantations, especially when the Koloa and East Maui holdings headed by Dr. R. W. WOOD began to succeed.

Hackfeld was appointed consul in Hawaii for Germany, Norway, and Sweden in 1852. He was a charter member of the Honolulu Chamber of Commerce. He retired in 1861, but his concern thrived and became one of the top companies in the islands; during World War I the assets of the German-owned firm were liquidated and acquired by a new corporation, American Factors, Ltd. (later Amfac), which became one of the so-called "Big Five." Hackfeld returned to Germany in 1863 because of the illness of his wife, and severed his connection with the firm in 1886, a year before his death.

HAGEMEISTER, LEONTH ANDREANOVICH.
See KRUSENSTERN.

HAILI, CLARISSA (HILO HATTIE) (1901–1979)

The outstanding comic-hula performer of her time began entertaining as a child, and sang in the choir of tiny Kealaula Oka Malamala Church on Cooke Street. She attended normal school and in 1923 began teaching for sixteen years at Waipahu Elementary School. On a ship on her way to a teachers' convention in Oregon in 1936 she performed a hula to the tune of Don McDiarmid's 1932 song, "When Hilo

Hattie Does the Hilo Hop." Show business beckoned, and in 1939 she gave up teaching and joined Harry Owens and his Royal Hawaiian Serenaders in San Francisco. For almost thirty years "Aunty Clara" was a familiar figure in her holoku and coconut hat, singing about Princess Pupule and the Cockeyed Mayor of Kaunakakai. After two brief early marriages she was Mrs. Theodore Inter for sixteen years. In 1949 she married Carlyle Nelson, a violinist from North Dakota who was eight years younger. Three years later Nelson had his own band and the couple was appearing together at the Roosevelt Hotel in Los Angeles. "Hilo Hattie" was also featured in several films. Her health began to fail in 1967, and ten years later she had a stroke from which she never fully recovered. See Milly Singletary, *Hilo Hattie: A Legend in Our Time* (Honolulu: published by the author, 1979).

HAKAU. See UMI and LILOA.

HALEOLE, S. N.
Haleole was born around 1819 and was a member of the Lahainaluna group under the Rev. Sheldon DIBBLE, entering the school in 1834. Haleole was author of a traditional work of fiction, *The Hawaiian Romance of Laieikawai*, translated by Martha W. BECKWITH.

HALL, EDWIN OSCAR (1810–1883)
Born at Walpole, New Hampshire, Hall was educated at Canandaigua Academy, New York, and trained for the printing trade at Detroit and New York City. He married Sarah Lyon Williams in 1834, a month before leaving with the Seventh Company of American missionaries to Hawaii. On arrival in 1835 the couple, who were to have four children, were stationed in Honolulu. On a visit to Oregon Territory in 1839 for the sake of his wife's health, Hall took as a gift from the First Church of Honolulu to the pioneer Oregon mission a "hand card" printing press, type, and paper. There Hall ran off the first printing from the Pacific Northwest. It was an eight-page primer in the Nez Percé language written by a missionary at Lapwai in what is now the state of Idaho.

On his return, Hall was appointed director of the official press of the kingdom and editor of the *Polynesian*, a government newspaper. Hall was released by the Boston mission in

1850 to head the Department of Finance of the kingdom in the absence of Dr. G. P. JUDD in 1849 and 1850. Hall left government service in 1855 to set up a mercantile business, the firm of E. O. Hall & Son, which operated until it was absorbed by Theo. H. Davies, Ltd., in 1873. In that year Hall was appointed minister of the interior and president of the Board of Health. On the death of his first wife he married Mary Lyon Dame in 1878 in Pennsylvania. Hall died in Falmouth, Maine, but was buried in Honolulu.

HALL, JOHN WAYNE (JACK) (1915–1971)
Born in Ashland, Wisconsin, Hall grew up in Southern California and at seventeen became a merchant seaman. He joined the Sailors' Union of the Pacific the following year, and in 1934 took part in a ninety-day strike on the San Francisco waterfront, against which were deployed tear gas and Army tanks. The strikers won pay increases. He began his career in Hawaii by helping to organize the Honolulu waterfront in 1935. He was involved in a ten-month longshoremen's strike on Kauai and began organizing sugar and pineapple workers for the International Longshoremen's & Warehousemen's Union (ILWU). By 1942 he had organized two Kauai plantations and had helped to get the first stevedoring contracts signed. He then drafted what became the Territory's first wage and hour law and acted as an inspector for the Wage and Hour Division of the Department of Labor and Industrial Relations. He married Yoshiko Ogawa of Olaa, Hawaii, in 1942.

Hall served on the Hawaii War Labor Board and the Hawaii War Manpower Commission. He was named Hawaii regional director of the ILWU in 1944, and served until 1969, with much assistance from

Harry Renton Bridges, president in San Francisco. Under Hall's direction this union competed with American Federation of Labor (AFL) organizers for worker members on plantations. In 1946 Hall was chairman of the local Congress of Industrial Organizations (CIO) Political Action Committee, which backed thirty-five successful candidates in that year's elections in Hawaii. Hall led the ILWU in the bitter six-month Honolulu waterfront strike of 1949, which bankrupted many small businessmen and brought about food shortages that occasioned strong protests, especially from housewives.

In 1953 Hall was convicted, along with six other defendants, of violations of the anti-Communist Smith Act, but the conviction was overturned by the United States Supreme Court in 1958. During the 1950s, supported by the Democrat Party under the leadership of John Anthony BURNS, Hall supported mechanization of local industries and negotiated contracts providing separation pay, higher pensions, improved medical plans, and job retraining for laid-off workers. He also served on the Honolulu Police Commission, the Aloha United Fund, and the Waikiki Improvement Association, and as a director of the Community Chest and the National Housing Conference. He was vice president of the Hawaii Visitors Bureau and president of the Hawaii Council for Housing Action. He became vice president and director of the ILWU on the West Coast in 1969 and died two years later in San Francisco. See *A Spark is Struck: Jack Hall and the ILWU in Hawaii* (Honolulu: University Press of Hawaii, 1979) by Sanford Zalburg.

HAMILTON, THOMAS HALE (1914–1979)

Born in Marion, Indiana, Hamilton obtained a bachelor's degree from DePauw University in 1936, a master's degree from the University of Chicago in 1940, and a doctorate from Chicago in 1947. He married Virginia Prindiville in 1940 and the couple had a son and a daughter. After teaching political science at several mainland universities he was named in 1959 president of the State University of New York, heading a system of fifty-four campuses.

Hamilton was appointed president of the University of Hawaii in 1963, following the retirement of Lawrence Hasbrouck Snyder. Hamilton led in the establishment of academic chairs, took part in the creation of the community college system, expanded science programs, and initiated new graduate degrees. When he assumed the presidency the statewide enrollment came to about 9,500 students; when he resigned the total approached 30,000. Grants to support the university were running at about five million dollars annually; they totaled sixty-four-million when he was in office. Hamilton resigned suddenly on December 23, 1967, when a faculty senate hearing committee protested his revocation of tenure of Oliver Lee, an assistant professor of political science. From 1968 to 1971, Hamilton was president of the Hawaii Visitors Bureau and then became a special adviser to the Kamehameha Schools/Bishop Estate, at a time when this campus-based institution expanded into statewide programs for the youth of Hawaii. Hamilton was a popular public speaker and his comments were always touched with humor. Hamilton Library on the Manoa campus bears his name.

HANDY, WILLOWDEAN CHATTERSON (1889–1965)

Born in Louisville, Kentucky, Willowdean Chatterson earned a bachelor's degree from the University of Chicago in 1909 and studied for two years at Radcliffe Graduate School. She was married on September 21, 1918, to E. S. Craighill Handy and was an associate in Polynesian folkways at the Bernice P. Bishop Museum from 1920 to 1930. Accompanying her husband on an expedition to the Marquesas Islands, she was drafted to record tattoo designs of the natives, living examples of this ancient art. She is author of *Forever the Land of Men: An Account of a Visit to the Marquesas Islands* (New York: Dodd, Mead, 1965) as well as a novel about the people of this Pacific group, *Thunder from the Sea* (Honolulu: University of Hawaii Press, 1973).

Mrs. Handy was a research analyst for the United States Office of Strategic Services during World War II and librarian of the Hawaiian Historical Society from 1950 to 1962. She was a regent of the University of Hawaii from 1943 to 1947 and a member of Phi Beta Kappa and the American Association of University Women. She was honorary life president of the Honolulu Branch of the Pan-Pacific and Southeast Asia Women's Association.

HARRIS, CHARLES COFFIN (1822–1881)

Born in Portsmouth, New Hampshire, Harris was educated at a school founded by his father in that town and graduated from Harvard University in 1841. He studied law and taught school before heading for California gold, and then joined two brothers in the operation of a schooner. He came to Hawaii in 1850 to practice law. He was appointed police magistrate in 1851 and studied Hawaiian. Under Kamehameha V he became advocate general and then Hawaii's first attorney general, a post created under the Constitution of 1864 that Harris had framed. During the next eight years he was minister of finance and foreign affairs. He left office because he had promoted the construction of the expensive Hawaiian Hotel downtown, but returned to service under Kalakaua. Harris was appointed vice chancellor and first associate justice of the Supreme Court in 1874; he became chief justice and chancellor of the kingdom in 1877 and served until the year of his death. Harris was one of the first communicants of the Episcopal Church in Honolulu.

HART, FRITZ (1874–1949)

Born in London, Hart was a composer and conductor of orchestras before becoming director of the Conservatorium of Music in Melbourne, Australia, in 1912. From 1931 to 1936 he acted as conductor for the symphony orchestras in both Melbourne and Honolulu, since their seasons did not overlap; thereafter he worked only in Honolulu. For fifteen years he lectured the week previous to a concert program. Hart also taught at the University of Hawaii for several years. During World War II he gave choral concerts at the Honolulu Academy of Arts. His compositions include chamber music, orchestral and choral works, more than four hundred songs, and twenty opera scores.

HARTWELL, ALFRED STEDMAN (1836–1912)

Born in Dedham, Massachusetts, Hartwell attended the public schools of that state; he earned a bachelor's degree from Harvard University in 1858 and a law degree in 1867. He enlisted in the Massachusetts Militia in 1861 and had an outstanding career in the Union Army as an officer in black regiments, and was brevetted as brigadier general in action.

Hartwell was recommended to Kamehameha V as an attorney to undertake the task of codifying the laws of the kingdom. The lawyer arrived in 1868 and served as first associate justice of the Supreme Court. When Kalakaua was elected, Hartwell acted as attorney general and played a large role in the 1876 treaty with the United States and the annexation proceedings in 1898. He was special agent for the Republic in 1899 and 1900 in Washington, D.C., where he remained the following year to work on the establishment of a cable connection between the islands and the mainland. As Supreme Court associate justice of the Territory, 1904, and chief justice, 1907–1911,

he handed down some notable decisions. Hartwell owned shares in several sugar plantations and at one time was the local representative of Claus SPRECKELS. Hartwell married Charlotte Elizabeth Smith of Koloa, Kauai, in 1872.

HEEN, WILLIAM HAEHAE (1883–1973)

Born in Olowalu, Maui, Heen was educated at Iolani School, Punahou School, and Hastings Law School in San Francisco (1902–1904). He was admitted to the bar of the territory in 1905. He married Mercy K. Akua in 1911 and the couple had five children. Heen served successively as deputy county attorney, Hawaii County, 1910–1915; deputy attorney general of the Territory, 1915–1917; third judge of First Circuit Court, Hawaii County, 1917–1919; and attorney of the City and County of Honolulu, 1919–1925. He was a senator in the Legislature from 1926 to 1957 and the first Democrat to be president of the Senate. He lost the bid for the Democrat nomination for the United States Senate to Frank Fasi in 1959.

Heen founded in 1925 the law firm of Heen & Kai (later Heen, Kai & Dodge), and was president of Heen Estates, Ltd. He was co-founder with Prince Kuhio KALANIANAOLE of the Hawaiian Civic Club and served as its first president in 1917. During the 1930s, Heen represented the five local defendants in the case of Thalia MASSIE. He was a director of several business concerns and was awarded the Order of the Splintered Paddle by the Honolulu Chamber of Commerce in 1962.

HEMENWAY, CHARLES REED
(1875–1947)
Born in Manchester, Vermont, of English descent, Hemenway earned a bachelor's degree from Yale University and studied law in New York City for two years. He married Jane Munson Colburn in 1901. He arrived in the islands in 1899 to teach at Punahou School and to practice law. He was appointed attorney general of the territory in 1907 and served for more than two years. Hemenway entered business in 1915 as a director of the "Big Five" firm of Alexander & Baldwin and from 1922 to 1938 he was vice president and assistant general manager. He was also president of Hawaiian Trust Co. from 1937 to 1945 and a director of half a dozen other enterprises. He is best known as a regent of the College of Hawaii (later the University of Hawaii) from 1910 to 1940; Hemenway Hall on the Manoa campus bears his name.

HEUCK, THEODORE C.
(1830–1877)
Born in Hamburg, Germany, Heuck was trained as an architect, engineer, and carpenter. He arrived in Hawaii from Australia in 1850 and during a decade was in business with Hermann J. F. VON HOLT. Heuck's first important work as Hawaii's first professional architect was the construction of the Queen's Hospital. While serving in the legislature of the kingdom from 1864 to 1867, Heuck designed the Royal Mausoleum and supervised its construction, as well as additions to the prison, custom's house, and Queen's Hospital. Iolani Barracks, later moved and rebuilt, was designed by Heuck in 1866 but not completed until 1871.

Heuck was a trustee of Queen's and secretary of the Board of Health. He also served as consul for the Kingdom of Prussia, for the North German Confederation, and for Denmark. He left Honolulu in 1874 after being created a Knight of the Order of Kamehameha I, and died in his native Hamburg.

HEWAHEWA (–1837)
The last high priest under the kapu system, Hewahewa was a lineal descendant of PAAO and served as kahuna for both Kamehameha I and Kamehameha II. Along with the latter and the queen regent KAAHUMANU, the priest overthrew the ancient system and helped to burn more than a hundred pagan idols. When the first American missionaries arrived at Kailua, Hawaii, in April, 1820, Hewahewa, on being introduced to the Rev. Hiram BINGHAM, "expressed much satisfaction in meeting with a brother priest from America." Hewahewa later became a devout Christian and attended the church of the Rev. John S. EMERSON at Waialua, Oahu. He wrote a Christian prayer antedating the use of the Lord's Prayer in the islands. He was associated with Anthony ALLEN in operating a farm on the road to Waikiki.

HILLEBRAND, WILLIAM
(1821–1886)
This Prussian medical man arrived in Hawaii in 1851 and opened a practice. He married Anna Post in 1852. He was named head physician in 1860 of the new hospital named for Queen EMMA and stayed on its staff until he left the islands in 1871. He was an expert botanist, and for many years his book (1888) was the only solid source for Hawaiian flora. The Foster Gardens in Honolulu are on the site of his former home, where he experimented with bringing in new plants, birds, and animals. Dr. Hillebrand was a member of the privy council of Kamehameha V. He was sent in 1865 by the Bureau of Immigration to China to arrange that laborers from that country be sent to Hawaii to work in the fields. The Bureau later followed Hillebrand's suggestion that a group of workers from the Madeira Islands be shipped to Hawaii; this was the beginning of the immigration of Portuguese laborers to these islands.

HILO HATTIE. See HAILI, Clarissa.

HIND, ROBERT ROBSON
(1832–1901)

Born in Newcastle, England, Hind married Mary Urwin and with their first son, John, went to Vancouver, British Columbia, to work as an engineer. After about a year he sought a warmer climate and came to the island of Hawaii, where he installed some machinery at a sugar mill near Hilo. He sent for his family and thereafter began a career as a pioneer planter and rancher in the islands. He engaged in a partnership on the island of Maui in 1869, and three years later joined forces with the growing firm of S. T. ALEXANDER and H. P. BALDWIN. He then turned his attention to the development of the Kohala region of the Big Island, and set up the Hawi Mill & Plantation Co. Hind also held coffee and sugar interests at Kona. In 1884, he decided to retire to San Francisco and turn over management to his son John. He was survived by his widow and six children, thus establishing a family whose achievements are still a part of Hawaii's ranching and business history. The name of Aina Haina, an eastern suburb of Honolulu, means "Hind's land"; it was named for Robert Hind, who started the Hind-Clarke Dairy there in 1924.

HITCHCOCK, DAVID HOWARD
(1861–1943)

One of the best-known artists born in the islands grew up in Hilo, grandson of the Rev. H. R. HITCHCOCK. Following attendance at Punahou School and Oberlin College, Ohio, the son studied at the National Academy of Design in New York and the Julienne Academy in Paris. He returned to the islands, married Hester Judd Dickson in Honolulu in 1898, and began producing much of his best work, especially scenes of the volcano region of the Big Island. His paintings are contained in many collections in the United States, Germany, and England. He taught art classes at Punahou School and in 1894 founded the Kilohana Art League, serving for twelve years as president. He also helped to bring the Boy Scout movement to Hawaii in 1919.

HITCHCOCK, HARVEY REXFORD (1800–1855)

Born in Great Barrington, Massachusetts, Hitchcock graduated from Williams College and Auburn Theological Seminary, where he was ordained in 1831. He married Rebecca Howard the same year and sailed with the Fifth Company of American missionaries, which arrived in Hawaii in May, 1832. In November the couple established the first mission station on the island of Molokai, at Kaluaaha, where Hitchcock's first pulpit was the broken stump of a lauhala tree. He was released from the mission at his own request in 1851 and died in 1855 after a trip to the United States. His wife moved to Hilo and died there in 1890, leaving four children. A grandson was David Howard HITCHCOCK.

HOAPILI (ULUMAHEIHEI) (1776–1840)

Son of the royal twin KAMEEIAMOKU and his wife Kealiiokahekili, he was renamed Hoapili because he was the "close companion" of Kamehameha I, entrusted with the task of concealing the dead king's bones. He was the father of LILIHA. After the death of Kamehameha, Hoapili married his sacred wife KEOPUOLANI, who retained him as her sole husband when she abandoned polygamy. He assisted in 1819 in the overthrow of the old religion, and supported the work of the American missionaries. After Keopuolani died, Hoapili married KALAKUA, daughter of KEEAUMOKU and NAMAHANA, in a Christian ceremony. This couple had a child, KEKAULUOHI (MIRIAM AUHEA), who became the mother of King LUNALILO. Other children were Queen KAMAMALU and KINAU. Hoapili was governor of Maui, Molokai, and Lanai from 1836 to 1840. He made education for children compulsory on Maui, and sent Moo, his pipe lighter, to teach at Puna on Hawaii.

HOLMAN, THOMAS (1793–1826)

First medical missionary to Hawaii, Holman was born in New Haven, Connecticut, and educated at Cherry Valley Medical School, New York. He spent the summer of 1819 at the Cornwall Mission School, Connecticut, before embarking in October on the *Thaddeus* as a member of the First Company to Hawaii. The previous month he had married Lucia Ruggles, a sister of his fellow worker and shipmate Samuel RUGGLES. After only four months in the islands, the Holmans had not adjusted to the spirit of the mission and he was excommunicated. The couple departed on a whale ship with their daughter (later they had two sons). The *Mentor* sailed via Canton, China, and the Cape of Good Hope to Boston. Lucia Holman is considered to be the first American woman to circumnavigate the globe.

HOLMES, OLIVER (HOMA) (–1825)

Holmes, an early American settler in Hawaii, was born in Plymouth, Massachusetts. He left New Bedford to trade in the Pacific and arrived in the islands in the *Margaret* in 1793. He was one of the first dozen foreigners to live in Hawaii, and the only one to have been in the service of KALANIKAPULE before joining that of Kamehameha I. After the victory of Kamehameha on Oahu, Holmes married Mahi Kalanihooulumokuikekai, daughter of a high chief of Koolau who was killed in the battle of the Nuuanu Pali. Holmes was made governor of Oahu and supported the establishment of the Protestant mission in 1820. Although said to be a member of the prominent Holmes family of New England, Oliver was content to live in a grass-roofed dwelling and his household was Hawaiian in every way. He provisioned visiting ships and sojourning ship captains were his paying guests. The couple had a number of pretty daughters. Hannah married Captain William Heath DAVIS and later his partner, John Coffin JONES.

HOOPER, WILLIAM NORTHEY (1809–1878)

Born in Boston, Hooper speculated in Puerto Rico and the Dutch East Indies before becoming a partner with Peter BRINSMADE and William LADD in the firm of Ladd & Co. in 1835. Obtaining a fifty-year lease on a tract of land on Kauai in 1835, the firm appointed Hooper as manager of Koloa Plantation, one of the first in the islands. He suffered heartbreaking troubles, especially in finding labor, and although Hooper replaced the fragile wooden rollers of the press with iron rollers, he produced in 1837 only two tons of sugar of poor quality. Twelve acres were cleared for cultivation with a plow drawn by forty Hawaiian workers until the invention of a deep-plow method by Samuel Burbank.

Hooper left Koloa in 1839, married the sister of Dr. R. W. WOOD the same year, and for a time was United States commercial agent and vice consul, beginning in 1845. Later he helped to establish San Francisco's first Chamber of Commerce. The Koloa Plantation was involved in the affairs of Brinsmade and the political problems of Ladd & Co. and was not successful until management was taken over by Dr. Wood.

HOPKINS, MANLEY (1818–1897)

Serving as Hawaiian consul in London from 1856 to 1896, Hopkins published *Hawaii: The Past, Present, and Future of Its Island-Kingdom* (London: Longman, Green, Longman & Roberts, 1862). Manley never visited Hawaii but his brother, Charles Gordon Hopkins, served in the island government for many years and furnished Manley with much material. Manley Hopkins was the father of the English priest-poet Gerard Manley Hopkins.

HOPU, THOMAS

On board the *Thaddeus* when it arrived off the island of Hawaii in 1820 were three young men of Hawaiian birth who had attended the mission school at Cornwall, Connecticut. They were Thomas Hopu, John Honolii, and William Kanui. (A fourth Hawaiian, George P. KAUMUALII, was listed as a passenger on the ship.) An engraving of all four of them, taken from portraits painted by Professor Samuel F. B. Morse, had been sold for the benefit of the mission.

Hopu had left the islands on the same ship that took Henry OPUKAHAIA. Hopu shipped on several privateering expeditions in the War of 1812, was shipwrecked in the West Indies, and became prisoner of the British. He returned to New Haven destitute, and there found his island friend Opukahaia. Converted to Christianity, Hopu walked sixty miles to find another Hawaiian, Honolii, in order to convert him. Other Hawaiians were sought to attend the school, among them William Kanui, who had reached Boston with his brother around 1809. They had both served on privateers, but when the brother died William went to New Haven to become a barber. Discovered by Yale College students, he also went to Cornwall.

Aboard ship and later in the islands, the three Hawaiians gave invaluable aid as teachers of the language and translators, and

53

smoothed the way for the peaceful reception of the American mission during the first weeks. Hopu later was assistant to the Rev. Asa THURSTON at Kailua, Hawaii, along with John Honolii, who died in 1838. Honolii served as a guide to David DOUGLAS during an ascent of Mauna Kea in 1834. Hopu left to join the California gold rush with William Kanui; the Rev. S. C. Damon encountered both of them at Sacramento. Kanui, who had served in the United States Navy and seen action against the Tripoli pirates in the Mediterranean, lost his gains from the gold fields in a bank failure and drifted about California, teaching the Bible and attending church. He lived for a while at Indian Creek, a colony of devout Hawaiian gold seekers, before returning to Honolulu to teach school; he died in 1864.

HOSMER, RALPH SHELDON (1874–1963)

Born in Deerfield, Massachusetts, Hosmer obtained a bachelor's degree at Harvard in 1894 and a master's degree at Yale. After working in the United States Department of Agriculture he became superintendent of forestry for the Territory of Hawaii from 1904 to 1914. He planned many of the present forest-reserve boundaries in the islands. He left in 1914 to become professor of forestry at Cornell University.

HOUSTON, VICTOR STEUART KALEOALOHA (1876–1959)

Houston was born in San Francisco, son of naval officer Edwin Samuel and Caroline Poor Kahikiola (Brickwood) Houston. The son graduated from the United States Naval Academy in 1897 and retired as commander in 1926 after thirty-two years in the Navy. He commanded the cruiser *St. Louis* in World War I. He married Pinao G. Brickwood in 1910. Houston was territorial delegate to Congress from 1927 to 1933. He was the first delegate to introduce an act enabling Hawaii to become a state. He was later chairman of the Hawaiian Homes Commission. An authority on Hawaiiana, Houston spoke the language and was a member of the Board of Trustees of the Liliuokalani Trust.

HUNNEWELL, JAMES (1794–1869)

Born in Charlestown, Massachusetts, Hunnewell first arrived in the islands on the *Bordeaux Packet* in 1817 and left as a passenger on the *Osprey*. He came again as first officer of the *Thaddeus* in 1820 with the First Company of American missionaries. Later he arranged for the sale of both a brig and a schooner to the Hawaiian government in exchange for a cargo of sandalwood. He traded between the West Coast and China for several years in command of the *Missionary Packet*, which he had sailed from Boston around Cape Horn. He set up a pioneer mercantile business in Honolulu as early as 1817, but left the islands in 1830 with Henry A. PEIRCE in charge of his affairs. The firm later became controlled by Charles BREWER; thus Hunnewell was the progenitor of one of the "Big Five" factors. Hunnewell is author of *Journal of the Voyage of the "Missionary Packet," Boston to Honolulu, 1826* (Charlestown, Mass.: privately printed, 1880).

HYDE, CHARLES McEWEN (1832–1899)

Born in New York City, Hyde graduated from Williams College in Massachusetts in 1852 and from Princeton Theological Seminary in 1860. He was ordained in 1862 and the degree of doctor of divinity was conferred upon him by Williams in 1872. After serving as pastor in Massachusetts, he arrived in Honolulu in 1877 with his wife, Mary T. Knight, whom he had married in 1865, and two sons. He was not a member of the Boston board that sent out twelve "companies" to the islands. Hyde reorganized the Theological School as the North Pacific Missionary Institute and served as its principal. He was secretary of the Board of the Hawaiian Evangelical Association; supported the Chinese, Japanese, and Portuguese Mission Churches; was trustee of five educational trusts; and initiated the Social Science Club for intellectual discussions. Hyde held a leading role in the organization and development of the Kamehameha Schools, of which he was an early trustee, and was an active civic influence. He translated hymns into Hawaiian and left a valuable collection of Hawaiiana now in the library of the Hawaiian Historical Society.

Hyde is best known, perhaps, as the recipient of the "Open Letter to the Reverend Dr. Hyde of Honolulu" by Robert Louis STEVENSON, a celebrated work of invective attacking Hyde for having written a slur on the character of Father DAMIEN. See *Dr. Hyde and Mr. Stevenson* by Harold W. Kent (Rutland, Vt. and Tokyo: Tuttle, 1973), a biography of Hyde.

IAUKEA, CURTIS PIEHU
(1855 – 1940)

A descendant of chiefs, Iaukea
was born at Waimea, Hawaii, son of
J. W. and Lahapa Nalanipo Iaukea.
The boy was reared in Honolulu
under the direction of his uncle,
Kaihupaa, an old-time retainer of
chiefs and a personal attendant upon
King Kamehameha III. The nephew
was educated at Iolani School under
the Church of England. Sent to Hilo
to learn the sugar business, Iaukea
was found there by King Kalakaua
on a royal tour and commanded to
resume his place at the palace.
Thereafter Iaukea was connected
with the monarchy until its overthrow
in 1893. In 1880 he was chief
secretary in the Department of
Foreign Affairs, and three years later
was special envoy to the coronation
of the Czar of Russia. He visited all
the courts of Europe and then went to
India and Japan to study the problem
of labor immigration; one result of
his efforts was the admission of
Japanese laborers to the plantations
of Hawaii.

Iaukea was collector general of
customs in 1884 and chamberlain of
the king's household. In the latter
office he took charge of the party
attending the jubilee of Queen
Victoria of England in 1887, which
visited President and Mrs. Grover
Cleveland en route. Ten years later
Iaukea attended Victoria's Diamond
Jubilee with the representatives of the
Republic of Hawaii, and in the same
year accompanied President
and Mrs. Sanford B. DOLE to
Washington, D.C., as secretary
and military attaché.

Iaukea was sheriff of the County of
Oahu from 1906 to 1908 and served a
term in the Territorial Senate from
1912. After 1909 he was managing
trustee of the Liliuokalani Trust and
business representative for the
former queen. One of the most
decorated men in Hawaii, he received
half a dozen orders from foreign
governments for his protocol
services. He was appointed secretary
of the Territory in 1917 and often
served as acting governor until his
retirement from the post in 1921. He
was chairman of the Hawaiian Homes
Commission from 1933 to 1935. In
1937 he became a member of the
Archives Commission and custodian
of the throne room of Iolani Palace.
In 1877 he married Charlotte K.
Hanks and they had a son and
a daughter.

II, JOHN PAPA (1800? – 1870)

Son of a chief of Kona and his
wife, the boy was born at Waipio,
Ewa, Oahu, and joined the royal court
at the age of ten, where he became
the companion of the future
Kamehameha II. He took the name of
"Papa" from his uncle, and the name
of "Ii" from an exclamation by Prince
Liholiho when he first saw his
future friend. Ii was converted to
Christianity soon after the arrival of
the American missionaries, and then
took the name of John. Ii
accompanied the young king to the
school of Hiram BINGHAM in 1820
and later helped the missionaries in
the translation of texts into Hawaiian.

Under Kamehameha III, Ii was
appointed to the House of Nobles and
the privy council, and from 1846 to
1852 was an associate justice of the
Superior Court. He was appointed in
1846 to the Board of Commissioners
to Quiet Land Titles under the second
organic act and was the only
Hawaiian member to serve the entire
term of the Board. He helped to draft
the Constitution of 1852 and under
the new Supreme Court served as a
justice from that year until he
resigned in 1864. Articles by Ii
appearing in the newspaper *Kuokoa*
from 1866 to 1870 were collected and
translated as valuable contributions
to Hawaiiana; see *Fragments of
Hawaiian History* (Honolulu: Bishop
Museum Press, 1959), translated by
Mary K. Pukui and edited by
Dorothy Barrère.

IMAMURA, YEMYO (1866 – 1932)

Born at Fukui Prefecture,
Japan, Imamura was trained as a
Buddhist priest. He came to Hawaii
to serve as the second bishop of the
Hawaii Hongwanji Buddhist Mission,
succeeding Hoju Tatsutani. He
arrived with ten thousand volumes on
Japanese culture, and sponsored the
English language section of the
Hongwanji Temple in order to
present to the general public a
non-sectarian form of Buddhism.
He worked to increase greater
understanding among the various
ethnic groups in the islands. He
retired after thirty-two years as
bishop, having added some thirty-six
Mission temples built in rural Oahu
and on other islands.

INGRAHAM, JOSEPH

Ingraham first saw the Hawaiian
Islands as second mate of the
Columbia in 1789, under Robert
GRAY, and returned twice as master
of the *Hope*. This brigantine barely
escaped being captured by
Kamehameha I. Ingraham wrote the
quite readable *Journal of the
Brigantine "Hope"* (Barre, Mass.:
Imprint Society, 1971), edited by
M. Kaplanoff.

IRWIN, WILLIAM G.
(1843–1914)

Born in England, Irwin was brought to Hawaii by his parents in early childhood from San Francisco. The father was at one time secretary of the Foreign Office under the monarchy. William, one of four children, was educated at Punahou School and worked for several Honolulu firms before setting out for himself as head of William G. Irwin & Co. In 1881 Irwin became the partner of Claus SPRECKELS, and the pair opened in 1885 the bank of Claus Spreckels & Co., later incorporated under the name of the Bank of Honolulu, Ltd., and still later merged with the Bank of Bishop & Co. Irwin acquired large sugar plantation holdings and other properties in the islands. He married Mrs. Fannie Holladay in 1886 and their daughter, Helene Irwin, married Charles Templeton Crocker of Burlingame, California. A close friend of King Kalakaua, Irwin was a member of the privy council in 1887. He incorporated his estate in San Francisco in 1913 and became a power in California business affairs, associated with the Mercantile National Bank of San Francisco in later years.

ISENBERG, HEINRICH PAUL
FRIEDRICH (1837–1903)

Paul Isenberg was born in Dransfeld, Germany, son of a Lutheran minister. With experience on a farm, he went to Hawaii and in the late 1850s was employed at Lihue Plantation as an overseer under William Harrison RICE. Isenberg married Rice's daughter Hannah Maria in 1861, and on the death of his employer became manager of Lihue in May, 1862. Two children were born, Dora and Paul, who at the time were the only white children in Lihue. Mrs. Isenberg died in 1867 and two years later Paul married Beta Glade in Germany. Of this couple six children were born. On his return from Europe, Isenberg began to develop the plantation heavily, and in the 1870s he also acquired an interest in Koloa Plantation. He retired from Lihue in 1878, having acquired a considerable fortune. In 1881 he was invited to obtain a half-share partnership with Captain Heinrich HACKFELD, and the firm developed into one of the "Big Five" as American Factors, Ltd. (Amfac).

Paul Isenberg was a friend of the native Hawaiian people and a welcome visitor at court, and he helped to prevent trouble over the proposed Constitution of 1887. For his service in the legislature, King Kalakaua decorated him with the Order of Kamehameha. He moved his family in 1878 to Germany, where his daughter Dora married in 1883 a first cousin, the Rev. Hans Isenberg. See Ethel M. Damon, *Koamalu* (Honolulu: privately printed, 1931).

JAGGAR, THOMAS AUGUSTUS
(1871–1953)

Born in Philadelphia, Pennsylvania, the future volcanologist obtained three degrees from Harvard University: A.B., 1893; A.M., 1894; Ph. D., 1897. After study at Munich and Heidelberg in Germany, he began teaching at Harvard. In 1906 he became head of the Department of Geology at Massachusetts Institute of Technology. In 1911 he established the Hawaiian Volcano Research Association and served for many years at Kilauea, Hawaii, co-operating with the United States Weather Bureau and the United States Geological Survey, as well as the National Park Service. Dr. Jaggar conducted research expeditions to volcanic areas in a dozen parts of the world. He was a member of various scientific societies and author of many articles and several books. See his *My Experiments with Volcanoes* (Honolulu: Hawaiian Volcano Research Association, 1956).

JANION, ROBERT
See DAVIES, Theophilus Harris.

JARRETT, WILLIAM PAUL
(1877–1929)

Jarrett was born in Honolulu of an old and distinguished family and educated at St. Louis College. He was deputy sheriff of the City and County of Honolulu for one term of two years, sheriff for three terms, and high sheriff of the Territory from 1914 to 1922. As warden of Oahu Prison during eight years he was noted for his reforms and his concern for his people. As a leader in the Democrat Party and winner of national recognition for his prison work, he was territorial delegate to Congress from 1923 to 1927. From 1926 until his death Jarrett was superintendent of the Lunalilo Home, an institution for aged Hawaiians. In 1907 he married Mary H. K. Clark and the couple had four children; his wife died in 1920 and he then married Mrs. Elizabeth Neal.

JARVES, JAMES JACKSON (1818–1888)
One of the first to write a history of Hawaii in English, Jarves was born in Boston; he was also a planter, merchant, editor, sketch writer, and author of the first novel with a Hawaiian setting. He came to Hawaii at the age of nineteen, and returned to Boston the same year, to marry his childhood sweetheart and bring her to Hawaii to share his life. Jarves founded the weekly *Polynesian* in 1840; it was re-established in 1844 as the official publication of the Hawaiian government. He left Hawaii for the last time in 1848, but in Washington, D.C., on December 6, 1849, he signed, as special commissioner, a treaty that recognized the independence of the Hawaiian kingdom. His books include *The History of the Hawaiian or Sandwich Islands* (Boston: Tappan & Dennet, 1843); *Scenes and Scenery in the Hawaiian Islands* (Boston: James Monroe, 1843); and the novel *Kiana: A Tradition of Hawaii* (Boston and Cambridge: James Monroe, 1857). For a biography see Francis Steegmuller, *The Two Lives of James Jackson Jarves* (New Haven, Conn.: Yale University Press, 1951).

JONES, JAMES (1921–1978)
Born in Robinson, Illinois, Jones served in the United States Army from 1939 to 1944, stationed at Schofield Barracks before and during the attack by Japanese warplanes on December 7, 1941. He studied at the University of Hawaii in 1942 and New York University in 1945, and for seven years worked with Mr. and Mrs. Harry E. Handy of Robinson, preparing the manuscript of his best-known novel, *From Here to Eternity* (New York: Scribner, 1951). It is the story of a group of people in Hawaii before and during the attack. Versions have appeared on film and on the television screen. A lesser-known and more unified novel by Jones is *The Pistol* (New York: Scribner, 1958), also dealing with the "blitz" and its aftermath. Jones published half a dozen other novels, written mainly during a residence in Paris, but in 1975 he returned to spend his last years in the United States.

JONES, JOHN COFFIN (1796–1861)
Jones, only son of a leading Boston merchant, left Harvard University to serve in the sandalwood trade under Captain Dixey Wildes. Jones arrived in Honolulu in 1821 as United States consular agent and representative of the Boston trading firm of Marshall & Wildes. He immediately collided with the missionary group led by the Rev. Hiram BINGHAM and for the next two decades he contended for commercial advantages to the neglect of native Hawaiian concerns. He set up his own trading firm in 1830 and made many voyages to California during the next ten years. The opposition of the Protestant mission finally succeeded in bringing about his dismissal from State Department office in 1839.

Jones's several marriages were also held against him. He took to wife in 1823 Hannah Holmes Davis, widow of his partner, William Heath DAVIS Sr. His younger stepson, William Heath Davis Jr., became a prominent California businessman. Jones continued to live with Hannah but also lived with Lahilahi Marín, daughter of Don Francisco MARÍN, and had children by both. He formally married in 1838 Manuela Carrillo of Santa Barbara, California, and deserted Hannah and Lahilahi. Jones settled in Santa Barbara in 1839 and continued as a merchant both in California and in Massachusetts. He died on Christmas Eve, 1861, leaving a goodly estate to his wife and six children.

The service of Jones as consular agent in Honolulu embroiled him in a number of commercial and political causes. Both as government representative and private trader during a formative period, he was an energetic figure and is credited with leadership in opening trade between Hawaii and Spanish California. On a visit to Hawaii in 1843, Jones authorized Stephen Reynolds to present a bill against the royal treasury for principal and interest on an unpaid note signed by the chiefs in 1829. This was the basis for visits to Hawaii by American gunboats and was the origin of the national debt. See Ross H. Gast, *Contentious Consul: A Biography of John Coffin Jones, First United States Consular Agent at Hawaii* (Los Angeles: Dawson's Book Shop, 1976).

JONES, PETER CUSHMAN
(1837 – 1922)

Born in Boston of old New England stock, Jones attended Boston Latin School and prepared to enter Harvard University, but the lure of business made him take a job as office boy at a salary of $50 a year. Seeking adventure, he followed many another New Englander to the Hawaii frontier and worked for several companies before becoming a partner with C. L. Richards in a ship chandlery. Jones became a partner in C. BREWER & Co. in 1871 and president in 1883, a position he held until 1891; he returned to the company a year later and served until 1899, when he was succeeded by Charles M. COOKE. With his son Edwin Austin Jones he formed a concern in 1892 that later became the Hawaiian Trust Co.

Of a strongly religious turn of mind, Jones served for years on church boards and built the Palama Chapel, out of which grew the Palama Settlement, an early social center. For twenty years he was treasurer of Punahou School. He was an adviser to the crown and in 1892 was appointed minister of finance to Queen Liliuokalani. He decided, however, that the best interests of the islands would be served by an overthrow of the monarchy, and he was one of the most influential leaders of the Revolution of 1893. In 1862 he married Cornelia Hall, daughter of E. O. HALL, and the couple had three children.

JONES, THOMAS AP CATESBY
(1769 – 1858)

Born in Boston, son of an Army major, Jones entered the United States Navy in 1805 and began a lifetime career of distinction. In the spring of 1826, Captain John PERCIVAL and the armed schooner *Dolphin* spent three months in Hawaii, the first American warship to visit Hawaii. In the autumn, a second vessel spent three months in the islands, with more lasting results. Captain Jones of the *Peacock* obtained a renewed pledge of payment of the debts piled up by the ruling chiefs; to raise the money the earliest written tax law was passed on December 27, 1826, requiring able-bodied Hawaiians to deliver payment in sandalwood or Spanish dollars. Jones also made, on behalf of the United States government, certain "articles of arrangement" that formed a rough treaty providing for peace between the Americans and Hawaiians, and for the protection of American interests. This first treaty between Hawaii and a foreign country was never ratified in Washington but was respected for many years, and Jones earned the sobriquet of "the kind-eyed chief." Jones returned to the islands in 1843 in command of the U.S.S. *United States*, aboard which Herman MELVILLE left Hawaii.

JOSEPH, BROTHER
See DUTTON, Ira Barnes.

JUDD, ALBERT FRANCIS
(1838 – 1900)

Son of Gerrit P. JUDD, Albert was born in Honolulu. He studied at Punahou School, obtained a bachelor's degree from Yale in 1862, and earned a law degree from Harvard Law School in 1864. He returned to practice in Hawaii, served several terms in the legislature beginning in 1868, and in 1873 was named attorney general under King Lunalilo. He was appointed a justice of the Supreme Court in 1874 and served as chief justice from 1881, presiding not only during the reigns of Kalakaua and Liliuokalani but also under the Republic of Hawaii. He was second president of the Hawaiian Board of Missions from 1883 to 1900. He married Agnes Hall Boyd in 1872 and was the father of nine children, including Albert Francis Judd II, James Robert Judd, Henry Pratt JUDD, Charles Sheldon JUDD, and Lawrence McCully JUDD.

JUDD, CHARLES SHELDON
(1881 – 1939)

Born in Honolulu, son of Albert Francis Judd, Charles attended Punahou School and graduated from Yale University in 1905; he obtained a master's degree in forestry from Yale in 1907. After several years in the United States Forestry Service he was appointed land commissioner for the Territory of Hawaii in 1911 and acted for eight months before returning to federal service. In January, 1915, he returned to the islands and became superintendent of forestry and chief fire warden, Board of Agriculture and Forestry. In 1927 he was given the title of territorial forester, which he retained until his death. He increased the ranger force greatly, added 183,000 acres to the area of forest reserves, and planted millions of trees in denuded areas. Judd accompanied the Bernice P. Bishop Expedition to Nihoa and Necker Islands in 1923 and took part in the Mauna Kea Expedition of 1935. He was a member of many professional and social groups. He married Louise Luquiens in 1910 and they had two children, Emma and Charles Sheldon Judd Jr.

JUDD, GERRIT PARMELE (1803–1873)

The medical missionary and adviser to the Hawaiian throne was born in Paris, New York. At the age of twenty-three he earned a medical degree from a school at Fairfield, New York. With his wife, Laura Fish JUDD, he arrived in Hawaii with the Third Company of American missionaries in 1828. He was a busy doctor in the community even after he left the mission in 1842 to become a leading counselor to KAMEHAMEHA III. He was made secretary of state for foreign affairs in 1845. He built a large home and with his wife reared no fewer than nine children, including Albert Francis JUDD.

Judd's courage was shown in 1843 when he quietly resisted the demands of Lord George PAULET. Judd resigned on May 10 as the king's deputy minister and secretly removed the public papers to the Royal Mausoleum in the palace grounds to prevent them from being taken by British naval officers. Using the coffin of KAAHUMANU as a writing desk, Dr. Judd prepared appeals to London and Washington to free Hawaii from the illegal rule of Paulet. As one result, Admiral Richard THOMAS arrived on July 26 to restore the kingdom to Kamehameha III.

Judd was chosen in 1849 to head a group going to France to obtain better relations. During his travels he took with him the two young princes who were to become KAMEHAMEHA IV and KAMEHAMEHA V, and the party also visited Great Britain and the United States. Fear of American filibusters in 1851, made worse by a bad smallpox epidemic that was blamed on foreign residents, resulted in the king's decision not to reappoint Dr. Judd as minister of finance, although he had served on a committee the previous year to write the Constitution of 1852. A novel in which the principal character is Dr. Judd is *The White King* by Samuel Harrison (Garden City, N.Y.: Doubleday, 1950).

JUDD, HENRY PRATT (1880–1955)

Widely known as a clergyman and teacher of the Hawaiian language, Judd was born at Rensselaer, New York, son of Agnes and Albert Francis JUDD. Henry graduated from Punahou School in 1897, from Yale in 1901, and from Auburn Theological Seminary in 1906. He worked with the Hawaiian Board of Missions from 1908 to 1935, and thereafter for ten years as a professor of Hawaiian at the University of Hawaii. He was pastor of several churches and chaplain of both houses of the Territorial Legislature. In later years he continued to teach Hawaiian. He was the author of a textbook on this language and co-author of an English-Hawaiian dictionary. He was a member of various professional and civic groups.

JUDD, LAURA FISH (1804–1872)

Laura Judd bore her husband, Gerrit Parmele JUDD, nine children. She taught school and was a friend of Queen KAAHUMANU. Laura Judd's diary includes dozens of views of life in Hawaii from 1828 to 1861. See her *Honolulu: Sketches of the Life, Social, Political, and Religious* (New York: Anson D. F. Randolph, 1880).

JUDD, LAWRENCE McCULLY (1887–1968)

Born in Honolulu, son of Albert Francis JUDD and grandson of Dr. Gerrit P. JUDD, Lawrence graduated from Punahou School in 1905 and in 1909 attended the University of Pennsylvania. He married Florence Hackett in 1909 and they had four children. Judd held several positions in mainland firms before returning to Honolulu in 1914 to work for Theo. H. Davies & Co., Ltd. He enlisted at the outbreak of World War I and made a noteworthy military record; by 1920 he was colonel in command of all the troops of the Hawaiian National Guard. He became a director of several leading commercial firms and supported education; he was a trustee of Palama Settlement and a warden of St. Andrew's Cathedral.

Judd was elected to the Territorial Senate from 1920 to 1928 and was president in 1923. While on the Board of Supervisors of Oahu County he was named seventh governor of the territory by President Herbert Hoover and served from 1929 to

1934. Soon after he took office, the depression began and it was his unpleasant duty to initiate drastic cuts in salaries and other spending. However, the government did carry out major public-works programs in parks and playgrounds, and the Waikiki Natatorium was built as a war memorial.

Perhaps the most dramatic act of Judd as governor was to commute the ten-year prison sentence of Thomas MASSIE and his co-defendants to one hour in his custody, thus averting in 1931 the possibility that the territory might be subjected to a carpetbagger regime. Previous to the Massie case, Judd in 1930 had set up a crime commission which made some recommendations similar to those made after the case had aroused wide comment, and additional corrective measures were passed by the legislature in 1932 and 1933. Judd spoke in favor of statehood for Hawaii and of an increased military presence in the islands previous to America's entry into World War II. He was head of the Civil Defense program in 1942 and city rent-control administrator in 1944. As superintendent of Kalaupapa Settlement on Molokai he was instrumental in legally relaxing the segregation of patients with arrested cases of leprosy. Later he was director of hospitals and settlements. He was president of the Hawaii Residents' Association (Imua), a conservative group, from 1951 to 1955. He was appointed governor of American Samoa in 1953, the only man to be governor of two American territories. His autobiography is entitle *Lawrence M. Judd and Hawaii* (Rutland, Vt. and Tokyo: Tuttle, 1971).

KAAHUMANU (1768?–1832)
This powerful chiefess was born at Hana, Maui, daughter of the elder KEEAUMOKU and NAMAHANA. Her brothers were KEEAUMOKU II and KUAKINI (Cox). She became one of the wives of KAMEHAMEHA I when he was ruling chief of the island of Hawaii. A breach between the pair was healed by Captain George VANCOUVER in 1793.

As foster mother of KAMEHAMEHA II she was named co-ruler with him and became the first kuhina nui, or regent. She led him in the celebrated breaking of the ancient religious tabu. In 1821, when King KAUMUALII of Kauai was brought to Honolulu as a virtual hostage, he was married to Kaahumanu, who also married the king's heir, Kealiiahonui. Kaahumanu was left in charge of the kingdom when the royal party left for London in 1823 and was assisted by KALANIMOKU, who put down the Kauai rebellion led by George P. KAUMUALII. She ruled her people, it was said, with "a rod of iron."

Kaahumanu allowed the American missionaries to land in 1820 for a trial period. At first she was disdainful of the strangers, but around 1825, as the most important person in the kingdom, she took the lead in promoting Protestantism, and was taught by the Rev. Hiram BINGHAM to read and write. On the first Sunday in December, 1825, she, along with Kalanimoku and several other chiefs, received communion at Kawaiahao Church for the first time. Six months after Kamehameha II departed for England, Kaahumanu proclaimed a code of civil laws, clearly based on missionary teaching, that prohibited murder, theft, fighting, and Sabbath-breaking. She opposed French efforts to introduce Catholicism into the islands (see MAIGRET) and ordered the priests that arrived in 1827 to be taken away, but later they were allowed to remain. She also strongly opposed the divisive efforts of BOKI and LILIHA. Kaahumanu received the first copy of the Hawaiian translation of the New Testament from Bingham shortly before her death on June 5, 1832.

KAEOKULANI (KAEO) (1748–1794)
Kaeo, son of KEKAULIKE and his wife Holau, was half-brother of KAHEKILI and ruler of the island of Kauai. At the death of the aged Kekaulike in 1794, his extensive domains were divided between his son KALANIKUPULE and his brother, Kaeo. At this time, Kaeo was on Maui and Kalanikupule was on Oahu, and they drifted into a war over the division of lands. After several skirmishes on Oahu, the opposing forces met in battle on December 12 near Aiea. With the aid of the crews of three foreign trading ships, Kalanikupule gained a clear victory and Kaeo was killed. Kaeo was the father of KAUMUALII.

KAEO, PETER (1836–1880)

A descendant of
KELIIMAIKAI of Maui and John
YOUNG, Peter was adopted when a
boy by John YOUNG II and attended
the Chiefs' Children's School. Later
he used the title of "Kekuaokalani."
He learned in the 1870s that he
suffered from leprosy. He arrived at
Kalaupapa, Molokai, in 1873 and
lived there most of the time until his
death. Queen EMMA was his full
cousin. See *News from Molokai:
Letters between Peter Kaeo and
Queen Emma, 1873–1876*
(Honolulu: University Press of
Hawaii, 1976), edited by
Alfons L. Korn.

KAHANAMOKU, DUKE PAOA (1890–1968)

Born in Haleakala, Maui, son
of Duke Halapu Kahanamoku and
Julia Paoakania Lonokahini
Kahanamoku, young Duke had six
brothers and three sisters. He
attended Waikiki Grammar School,
Kaahumanu School, and the
Kamehameha School for Boys. As a
youth he became a master surfer on a
sixteen-foot koa-wood board
weighing 114 pounds. In 1910 he
developed what he called "the
Hawaiian crawl," a basic swimming
competition stroke today known as
"the American crawl."

Kahanamoku won an AAU meet in
Honolulu Harbor, breaking United
States records for the 100- and
50-yard sprints. He went to the
Stockholm Olympics in 1912 and
swept the swimming events, setting a
world record for the 100-meter event;
in the same year he broke his own
record at Hamburg. Returning to
Hawaii, he worked as a reader of
water meters, on surveying jobs, and
as a beach boy. He entered

competition again in 1916 and broke
more records with his distinctive
style. During World War I, when the
1916 Olympics were cancelled,
Kahanamoku made a tour of the
mainland United States,
demonstrating his skill to raise
money for the Red Cross. At almost
thirty years of age, he beat his own
100-meter freestyle record at the
Antwerp Olympics in 1920 by
making the course in one minute flat.

Kahanamoku began a Hollywood
film career in 1922, playing
Polynesians, American Indians, or
Hindus—everything except
Hawaiians. He lost his title in the
1924 Olympics in Paris to Johnny
Weissmuller, who set a new record of
59 seconds. Kahanamoku became a
national hero when, on June 14,
1925, he rescued on his surfboard
eight of the twelve men saved from a
capsized fishing boat in high surf off
Newport Beach, California. He won
medals in the 1928 Olympics and
continued acting until 1929, when he
returned to Honolulu and worked as a
janitor at City Hall. In 1932 he failed
to place in the Olympic swimming
trials but won a spot on the United
States water-polo team and thus
appeared in four Olympic
competitions in twenty years. While
running a gasoline service station in
1934, he was elected sheriff of
Honolulu, a largely ceremonial post
that he held until it was abolished in
1961; he was then appointed official
city greeter.

Kahanamoku married Nadine
Alexander in 1940. He was a familiar
figure at the Outrigger Canoe Club
on Waikiki Beach and was known to
thousands of visitors to the islands.
He was selected in 1965 as a charter
member of the Swimming Hall of
Fame. He became one of twenty-six
all-time sports champions in 1967,
the year after he was named to the
first Surfing Hall of Fame.
Kahanamoku's name is perpetuated
in the annual World Surfing
Championships.

KAHEIHEIMAILE

A wife of KAMEHAMEHA I
and the mother of KINAU.

KAHEKILI (1713–1794)

A son of KEKAULIKE,
Kahekili was ruler of Maui, father of
KALANIKUPULE and
KOALAUKANI, and enemy of
KALANIOPUU. He was said by
some to be the father of
KAMEHAMEHA I, who later fought
against him. Kahekili visited the
flagship of James COOK in
November, 1778. With the aid of his
half-brother KAEO, Kahekili
extended his rule to the island of
Oahu and set up court at Waikiki,
leaving his son Kalanikupule to rule
over Maui. Challenged from Molokai
by the conquering Kamehameha,
Kahekili declared that he would
defend his kingdom to the death.
Later he recaptured Molokai and
Maui, but his canoe fleet was
defeated off northern Hawaii in the
spring of 1791 by Kamehameha's
fleet; this was the first native
engagement using on both sides the
cannon of the white men. Kahekili
died in Waikiki in 1794, leaving his
domains to Kaeo and his son
Kalanikupule, whose conflict
proved fatal to both.

KAIANA (1756?–1795)

Kaiana was the son of Ahuula and Kaupekamoku and a half-brother of KAHEKILI. This prince of Maui was more than six feet tall, and was the first chief to travel to foreign lands. He went with Captain John MEARES in the *Nootka* to Canton in 1787 and returned with Captain William Douglas in the *Iphigenia* in December, 1788, the first ship to visit Kealakekua Bay after the departure of the Cook expedition. Kaiana plotted to kill Douglas in 1789 and seize his ship, but the captain learned of the plot and foiled it, despite Kaiana's efforts to blame Kamehameha.

Kaiana's high rank, his fame in war, and his knowledge of the use of foreign weapons—he brought back with him muskets and cannon—gave him much prestige and he was a valuable ally to Kamehameha for several years. He led the forces of the conqueror against KEOUA KUAHUULA. Kaiana was suspected of having an affair with Queen KAAHUMANU in 1793, however, and Kamehameha became less friendly. During the invasion of Oahu in 1795, Kaiana and his brother Namakeha feared a plot and deserted to the side of Kahekili. Kaiana was killed fighting against Kamehameha at Nuuanu Pali in 1795.

KAIKIOEWA (1765–1839)

A high chief, born at Waimea, Kauai, he was son of Kaianakukue Kaolohaka-a-keawe and his wife Kekikoola Lalanikauleleaiwi; he was thus a cousin of KAMEHAMEHA I on both sides. He was a supporter of Kamehameha in the civil wars and married his sister Kalanikaulihi-wakama; their daughter was Kuwahine. Kaikioewa had another daughter, Likelike, by Nahaukapu.

Kaikioewa was the guardian of Kauikeaouli, the future KAMEHAMEHA III. In 1825, when the rebellion on Kauai was put down, Kaikioewa was made governor and served until his death. He was among those chiefs who went into debt during the sandalwood era to buy expensive novelties. He became a vigorous convert to Protestantism and in 1830 proposed the expulsion of the Catholic priests (see MAIGRET); he opposed that sect all his life. Kaikioewa was a co-signer of the lease to Ladd & Co. (see BRINSMADE). At his death he was replaced as governor by his wife, KEAWEAMAHI.

KAISER, HENRY JOHN (1882–1967)

Born at Sprout Brook, New York, the future industrialist barely finished the eighth grade before becoming a salesman of photographic equipment. He set up his first construction company in 1914 and began a meteoric career as an international builder of highways, dams, bridges, ships, and automobiles. By 1966 he had founded sixty companies, operating 176 major plants in thirty-two states and thirty countries.

Kaiser first visited Hawaii in 1930 and gradually became interested in developing the island economy. He began shipping cement to Hawaii from his Permanente plant in California in 1940, and in 1958 set up one of the two important cement works in Hawaii at the Campbell Industrial Park in Waianae, Oahu. With Fritz Burns of the Kaiser-Burns Development Corp., Kaiser established a twenty-acre resort center that included the Hawaiian Village Hotel, later sold to the Hilton interests. Kaiser also owned KHVH radio and television stations. He erected and operated the Kaiser Foundation Medical Center with several clinics on Oahu, serving thousands of patients under a prepaid health plan. He will probably be best remembered as the developer of Hawaii Kai, a growing suburb east of Honolulu. Kaiser married Bess Fosburgh in 1907 and had two sons; after her death in 1951, he married her thirty-three-year-old nurse, Alyce Chester, and the pair had two sons. For a time their home on Portlock Road was a showplace. Kaiser was named Father of the Year in Hawaii in 1962.

KAIULANI (VICTORIA KAWEKIU KAIULANI LUNALILO KALANINUIAHILAPALAPA) (1875–1899)
This princess was born in Honolulu, daughter of Governor Archibald Scott CLEGHORN and Princess Miriam LIKELIKE and niece of King KALAKAUA and Queen LILIUOKALANI. When Kalakaua was in Japan on his world tour in 1881 he proposed that Kaiulani, then five years old, might in the future marry a Japanese prince, to make a royal alliance.

Kaiulani was given the Ainahau estate in Waikiki by her godmother, Princess RUTH, and there she entertained Robert Louis STEVENSON in 1889. He wrote a celebrated poem, "Forth from her land to mine she goes," on the occasion of her departure to attend school in England under the guardianship of Theophilus H. DAVIES, after which she traveled in Europe with her father.

The princess was widely loved as a linguist, musician, artist, horsewoman, and swimmer, and was active in many charities. At the accession of Liliuokalani, she was proclaimed heiress apparent of the kingdom. After the overthrow of the monarchy in 1893, Kaiulani went to Washington, D.C., with Davies to argue for the restoration of the throne. She died on March 6, 1899. See *Princess Kaiulani: The Last Hope*

of Hawaii's Monarchy (Honolulu: Mana Publishing Co., 1976; rev. 1982) by Kristin Zambucka.

KALAIMOKU. See KALANIMOKU.

KALAKAUA, DAVID (1836–1891)
The future elected king was born in Honolulu at the foot of Punchbowl Crater, where his grandfather, the high chief AIKANAKA, had been in charge of the gun battery. David was not a member of the Kamehameha dynasty. His ancestors had been prominent chiefs on the island of Hawaii. His great-grandfather was KEAWEAHEULU, and he was one of the seven children of Kapaakea and his wife Keohokalole; two younger sisters were LILIUOKALANI and LIKELIKE.

David was educated at the Royal School, and could speak and write well in both English and Hawaiian; he had practised public speaking and was adept at winning votes under the universal suffrage amendment passed in 1874. He once edited a newspaper, *Hoku i ka Pakipaka (Star of the Pacific)*. He married KAPIOLANI in 1863.

Kalakaua first became a candidate for the crown after the death of KAMEHAMEHA V, who had named no successor. During the election of 1872, he was badly beaten by the supporters of LUNALILO. At the death of this short-lived ruler, Kalakaua ran against the queen dowager, EMMA, widow of KAMEHAMEHA IV. After the stormiest election in Hawaiian history, the supporters of Emma attacked the legislators who had given her only six of the forty-five votes, and the courthouse was the scene of a bloody riot that left several members injured severely; one died as a result of his wounds. Public order was restored only when armed marines were landed from two American ships and one British ship.

Kalakaua took the oath of office on February 13, 1874, and began a reign that earned him the title of "the Merry Monarch."

Kalakaua began by making a royal progress around the islands, and before his first year ended he went to the United States to help promote the signing of the long-deferred reciprocity treaty in Washington. He was the first king in history to visit that country and was royally received. He made history again when in 1881 he set out on a tour of the world to visit fellow heads of state. He conceived the idea of being publicly crowned, although no previous Hawaiian ruler had received such a ceremony. On February 12, 1883, the ninth anniversary of his election, in front of the fine new Iolani Palace whose cornerstone had been laid in 1879, Kalakaua the elected king placed a jeweled crown on his head and another on that of his queen. Two days later, the celebrated statue of Kamehameha I that still stands in front of Aliiolani Hale in downtown Honolulu was unveiled by the king; the funds for its erection had been voted by the legislature in 1879 to commemorate the centennial of the death of Captain James COOK, but the effort somehow resulted in a statue to a Hawaiian.

The latter reign of Kalakaua was marred by growing ineptness and forms of corruption not uncommon

63

in the United States during the same period. Incidents such as land deals for the benefit of Claus SPRECKELS, the king's poker-playing friend; repeal of the laws against furnishing Hawaiians with liquor; minting of the Kalakaua coins of 1884, another Spreckels deal; a "national bank"; a lottery; licensing of the sale of opium; formation of a "Hawaiian Board of Health" to revive the role of the ancient kahuna—such actions gave reason for anti-monarchy movements like the founding of the Reform Party. The role of advisers Celso Caesar MORENO and Walter Murray GIBSON resulted in the fiasco of the "primacy of the Pacific" movement and the Samoan mission of John E. Bush and led to the forced signing on July 6 of the "Bayonet Constitution" of 1887. During renewal of the reciprocity treaty, one provision gave the United States the exclusive right to set up a coaling station at Pearl Harbor, but the American government never exercised this right during the remaining years of the monarchy.

Growing opposition by Hawaiians to the diminished position of their leader resulted in bloodshed in 1889 in the insurrection led by Robert W. WILCOX. The Hui Kalaiaina, a party made up of native Hawaiians, prevented the formation of a majority in the legislature of 1890, and its cabinet was forced to yield to a compromise coalition. When the session closed in November, Kalakaua, hoping his health would improve, left for San Francisco, where he died on January 20, 1891. His body was brought to Honolulu by an American warship, and after a ceremonious lying-in-state was buried in the Royal Mausoleum, leaving his younger sister LILIUOKALANI to ascend the throne. See *Kalakaua, Hawaii's Last King* (Honolulu: Mana Publishing Co., 1983), by Kristin Zambucka.

KALAKUA (–1842)
A wife of Kamehameha I, afterwards married to HOAPILI.

KALAMA, HAKALELEPONI KAPAKUHAILI (1817–1870)
Born near Kailua, Kona, daughter of Naihekukui, she began the longest reign of a Hawaiian queen on February 14, 1837, when the Rev. Hiram BINGHAM married her to KAMEHAMEHA III. She took part in the many events of his reign; in 1847 she was hostess to as many as ten thousand people at the luau celebrating Restoration Day. After the death of the king in 1854 she seldom appeared in public, but occupied herself in the development of her property, including a tract in windward Oahu that she hoped to convert into a sugar plantation.

KALANIANAOLE, JONAH KUHIO (1871–1922)
Prince Jonah was descended from the kings of Kauai; KAUMUALII was his grandfather. Jonah was born at Koloa, Kauai, on March 26, 1871. His parents were the high chief David Kahalepouli Piikoi and Princess Kinoiki Kekaulike. He was a cousin of King KALAKAUA and Queen LILIUOKALANI and a nephew of Queen KAPIOLANI, consort of Kalakaua. His elder brothers were Prince Edward Keliiahonui (1869–1887) and Prince David KAWANANAKOA.

At school his French teacher gave Jonah the lifelong nickname of "Prince Cupid." Jonah was an athlete at Punahou School and was interested in sports from an early age. He and his brothers were made princes by royal decree when he was thirteen. He was educated at San Mateo, California, and at the Royal Agricultural College, Cirencester, England. On his return to Hawaii he worked in the ministry of the interior and the customs service. He was trained as a successor to the royal throne. But when he was twenty-one the monarchy was overthrown. He was arrested and charged with treason for his part in the counter-revolution of 1895 and served, not unhappily, as a political prisoner for about a year. He married Elizabeth Kahanu Kaauwai, daughter of a chief of Kauai, in 1896, and after the death of Queen Kapiolani in 1899 the couple spent two years in world travel. Elizabeth died in 1932.

Jonah was a member of the Republican Party and was elected in 1902 as the second Hawaii delegate to Congress, succeeding Robert W. WILCOX, and served until his death in 1922. He attained a number of political gains for Hawaii during his long term, and is remembered best as the father of the present Hawaiian Homes Commission. He introduced a bill on February 11, 1919, asking that Hawaii be admitted to the Union as a state. Kuhio in 1903 organized the Order of Kamehameha and officiated at the first observance of Kamehameha Day in 1904. He also organized the Chiefs of Hawaii and the Hawaiian Civic Club. He died on January 7, 1922, at the age of fifty, and was given the last state funeral held in Hawaii for an alii. He was buried in the Royal Mausoleum.
See *The Empty Throne: A Biography of Hawaii's Prince Cupid* (Honolulu: Topgallant, 1980), by Lori Kamae.

KALANIKUPULE (1760–1795)
Son and heir of KAHEKILI, Kalanikupule became ruler of Maui and Oahu at the death of his father in 1794. In a dispute about the inheritance he fought his uncle, KAEO, and the latter was killed in battle on Oahu in the same year. In the decisive battle of the Nuuanu Pali in 1795, the invading forces of KAMEHAMEHA I overcame the defenders and Kalanikupule, after wandering in the mountains for several months, was captured and sacrificed to Kamehameha's war god, leaving the islands (except Kauai) virtually united under one ruler.

KALANIMOKU (KALAIMOKU, CRYMOKU, BILLY PITT) (1768?–1827)
High chief of Maui, Kalanimoku was present at the death of Captain James COOK. He was the right hand of KAMEHAMEHA I, acting as his treasurer and principal adviser or "kalaimoku," which might best be translated as prime minister. The office of kalaimoku, however, was of less high rank than that of kuhina nui, held by KAAHUMANU. Kalanimoku took for himself the nickname of "Billy Pitt," after the great English prime minister William Pitt. He was also called "the iron cable of Hawaii."

Kalanimoku was baptized into the Roman Catholic faith in August, 1819, on board the visiting French ship *L' Uranie*, commanded by Captain FREYCINET, in the presence of KAMEHAMEHA II and the queen dowager. A celebrated drawing of the scene was made by the ship's artist ARAGO.

Kalanimoku commanded the Hawaiian army from the death of Kamehameha until 1824. He took a leading role in the breaking of the ancient kapu in 1819; he defeated the rebellion of KEKUAOKALANI in that year and the rebellion on Kauai in 1824 led by George P. KAUMUALII. More than anyone else, Kalanimoku held the kingdom

together after the death of the founder, and was the prime councillor of Kaahumanu during the first three years of her term as kuhina nui. He was treasurer of the realm and supervised collection of all taxes and revenue. From 1821 he sent ships on trading voyages to the Russian-American colonies, the South Seas, and America. He was the first chief to greet the arrival of the first American missionaries off Kawaihae in 1820, and strongly supported their settling in the islands. Along with Kaahumanu, he was admitted to the church in 1825, the year he became guardian of the boy king KAMEHAMEHA III. Kalanimoku recognized the need for a written code of laws and proposed the adoption of the Ten Commandments as a first step in such a program. Richard CHARLTON averred that the basis for his troublesome land claim was a grant of land to him by Kalanimoku in 1826, a year before the death of the "kalaimoku."

KALANIOPUU (–1782)
A son of Kalaninuiiamamao, ruling chief of Ka'u, and Kamakaimoku, Kalaniopuu rose to power as a war leader under ALAPAINUI, but turned against him and fought for his own ambitions. In 1754 he defeated Keaweopala, son and successor of Alapainui, and became ruler over the entire island of Hawaii. He failed, after several attempts, to subdue the neighboring

island of Maui. Kalaniopuu's chief wife was KALOLA. He was also the husband of KANEKAPOLEI and by her was father of twin sons, KEOUA KUAHUULA and KEOUA PEEALE. Kalaniopuu took a leading part in the drama at Kealakekua Bay in 1779 when Captain James COOK was killed. In 1780 Kalaniopuu made his son KIWALAO his heir and named his nephew, KAMEHAMEHA, the custodian of the war god Kukailimoku. Kalaniopuu died in 1782 at Waiohukini in Ka'u, but his body was taken, as he requested, for burial at Hale-o-Keawe at Kona.

KALELEONALANI. See EMMA.

KALOLA
She was the daughter of KEKAULIKE and sister of KAHEKILI, and the mother of KIWALAO by her husband, KALANIOPUU. After his death she wedded Keopuili and returned to Maui. Later she fled to Molokai and died there.

KAMAKAU, SAMUEL MANAIAKALANI (1815–1876)
Born at Mokuleia, Oahu, Kamakau entered Lahainaluna School in 1833. He remained there for seven years as student and teaching assistant. He collected Hawaiiana under the direction of the Rev. Sheldon DIBBLE. He married S. Hainakolo and began teaching on Maui, where he acted briefly as a judge. In 1841 he helped to form the Royal Hawaiian Historical Society. From 1851 until his death he served many times in the legislature of the kingdom. He began in 1865 to publish more than two hundred articles in newspapers. From these, two volumes have been published, both translated by Mary K. Pukui: *The Ruling Chiefs of Hawaii* (Honolulu: Kamehameha Schools Press, 1961), and *Ka Po'e Kahiko: The People of Old* (Honolulu. Bishop Museum Press, 1964).

KAMAMALU (1802–1824)

Kamamalu was a daughter of HOAPILI and KALAKUA and a sister of KEKAULOHI and KINAU. The favorite wife of KAMEHAMEHA II, she accompanied him to London and died there a few days before his own death.

KAMAMALU, VICTORIA KAAHUMANU (1838–1866)

Princess Victoria was the daughter of KINAU and KEKUANAOA and sister of KAMEHAMEHA IV and KAMEHAMEHA V. She attended the Chiefs' Children's School (later the Royal School) operated by American missionaries, and became a skilled poet and chanter in the old Hawaiian style. Kamehameha IV appointed her as kuhina nui to replace John YOUNG II. She was once engaged to Prince William C. LUNALILO but it is said that the marriage was opposed by Kamehameha IV. It is also reported that David KALAKAUA proposed to her but was rejected, and she never married. Robert C. WYLLIE believed that the annexation movement of 1854 was designed to substitute Victoria on the throne for Kamehameha IV, since she was thought to be pro-American. Her death in 1866 was the occasion for a great state funeral, described in one of the letters of Mark Twain (Samuel L. CLEMENS). Victoria was a composer of native chants, some of which have survived.

KAMANAWA

Son of Keawepoepoe and Kanoena and twin brother of KAMEEIAMOKU, he and his brother were two of the four great chiefs of Kona (the others being KEEAUMOKU and KEAWEAHEULU) who supported KAMEHAMEHA I through his wars. Kamanawa and Keaweaheulu were the two emissaries sent to summon KEOUA KUAHUULA to his death in 1791. Kamanawa and his twin were made governors of wide lands after the conquest of the island of Hawaii. They were half-brothers of KAHEKILI and hid his bones after his death in 1794. They were also half-brothers of KEEAUMOKU; they shared the same father but the mother of Keeaumoku was Kumaaiku.

KAMEEIAMOKU (–1804)

Twin brother of KAMANAWA. Kameeiamoku was the father of Ulumaheihei HOAPILI. He was killed at Lahaina in 1804 defending the peleliu fleet of KAMEHAMEHA I.

KAMEHAMEHA I (1758?–1819)

"The Lonely One," the chief who first united all the main islands under one rule, was born in North Kohala on a November night. His mother was KEKUIAPOIWA, a niece of KAHEKILI, and his father was KEOUAKALANI, a stepson of ALAPAINUI. It is said, however, that the real father was Kahekili, against whom Kamehameha would later battle. It was foretold that the baby would be a danger to the chiefs, and the mother arranged that he should be taken away and reared by NAEOLE. After five years the child was returned to the court, and

was trained in warfare by KEKUAHAUPIO (whose life Kamehameha later saved in battle). By the time Kamehameha's uncle, KALANIOPUU, became ruler of Kohala, the young man was a celebrated warrior. When Captain James COOK returned from the Arctic in November, 1778, Kamehameha visited the English ships along with his uncle. The young chief observed the power of the visitors' cannon and gunpowder, and he was wounded by gunfire on the beach when Cook was killed at Kealakekua Bay the following February. A year later, Kalaniopuu named his son KIWALAO as his heir, and named Kamehameha guardian of the war god Kukailimoku. After boldly asserting his rights, Kamehameha was advised to retire from the court for a time.

Civil war broke out on the Big Island at the death of Kalaniopuu in 1782. Prominent among the supporters of Kamehameha were KEEAUMOKU, KEAWEAHEULU, and the twin brothers KAMEEIAMOKU and KAMANAWA. Kiwalao was killed, and the followers of Kamehameha urged him to fight against KEOUA KUAHUULA, a younger son of Kalaniopuu. Keoua was supported by Kahekili, and a ten-year war began. Kamehameha in 1790 invaded the eastern end of Maui, and after a battle at Iao Valley took over the entire island of Maui as well as neighboring

Lanai. He was forced to return to Hawaii, however, to defend his troops against those of Keoua. Kahekili recaptured Molokai and Maui, and invaded northern Hawaii with a large fleet of canoes. This fleet was driven back by the canoes of Kamehameha, armed with swivel guns manned by crews under John YOUNG and Isaac DAVIS. Only Keoua stood in the way of Kamehameha's domination over the whole of the Big Island. Following the advice of a soothsayer, Kamehameha led in the building of a great heiau or temple at Kawaihae, and then summoned Keoua to attend him there. Fatalistically, Keoua came and was killed along with his followers; the fatal spear was thrown by Keeaumoku.

Thereafter Kamehameha ruled the Big Island and was visited by George VANCOUVER, who found that the chief had changed his character for the better. The English captain made peace between the ruler and his favorite wife, KAAHUMANU, after a quarrel. When KAEO and his nephew KALANIKUPULE began fighting against each other and Kaeo was killed in 1794 in a battle near Pearl Harbor on Oahu, Kamehameha saw his chance to add that island to his growing kingdom. His fleet captured Maui, then Molokai, and landed on the southern shore of Oahu in 1795. The invaders then fought their way up Nuuanu Valley behind Honolulu. The forces of Kalanikupule were defeated and their fugitive leader was captured and sacrificed to the war god. Thereafter Kamehameha was undisputed monarch of all the islands except Kauai and Niihau, which fell to the crown under an agreement in 1810 with KAUMUALII.

The reign of Kamehameha I was marked by peaceful expansion and trade with the foreign ships that continued to arrive, bringing more strangers who were enlisted in the royal service. Kamehameha was a shrewd bargainer and increased the wealth of his family. Visiting vessels plying between the Northwest Coast of America and Asia were supplied with pork and yams, and later the export of precious sandalwood to the Orient brought the chiefs the ability to purchase merchandise from abroad. Kamehameha defended the islands against the incursion of Russian forces in 1816 and 1817 under Georg Anton SCHEFFER, and he cultivated the abilities of such settlers as Francisco de Paula MARÍN, John Palmer PARKER, Alexander ADAMS, and Archibald CAMPBELL.

Kamehameha I, founder of the dynasty that was to last until 1872, died on May 8, 1819, at Kailua, Hawaii, where he had set up his court in 1811. All his life he had been loyal to the religion of his ancestors. However, when the priests told him that a human sacrifice was demanded at his death, he refused, saying: "The men are kapu for the king"— meaning that his followers should live to serve his son Liholiho, who would succeed him on the throne as KAMEHAMEHA II. The bones of the father, as was customary, were taken and concealed in a secret cave. "Only the stars of the heavens know the resting place of Kamehameha." He was followed as ruler of the islands by two of his sons, children of his sacred wife KEOPUOLANI, and two grandsons. After this family died out, the kings of Hawaii were elected by the people.

KAMEHAMEHA II (LIHOLIHO) (1796–1824)

Son of KAMEHAMEHA I by KEOPUOLANI, Liholiho was somewhat spoiled at the court. When his father died in the critical year 1819, Liholiho was told by the favorite queen, KAAHUMANU, that by the will of Kamehameha I she was to share the kingdom as kuhina nui or joint ruler. Liholiho and his advisers

soon overthrew the ancient kapu system by having men and women of the court eat at the same table. At the end of this ceremony he announced that the heiau temples should be destroyed and all the old idols overthrown. A chief named KEKUAOKALANI led a brief revolt but was defeated and killed by royal forces led by KALANIMOKU.

The reign of Kamehameha II was noted for the large income to the chiefs from the trade in sandalwood and for the beginning of whaling in the islands. The arrival in 1820 of the first company of American missionaries added to the problems of the kingdom. Liholiho also led a stormy voyage to Kauai and brought back as his vassal the king of that island, KAUMUALII. Liholiho believed, like his father, that his kingdom was under the protection of Great Britain, and decided to visit the capital of that country to increase his knowledge of the world. He left in the English whaling ship L'Aigle on November 27, 1823, along with his favorite wife KAMAMALU, Governor BOKI of Oahu and his wife LILIHA, KEKUANAOA, several other chiefs, and his secretary, a Frenchman named John RIVES.

The ship arrived in England in May, 1824, and the captain led the group to London. Here they were

67

lodged in a luxury hotel and the government of King George IV planned for them a program of royal entertainment. Sadly, the party was attacked by a disease unknown to them—measles—and despite every care, Kamamalu died on July 8. Liholiho, stricken with grief as well as the disease, died on July 14, after a short but important reign. The bodies were brought back to the islands on a British vessel commanded by Lord BYRON.

KAMEHAMEHA III (KAUIKEAOULI) (1813–1854)

The ruler who held the throne of the islands for the longest reign in history was a son of KAMEHAMEHA I and KEOPUOLANI and a younger brother of KAMEHAMEHA II. He was nine years old when his brother left for England, naming him heir to the monarchy, and was proclaimed king in 1825 under a regency with KAAHUMANU as kuhina nui. When she was succeeded by KINAU, the young man threw off the control of his half-sister and began a two-year period of dissipation; gambling, drunkenness, and dancing the hula

were a reaction to the puritanism preached by the American missionaries. However, the king was reconciled to Kinau and the council of chiefs began to face the need for written laws to control growing problems—especially those caused by the increasing settlement of foreigners in the kingdom. As early as 1836 the chiefs employed William RICHARDS to teach them political science. The first result was the declaration of rights of June 7, 1839, which has been called the Hawaiian Magna Charta. Persecution of Catholics was stopped when the king issued an oral "edict of toleration" the same month. The rights of residents were repeated in the Constitution of 1840, the first of several such documents, which was signed by the king on October 8.

Other improvements in government were carried out. In 1842 the king appointed a treasury board consisting of Dr. Gerrit P. JUDD, Timothy HAALILIO, and John II that separated the private property of the king from government property and reformed the system of taxation; by 1846 the national debt was paid off. John RICORD was appointed attorney general in 1844, and worked out a series of organic acts that included the "Great Mahele," the first legal basis for land ownership in the kingdom. In 1846 the executive branch was organized and divided into five departments with a minister in charge of each; Robert C. WYLLIE, who had taken over from Dr. Judd in 1845, was the first minister of foreign relations. The third organic act made badly needed improvements in the judiciary system; the work of Ricord was completed by a young American lawyer, William L. LEE. Lee also incorporated many political gains in the Constitution of 1852.

The need for international recognition of Hawaii's independence was even more pressing, and a series of threatening visits by French gunboats under the command of captains like A. du PETIT-THOUARS (1838), C. P. T. LAPLACE (1839), S. MALLET (1842), Legoarant de TROMELIN (1849), and Louis Emile PERRIN (1851) made it appear that Hawaii was doomed to become a colony of France, as had happened to the Society and Marquesas Islands in the South Pacific. Moreover, for five months in 1843 Hawaii was annexed by the British Empire under the domination of Lord George PAULET. The threat of a takeover by American filibusters in 1851 was averted by strong action by Marshal William C. PARKE. The question of annexation by the United States was first discussed during the troubled year of 1853, but the death of the king the following year put an end to this possibility for decades.

During the long reign of Kamehameha III the economy of the kingdom was put on a much firmer footing. It saw the decline of the sandalwood trade, the rise and decline of whaling, and the rise of the profitable sugar-growing industry that is still important today. Churches and schools were built, and life in the islands was influenced even more than before by foreign customs.

Kamehameha III married KALAMA on February 14, 1837, but they were childless, and at his death, the throne was occupied by his named successor, his younger nephew Alexander Liholiho, who became KAMEHAMEHA IV.

KAMEHAMEHA IV (ALEXANDER LIHOLIHO) (1834–1863)

Son of Mataio KEKUANAOA and KINAU, grandson of KAMEHAMEHA I, Alexander was the younger brother of Lot Kamehameha (KAMEHAMEHA V) and elder brother of VICTORIA KAMAMALU. Like his brother Lot, Alexander attended the Royal School and went with Dr. G. P. JUDD on a mission to Paris, London, and the United States. During his visit to New York City, the young prince had been mistaken for a servant by a railway conductor and ordered out of the car. His anger at racial discrimination was deepened by fear that his country might be taken over by the United States as part of its "manifest destiny," and he gradually swung away from using Americans as his closest advisers and toward a revival of British influence in the kingdom.

Alexander was proclaimed king at the death of his uncle, Kamehameha III, in December, 1854. An early event of the reign was the marriage of the king on June 19, 1856, to EMMA, to whom he had long been engaged. She had been adopted as a child by Dr. T. C. B. Rooke, an English medical man who had married Emma's aunt, and she also inclined toward the British way of life. Emma was thereafter to play an important role in Hawaiian politics. The birth of a son, ALBERT, was an even more joyous event for the royal pair, who held court in European style.

Like his brother Lot, Kamehameha IV was concerned about the decimation of his subjects by disease, and on April 20, 1859, signed a law setting up a hospital in Honolulu for sick and destitute Hawaiians. Along with Emma, he personally solicited funds to erect Queen's Hospital, named in her honor; this building was the first to stand on the same site in downtown Honolulu.

This hospital, of which Dr. William HILLEBRAND was the first head, is one of the two monuments to the reign of Kamehameha IV. The other is the establishment of the Anglican Church in Hawaii, under the direction of Thomas N. STALEY. The king was an intelligent and articulate gentleman, fluent in both English and Hawaiian, and translated into the latter language the English Book of Common Prayer. The reign was marred by a personal scandal at Lahaina when the king, unjustifiably jealous, shot and wounded his secretary, a young American named Henry A. Neilson. Remorse over this affair was aggravated by grief when the promising little prince died in August, 1862. Weakened by asthma and sorrow, Alexander Liholiho died on November 30, 1863, at the age of twenty-nine, and was succeeded by his elder brother, Lot Kamehameha, as KAMEHAMEHA V.

KAMEHAMEHA V (LOT KAPUAIWA KAMEHAMEHA) (1830–1872)

Son of Mataio KEKUANAOA and KINAU, Lot was four years older than his brother KAMEHAMEHA IV, and like him was to reign for nine years. Lot attended the Royal School and along with his brother accompanied Dr. G. P. JUDD on a mission to Paris, London, and the United States. During the last six years of his brother's reign he served as minister of the interior and for more than a year as minister of finance. He traveled in 1850 to the Pacific Coast to visit California and British Columbia. Lot was the first president of a graziers' association started on Oahu in 1856 to promote the cattle industry.

When Kamehameha IV died on November 30, 1863, Lot was immediately proclaimed his successor. Kamehameha V has been called "the last great chief of the olden type." He believed that the example of his grandfather, KAMEHAMEHA I, gave him the right to lead the Hawaiian people personally, and favored a stronger monarchy that verged on despotism. He was, however, a kindly despot, and wanted to protect his subjects from waste and idleness. When it was proposed that the law against selling strong liquor to the Hawaiians should be repealed, he defeated the proposal by saying, "I will never sign the death warrant of my people." He tried to restrict hula dances and other parties that would keep workers away from their crops. He liked to visit his friend John CUMMINS at his plantation at Waimanalo, and to avoid the harsh Pali trail purchased a small steamboat in which to ride around the shore in royal style. He also had a small railway built between the boat landing and Cummins's house. "There was no trivial royal nonsense about him," wrote Mark Twain on Kamehameha V in 1866; "he dressed plainly, poked about Honolulu, night or day, on his old horse, unattended; he was popular, greatly respected, and even beloved."

Lot Kamehameha's action in 1864 resulted in the formation of two political parties in the kingdom. On August 13, when it appeared that a new constitution could not be agreed on, he declared that the Constitution of 1852 should be replaced by one he wrote himself. Although the Constitution of 1864 freed the king from the control of the privy council and the kuhina nui and limited the privilege of voting, the new law remained in force for twenty-three years—a longer period than that of any other constitution before annexation. Only one minor amendment was made during the reign. But the strengthening of the throne at this time aroused opposition that eventually overthrew the monarchy.

Kamehameha V was known as "the bachelor king." His sister, VICTORIA KAMAMALU, was named as his successor, but she died in 1866 and it was often suggested that he should marry and give the kingdom an heir. It is said in his youth he was engaged to marry Bernice Pauahi, but she chose instead to marry Charles Reed BISHOP. An hour before his death on December 11, 1872, Lot called Bernice to his bedside and asked that she become his successor, but she modestly declined this offer. The king's body lay in state in the shadow of dark kahili standards, and was then conveyed to the Royal Mausoleum. The decision of Kamehameha V not to name a successor to the throne resulted in invoking the constitutional provision for electing kings of Hawaii (see LUNALILO).

KANAHELE, BENEHAKAKA
On December 7, 1941, a Japanese plane attempting to return to its carrier crash-landed on the small island of Niihau. Kanahele and his wife were held as hostages by the pilot. During a fight several days later, the middle-aged Kanahele was shot three times but crushed the Japanese to death, while his wife grappled with the pilot's supporter, a beekeeper named Harada. At the end of World War II, Kanahele was awarded the Purple Heart and the Medal of Merit for his defense of Niihau; this was the only act of conflict with an enemy in the islands during the entire war. See Blake Clark, *Remember Pearl Harbor!* (New York: Harper, 1943), "The Battle of Niihau."

KANAINA, CHARLES (1801?–1877)
A friend of Kamehameha, in 1821 he was given KEKAULUOHI, the fifth wife of Kamehameha II. Her first male child became King LUNALILO. Kamehameha III married Kanaina's adopted daughter, KALAMA.

KANEHOA, JAMES YOUNG (1797–1851)
Son of John YOUNG, he left for England with KAMEHAMEHA II and his party to serve as interpreter and bearer of official papers. Kanehoa missed the *L'Aigle* at Rio de Janeiro and the party arrived without the documents that would convince George IV that this was the ruler of the Sandwich Islands. Kanehoa turned up later on a coaling vessel. In 1845 he was a member of the board to quiet land titles.

KANEKAPOLEI
A chiefess of high rank, she was the wife of KALANIOPUU and her fears aroused the crowd to attack Captain James COOK on February 14, 1779. She was the mother of twin sons, KEOUA KUAHUULA and KEOUA PEEALE. After the death of Kalaniopuu she became a wife of KAMEHAMEHA I and by him had his first-born son, Pauli Kaoleiku, who died mysteriously in 1816.

KANOA, PAUL (1802–1885)
Kanoa was born at South Kona; his mother was named Kepaa. He lived with Dr. Gerrit P. JUDD and was clerk to Governor Mataio Kekuanaoa. Kanoa served as governor of Kauai from 1847 to 1877, when he resigned. He was a member of the House of Nobles until 1882, and of the privy council until his death.

KANUI, WILLIAM
See HOPU, Thomas.

KAPAAKEA, CAESAR (1817?–1866)
A son of KAMANAWA and Kamokuiki, Kapaakea married Keohokalole in 1835. Among their six children were Lydia Kamakaeha LILIUOKALANI, Miriam LIKELIKE, David KALAKAUA, and William Pitt LELEIOHOKU.

KAPENA, JOHN MAKINI
(1843–1887)

Born at Lahaina, son of
Maniki, adviser to kings, Kapena was
educated at the Royal School and
Punahou. In 1863 he married Emma
Malo. He was appointed a circuit
judge of Oahu in 1873 and as
governor of Maui the following year.
He accompanied King Kalakaua to
the United States in 1874 and served
as minister of finance in 1876 and
minister of foreign affairs in 1878.
He left for Tokyo in 1882 as envoy
extraordinary and minister
plenipotentiary to Japan. On his
return he again served as minister of
finance and, in 1883, as a member of
the Board of Education. He acted as
collector general of customs until his
resignation in 1887, the year of his
death. He was a scholar of Hawaiiana.

KAPIOLANI (1781–1841)

She was the daughter of kapu
chief KEAWEMAUHILI; her mother,
Kekikipaa, was the daughter of
KAMEEIAMOKU. Married to
NAIHE, she was converted by the
Protestant missionaries and carried
out a testament to her new faith by
leading a march from Kona to the
edge of Kilauea Volcano in 1824.
There she defied the goddess Pele by
breaking the usual tabu and
proclaiming the might of Jehovah.
The party withdrew without being
overwhelmed by fire from an enraged
deity, and the Hilo mission was
enlarged by ninety converts. Lord
Tennyson, the English poet laureate,
wrote a dramatic poem, "Kapiolani,"
about the incident.

KAPIOLANI, QUEEN
(1834–1899)

Kapiolani, a niece and
namesake of the chiefess who defied
Pele, was a granddaughter of King
KAUMUALII of Kauai. Two of her
sisters were Virginia Kapooloku
Poomaikelani and Esther Kinoike
Kekaulike (who married
David Piikoi).

During her first marriage—
to a chief named Bennett (Benet)
Namakeha—she acted as governess
of the little Prince ALBERT. She
married David KALAKAUA in 1863
and was crowned with him in 1883 on
the ninth anniversary of his accession
to the throne. She received royal
honors when she attended the jubilee
of Queen Victoria of Great Britain in
1887, visiting the American
president, Grover Cleveland, on the
trip. Kalakaua and Kapiolani had no
children. After his death, the queen
dowager concerned herself with the
welfare of Hawaiian women. She
established and helped to support the
Kapiolani Maternity Home and the
Kapiolani Home for Leper Girls.

KAPULE, DEBORAH
(1798–1853)

Kapule was the favorite queen
of King KAUMUALII of Kauai.
Widowed by his death in 1824, she
married Simeon Kaiu. Although she
helped to contain the abortive Kauai
rebellion led by George P.
KAUMUALII, she suffered
imprisonment on Oahu for a time and
loss of most of her property.

KATSUKI, ICHITARO
(1866–1967)

Born in Osaka, Japan, the son
of an industrialist, Katsuki graduated
from San Francisco High School in
1888 and was the first Japanese
physician educated in the United
States. He graduated from the
University of California School of
Medicine in 1896. He was sent to
Hawaii by the San Francisco Health
Department to investigate the
outbreak of bubonic plague in 1900.
He remained as a pioneer physician
among the Japanese plantation
workers on Oahu. After thirty-six
years of practice he retired and
traveled to the Far East, studying
genetics. He was honored by the
Hawaii Medical Association in 1963
and was a life member of the
American Red Cross from 1919. A
variety of hibiscus is named
for Katsuki. Dr. Katsuki lived to the
age of 101 years.

KAUIKEAOULI

See KAMEHAMEHA III.

KAUMUALII (TAMOREE)
(1780?–1824)

The future king of the island of
Kauai was the son of KAEO and his
wife Kamakahelei. In 1779 a certain
Keawe, Kamakahelei's son by a
previous marriage, was placed on the
throne, but Kaeo thereafter
supported his son Kaumualii. During
the three visits of George
VANCOUVER, this British captain
found the young prince Kaumualii
ruling the island, aided by a chief
named Inamoo acting as a regent in

71

the absence of Kaeo (who was killed on Oahu at the end of 1794). Vancouver gave the prince the name of "George" in honor of his fellow monarch of England. In February, 1796, Keawe was attempting to dethrone Kaumualii and succeeded in this effort, but Keawe died a year or two later and the prince was restored to power.

Young Kaumualii was handsome and accomplished, and learned to speak English; he was one of the best swimmers in all the islands. By gathering arms and enlisting foreigners in his defense efforts he resisted the aims of Kamehameha I to conquer Kauai by force. However, in 1810 Captain Nathan WINSHIP persuaded Kaumualii to go to Oahu. There he faced Kamehameha and, perhaps overawed by the growing fleet off Honolulu, agreed to become his subject; after his death Kauai would peacefully become a part of the realm of the conqueror. Some of the chiefs plotted to kill Kaumualii at this time; when Isaac DAVIS revealed their plans, he was poisoned but the young king escaped back to Kauai.

Kaumualii took a leading role in the movement led by Georg Anton SCHEFFER which resulted in Russian occupation of Kauai in 1816 and 1817. However, in the latter year Kaumualii supplied sandalwood when Kamehameha desired to purchase the vessel *Columbia*, and later he joined with Boki and others in trading ventures in the Pacific. Kaumualii approved the breaking of the ancient kapus by Kamehameha II in 1819, and was overjoyed when his long-lost son George P. KAUMUALII turned up on the first missionary vessel to the islands in 1820.

In 1821, Kamehameha II made a visit to Kauai and was received royally, and some weeks later he persuaded Kaumualii to return to Honolulu with him as a feudal subject. Thereafter Kaumualii was a virtual prisoner of state. He also endured a marriage with the dowager queen KAAHUMANU on October 9, 1821; to make the affair more binding, the queen also married her husband's son Kealiiahonui. Kaumualii died in Honolulu in May, 1824. His son George claimed that the death was caused by poison, and led a brief revolt on Kauai. Thus ended the traditional rulership of one of the main islands of the group; thereafter Kauai was part of Kamehameha's kingdom.

KAUMUALII, GEORGE P(RINCE) (1798?–1826)

Son of King KAUMUALII of Kauai, the boy, around the age of seven, was sent to America to save him from the malice of the queen. He enlisted in the United States Navy and was wounded in action. He found himself at the Cornwall School in Connecticut along with three other young men from Hawaii (see HOPU), and there obtained further education. He had acquired his father's name "George," and the initial *P* to stand for "prince."

George landed on Oahu with the First Company of American missionaries in 1820. Soon afterwards he was taken to Kauai, where his grateful royal father rewarded the ship's captain with a load of sandalwood worth a thousand dollars. The king placed George second in command only to himself on Kauai, and was pleased when his son showed such accomplishments as playing on a bass viol during hymn-singing sessions. George fell

into bad habits, however, and once set fire to the house of a ship captain because he had been denied a bottle of gin. After the death of his royal father in 1824 under suspicious circumstances, George led a brief rebellion on Kauai. It was soon put down and he and his wife Betty, a daughter of Isaac DAVIS, were taken prisoners of KAAHUMANU to Honolulu. He died there of influenza on May 3, 1826, the long-lost "prince" who had inspired high hopes among the mission band.

KAWANANAKOA, ABIGAIL WAHIIKAAKUULA CAMPBELL (1882–1945)

Born in Honolulu, she was the daughter of James CAMPBELL and Abigail Kuaihelani Maipinepine of Lahaina, Maui. She married Prince David KAWANANAKOA in San Francisco on January 6, 1902. Her husband was an active member of the Democrat Party and she shared his interest in politics. As a member of the Hawaiian Homes Commission she urged those of Hawaiian blood to return to work on homesteads. She was an advocate of home rule, jury service for women, and female suffrage. She entertained many prominent visitors at her Punaluu home and during World War II made it available for recreation by servicemen. She was a member of a number of civic and charitable groups.

KAWANANAKOA, DAVID LAAMEA KAHALEPOULI PIIKOI (1868–1908)
Prince David, elder brother of Edward Keliiahonui (1869–1887) and Jonah Kuhio KALANIANAOLE, was like him the son of high chief David Kahalepouli PIIKOI and Kinoiki Kekaulike. David and his brothers were proclaimed princes of the realm in 1883 by KALAKAUA; the title could not, however, be inherited.

David was educated under Alatau ATKINSON at St. Alban's College, at Punahou School, and at a military school in San Mateo, California. Like his brother Jonah, he also attended the Royal Agricultural College in Cirencester, England, and with him traveled to many of the royal courts of Europe. In 1900, David ran as a Democrat in opposition to Colonel Samuel Parker, Republican, and Robert W. WILCOX of the Home Rule Party; Wilcox was elected for one term only and was succeeded by David's brother Jonah, a Republican. For the remainder of his life, David was active in the Democrat Party, rivalling that headed by his brother.

David Kawananakoa married Abigail Wahiikaahuula Campbell, daughter of James CAMPBELL, in 1902. They had three children: Abigail Kapiolani, David Kalakaua, and Lydia Liliuokalani Kawananakoa.

KEALIIMAIKAI
A brother of Kamehameha I.

KEAWE
This ruler of Kona was the son of Kanaloakapulehu and Keakealani. He was the father of KEEAUMOKU and other offspring and grandfather of KALANIOPUU. He traveled widely, and built a house to contain the remains of the chiefs at Honaunau, still called Hale-o-Keawe, at the City of Refuge.

KEAWEAHEULU
An uncle and supporter of KAMEHAMEHA I and one of the four great chiefs of Kona, he escorted KEOUA KUAHUULA to his death at Kawaihae. Keaweaheulu was the great-grandfather of KALAKAUA and LILIUOKALANI. The family was considered the rightful custodians of the bones of Kamehameha.

KEAWEAMAHI
A converted chiefess, wife of KAIKIOEWA, she was made governor of the island of Kauai in 1839, following the death of her husband.

KEAWEMAUHILI (–1790)
The father of this kapu chief was a son of KEAWE and his mother was a granddaughter of KEAWE; the son's name means "Keawe of the double twist," because of this descent on both sides. He was a supporter of KALANIOPUU, along with whom he fought in battle on the island of Maui in 1776. As an uncle of KIWALAO, he urged this nephew to fight for his rights after the death of Kalaniopuu in 1782, and he divided up the conquered lands in favor of Kiwalao. Keawemauhili was captured by the forces of KAMEHAMEHA I after the death of Kiwalao in 1782 but was

allowed to escape because of his high rank. He became ruling chief of the Hilo region, continued to resist Kamehameha, and sent canoes to aid KAHEKILI on the island of Maui. However, Keawemauhili also sent arms and men to aid Kamehameha in the capture of the snow *Eleanora* in 1790 (see METCALF). For thus breaking his vow of neutrality, he was attacked by KEOUA KUAHUULA and killed in the same year. Keawemauhili was the father of KAPIOLANI, the chiefess who broke the kapu of Pele at Kilauea Volcano in 1824.

KEEAUMOKU (1736?–1804)
Son of Keawepoepoe and Kumaaiku, Keeaumoku was foremost among the four high chiefs of Kona who supported KAMEHAMEHA I in the civil wars. He commanded both on land and in the canoe fleet. He was a younger brother on his father's side of the twins KAMANAWA and KAMEEIAMOKU, his comrades in arms. Keeaumoku was the husband of NAMAHANA and father of their daughter KAAHUMANU and their son KUAKINI (JOHN ADAMS). He was also the father of KEEAUMOKU II (GOVERNOR COX). After various adventures in the interisland battles, Keeaumoku joined forces with the rising conqueror, and was the slayer of KEAOUA KUAHUULA at the heiau of Kawaihae in 1791. Keeaumoku was made governor of wide lands after the island of Hawaii was subdued. During Kamehameha's invasion of Oahu in 1804, Keeaumoku died of a plague, probably bubonic.

KEEAUMOKU II (GOVERNOR COX) (–1823)

Kahekili Keeaumoku was a son of KEEAUMOKU and NAMAHANA and a brother of KUAKINI (JOHN ADAMS) and KAAHUMANU. His wife was Kekuaiaea, who died on Kauai. He was governor of the island of Maui for many years. Like his brother Kuakini, he learned English and joined foreigners in various enterprises, such as gathering sandalwood. He proposed the abolition of the old religion even before the breaking of the kapu in 1819. His hand pulled the lever of the press on the occasion of the first printing in the islands (see LOOMIS).

KEELIKOLANI. See RUTH.

KEKAULIKE (–1736)

A ruler of Maui, he was fond of warfare and although related to ALAPAINUI, invaded Kohala and died of epilepsy on his return. Even though he had many children, including KALOLA, KAHEKILI, and NAMAHANA, he decreed that his lands should go to KAMEHAMEHA I.

KEKAULUOHI, MIRIAM AUHEA (1794?–1845)

Miriam was a daughter of HOAPILI and KALAKUA and a sister of Queen KAMAMALU and KINAU. Brought up at Kahuluu, Oahu, by her grandparents, KEEAUMOKU and NAMAHANA, in 1809 she became one of the five wives of KAMEHAMEHA I and at his death became a wife of his son, KAMEHAMEHA II. She married Kanaina in 1834 and bore a male child, the future King LUNALILO.

Miriam was a stern chiefess but, according to the Rev. Amos Starr COOKE, an over-indulgent mother. She loyally supported the Royal School of the Protestant missionaries but was equally tolerant of other faiths. She succeeded KINAU as kuhina nui from 1839 to 1845.

KEKAUONOHI (1805?–1851)

A daughter of KINAU and a granddaughter of KAMEHAMEHA I, Kekauonohi was one of the wives of KAMEHAMEHA II but after his death ran away with a chief named Keliiahonui. Later she married Levi Haalelea, who inherited her lands. She was governor of the island of Kauai in 1842.

KEKELA, JAMES HUNNEWELL KEKELAOKALANI (1824–1904)

First ordained Protestant minister of Hawaiian blood, Kekela preached at Kahuku and Hauula on Oahu before going to the Marquesas Islands when Hawaii became a "home mission." In 1853 he and his wife Naomi first went to Fatuhiva. The people were cannibals who carried on perpetual tribal warfare, but missionaries were given tabu status. The Kekelas were, however, forced to leave the island of Hivaoa in 1864. The first officer of the whale ship *Congress,* Francis Whalon, was the victim of the local chief's vengeance for the loss of a son. Whalon was bound and tortured and would have been eaten as a warning to others, but Kekela bargained for the captive's life. For this brave act, Kekela was rewarded by the gift of an inscribed gold watch by Abraham Lincoln in the final year of the American president's life. Thereafter the Kekelas worked on the island of Puamau, running a school for boys, until 1899, when they returned to Hawaii after forty-seven years in the mission field.

KEKUAIWA, MOSES (1829–1848)

A son of KINAU and KEKUANAOA, Moses was the brother of KAMEHAMEHA IV and KAMEHAMEHA V. He was adopted by KAIKIOEWA of Kauai.

**KEKUANAOA, MATAIO
(1794–1868)**
Mataio was descended on his
father's side from chiefs of Oahu and
on his mother's side from a family of
tutors who attended
KAMEHAMEHA I. He was a
punahele or intimate companion of
the future KAMEHAMEHA II, and
attended him on the journey to
London in 1823. On his return
Kekuanaoa married in 1827 KINAU,
daughter of KAMEHAMEHA I, who
after 1832 was kuhina nui and
governor of Oahu. The pair had five
children: Kamehameha, who died
early; Moses KEKUAIWA, who died
in 1848; Lot Kamehameha, who
became KAMEHAMEHA V;
Alexander Liholiho, who became
KAMEHAMEHA IV; and
VICTORIA KAMAMALU. By an
earlier marriage to Pauahi, formerly
a queen of Kamehameha I, he was
also the father of RUTH
KEELIKOLANI.

At the death of Kinau in 1839,
Kekuanaoa became governor of
Oahu. He was a member of the House
of Nobles and the privy council and
president of the Board of Education.
Mark Twain, who observed
Kekuanaoa presiding over the
Legislative Assembly in 1866, said:
"He bears himself with a calm, stately
dignity, and is a man of noble
presence . . . a grave, dignified,
statesmanlike personage, and as
seemingly natural and fitted to the
place as if he had been born to it and
had never been out of it in
his lifetime."

KEKUAOKALANI (–1819)
Born at Kona, son of
KELIIMAIKAI, Kekuaokalani was a
cousin of KAMEHAMEHA II. At the
death of KAMEHAMEHA I in 1819,
the chief became keeper of the war
god KUKAILIMOKU. Angered at
the breaking of the ancient kapu, he
retired to Kaawaloa on Hawaii and
raised a rebellion against Liholiho.
Two precedents in history justified

this act; the overthrow of HAKAU by
UMI and the defeat of KIWALAO by
Kamehameha I. The precedent failed
when Kekuaokalani faced the army
of KALANIMOKU, reinforced by
American swivel guns mounted on
double canoes. The chief and his
wife, Manono, fought bravely but
were killed in the battle of Kuamoo in
December, 1819.

KEKUHAUPIO (–1784)
This chief was a noted fighter
who tutored KAMEHAMEHA I in
the arts of war and defense, and was
one of his foremost supporters. On
one occasion, his pupil repaid him by
saving his life in battle. Kekuhaupio
was at Kealakekua Bay on the day of
the death of Captain James COOK
and brought to KALANIOPUU the
critical news that a chief named
Kalimu had been killed by the cordon
of boats across the bay. Kekuhaupio
lost his life during a sham battle
at Napoopoo.

KEKUIAPOIWA LILIHA
Daughter of KALOA and niece
of KAHEKILI, she was the wife of
KEOUAKALANI
KUPUAPAIKALANINUI and
mother of KAMEHAMEHA I.

KEKUPUOHI
A wife of KALANIOPUU, she
was a great beauty of the time and
later married KAIANA. She was one
of the first chiefs to learn from the
missionaries to read and write.

KELIIMAIKAI (–1809)
The favorite younger brother of
KAMEHAMEHA, he was given the
name of "the good chief" because of
his fair treatment of the common
people as ruler of Maui.

**KELIINOI, ROSALIE A.
(1875–1952)**
The first woman elected to
public office in the Territory of
Hawaii, Rosalie Keliinoi was born at

Wailuku, Maui. She took office in
1925, and was instrumental in
enacting a bill to give women full
right, without the consent of their
husbands, to dispose of property
owned at the time of their marriage.
She was a member of various
Hawaiian civic groups. Of her seven
sons, three served on government
boards. Her favorite hobby in later
years was making Hawaiian quilts,
which she entered in competitions at
the Honolulu Academy of Arts.

**KELLER, ARTHUR RIPONT
(1882–1961)**
Born in Buffalo, New York,
Keller obtained degrees at Cornell,
National University Law School,
Massachusetts Institute of
Technology, and Harvard University.
After experience on the mainland as a
civil engineer he came to Hawaii in
1909 as professor at the College of
Hawaii; he retired as vice president
of the University of Hawaii in 1946.
During World War I he served on the
mainland and retired with the rank of
major in the United States Army
Reserve. Keller devoted time to civic
affairs and served on several
territorial commissions. He married
Lora T. Keegan in 1908.

**KELLY, JOHN MELVILLE
(1879–1962)**
Born in Oakland, California,
son of a rancher, Kelly had his first
drawing published at the age of
seventeen, and at the age of twenty
attended Partington Art School in
San Francisco. In 1908 he married
Katharine Howland, who later won
recognition as a sculptor. Kelly
worked for Charles R. Frazier in
Honolulu in 1923 and was art director
of the *Star-Bulletin* from 1927 to
1935. Thereafter he spent all his time
as an etcher, first with Hawaiian
subjects and later with Oriental. His
work was displayed at galleries in
Hawaii and on the mainland.

75

KENDALL, CHARLES RUSSEL (1905–1965)

Born in Logansport, Indiana, Kendall graduated from Dayton University in 1929 and came to Hawaii the same year to teach and coach football at St. Louis High School until 1932. He was a clerk in the Circuit Court until 1943. In 1946 he became executive director of the Hawaiian Government Employees' Association and thereafter was a most active lobbyist for this state employees' union. He was an authority on civil service and retirement systems and on pay schedules. He was a member of a number of professional and fraternal groups. Kendall Hall, headquarters of the Association, bears his name.

KENDRICK, JOHN (1740?–1794)

A former privateering captain in the American Revolution, Kendrick was sent out from Boston in company with Robert GRAY to trade for furs on the Northwest Coast of America. On that coast Kendrick, master of the *Columbia Rediviva,* traded commands with Gray of the *Lady Washington.* The latter vessel first arrived in the Hawaiian Islands in the autumn of 1791; it returned under Kendrick in 1793 and 1794. Kendrick and several of his officers were killed in December, 1794, when William BROWN fired a victory salute after the battle in which KAEO was killed near Pearl Harbor. A gun from a nearby ship, accidentally loaded with grapeshot, crashed through the side of the *Lady Washington,* which had to sail to China under another captain. Kendrick may have been a pioneer in the sandalwood trade; in 1790 he left two men on the island of Kauai to collect a cargo of this valuable wood.

KENNEDY, STANLEY CARMICHAEL Sr. (1890–1968)

Kennedy was born in Honolulu, son of James A. Kennedy of the Inter-Island Steam Navigation Co. The young man attended Punahou School and graduated from Stanford University in 1912. He joined the Naval Aviation Service in 1917 and was one of the few residents of Hawaii to see active service overseas in World War I, on duty in the North Sea as a pilot of flying boats. He saw the possibilities of introducing commercial aviation to Hawaii and helped to form Inter-Island Airways, Ltd., in 1929. Kennedy became president and general manager of the airline in 1932, and head of the Inter-Island shipping line the following year. The airline was later incorporated as Hawaiian Airlines, one of the three inter-island firms of today.

Kennedy helped to establish regular trans-Pacific air service by Pan American Airways. He was also president of the Hawaii Transportation Co., the Coca-Cola Bottling Co., and the Honolulu Chamber of Commerce. He married Martha Davenport in 1919 and their son, Stanley C. Kennedy Jr., carried on the family tradition of inter-island transportation.

KEOHOKALOLE

Wife of KAPAAKEA and mother of KALAKAUA, LILIUOKALANI, and LELEIOHOKU.

KEONI ANA.

See JOHN YOUNG II.

KEOPUOLANI (HOAPILI WAHINE) (1778–1823)

Daughter of KIWALAO and KEKUIAPOIWA LILIHA, she became the sacred wife of KAMEHAMEHA I and held the highest royal rank. She was the mother of KAMEHAMEHA II, KAMEHAMEHA III, and NAHIENAENA. After the death of the conqueror she married his closest companion, HOAPILI, whom she retained, alone among her husbands, after she rejected polygamy. She advised KAMEHAMEHA II to break the ancient tabu in 1819. She was one of the first Hawaiian converts to Christianity, and was baptized by the Rev. William ELLIS at Lahaina an hour before her death on September 16, 1823. See William Richards, *Memoirs of Keopuolani, Late Queen of the Sandwich Islands* (Boston: Crocker & Brewster, 1825).

KEOUAKALANI KUPUAPAIKALANINUI

This chief was a stepson, along with KALANIOPUU, of ALAPAINUI, king of Kohala. He married KEKUIAPOIWA LILIHA, niece of KAHEKILI, and was the father of KAMEHAMEHA I, although it was rumored that the future conqueror was a son of Kahekili.

KEOUA KUAHUULA

This Keoua was the son of
KALANIOPUU of the island of
Hawaii and half-brother of
KIWALAO. Keoua was of lower rank
among the alii than Kiwalao, his
mother KANEKAPOLEI not being
as high-born as KALOLA, mother of
Kiwalao.

Disgruntled at the division of the
heritage after the death of
Kalaniopuu in 1782, Keoua joined
Kiwalao against KAMEHAMEHA I
and Kiwalao was killed the same year.
After a battle, the island of Hawaii
was held by three forces. Keoua took
Ka'u and part of Puna;
KEAWEMAUHILI, the uncle of
Keoua, kept Hilo and southern
Hamakua; and Kamehameha held
Kona, Kohala, and northern
Hamakua. In 1790 Keoua killed his
uncle and invaded northern Hawaii
while Kamehameha was fighting
elsewhere. He conquered Hilo and,
while returning to Ka'u, was caught
in an explosive eruption of Kilauea in
1790 when some four hundred
warriors and their families were
killed by suffocation and
falling rocks.

After Kamehameha built his great
heiau near Kawaihae in the summer
of 1791, only Keoua stood in the way
of his domination of the Big Island.
Fatalistically, Keoua came to the
shore to discuss peace and was
speared to death by KEEAUMOKU.
His companions were also killed,
Keoua was sacrificed on the altar of
Kukailimoku, and Kamehameha was
master of the island of Hawaii.

KEOUA PEEALE

Another son of
KALANIOPUU.

KEPELINO (ZEPHYRIN) (1830?–1876)

Kepelino came from a family
descended from the legendary priest
PAAO, but he was brought up as a
Catholic and trained to become a lay
teacher. When he received his
diploma in 1845, however, no
position was open to him. He
accompanied Father Ernest Meurtel
in 1847 to work at a mission in Tahiti
but grew bored and was sent home.
In time he became private secretary
to the dowager Queen EMMA, and
campaigned so vigorously for her
election in 1874 that he was brought
to trial by the victor, KALAKAUA,
on a charge of high treason, and on
October 17 of that year was sentenced
to be hanged. His death sentence was
commuted but he served in prison
until 1876. He left half a dozen
works in the Hawaiian language,
the most important of which is
Kepelino's Traditions of Hawaii
(Honolulu: Bernice P. Bishop
Museum, 1932), translated by
Martha W. BECKWITH.

KIAMAKANI (–1824)

A blind chief of Kauai, he was
killed as an insurgent after the
breaking of the old kapu in 1819.

KIHAAPIILANI

Son of PIILANI by
Laieloheloheikawai. After victory
in wars, he asserted his right to rule
Maui, where he divided the lands
and built walls and roads.

KIMBALL, CLIFFORD (1875–1941)

Born in Newton,
Massachusetts, Kimball was a
high-school classmate in that town of
Walter DILLINGHAM. Kimball
came to Hawaii in 1901 and married
Juliet M. King in 1902. Dillingham
offered Kimball the managership of
the Haleiwa Hotel in 1908. In 1917
the couple were able to borrow
enough to take over the lease of the
Hau Tree Hotel on Waikiki Beach,
on the site of the family home of
Robert LEWERS. Thus began years
of operation of the celebrated
Halekulani (House Befitting Heaven)
Hotel, which acquired adjoining
property such as Gray's Inn. Two
sons, George Pulsifer and Richard
(Kingie) Kimball, continued to carry
on the gracious tradition after the
death of their father in 1941; Richard
was in charge until 1962, five years
after the property was optioned to
Norton Clapp of Seattle.

KIMMEL, HUSBAND EDWARD (1882–1968)

Kimmel was born in
Henderson, Kentucky, son of an
army officer and businessman. After
graduation from the local high school
he was appointed to the United States
Naval Academy and graduated in

1904. He married Dorothy Kinkaid, daughter of a naval officer, in 1912. After an outstanding career, especially as a gunnery specialist, Kimmel was promoted to the rank of admiral in 1941 and assumed command of the United States Pacific Fleet, with the U.S.S. *Pennsylvania* as his flagship.

Kimmel was in command when the fleet was attacked by Japanese aircraft at Pearl Harbor on the morning of December 7. He and Walter C. SHORT, then United States Army commander in Hawaii, bore the brunt of the blame for the disaster that plunged the United States into World War II. Kimmel was relieved of his command ten days later and replaced by Chester W. NIMITZ. Kimmel retired from the Navy on March 1, 1942, at the request of the Chief of Naval Operations, and reverted to his permanent rank of rear admiral. The 1944 Naval Court of Inquiry found him guilty neither of wrongdoing nor incompetence; the 1945–1946 joint Congressional investigation accused him, finally, only of errors of judgment. After his retirement he worked with a marine engineering firm and helped to design the first large sectional drydock capable of holding a battleship; the dock saw much service during the Pacific fighting. See his book, *Admiral Kimmel's Story* (Chicago: Regnery, 1955).

KINAU (1805–1839)
Kinau was a daughter of KAMEHAMEHA I and KALAKUA and a sister of KEKAULUOHI and KAMAMALU. She married Mataio KEKUANAOA and was the mother of KAMEHAMEHA IV and KAMEHAMEHA V, as well as VICTORIA KAMAMALU. Kinau succeeded KAAHUMANU as kuhina nui in 1832 and continued the policy of strictly enforcing laws inspired by missionary teachings. In this way she often collided with the young and willful king, KAMEHAMEHA III, who resented her authority and, in particular, land laws which prevented him from recovering certain holdings. Around 1835, however, he became reconciled with Kinau and agreed to proclaim a code that would punish evildoers.

KING, CHARLES EDWARD (1874–1950)
Born in Honolulu, the future composer of many songs of Hawaii was educated at the Kamehameha Schools, Oswego State Normal School, and Pratt Institute. He was principal of Waiahole School, Oahu, from 1895 to 1899; instructor at Kamehameha, from 1900 to 1902; and inspector of private schools, Territory of Hawaii, from 1902 to 1913. Thereafter he was an agent for an insurance company.

King did not begin composing until 1911. He moved to New York City to be near the center of music publishing and to supervise the Charles E. King Music Co., which he established in 1916. He composed more than four hundred songs, including "The Kamehameha Waltz" and "Ke Kali Nei Au," the Hawaiian wedding song. He wrote the libretto and music of the operetta "The Prince of Hawaii," which was produced both in Honolulu and on the mainland. King published three collections of his songs. He also did considerable research and transcription work to preserve old melodies. At various times he conducted the Royal Hawaiian Band.

King served as a Republican in the territorial senate in the 1919 and 1921 sessions, introducing legislation that transformed the College of Hawaii into the University. He was married four times.

KING, JAMES (1750–1784)
Born at Clitheroe, Lancashire, son of a curate, King served in the Royal Navy off Newfoundland and in the Mediterranean and studied astronomy at Oxford. He was second lieutenant of the flagship of Captain James COOK on the voyage to Hawaii. The day after Cook's death on February 14, 1779, King was made first lieutenant by Captain Charles CLERKE; he was put in command of the *Discovery* on August 22, 1779, after Clerke's death, and took the expedition back to England.

King was quite active during the Hawaii visits and was so well liked by the natives that they asked him to remain in the islands after the ships departed. He finished the official account of the voyage as collaborator with Cook; see James Cook and James King, *Voyage to the Pacific Ocean . . .* (London: W. & A. Strahan for G. Nicol and T. Cadel, 1784).

KING, SAMUEL WILDER (1886–1959)

King was born in Honolulu, son of Captain James A. King, pioneer in interisland shipping and minister of the interior during the Republic, and Charlotte Holmes Davis, great-granddaughter of Oliver Holmes. The son was educated at St. Louis College and Honolulu High School (now McKinley), and graduated from the United States Naval Academy in 1910. He served in the Navy until 1924, including the full period of World War I, and resigned as a lieutenant commander to make his home in the Islands.

King developed extensive business in real estate and for a time was president of the Honolulu Realty Board. He entered politics in 1932; appointed to fill out an unexpired term on the Board of Supervisors of Honolulu, he ran successfully for the term of 1933 to 1935. He was the Republican candidate for delegate to Congress in 1934 and served from 1935 to 1942, withdrawing from the race in that year in order to return to the Navy in World War II. He retired with the rank of captain in 1946.

King was elected unanimously as president of the Constitutional Convention of 1950. He was a charter member of the Hawaii Statehood Commission from 1947 and chairman from 1949 until he was named governor of the territory in February, 1953. He was governor until 1957 and helped to defeat the Rankin Bill which would have permitted non-residents of Hawaii to hold high office in the territory. King returned to his real-estate business and was appointed a trustee of the Bernice P. Bishop Estate. He was elected as a representative to the state legislature in 1958 and was planning to run in the first election for state governor when he died of a heart attack on March 24, 1959.

King married Pauline Nawahineokalai Evans in 1912 and the pair had five children, including Samuel Pailthorp King, later a federal judge, and Pauline Nawahineokalai King Joerger, author and teacher.

KINNEY, RAY (1900–1972)

Born in Hilo, Kinney graduated from high school and spent a year at Brigham Young University in Utah. At the age of fifteen he composed his first song, "Across the Sea." The following year he began many years of touring the mainland as a leading vocalist. Engagements included six weeks at the Roxy Theater in New York and an eleven-month stint at the Palace Hotel in San Francisco. His band played for four years, from 1938 to 1942, at the Hawaiian Room of the Hotel Lexington in New York.

During World War II Kinney performed at 157 American military bases and clubs. After the war he was entertainment director for Matson ships and hotels. His active career lasted for more than half a century, and he was known not only as a singer and composer but also as a recording artist (he made almost six hundred sides), radio and stage performer, orchestra leader, and master of ceremonies. His influence on the popularization of Hawaiian music, especially on the United States mainland, was immeasurable. Kinney married Dawn Holt in 1925 and the pair had two sons and three daughters.

KIWALAO (–1782)

Son of KALANIOPUU, Kiwalao was a chief of very high rank through his mother, KALOLA—perhaps of slightly higher rank than his cousin KAMEHAMEHA I, who was next in line for the title. Kiwalao at the death of his father in 1782 received the greater part of his lands and the title to his throne, but Kamehameha was entrusted with custody of the war god, Kukailimoku. Kiwalao fought against the growing power of Kamehameha and was joined by another disgruntled half-brother, KEOUA KUAHUULA. Kiwalao was killed at Keei, Hawaii, in battle against Kamehameha.

KNUDSEN, ERIC ALFRED (1872–1957)

Born in Kauai, son of Valdemar KNUDSEN, Eric was educated at Auckland, New Zealand; Vienna; Berlin; Boston; and Harvard University, where he graduated from the law school in 1897. He returned to Hawaii in 1900 and became manager of Knudsen Brothers' Ranch. He entered politics in the territorial house of representatives as vice speaker in 1903 and speaker in 1905; he was a senator from 1907 to 1915, acting as president during the 1911 and 1913 sessions. He was a member of the Kauai Board of Supervisors from 1923 to 1932. He became celebrated during World War II for his radio show on KTOH, Lihue, on which he told Hawaiian tales, history, and legends. He was also an authority on the mountain trails of Kauai and blazed one of the earliest routes up to Mount Waialeale. He is author with Gurre P. Noble of *Kanuka of Kauai* (Honolulu: Tongg, 1945), about the Knudsen and Robinson families of that island. Knudsen married Cecilie L'Orange in 1905 and they had three daughters and a son. By his second wife, Helen Lewis, whom he married in 1935, he had one son and one daughter.

KNUDSEN, VALDEMAR
(1820–1898)

Knudsen was born at Kristiansand, Norway, son of the premier of that country. After an education at the University of Norway, he went to New York and was connected with book publishing. He joined the California gold rush of 1849, and with his gains from mining started a business at Sacramento. When returning from a visit to Norway he contracted Panama fever and it was impossible for him to remain in California. By chance his ship stopped at Kauai and, hearing that he had been cheated of his mainland holdings, he began a third career by pioneering in the growing of sugar cane. For some time he was manager of Grove Farm at Lihue, but gradually he acquired properties in southern Kauai that are still retained in the family.

Knudsen married in 1867 Anne McHutcheson Sinclair, daughter of Captain Francis Sinclair, R.N., and Eliza McHutcheson Sinclair. The couple had five children, including Eric Alfred KNUDSEN. Valdemar took part in civic affairs, served in the legislature between 1860 and 1890 under the monarchy, but was one of the first to pledge allegiance to the Provisional Government in 1893. See Eric A. Knudsen and Gurre P. Noble, *Kanuka of Kauai* (Honolulu: Tongg, 1945).

KOALAUKANI
(KAHOLOKALANI)

Son of KAHEKILI by Kauwahine and younger brother of KALANIKAPULE, Koalaukani supported his father in the civil wars. He was the hero of a battle at Paukukalo on Maui. He commanded the right wing of his father's forces on Oahu in 1794 but escaped from the defeat by KAMEHAMEHA I at the battle of Nuuanu Pali in 1795.

KONIA (1807–1857)

A granddaughter of Kamehameha I, she was the wife of PAKI and mother of Bernice Pauahi BISHOP. She was a member of the legislature from 1840 to 1847.

KOOLAU (1862?–1896)

In the revolution year of 1893, Koolau, a cowboy on the Gay & Robinson Ranch on Kauai, helped to round up fellow lepers who were to be shipped to Molokai for isolation. His wife, Piilani, agreed to accompany him as a kokua or healthy helper, but she was kept behind when the vessel sailed. Koolau swam ashore and with his wife and five-year-old son took refuge with other fugitives in remote Kalalau Valley. During an attempt to capture Koolau by Deputy Sheriff Louis Herbert Stolz, son-in-law of the Rev. George B. ROWELL of Waimea, the leper shot and killed Stolz after warning him not to cross a boundary line.

Exaggerated reports of the size of the refugee band caused the landing at Kalalau beach on July 1 of a score of men of Company A, Hawaiian National Guard Auxiliary, armed and carrying a small mounted B. L. Krupp gun. Koolau defended the heights during several attacks and was accused of murdering four soldiers. In the night he and his family retreated from the ledge that had been their home. Next morning a bombardment by the Krupp gun convinced the attackers that the outlaws could not have survived, and the force departed.

However, Koolau lived on for three years under rigorous conditions. The child, Kaleimanu, came down with leprosy and was buried in a grave hollowed out in the rocky soil by the hands of his parents. Two months later Koolau also died and was buried by his wife, with his rifle beside him. She later was able to ascend the rugged heights to Kokee and relate the story of their sufferings to the police. The adventures of the indomitable Hawaiian was the inspiration for "Koolau the Leper," one of the most impressive tales by Jack LONDON.

KOPP, BARBARA (MOTHER MARIANNE) (1836–1918)

In 1862 Barbara Kopp became a novice in the Motherhouse of the Sisters of the Third Order of St. Francis in Syracuse, New York. She became a teacher at Assumption School in that city and at St. Peter's School in Oswego. She returned to Syracuse to take charge of St. Joseph's Hospital. When six nuns answered the call to serve at the leper settlement on the island of Molokai, Mother Marianne, as she was known, accompanied them to Hawaii in 1883. Permission to work on Molokai was delayed for five years, and they worked at the Kakaako Branch Hospital before being allowed to go to the settlement in 1888, to assist the failing Father DAMIEN and supplement the labors of Brother Joseph DUTTON.

Under the guidance of Mother Marianne, who continued to work at the colony throughout the remainder of her life, a home for girls was built and hospital care was given to the sufferers. See Leo V. Jacks, *Mother Marianne of Molokai* (New York: Macmillan, 1935).

KOTZEBUE, OTTO VON (1787–1846)

A Baltic German and Russian subject, Otto was the son of a famed German playwright. The son devoted the best years of his life to service in the Russian Imperial Navy. He first visited Hawaii in 1804 on the *Nadeshda*, a round-the-world vessel commanded by his uncle, Adam Johann von KRUSENSTERN. In command of his own ship, *Rurik*, Kotzebue arrived from California off the island of Hawaii in November, 1816. On the staff of the captain were three "scientific gentlemen": Adelbert von Chamisso, botanist; Johann Friedrich Eschscholtz, naturalist; and Ludwig (Louis) CHORIS. The *Rurik* arrived during the filibustering exploits of Georg Anton SCHEFFER, about which Kotzebue knew nothing, and at first KAMEHAMEHA I mistook his ship for an invading vessel of war. On November 2 the captain and his gentlemen were regally received before sailing off to visit Honolulu. A translation of his account of the voyage appeared in three volumes under the title of *A Voyage of Discovery into the South Sea and Beering's Straits* (London: Longman, Hurst, Rees, Orme & Brown, 1821).

On his third visit, Captain Kotzebue arrived in Honolulu late in 1824, in command of the *Predpiyatie*. On this circumnavigation the Russians explored a number of Pacific groups. Kotzebue was received in Hawaii by former acquaintances such as KINAU and the queen dowager NAMAHANA. He felt that the pious atmosphere of post-missionary Hawaii had killed the former liveliness of the island people. His account of this voyage is found in a two-volume translation, *A New Voyage Round the World* (London: H. Colburn & R. Bentley, 1830). As a son of his father, Otto was a graphic writer and his notes on Hawaiian life are well worth study.

KRAUSS, FREDERICK GEORGE (1870–1962)

Born in San Francisco, Krauss graduated from Stanford University in 1894 and the University of California in 1901. He came to Hawaii in that year to teach agriculture at the Kamehameha Schools. He was professor of agronomy at the College of Hawaii from 1911 and agronomist at the Hawaiian Agricultural Experiment Station, Haiku, Maui, from 1915. He was owner and developer of New Era Homestead Farms, an experimental headquarters, from 1913 until 1921. He became professor of agronomy and genetics at the University of Hawaii from 1921 to 1936 and director of the Agricultural Extension Service from 1930 to 1936. He was author of a number of agricultural bulletins and articles, specializing in field crops, especially legumes. Krauss Hall on the Manoa campus bears his name. He married Elizabeth Hilmer in 1897 and they had four children.

KRUSENSTERN, ADAM JOHANN VON (1770–1846)

This Russian navigator was the first from his country to visit Hawaii, on a round-the-world cruise from 1803 to 1806. Its purpose was to stimulate the Pacific fur trade and to revive relations with China and Japan. He arrived in June, 1804, in command of the *Nadeshda*; his consort was the *Neva* under Urey Lisiansky. Krusenstern soon left for Alaska, but the *Neva* visited Kealakekua Bay and Kauai, where Lisiansky met the young King KAUMUALII. More than a year later, when the *Neva* was on the way to Canton with a cargo of furs, it grounded on a shoal near Midway Island; a nearby islet still bears the name of Lisiansky. The *Neva* was again seen in the islands in 1809, commanded by Leonth Andreanovich Hagemeister. See

Krusenstern's *A Voyage Round the World* (London: printed by C. Roworth for J. Murray, 1813), translated from the German by R. B. Hoppner.

KUAKINI (JOHN ADAMS) (1791–1844)

Youngest son of KEEAUMOKU and NAMAHANA and brother of KAAHUMANU, he was also known as KUAKINIOKALANI or KUAKINIIKONAHALE. He was a high chief and governor of the island of Hawaii from 1820 until his death. He was one of the first chiefs to read and write English and Hawaiian. He became acting governor of Oahu in 1831 and was a diligent supporter of missionary ideals. He had a wagon road built from Waimea to Kawaihae on the Kona cost with a labor force comprised of men sentenced for breaking the Seventh Commandment. Kuakini built a fort at a site near the official temple of KAMEHAMEHA I and armed it with cannon. He also built many schools and a large meetinghouse near the mission at Waimea, Hawaii. He conceived in 1835 an attempt to grow cotton and set up a textile industry on that island, and two years later had a spreading field of cotton at Waimea and a factory that produced and wove yarn, but the projected industry came to nothing.

KUALII
One of the last great chiefs, Kualii was a descendant of PINEA, wife of LILOA. He is said to have subjugated first his own island of Oahu and later the other Hawaiian Islands. One report says he died in 1730 at the age of 175. He was succeeded by his son Peleioholani.

KUHIO. See KALANIANAOLE.

KUYKENDALL, RALPH SIMPSON (1885–1963)
Born in California, the future historian of the Hawaiian kingdom earned a bachelor's degree from the College of the Pacific in 1919 and a master's degree in history from the University of California at Berkeley in 1921. He came to Hawaii in 1922 as executive secretary of the Historical Commission of Hawaii and began a career of forty years as a teacher and researcher. The first result of his studies was an elementary textbook, *A History of Hawaii* (New York: Macmillan, 1926), with Herbert E. GREGORY. Kuykendall became a professor of history at the University of Hawaii in 1932 and worked at his desk for some years after he was officially retired in 1950. Aside from publishing some fifty historical articles, he collaborated with A. Grove Day on a one-volume account, *Hawaii: A History* (New York: Prentice-Hall, 1948, 1961). His monumental three-volume work, *The Hawaiian Kingdom* (Honolulu: University Press of Hawaii, 1943, 1956, 1967) is a storehouse of information for anyone wishing to do serious study of the period from 1778 to 1893.

LAANUI
The husband of Kekuaipiaa, he escaped at the death of KEOUA KUAHUULA at Kawaihae in 1791 by jumping overboard secretly. He joined KAAHUMANU in taking part in communion at Kawaiahao Church in 1825 for the first time.

LADD, WILLIAM
See BRINSMADE.

LA FARGE, JOHN (1835–1910)
A painter and writer, La Farge in 1890–1891 traveled in company with Henry ADAMS and made a number of sketches of the islands. He wrote and illustrated *Reminiscences of the South Seas* (New York: Doubleday, Page, 1912).

LAFON, THOMAS (1801–1876)
Born in Chesterfield County, Virginia, Lafon studied medicine at Transylvania University and was ordained as a minister at Marion College, Missouri, in 1835. He married Sophia Louisa Parker in 1836 and the couple arrived in Hawaii with the Eighth Company of American missionaries in 1837. They were stationed at Koloa, Kauai, where he acted not only as physician but also as minister and teacher. He later became head of the church set up at Nawiliwili. He resigned from the Boston mission because of an almost fanatical devotion to the abolition of slavery, and the couple left the islands in 1842. After his wife's death in 1844, Dr. Lafon married Ruth Ann Atwell Tweedy in 1846 and they had three children.

LANE, JOHN CAREY (1872–1958)
Born at Makao, Oahu, Lane was educated at Hauula School and St. Louis College. He held various jobs as a clerk, and from 1893 to 1900 farmed near Honolulu. He married Alice Kalakini in 1909. Lane was a member of the territorial senate from 1905 to 1907 and introduced the bill establishing the City and County of Honolulu. He failed to win the post of mayor in 1908 and 1910, but was elected by an overwhelming majority in 1914. He was defeated in his bid for re-election in 1917. Appointed high sheriff of the territory and warden of Oahu Prison in 1922, he resigned in 1932 during charges of lax administration and because of ramifications of the case of Thomas MASSIE.

LA PÉROUSE, JEAN FRANÇOIS DE GALAUP (1741–1788?)
The Count de la Pérouse was the most celebrated French navigator of the eighteenth century. He entered the French Navy as a royal cadet in 1756 and spent most of his life at sea. He was chosen in 1785 to head an expedition into the Pacific that King Louis XVI hoped would rival those of Captain James COOK. The count commanded two five-hundred-ton armed frigates, *Boussole* and *Astrolabe*, which sailed from Brest in August, 1785. The ships entered the Pacific the following January and touched at Easter Island before reaching Hawaii.

These French crews were the first Europeans to go ashore on the island of Maui, which Cook had sighted on November 26, 1778. A ceremonious landing was made on May 30, 1786, at the spot now called La Pérouse Bay. But the commander judged that taking possession of the island for the French Empire would not be a humane act. After exploring the American coast from Alaska down to California, the ships were again in Hawaiian waters. Necker Island was

named by La Pérouse after the French statesman. The ships were almost wrecked on French Frigate Shoal, whose name commemorates the event. After many other adventures in the Pacific, the ships left Port Jackson, Australia, on January 26, 1788, and thereafter disappeared from history for forty years. The mystery of their fate was solved by Captain Peter Dillon, an Irish adventurer. The two vessels had foundered in a storm off the island of Vanicoro, in the Santa Cruz group. See *Voyages and Adventures of La Pérouse* (Honolulu: University of Hawaii Press, 1969), translated by F. Valentin.

LAPLACE, CYRILLE-PIERRE-THÉODORE

Captain Laplace arrived off Honolulu on July 9, 1839, in command of the French frigate *L'Artemise*, with orders from Paris to teach the people of Hawaii a salutary lesson. Having consulted only with Jules DUDOIT, he submitted to King KAMEHAMEHA III a "Manifesto" that included five demands concerning Catholic worship in the islands. The sum of $20,000 had to be deposited with Laplace to guarantee that the treaty would be carried out. War would instantly follow if the demands were refused.

The king was at Lahaina but the treaty was signed on the 12th on his behalf and the money, raised from local merchants, was paid. Not satisfied, Laplace paraded his forces under arms at a military mass ashore and then forced the king on July 17 to sign an additional convention giving special privileges to French residents and French imports, particularly wines and brandies. These acts put Great Britain and the United States at a disadvantage and such demands eventually led to recognition of Hawaiian independence by the three foreign powers.

LARSEN, NILS PAUL (1890–1964)

Born in Stockholm, Sweden, young Larsen was brought to the United States by his parents at an early age. He graduated from Cornell University Medical College in 1916 and saw action in France and Belgium as a medical officer with the 106th Infantry. On receiving his honorable discharge with the rank of major, Dr. Larsen made his first trip to Hawaii in 1919 to visit his brother, L. David Larsen, manager of Kilauea Plantation, Kauai. After teaching at Cornell University, Dr. Larsen returned to Hawaii in 1922 as a pathologist at Queen's Hospital and thereafter became medical director.

Larsen served two terms as president of the Honolulu County Medical Society and was for one term president of the Hawaii Medical Association, as well as president of the Hawaii Academy of Sciences. He was author of many important medical papers; he co-operated in a wide range of researches, including studies of ancient Hawaiian medicine and food, and led in various community activities. For eleven years he was Swedish vice consul in Hawaii. In 1921 he married Sara Elizabeth Lucas and they had two children.

LEDYARD, JOHN (1751–1789)

Born in Groton, Connecticut, son of a sea captain, Ledyard studied at Dartmouth College, lived among the Iroquois Indians, and paddled down the Connecticut River wrapped in a bearskin. After a voyage to the Mediterranean, Ledyard signed on as corporal of marines on the flagship of Captain James COOK, unaware that his native country was at war with England. At the time of Cook's death at Kealakekua Bay, Ledyard was in charge of the squad that defended the *Resolution*'s foremast ashore and was bombarded by stones hurled by angry Hawaiians.

Ledyard remained in the Royal Navy for two years after returning to England, but toward the end of 1782 he deserted off Long Island. He wrote his own account of the Hawaiian adventure in *Journal of Captain Cook's Last Voyage to the Pacific Ocean* (Hartford, Conn.: Nathaniel Patten, 1783). Ledyard ended his career as a celebrated explorer on land who had walked across Siberia. He died in Cairo, Egypt, on his way to seek the sources of the Niger River. See Jared Sparks, *The Life of John Ledyard, the American Traveler* (Cambridge Mass.: Hilliard & Brown, 1828) and Kenneth Munford, *John Ledyard: An American Marco Polo* (Portland, Ore.: Binfords & Mort, 1939).

LEE, KUIOKALANI (KUI) (1932–1966)

Lee was born in Shanghai, where his parents, both professional entertainers, were on tour. He was educated at the Kamehameha School for Boys and Roosevelt High School. He began performing as a knife dancer in 1950 and, although told that he did not have a good voice, was determined to succeed as a vocalist as well as a dancer. He performed in various spots on the mainland from the Lexington Hotel in New York to the Seven Seas in Los Angeles. He is best known, however, as a composer of some forty songs, mostly between 1956 and 1961. Among these compositions are "Lahainaluna," "One Paddle, Two Paddle," and "I'll Remember You." His nonconformist nature led him to leadership in a break with the smooth harmonic progressions of the past; the driving beat of rock shows up in such songs as "Ain't No Big Thing" and "Going Home." Lee married Nani Naone, and the couple had one son and three daughters.

LEE, WILLIAM LITTLE (1821–1857)

A young American lawyer, Lee arrived in Hawaii in the winter of 1846 and was appointed on December 1 as a judge in Honolulu. This began a new era in the history of the judiciary, and he was to serve with distinction. Along with John RICORD, Lee took a lead in the framing of the organic acts of 1845–1847. He was named chief justice under the third organic act in September, 1847, and helped to draft the Constitution of 1852. Because of his leadership in promoting the Great Mahele of 1846, Lee may be considered the father of Hawaii's present land laws. He was interested in agriculture, was a partner in the firm of H. A. PEIRCE that established Lihue Plantation, was the author of the "Act for the Government of Masters and Servants" of 1850 setting up laws concerning immigrant labor, and was

a guiding spirit in the Royal Hawaiian Agricultural Society founded the same year. Along with Dr. G. P. JUDD, Judge Lee was appointed to treat with French Admiral Legoarant de TROMELIN in 1849, and he was consulted when annexation by the United States was being considered by the Hawaiian government in 1854.

LELEIOHOKU (–1848)

A son of KALANIMOKU, he became governor of the island of Hawaii in 1846. He married Princess Harriet NAHIENAENA on November 25, 1835. After her death in 1836 he married Princess RUTH and fathered two sons. Leleiohoku died during the measles epidemic of 1848.

LELEIOHOKU, WILLIAM PITT KALAHOOLEWA (1835–1877)

Brother of two future rulers of the kingdom, Leleiohoku was the youngest son of KAPAAKEA and his wife KEOHOKALOLE and brother of David KALAKAUA and Lydia LILIUOKALANI. The child was adopted at birth by Princess RUTH, who named him Leleiohoku in memory of her first husband and made him heir to her large estate. The boy grew up to be a gifted poet and musician, and in 1876 founded a choral society, the Hui Kawaihau (the name means "Ice Water Club").

Some of his compositions are still sung in the islands.

Soon after Kalakaua became king he named Leleiohoku as his successor. The American minister in Honolulu wrote that Leleiohoku was "of correct morals, well-educated and accomplished," and "promised to become, had he lived to ascend the throne, a wise and popular sovereign." Sadly, he died of pneumonia on April 9, 1877, leaving Liliuokalani as the heir of her brother, with results not always fortunate for the royal family.

LEWERS, ROBERT (1836–1924)

Born in New York City, Lewers landed in Honolulu in 1856 and was employed as a carpenter. In 1860 he joined the lumbering firm of his cousin, Christopher H. Lewers, founded in 1852. In 1877, following the death of Christopher, Robert and Charles Montague COOKE Sr. became partners with J. G. Dickson in the thriving firm. When Dickson died in 1880, the company became Lewers & Cooke—still an important name in the economy of Hawaii. Lewers married Catherine B. Carter in 1867 and the couple had a son and a daughter.

LIHOLIHO. See KAMEHAMEHA II and KAMEHAMEHA IV.

LIKELIKE

Wife of Kalanimoku.
See also LIKELIKE, Miriam Kapili.

LIKELIKE, MIRIAM KAPILI (1851–1887)

Miriam was a younger child of KAPAAKEA and KEOHOKALOLE, and therefore sister of David KALAKAUA and Lydia LILIUOKALANI. She was married on September 22, 1870, to Archibald Scott CLEGHORN, and their only child was Princess Victoria KAIULANI.

LILIHA (–1842)

Liliha was the daughter of HOAPILI KANE and a granddaughter of KALOLA. She was the wife of BOKI and accompanied him to England in 1823. After his departure on a voyage to the South Pacific, she succeeded him as governor of Oahu. Hearing in 1831 that KAAHUMANU and her missionary advisers were planning to remove her from the office, Liliha bought guns and ammunition and with armed men occupied the fort at Honolulu and the battery on top of Punchbowl Hill. Her father, Hoapili, governor of Maui, persuaded her to resume loyalty to KAMEHAMEHA III. The chiefs decided on April 1, however, to put Oahu under Kaahumanu, who in turn appointed her brother KUAKINI, governor of the island of Hawaii, as acting governor. Liliha then retired to Lahaina, Maui, but remained the center of the anti-missionary faction. Kamehameha III tried to replace KINAU with Liliha, but failed. In 1839, during the "Great Revival," Liliha was converted to the Protestant faith, along with many other chiefs.

LILIUOKALANI, LYDIA KAMAKAEHA KAOLAMALII (1839–1917)

Last of the rulers of the kingdom of Hawaii, Liliuokalani was born in Honolulu, one of seven children of KAPAAKEA and his wife KEOHOKALOLE. Her great-grandfather was KEAWE-A-HEULU, who, she claimed, was first cousin to the father, of KAMEHAMEHA I. The child was adopted by PAKI and KONIA and reared as foster sister to Bernice PAUAHI. Lydia was two years younger than her brother KALAKAUA, and she was also a sister of Miriam LIKELIKE, who was much younger. Lydia attended the Royal School and had a good education.

On September 16, 1862, Liliuokalani married John Owen DOMINIS, shortly before he was made governor of the island of Oahu. The couple lived at his mother's home, Washington Place, named by Anthony TEN EYCK. She acted as regent of the kingdom during the world tour of Kalakaua, and the childless king made his sister the heiress apparent on April 10, 1877, after the death of William Pitt LELEIOHOKU. Liliuokalani attended the jubilee of Queen Victoria of England with her sister-in-law, Queen KAPIOLANI, in 1887.

A strong-willed woman who firmly believed in the rights of royalty, Liliuokalani swore that had she been at home, her brother would never have signed away his powers in the "Bayonet Constitution" of 1887, as she called it. After the death of Kalakaua, Liliuokalani was proclaimed queen on January 29, 1891. Her desire to restore the old authority of the crown led to the downfall of that crown. The wise

restraint of her husband, Dominis, was lost when he died seven months after her accession. Revolution was in the air, and her efforts to overthrow the Constitution of 1887 which she had taken an oath to maintain was only one of the complicated causes of the bloodless overthrow of the monarchy. Deposed on January 17, 1893, she continued to obtain support from firebrands like Robert W. WILCOX. When, during the counter-revolution of 1895, a small arsenal of arms and dynamite bombs was uncovered at Washington Place, the lady was comfortably confined in an upper room of her former palace. "Mrs. Dominis" signed a formal abdication and pledged allegiance to the Republic of Hawaii. Her efforts to be reseated on the throne are described by her in *Hawaii's Story by Hawaii's Queen* (Boston: Lothrop, Lee & Shepard, 1898).

Liliuokalani attended the celebration at the opening of the Pearl Harbor Naval Base in 1911, seated with her old enemy and successor Sanford B. DOLE. When the United States entered World War I, she flew the Stars and Stripes over Washington Place for the first time, to announce her loyalty in this global conflict. Liliuokalani is remembered as the author of a number of songs, especially "Aloha Oe"; the words are preserved on a bronze plaque inlaid in a lava boulder at Washington Place.

LILOA

Son of Kiha and father of UMI, Liloa built the heiau of Honuaula in Waipio Valley, his home. Before he died, Liloa gave Umi the custody of the war god while making HAKAU, Umi's half-brother, his heir. Umi defeated Hakau in battle and sacrificed the loser and his attendants at the heiau. Thus began a tradition upheld by KAMEHAMEHA I when he defeated his half-brother, KIWALAO.

LISIANSKY, UREY. See KRUSENSTERN.

LONDON, CHARMIAN. See LONDON, John Griffith.

LONDON, JOHN GRIFFITH (JACK) (1876–1916)

With an international reputation as an adventurer and popular author, London sailed his self-designed ketch *Snark* from San Francisco to Honolulu in 1907, and with his wife Charmian Kittredge

London spent five months touring the Hawaiian Islands before embarking on a two-year cruise of the South Seas. London learned to ride a surfboard at Waikiki, was entertained by Prince KALANIANAOLE and the deposed Queen LILIUOKALANI, and with his wife rode around Oahu. They then visited Haleakala Ranch on the island of Maui, and Jack wrote a graphic chapter in *The Cruise of the "Snark"* (New York: Macmillan, 1911) concerning their trip through the "House of the Sun," the dormant crater of Haleakala. They went to the Big Island, stayed at the Parker Ranch, and watched the bubbling fire pit of Halemaumau at Kilauea Volcano. A visit to the isolation colony on Molokai elicited another chapter, about the lepers resident there. London decided that the horrors of Molokai had been exaggerated, but three of the six stories in his *The House of Pride* (New York: Macmillan, 1912) concern leprosy, and after publication of the book his former hosts in Hawaii scolded him in print for dwelling on this aspect of island life. Two stories in this collection are based roughly on the careers of Chun AFONG and KOOLAU.

The Londons fell in love with Hawaii and returned there in 1915 and 1916. *On the Makaloa Mat* (New York: Macmillan, 1919), a posthumous collection of stories of Hawaii, is on the whole superior to *The House of Pride*. At the death of London at the age of forty, the unfinished manuscript of a novel about Hawaii's multiracial community was found on his desk.

London's second wife, Charmian (1871–1955), whom he married not long before they voyaged to the islands in 1907, was an enthusiastic later visitor. She intentionally omitted from her book *The Log of the "Snark"* (New York: Macmillan, 1915) her comments on the sojourn in the islands in 1907; this was reserved for her book *Our Hawaii* (New York: Macmillan, 1917; rev. ed., 1922). It contains three articles by Jack, written in 1916 and entitled "My Hawaiian Aloha." More information on the islands is found in Charmian's two-volume *The Book of Jack London* (New York: Century, 1921). See also *Stories of Hawaii by Jack London* (New York: Appleton-Century, 1965, 1984), edited and with an introduction by A. Grove Day.

LONG, OREN ETHELBERT (1889–1965)

Born in Altoona, Kansas, Long received a master's degree from the University of Michigan in 1916 and another from Columbia University in 1922. He came to Hawaii in 1912 and served as a high-school teacher and principal until 1925; he was deputy superintendent of public instruction from 1925 to 1934 and superintendent from 1934 to 1946. He was secretary of the territory from 1946 to 1951 and governor from 1951 to 1953, appointed by President Harry Truman. Long was one of the first two senators to represent Hawaii in Congress in 1959, the year of statehood, and retired from candidacy in 1963. He was an early advocate of statehood, was a member of the Constitutional Convention of 1950, and was chairman of the Statehood Commission from 1954 to 1956.

Long was a member of a number of professional, business, civic, and political groups, and a regent of the University of Hawaii from 1935 to 1946. He married Geneva Rule in 1917.

LOOMIS, ELISHA (1799–1836)

Born in Rushville, New York, Loomis became at the age of sixteen an apprentice printer in Canandaigua. In 1819 he attended the Foreign Mission School at Cornwall, Connecticut, during the summer before he and his wife, Maria Theresa Sartwell Loomis, whom he married in September, sailed with the First Company of American missionaries to Hawaii in October.

The couple were stationed at Kawaihae, Hawaii, on their arrival, but moved their school to Honolulu in November, 1820. After the missionaries worked out a roman alphabet for writing the Hawaiian language, Loomis set up his second-hand Ramage press and composed a few pages of type for an elementary spelling book. On January 7, 1822, in a grass-roofed hut at Kawaiahao, the first printing in the North Pacific region was struck off. Chief KEEAUMOKU II (GOVERNOR COX) pulled the lever that put pressure on the form, and the first page of millions put out by the Mission Press was lifted off. In December, 1823, the press was moved into the first building regularly used as a printing office.

The Loomis family (their son Levi was the first white child born in the islands) left for the United States in 1827, but Elisha supervised the printing of books in Hawaiian from 1828 to 1829 at Rochester, New York. For two years he was a missionary with the Ojibway Indians at Mackinac Island, Michigan. See *Grapes of Canaan* (New York: Dodd, Mead, 1951) by Albertine Loomis, a documentary novel by a great-granddaughter of Elisha and Maria.

LOT KAMEHAMEHA. See KAMEHAMEHA V.

LOW, EBENEZER PARKER (EBEN) (1864–1954)

Born in Honolulu, grandson of John Palmer PARKER, Low attended Iolani School. He joined Theo. H. Davies & Co. in 1881 as office boy and rose to become cashier and plantation accountant in 1887. From 1890 to 1893 he managed the Kohala Ranch; he then became a partner with Robert HIND and started Puuwaawaa Ranch, but the arrangement soon ended. In 1900 he managed the Woods cattle ranch. Previous to losing one hand in a roping accident, Low was a star rider and hog-tier, and in 1908, when he took some Hawaiian cowboys or paniolos to the Cheyenne Roundup, he was crowned as the "one-handed champion roper of the world."

From 1908 to 1910 Low managed the Humuula Ranch and in 1909 began a shipping business with Miller Salvage Co. In 1913 he established the Oahu Shipping Co. with J. B. Castle, whose interests he bought in 1917. Low was a member of the Honolulu Board of Supervisors, a founder of the Kamehameha Day celebration, and a yachtsman who made several cruises to the South Pacific and who was a crew member of the yacht *Lurline* when it won a trans-Pacific race.

LOWREY, CHERILLA LILLIAN (1861–1918)

Born in Utica, New York, Cherilla L. Storrs came to Honolulu in the early 1880s and taught at Punahou School from 1882 to 1884. She married Frederick J. Lowrey in 1884 and the couple had four children; her husband was later speaker of the House of Representatives, member of the Board of Health, and president of Lewers & Cooke, Ltd. During World War I Mrs. Lowrey was president of the Women's War Council. In 1930 she became the first president of Hui Hana, a movement to restock Hawaiian birds. She was also a founder of the Outdoor Circle and served on the City Planning Commission.

LUAHINE, IOLANI (1915–1979)

Luahine first learned Hawaiian dancing at the age of three from her grandmother, Keahi, former dancer at the royal court. She continued her studies at the age of fourteen under Mary Kawena Pukui, and made her professional debut as a solo dancer in 1947. She performed and taught during the rest of her life. In 1956 she was made curator of Hulihee Palace at Kailua, Kona. She retired as custodian of the Royal Mausoleum in Honolulu in 1965. In 1960 "Hoolaulea," a film demonstrating her art, was made by Francis Haar. During her life Iolani Luahine was considered the foremost preserver of the ancient Hawaiian dance repertory.

LUNALILO, WILLIAM CHARLES (1833–1874)

Lunalilo was a chief of high ancestry. He was a grandson of a half-brother of KAMEHAMEHA I. His parents were Charles KANAINA and KEKAULUOHI, a sister of KINAU. The mother of Lunalilo died when he was ten, and he was brought up as a spoiled prince. He was educated at the Royal School, spoke English even better than he did Hawaiian, and was popular among the American colony.

When KAMEHAMEHA V died without naming a successor, the Constitution provided that the throne should be filled by a vote of legislators. Lunalilo, the outstanding survivor of the royal line, offered himself as a candidate when a mass meeting of Hawaiians voted unanimously that he was their choice. It was known that Lunalilo did not favor the Constitution of 1864, and he had held no posts under Kamehameha V. His opponent was David KALAKAUA. The voters on January 1, 1873, were almost unanimous in favor of "Prince Bill," and he took the throne on January 8.

King Lunalilo began at once to offer many amendments to the Constitution of 1864, especially to abolish the property qualification for voting. Like the three previous kings, Lunalilo tried to obtain a reciprocity treaty with the United States, and at this time the idea arose of offering a lease on the lagoon at Pearl Harbor. A storm of protest arose, causing the legislature and the king to take back such a proposal. The short reign of Lunalilo was marked mainly by a mutiny of the Household Troops, who rebelled against their officers on Sunday, September 7, and remained in their barracks until a carefully worded message from the king, asking that they lay down their arms, was obeyed on the following Friday. The king then disbanded what Dr. Gerrit P. JUDD called "a useless and expensive army."

A description of the king soon after he ascended the throne was given by Isabella Bird BISHOP, who wrote, in part: "The king is a very fine-looking man of thirty-eight, tall, well formed, broad-chested, with his head well set on his shoulders and his feet and hands small. His appearance is decidedly commanding and aristocratic; he is certainly handsome even according to our notions. He has a fine open brow, significant at once of brains and straightforwardness, a straight, proportionate nose, and a good mouth." He had been engaged in his youth to Princess VICTORIA KAMAMALU, but the wedding was opposed by Kamehameha IV.

Poor health aggravated by heavy drinking developed in Lunalilo a serious case of tuberculosis. He died in Honolulu on February 3, 1874, a little more than a year after his election. He wished to have his own tomb instead of joining others in the Royal Mausoleum, and this tomb still stands on Punchbowl Street in Kawaiahao Churchyard. Lunalilo is best remembered as the first Hawaiian to leave his property to a work of charity. His will created the Lunalilo Home, "for the use and accommodation of poor, destitute, and infirm people of Hawaiian blood or extraction, giving preference to old people." He was succeeded on the throne by the election of Kalakaua.

LUQUIENS, HUC MAZELET (1881–1961)

Born in Auburndale, Massachusetts, Luquiens studied art at the Yale University School of Fine Arts, the Ecole des Beaux Arts, and the Julian Academy in Paris. He came to Hawaii shortly after World War I ended and joined the University of Hawaii Art Department in 1924. He retired in 1946 after serving as chairman of the department. Luquiens was the first president of the Honolulu Print Makers, and was nationally known as a master etcher. His work has been displayed at the Yale School of Fine Arts, the National Museum, the New York Public Library, the Library of Congress, the Honolulu Academy of Arts, and the University of Hawaii.

LYCURGUS, GEORGE ANASTASIOS (1859–1960)

Born in Sparta, Greece, the future innkeeper at Kilauea Volcano served for eighteen months in the Greek Army before leaving for New York. He visited some relatives in San Francisco and opened an oyster grotto there. In 1889 he came to Honolulu to join his brother John Lycurgus and cousin Peter Camarino in a fruit business. The company bought the California Wine Co. and pioneered as exporters of bananas and pineapples.

An outgoing personality, George Lycurgus was a friend of Claus SPRECKELS, King KALAKAUA, and Queen LILIUOKALANI. He acquired the Union Grill restaurant in Honolulu and the Sans Souci Hotel at the Diamond Head end of Waikiki Beach; Robert Louis STEVENSON stayed there in 1893. Lycurgus was imprisoned, not uncomfortably, for his part as a royalist in the counter-revolution of 1895. In 1902 he moved to Hilo, where he operated the Demosthenes Cafe, later replaced by the Lycurgus Building. He married Athena Geracimos of Sparta in 1903, and their sons, Nicholas George and Leonidas George

Lycurgus, carried on the family businesses after the father retired.

George Lycurgus acquired the old Volcano House in 1904; it had been built on the edge of the Kilauea caldera forty years earlier on the site of the original building of 1846. Through the years, Lycurgus was an affable host to hundreds of distinguished patrons of the hotel. He acquired the Hilo Hotel, formerly the summer palace of King Kalakaua, from Spreckels, and operated it for some years. Visiting Greece in 1914, Lycurgus was caught by World War I and did not return to Hawaii until 1920. He then sold the Volcano House to the Inter-Island Steam Navigation Co., which went bankrupt after spending $150,000 in remodeling and expanding the hotel. It was repurchased by Lycurgus for $300. It burned down in 1940, but he rebuilt and reopened it in 1941, just before the outbreak of World War II. Lycurgus was a champion cribbage player, and was also noted for conducting rites to placate the volcano goddess PELE. He died soon after his hundredth birthday.

LYDGATE, JOHN MORTIMER II (1854–1922)

Born at Gore's Landing, Rice Lake, Ontario, Canada, son of John Mortimer and Helen Elwell Lydgate, Lydgate came to Hawaii with his parents in 1865, in company with Alexander YOUNG and family. The elder Lydgate joined Young in founding the Hilo Iron Works but later sold his interest to Young and moved to Laupahoehoe, Hawaii, where he started a sugar plantation subsequently sold to Theo. H. Davies & Co. The younger Lydgate attended Punahou School and was employed from 1873 to 1875 as a government surveyor, laying out the first wagon road from Hilo to Kilauea Volcano. Heeding a call to the ministry, he received a bachelor degree in 1880 from Toronto University and despite family problems graduated from the

Yale Divinity School in 1891. For four years he was pastor of the Congregational Church at Stellacoom, Washington, but returned to Hawaii and founded the Lihue Union Church in 1898, where he served until 1919.

On the secular side, Lydgate proposed to the McBryde family that their cattle ranch should be turned into a sugar plantation; this was done in 1903 and Lydgate served as managing director until 1910. He was also active in land and engineering developments on Kauai, and was a collector of botanical specimens. He spoke Hawaiian fluently and published a dozen versions of native legends. He founded the Kauai Historical Society in 1914. Lydgate was instrumental in obtaining several park sites for the people of Kauai; the largest and most beautiful of these was named for him officially after his death. Lydgate married Helen Elwell in 1898 and the couple had four sons.

LYMAN, CHESTER S.

Lyman visited the islands at mid-century and gave in his book, *Around the Horn to the Sandwich Islands and California, 1845–1850* (New Haven, Conn.: Yale University Press, 1924), some fine vignettes of adventure. He described surfing at Waikiki with royal children; the preaching of Titus COAN during the "Great Revival"; a trip to Kilauea Volcano; and Hawaiian "thugs."

LYMAN, DAVID BELDEN (1803–1884)

Born in New Hartford, Connecticut, Lyman graduated from Williams College in 1828 and Andover Theological Seminary in 1831, the year he was ordained. He married Sarah Joiner in the same year and the couple sailed with the Fifth Company of American missionaries to Hawaii. They were stationed at Hilo and spent the remainder of their lives in that town.

Lyman established the Hilo Boys' Boarding School in 1836 and was principal until 1874. He performed pastoral duties during the frequent absence of the Rev. Titus COAN on preaching tours. Mrs. Lyman was a teacher at the school and promoted musical performances. The pair had eight children, and founded a family still prominent in the islands today. One son was Henry Munson Lyman (1835–1904), who spent most of his life in Hilo as a physician, educator, and writer; see his *Hawaiian Yesterdays: Chapters from a Boy's Life in Hawaii in the Islands in the Early Days* (Chicago: A. C. McClurg, 1906).

LYON, HAROLD LLOYD (1879–1957)

Born in Hastings, Minnesota, Lyon studied botany at the University of Minnesota and earned three degrees, including a doctorate in 1903, while teaching there from 1900 to 1907. He came to Hawaii in the latter year as assistant pathologist at the Hawaii Sugar Planters' Association Experiment Station in Honolulu. He became head of the Department of Botany and Forestry and directed research on sugar cane, pineapples, and forestry in a dozen parts of the world. Lyon helped to organize the Pineapple Research Institute in 1914.

Lyon retired in 1948 after twelve years as director of the Experiment Station. He then became director of both the Foster Botanical Gardens and Manoa Arboretum. He was author of numerous papers on plant pathology, embryology, and evolution. After his death, Manoa Arboretum was renamed for him, as were the botanical garden in Koko Head Crater, the University of Hawaii Arboretum, and the Orchid Garden in the Foster Botanical Gardens. His wife, Maude Fletcher Lyon, whom he married in 1906, was a botanist in her own right.

LYONS, LORENZO (1807–1886)

Born in Colerain,
Massachusetts, Lyons was educated
at Union College, New York, and
Auburn Theological Seminary,
Massachusetts. He was ordained in
1831 and married Betsey Curtis two
months before the couple sailed for
Hawaii with the Fifth Company of
American missionaries. On arrival in
1832 they were stationed at Waimea,
Hawaii, where he labored for the
following fifty-four years. His first
wife died in 1837 having borne one
living son, and the following year he
married Lucia Garratt Smith, who
bore him two daughters and a son.
Lyons became an expert in the
Hawaiian language, established
popular singing schools, and
composed hymns. His career is given
a full account in *Makua Laiana: The
Story of Lorenzo Lyons* (Honolulu:
privately printed, 1945), by Emma
Lyons Doyle.

McCANDLESS, LINCOLN LOY (1859–1940)

Born in Indiana, Pennsylvania,
son of a merchant, Lincoln was one of
three brothers who were early
developers in the islands. John A.
McCandless was born in 1853 and
James S. McCandless was born in
1855. James, who had experience in
drilling for oil in West Virginia, heard
from Samuel G. WILDER in San
Francisco in 1880 that artesian wells
were needed in Hawaii. He
immediately headed for Honolulu; a
year later James was joined by John,
and the next year Lincoln followed.
The three formed the firm of
McCandless Brothers in 1882 and
thereafter drilled more than six
hundred wells in the various islands
to provide water for the spreading
sugar plantations; the very existence
of B. F. DILLINGHAM's Ewa
Plantation west of Honolulu was
owed to the discovery of

subterranean water there. Lincoln
conceived the successful idea of
diverting water from Waiahole,
Waikane, and Kahana, on the
windward side of Oahu, and
converting it by tunnel through the
Koolau Range to the central
sugar lands.

The brothers also invested in
California mines, ranching, and
construction. Lincoln was one-third
owner of the McCandless Building
erected in 1907, one of the first
modern office structures in
Honolulu; he was full owner of the
Armstrong and L. L. McCandless
Buildings. He participated as a
Democrat in every political campaign
during the years of the territory until
1940; he was a representative from
1889 to 1900 and a senator from 1902
to 1906. He helped convince
Congress to exclude a property
qualification for voting under the
Organic Act in 1898 and sponsored
the Torrens Land Court Act. He was
territorial delegate to Congress from
1933 to 1935, when he worked for
statehood for Hawaii. He also
advocated government aid for
homesteaders and making Honolulu a
free port. McCandless was married
to Elizabeth Jane Cartright of New
York and they had one daughter.

McCARTHY, CHARLES JAMES (1861–1929)

Born in Boston, McCarthy was
educated in the schools of San
Francisco and came to Hawaii in 1881
to represent a fruit wholesaler.
During the monarchy he was a
member of the House of Nobles in
1890 and secretary of the legislature
in 1892. He was a captain in the
Honolulu Rifles during the troubles
raised by Walter Murray GIBSON
and Robert W. WILCOX and
opposed the dethronement of Queen
LILIUOKALANI. However, he was a
lieutenant colonel in the National
Guard during the period of
reconstruction.

All this time he was engaged in
business. His political career opened

in 1907 when he began serving in the
senate of the territory; he left in 1912
and was elected city treasurer until
1914. In that year he was appointed
as treasurer of the territory until
1918. He was appointed fifth
governor of Hawaii by President
Woodrow Wilson on June 22, 1918,
and served until July 5, 1921.
McCarthy helped to get the islands
back to a peacetime basis after World
War I. He believed that after two
decades as a territory, Hawaii was
ready for statehood and
recommended to the legislature in
1919 that a memorial be sent to
Congress to that effect. He was the
first governor to recommend
statehood. For the next two years he
represented the Honolulu Chamber
of Commerce in Washington, D.C.
He then worked for the land
department of the Hawaiian
Dredging Co. to reclaim sections of
Waikiki. In 1925 McCarthy was
general manager of the water and
sewer department of Honolulu. He
married Margaret Teresa Morgan in
1889 and they had five daughters.

MacDONALD, GORDON ANDREW (1911–1978)

Born in Boston, the future
volcanologist obtained a bachelor's
degree in 1933 from the University of
California in Los Angeles and a
master's degree in 1934; his doctorate
was granted by the University of
California in 1938. MacDonald came
to Hawaii with the United States
Geological Survey in 1948 and
served until 1956. In 1958, after two
years at work in Denver, he returned
to the islands as a professor of
geology and geophysics at the
University of Hawaii, retiring in
1976. In addition to publishing a
number of scientific papers, he was
author with Will Kiselka of *Anatomy
of an Island: A Geological History of
Oahu* (Honolulu: Bishop Museum
Press, 1967) and with Agatin T.
Abbott of *Volcanoes in the Sea: The
Geology of Hawaii* (Honolulu:
University of Hawaii Press, 1970).

McGREW, JOHN STRAYER (1825–1911)

Born in Lancaster, Ohio, the future "Father of Annexation" was taken at an early age to Cincinnati, where his father founded the local *Inquirer*. McGrew earned a medical degree at the Ohio Medical College in 1847. He rose to the rank of lieutenant colonel as a surgeon in the Union Army in the Civil War. On a world tour with his bride, Pauline Gillet, he arrived in Hawaii in 1866 and settled in Honolulu to enter medical practice. For many years, Dr. McGrew was in charge of the Marine Hospital and was the first president of the Honolulu Medical Society.

The doctor prospered, and his home, on the site of the future Alexander Young Building, was a center of hospitality. He was a member of the commission that co-operated with J. M. SCHOFIELD and B. S. Alexander in making a survey for an American naval base at Pearl Harbor, as provided for by the reciprocity treaty. Although filibusters from California had dreamed of conquering the islands, McGrew is believed to have been the first political proponent of the idea that Hawaii should be an American possession. He was called "Annexation McGrew" by King KALAKAUA, who opposed his efforts but could not deny his sincerity. Immediately after the deposition of Queen LILIUOKALANI, McGrew was named by the Annexation Club as honorary editor of the *Hawaiian Star*. During this period, the life of the doctor was threatened but he did not waver in his purpose, which was eventually fulfilled.

McINERNY, JAMES D. (1867–1945)

Twin brother of William McINERNY, James was the son of Michael McInerny, who had founded a store in Honolulu in 1850. Like his brother, James was educated in Honolulu and San Francisco and entered the family business. He specialized in the clothing half of the enterprise, whereas William specialized in managing the shoe store after the business expanded to two locations. The twins managed the firm after the death of their elder brother in 1923. James was a director of the Tourist Bureau for fourteen years and a director of half a dozen business concerns. The McInerny stores, under different management, are found today in a number of island centers. See *McInerny* (Honolulu: University Press of Hawaii, 1982), by Bob Krauss.

McINERNY, WILLIAM H. (1867–1947)

Twin brother of James D. McINERNY, William was educated, like his brother, in Honolulu and San Francisco, and managed the shoe department of the family business. William was a Republican senator in the legislature for four terms, ending in 1934. He helped to found the San Carlos Milling Co. in 1912 and was elected its president in 1945.

McKENZIE, TANDY (1892–1963)

Born at Hana, Maui, the future opera singer graduated from the Kamehameha Schools in 1911. Planning to study medicine, he enrolled in Northfield Seminary, Massachusetts. There the manager of a light opera company heard him sing, and MacKenzie began a career that took him from 1912 through the United States, the Middle East, Europe, South America, and Australia, singing dramatic roles. He sang his last series of concerts in Hawaii in 1933 and his last visit to Hawaii was in 1960. He died in Hollywood, California. See the biography by his wife, Jean S. MacKenzie, *Tandy* (Norfolk Island, Aus.: Island Heritage, 1975).

MACHADO, LENA (1903–1974)

Born in Honolulu, daughter of Louise Keoneula and Robert Waialeale, Lena became known as "Hawaii's songbird" because of her soprano-falsetto voice. She was discovered at the age of sixteen and a few years later appeared on radio station KGU. Thereafter she began singing with the Royal Hawaiian Band for many years, and also appeared as an entertainer in many mainland cities. During World War II she entertained thousands of servicemen. Through radio appearances and recordings and her stage and nightclub shows, and in such films as "Bird of Paradise," Lena Machado became one of the best known personalities in the world of Hawaiian music. She composed many songs especially suited to her voice and style, and was also a fine performer able to play all the basic Hawaiian strings as well as using the piano and other percussion instruments. Lena was the wife of Luciano Machado and the couple had one daughter.

MACKAY, JOHN

Mackay (or McKey) arrived on the *Imperial Eagle*, under Captain C. W. BARKLEY, in May, 1787. Mackay had been surgeon's mate of a trading ship who by his own wish had spent a year among the Indians of the Nootka Sound country as the first European resident of that region. This Irish "doctor" was also to become the first white resident of the Hawaiian Islands. He was living on the Kona Coast when Thomas METCALFE's schooner *Fair American* was captured in 1790.

MAHUNE, BOAZ (–1847)

A cousin of Governor Paul KANOA of Kauai, Mahune was a graduate of the first class of students at Lahainaluna Seminary in 1835. He was one of the ten chosen to remain as teachers and translators. Mahune later served as secretary to Kamehameha III and drafted a number of tax laws adopted in 1842. He became manager of the king's Wailuku sugar plantation, which failed. Mahune returned to Lahaina and acted for a time as a judge; he then went back to Honolulu as a civil servant.

MAIGRET, LOUIS DESIRE (1804–1882)

Maigret was a leader in the founding of the Catholic Church in Hawaii and was its first bishop, serving for more than thirty years. He was educated in France and was ordained at Rouen in 1828. He left for the South Pacific in 1834 and at Mangareva in the Gambier Group and in Chile he served until he first arrived in Hawaii in 1837, scene of his future labors.

The American Protestant mission that began work in the islands in 1820 soon became so firmly established among the chiefs that it was virtually the state religion. The incursion of Catholic missionaries under French auspices was therefore opposed and freedom of worship was not soon attained. The idea of French colonization of Hawaii originated with Jean RIVES. The pioneer mission arrived in Honolulu on July 7, 1827. It consisted of three priests of the Order of the Sacred Hearts of Jesus and Mary: Fathers Alexis Bachelot, Abraham Armand, and Patrick Short, an Englishman. They were supported by half a dozen other Frenchmen. KAAHUMANU ordered the ship's captain to take them away, but he refused and the group remained on shore. Their first mass was celebrated on Bastille Day, July 14, and the first baptism was given on November 30, to a child of MARIN. A lawyer accompanying the group obtained from Kamehameha III a piece of land in Honolulu on which the first Catholic chapel was opened. They had the protection of Governor BOKI, who had been baptized on the French ship *Uranie* under Captain FREYCINET in 1819, but he disappeared in 1830 and his wife LILIHA was removed from power in 1831. On April 2 of that year, the chiefs read a decree of banishment to Fathers Bachelot and Short, and after several months fitted out a vessel and shipped the priests to Mexican California.

The second attempt to found a Catholic mission in the islands was made in 1835. The church had created the Vicariate Apostolic of Eastern Oceania, and Father Bachelot had been made prefect of the area north of the equator. Brother Columba Murphy, a jolly Irishman who was a British subject, arrived in 1835 to look over the situation. As a result, Father Arsenius Walsh, also a British subject, arrived on September 30, 1836, and through the influence of the captain of a French warship then in port was allowed to stay and minister to foreigners but not to native Hawaiians. Bachelot and Short returned on April 17, 1837, but on April 30 a decree ordered that they return on the same ship that had brought them. The English and American consuls sided with Jules DUDOIT against the chiefs, and the priests were escorted ashore in early July by the captains of a British and a French warship.

Father Short did leave Honolulu at the end of October, but a few days later two more priests arrived on the scene. They were Murphy and Maigret, who for the first time saw the field of his future works. The fact that Murphy had been ordained since his visit in 1835 was not revealed and he was allowed to land, but Maigret and Bachelot sailed on November 23 for the South Pacific, where Bachelot died at sea.

Soon after their departure, Kamehameha III issued a ban against the teaching or practice of Catholicism in the islands, but in June, 1839, what amounted to an edict of toleration was issued. As a result of changing conditions and the demands of the French captain C. P. T. LAPLACE, the Catholic mission was finally established when on May 15, 1840, the vicar apostolic of the Pacific, Bishop Rouchouze, arrived with three other priests—one of them the exiled Father Maigret. A church of stone was soon begun, and schools and churches were erected on other islands to advance the mission labors. The first Catholic printing press was set up in November, 1841, and operated for fifty years. In 1847 Maigret was named Vicar Apostolic to the Sandwich Islands under the title of Bishop of Arathia and served as head of the mission until his death in 1882.

MAKEE, JAMES (1812–1879)

Makee was born in Woburn, Massachusetts, and in 1836 in New York married Catherine McNiven. As master of a whale ship off the port of Lahaina, Maui, Makee was nearly killed by the cleaver of his Chinese cook and left for dead. He was saved by the surgeons of an American warship in the roads, and after recovering decided to bring his wife to Hawaii and spent the rest of his life in the islands. He set up a partnership in a trading business in Honolulu that acted as agents for many whalers using the port.

Makee was a member of the first group to embark on the business of whaling from a Honolulu base; in 1851 he and his associates sent the ship *Chariot* to seek whales in the Arctic, and in 1854 the company sent out the whaler *Black Warrior* on a three-year operation. Captain Makee erected the first three-story brick building in Honolulu and resided with his growing family on Nuuanu Avenue, but in 1856 he sold the house to King Kamehameha IV and purchased "Torbert's Plantation" at Ulupalakua on the south shore of the island of Maui. There he continued the cultivation of sugar cane and the milling of sugar, and brought in thoroughbred cattle and dairy stock on a large scale. During the American Civil War he helped the Union cause by contributing molasses and produce for the benefit of the Sanitary Fund, predecessor of the Red Cross. Makee took the lead in 1877 in the construction of a breakwater at the harbor of Makena, Maui, and two years later engaged in a cane-growing venture with King Kalakaua that became part of the Makee Sugar Co.; his interest in this firm was acquired at his death by his son-in-law, Z. S. SPALDING. The Ulupalakua residence, called "Rose Ranch" because of the gardening efforts of Mrs. Makee, was a center of hospitality for countless important people in the region; the king was a frequent visitor. Today the ranch is the site of a venture in growing wine grapes on the southwestern slopes of Mount Haleakala. At Makee's death he was survived by his widow and eight children.

MAKINO, FREDERICK K. (1877–1953)

Born in Yokohama, Makino arrived in Hawaii in 1899 and worked in the general store of his brother Jo at Naalehu, Maui. Fred began as an assistant bookkeeper, first for the Kona Sugar Co. and then for the Honokaa Sugar Co. In 1903 he opened the Makino Drug Co. in Honolulu and married Michiye Okamura of Kauai.

Makino became a publisher; he founded the *Hawaii Hochi* in Japanese on December 7, 1912, adding an English section in 1925. He fought for the rights of Japanese aliens and was a leader of the Oahu sugar plantation strike of 1909, which brought increased pay for laborers; as head of the strike committee he was jailed from March to July, 1911. In 1920 Makino brought a successful Supreme Court suit to have Japanese schoolteachers admitted into the islands. In 1927 he brought another successful suit in the Supreme Court on behalf of eighty-seven Japanese language schools.

MALLET, S.

In command of the French sloop-of-war *Embuscade*, Captain Mallet was sent from Tahiti by Admiral PETIT-THOUARS and arrived off Honolulu in August, 1842, to investigate charges that the Hawaiian government had violated the 1839 treaties with LAPLACE. Mallet was mainly concerned with the free import of French wines into the islands and permission for the Catholic priests to work without interference (see MAIGRET). The ship departed in September, allaying fears that Mallet would take possession of the islands for France. Ahuimanu School was started on Oahu for Catholic education as one result of the visit. Two months after Mallet's departure, news was received in Honolulu that Petit-Thouars had set up a French protectorate over the Society and Marquesas Islands.

MALO, DAVID (1793?–1853)
Malo was brought up in the household of the high chief KUAKINI (JOHN ADAMS), brother of KAAHUMANU. Then, having become a Christian, he lived with the Rev. William RICHARDS at Lahaina, Maui. In his late thirties, Malo entered the first class at Lahainaluna Seminary. He had learned to read and write in the Hawaiian language, and helped Richards in his translations of part of the Bible. Ordained as a minister, Malo in his later years was pastor of the Congregational Church at Kalepolepo, Maui. Malo favored the land division called the Great Mahele and encouraged people to survey and register their lands. He tried to introduce cotton growing and cloth manufacture in the islands, but warned KINAU against the influx of foreigners who might take over land and industry from the natives. He put down many chants, genealogies, and other Hawaiian traditions which, written around 1840, were not translated until 1903; see his book, *Hawaiian Antiquities (Ka Moolele Hawaii)* (Honolulu: Hawaiian Gazette Co., 1903), translated by N. B. EMERSON.

MANINI. See MARIN.

MANJIRO. See NAKAHAMA.

MANLAPIT, PABLO (1890–1969)
Born in the Philippines, Manlapit arrived in Hawaii in 1910 as a recruited worker and soon became involved in labor disputes concerning plantation hands and Honolulu stevedores. He led an eight-month strike in 1924 that resulted in the death at Hanapepe, Kauai, of four policemen and seventeen strikers, and the jailing of sixty strikers. For his part, Manlapit served four years in Oahu Prison until pardoned by Governor Oren E. LONG.

Manlapit then went to California, where he was accused of helping Communists foster strikes among Filipino agricultural workers. He returned to Hawaii and formed the Hawaii Labor Association in 1933, but was expelled the following year. He went to the Philippines, became president of the American-Hawaiian-Philippines Labor Federation and helped to elect General Manuel Roxas as president of the Republic in 1946. Manlapit attempted to return to Hawaii in 1949 but was barred because of his 1924 conviction.

MANONO. See KEKUAOKALANI.

MANUIA (–1830?)
A son of Kaulunae, Manuia was a younger cousin of BOKI and went with the party of KAMEHAMEHA II to England. After his return Manuia was made commander of the harbor of Honolulu and the fortifications on Punchbowl Hill. Like Boki, he took part in the enterprises of foreigners and went with him in search of sandalwood in the South Pacific—an enterprise from which he did not return.

MARCHAND, ETIENNE (1755–1793)
In command of the *Solide*, the first French ship to visit the islands after those of LA PÉROUSE, Marchand arrived off the island of Hawaii on October 4, 1791, en route from the Northwest Coast of America to China. After a voyage around the world, Marchand sailed as an officer of the French National Guard to the island of Mauritius, where he died.

MARIANNE, SISTER. See KOPP, Barbara.

MARÍN, FRANCISCO DE PAULA (MANINI) (1774–1837)
Marín was born in Jerez, Andalusia, Spain, and deserted from the Spanish Navy at Nootka Sound, Vancouver Island, on the Northwest Coast of America. He arrived in Hawaii in 1793 or 1794, and probably served in the forces of KAMEHAMEHA I. He settled in Honolulu and began a family; at least three children were born before 1800. He may have traveled as a pilot to the South Pacific and China as well as to California, but was back in Honolulu by 1805. Marín began keeping a journal in Spanish in 1809; surviving portions have been translated, and contribute valuable documentary sidelights on the history of Hawaii through 1826. A man of great versatility, Marín served his friend the king throughout his life as interpreter, business adviser, accountant, physician, and supplier of rum. He attended Kamehameha at the royal deathbed.

Marín's home on the waterfront, at the junction of the Nuuanu and Pauoa Streams, was opened to ship captains and other paying guests, and he began a business of supplying vessels with many staples that he manufactured. His role as an introducer of dozens of plants from many parts of the Pacific may have been exaggerated by legend, but he certainly was adept at making such useful products as coconut oil, soap, molasses, pickles, lime, tiles, nails, candies, and cigars. He experimented with raising pineapples and milling sugar, and his vineyard—which gave its name later to a busy boulevard —supplied wine and brandy. He kept a large herd of dairy cattle, from which he got milk, butter, and cheese. He owned what later came to be called Ford Island in Pearl Harbor and on it raised hogs, goats, and rabbits.

Marín's mind was a strange mixture of pagan beliefs soaked up from his wives and friends and a pragmatic trust in experiment; but he never forgot his boyhood faith, and as a visiting doctor in the community was said to have "saved more than three hundred souls from hell" by secretly baptizing patients. He was cautiously friendly with the Protestant missionaries who arrived in 1820 but became suspicious of their strictness; nor was he trusted by the Catholic clergy when he was reluctant to aid them. He had three wives and fathered more than twenty children during his forty-five pioneer years in Hawaii. See Ross H. Gast, *Don Francisco de Paula Marín: A Biography*, with *The Letters and Journal of Francisco de Paula Marín*, edited by Agnes C. Conrad (Honolulu: University Press of Hawaii, 1973).

MARQUES, AUGUSTE J. B. (1841–1929)
Born in Toulon, France, Marques grew up in North Africa, son of a general in the French Army. He was educated in medicine and music at the University of Paris. He arrived in Hawaii in 1878, bought a tract near Punahou School in 1880, and taught music at that school. He was a charter member of the Philharmonic Society and organized the Theosophical Society in 1893. He was responsible for the boring of the first artesian well in Honolulu. He served in the legislature from 1890 to 1891 and at various times was consul for France, Russia, Panama, and Belgium. He was honored for his work by several decorations, and served in Belgium during World War I.

MARSHALL, JAMES F. B. (1819–1891)
A New England merchant who came in 1839 to Honolulu, Marshall was chosen in 1842 to carry to Washington and London the royal dispatches concerning the PAULET episode, drafted by Dr. G. P. JUDD. Marshall traveled to Mexico on the same ship with Alexander SIMPSON, and the documents each carried were deposited together in June, 1843, on the same desk in the British Foreign Office. Joined by William RICHARDS and Timothy HAALILIO, Marshall pursued successful efforts to obtain recognition of the independence of the Hawaiian kingdom. He returned to Hawaii, was elected to the legislature, and helped Richard ARMSTRONG in establishing a system of public education. Marshall left the islands in 1859 to reside in Massachusetts. In 1870 he became manager of Hampton Institute, Virginia, founded by Samuel G. ARMSTRONG.

MASSIE, THALIA FORTESCUE (1910 or 1911–1963).
After a party at the Ala Wai Inn on the night of September 12, 1931, Mrs. Thomas Massie, wife of a Navy lieutenant, disappeared for several hours and turned up near Waikiki Beach. She had been beaten and her jaw was broken in two places; there was no evidence of rape. She claimed that she had been attacked by five "local boys." Five youths were tried on charges of criminal assault: Joseph Kehahawai (Joe Kalani), Hawaiian; Shomatsu (Horace) Ida, Japanese; Henry Chang, Chinese-Hawaiian; Ben Ahakuelo, Hawaiian; and David Takai, Japanese-Hawaiian. On December 6 a jury could not agree on a conviction.

While a retrial was pending, Ida was kidnapped and beaten on December 12. Kehahawai was kidnapped on January 8, 1932, taken to the Manoa Valley house rented by Mrs. Grace Granville Fortescue, Thalia's mother, and shot to death by one of three Navy men present. During a trial in April, in spite of the pleas presented by the celebrated but aging Clarence Darrow, the defendants—Mrs. Fortescue; Lieutenant Massie; and two enlisted Navy men, Albert O. Jones and Edmund J. Lord—were all judged guilty of manslaughter, with a jury recommendation for leniency. On the morning of May 4, the defendants were sentenced under the mandatory law to ten years at hard labor in Oahu

Prison. They were then taken to the office of Governor Lawrence M. JUDD, who handed each of them a document commuting their sentences to one hour.

Although no jury found clear evidence against the local youths and no jury believed Thalia Massey's story, and although the obvious charges were the beating of one suspect and the murder of another, lurid treatment of the Massie case in the nation's newspapers suggested that a carnival of crime was happening in placid Hawaii. Proposals were made that the islands should be ruled by a commission in which the Army and Navy would have a part. The case almost ended self-government in Hawaii and probably delayed the attainment of statehood for twenty years. For a time there was serious danger that the territory, as a result of action by Congress, would be subjected to a carpetbag regime. Governor Judd resisted such actions. An investigation by an assistant United States attorney general, Seth W. Richardson, failed to find evidence justifying the wild reports circulating on the mainland, but did reveal some laxity in crime enforcement, and corrective measures were passed by the Hawaii legislature. See Peter Van Slingerland, *Something Terrible Has Happened* (New York: Harper & Row, 1966) and Theon Wright, *Rape in Paradise* (New York: Hawthorn, 1966). See also *Lawrence M. Judd: An Autobiography* (Tokyo and Rutland, Vt.: Tuttle, 1971).

MASSIE, THOMAS. See MASSIE, Thalia.

MATSON, WILLIAM (1849–1917)
Born in Lysekil, Sweden, the boy, like his Viking ancestors, went to sea at the age of ten. At twenty-one he was captain of a San Francisco schooner and for some years operated a fleet between that city and Puget Sound ports. He saw the need for a shipping line between Hawaii and California, and obtained support for the effort that still links his name with a fine fleet under the American flag, a subsidiary of Alexander & Baldwin (A&B).

In 1882 Matson acquired the 200-ton schooner *Emma Claudine*, nucleus of the Matson Navigation Co., Ltd. Other sailing vessels were added to carry bulk sugar, canned pineapple, other cargo, and passengers—*Lurline, Falls of Clyde* (now a floating museum in Honolulu Harbor), *Harvester*, and others. In 1902 Captain Matson acquired his first steamer, *Enterprise*, which with rare foresight he immediately converted into a burner of fuel oil. He was also the first Pacific operator to equip his ships with radio telegraphy. The first steamer built by the company was the *Lurline*, named for the captain's daughter, which went into service in 1908. Other steamers were soon added—*Wilhelmina, Matsonia, Manoa*, and *Maui*. When America entered World War I in 1917, Matson offered his entire fleet to the government, and several made splendid records as troop transports.

In 1923 the Matson Building, one of the largest in San Francisco at the time, became the firm's headquarters. During his shipping career, Matson also found time to become a developer of California petroleum; in 1903 he put five oil tankers into service to make deliveries from Monterey, California, to various Pacific Coast ports as far north as Nome, Alaska. In 1910 he amalgamated all his petroleum interests under the name of the Honolulu Consolidated Oil Co. Matson was also instrumental in substituting oil for coal on the Hawaiian sugar plantations served by his fleet.

MEARES, JOHN
A former lieutenant in the British Navy, Meares was one of the earliest fur traders on the Northwest Coast. He first came to Hawaii in 1788 in the Calcutta snow *Nootka* on his way to China. He returned as master of the *Felice Adventurer* in 1788, in company with the *Iphigenia*, one of his vessels, captained by William Douglas. See John Meares, *Voyages Made in the Years 1788 and 1789* (London: Logographic Press, 1790).

MELVILLE, HERMAN (1819–1891)
Melville, one of the foremost American authors writing about the Pacific, was born in New York City. He went to sea and in July, 1842, with one companion deserted the forecastle of the whale ship *Acushnet* at the island of Nukuhiva in the

Marquesas group. After less than a month in the valley of "Typee" he signed on another vessel, *Lucy Ann*, and as described in his novel *Omoo* was put ashore at Tahiti as a mutineer. He was discharged from a third whaler, *Charles and Henry*, at Lahaina, Maui, in May, 1843. He soon went to Honolulu, where after serving as a pinsetter in a bowling alley he signed on as a clerk in a general store run by a young English merchant, Isaac Montgomery. Melville sided with the British view during the occupation of the islands by Lord George PAULET. In an appendix to his novel *Typee*, Melville describes his shock at the celebrations following the restoration of the monarchy by Admiral Richard THOMAS. After ten weeks, Melville enlisted in an American warship and returned home to become author of *Moby Dick* and a number of other works of fiction. See A. Grove Day, *Melville's South Seas* (New York: Hawthorn Books, 1970).

MENZIES, ARCHIBALD (1754–1842)

Born in Scotland, Menzies first came to Hawaii on the *Prince of Wales* in 1788. As naturalist with Captain George VANCOUVER, he returned in 1792, 1793, and 1794 and supplied seeds to the people. He was the first non-Hawaiian to climb to the summit of Mauna Loa, almost fourteen thousand feet above sea level. The party required ten days in 1794 to reach the top, over a trail still bearing his name. His journal reveals much about Hawaiian agriculture; he believed that sugar cane could be cultivated in the islands without resort to slave labor. See his *Hawaii Nei 128 Years Ago* (Honolulu: New Freedom Press, 1920), edited by W. F. Wilson.

METCALFE, SIMON

Metcalfe was one of the earliest traders on the Northwest Coast of America. He may have been the first captain to take sandalwood from Hawaii to Asia. In February, 1790, when he was in command of the snow *Eleanora*, one of his boats was stolen and in revenge he committed the "Olowalu Massacre" off the island of Maui. He attracted scores of canoes to one side of his ship and his cannon fire killed at least a hundred Hawaiians.

Later, off the coast of the Big Island, he whipped Chief KAMEEIAMOKU for some offense aboard ship. Several weeks later, Simon's eighteen-year-old son Thomas, in command of the little schooner *Fair American*, was attacked by Kameeiamoku, and Thomas and all his crew were killed except Isaac DAVIS. Metcalfe left his boatswain, John YOUNG, ashore and sailed from the islands without learning the fate of his son. The *Fair American* was taken over by KAMEHAMEHA I, who also enlisted Young and Davis in his corps of foreign supporters.

METZGER, DELBERT EVERNER (1875–1967)

Born in Ozawakie, Kansas, Metzger attended Washburn College and received a law degree from Indiana Law School. After various posts on the mainland he came to Hawaii in 1899 with the United States Army and worked on the first map of the lochs of Pearl Harbor. He also drilled artesian wells on Oahu and Niihau.

Metzger helped to organize the Democrat Party on Kauai in 1900, and from 1913 to 1915 was territorial senator from the Big Island. He was named Fourth Circuit Court judge at Hilo from 1934 to 1939. During World War II he took a leading role in fighting the encroachment of martial law in Hawaii. The defenders of civil rights were not vindicated until four years of litigation ended with a United States Supreme Court decision on February 25, 1946. Metzger was not reappointed in 1952 by President Harry Truman, probably because of the political effect of some of the judge's decisions. During wartime Metzger had fined General Robert S. RICHARDSON Jr. the sum of $4,000 for contempt of court. In another case, Metzger ruled that Navy enlisted men do not lose their constitutional rights simply because they are in the Navy. He also reduced the bail of the "reluctant seven," including Jack HALL, from $75,000 to $5,000, saying: "The practice of setting bail was never intended as a punishment of defendants before trial."

MILLER, WILLIAM (1795–1861)

General Miller, an English soldier who had taken part in a revolution in Peru, became British consul general in Hawaii in 1844. He arrived just before the departure of Admiral Richard THOMAS after the restoration of KAMEHAMEHA III. Miller brought with him a treaty almost the same as the one that the king had been forced to sign in 1839, but the government had no choice except to affirm it on February 12.

MIRIAM LIKELIKE. See
LIKELIKE.

MOIR, JOHN TROUP
(1859–1933)
Born in Cookney, Kincardine-
shire, Scotland, Moir left school
before he was twelve to labor on his
father's farm. He worked on a
railroad for four years before
returning to the farm. He arrived in
Honolulu in 1888 and began serving
as a field foreman at the Waiakea
Plantation near Hilo. After rising in
rank on several other plantations,
Moir finally became manager of the
Onomea Sugar Co. at Papaikou. He
was also president of the Hilo
Electric Light Co. and a director of
several other local concerns. He
married Louisa Silver in 1889 and the
couple had five sons, several of whom
continued the family tradition
in agriculture.

MONSARRAT, JAMES
MELVILLE (1854–1943)
Born in Honolulu, Monsarrat
was descended on his father's side
from a noble French family that
emigrated to Ireland in 1755. The
father came to Hawaii from Canada
and in the 1850s was at one time
deputy collector of customs and a
member of the lumber firm of
Dowsett & Co. The mother of James
was Elizabeth Jane Dowsett, daughter
of Samuel James DOWSETT. James
attended Punahou School, studied
for two years at Kilkenny College in
Ireland, and obtained a law degree
from Harvard in 1878. He opened a
practice in Honolulu the following
year, and was secretary of the
legislative assembly in 1880. He
drew up the wills of Queen Dowager
EMMA and of Princess Miriam
LIKELIKE. After annexation he was
district magistrate in Honolulu
from 1911 to 1917.

MORENO, CELSO CAESAR
(1830–1901)
The Italian adventurer whose
influence on King KALAKAUA
paralleled that of Moreno's friend
Walter Murray GIBSON was born in
the Piedmont and educated by his
uncle, a Catholic bishop. He was
highly gifted as a linguist. He
graduated from the Italian naval
academy in Genoa and served in the
Crimean War. He obtained a degree
in civil engineering at the University
of Genoa and began a career as a
filibuster in Sumatra and a promoter
of a trans-Pacific cable from
California to China. Moreno arrived
in Honolulu in November, 1879, to
seek support for this floundering
cable project, and fed the king a
proposal for a Pacific steamship line
and other dubious programs, such as
the importation and sale of opium.
When several such suggestions were
opposed by the cabinet in 1880,
Kalakaua on August 14 dissolved the
body and appointed Moreno as
minister of foreign affairs.

Moreno's term lasted only five
days; he resigned under pressure,
revolution loomed, and the Italian
was threatened with lynching. At the
end of the month Kalakaua sent
Moreno to Italy to supervise the
education of three young Hawaiians
at crown expense; one of the three
was Robert W. WILCOX. Moreno
carried letters to the governments of
the United States, Great Britain, and
France, asking them to recall their
consuls from Hawaii for their failure
to recognize Moreno, but the cabinet
forestalled such acts. Moreno's
guardianship ended in scandal
when Kalakaua visited Italy in 1881.
His career collapsed when he
was a small-time lobbyist in
Washington, D.C.

MOTT-SMITH, JOHN
(1824–1895)
Born in New York, Mott-Smith
was educated in the public schools.
He taught himself to pass the state
dental examinations and practised in
Albany until news of the gold rush
caused him to depart for California.
He arrived in Hawaii in 1851 and
opened an office at the corner of Fort
and Hotel Streets in Honolulu; for
many years he was the only dentist in
the islands. He became first editor of
the *Hawaiian Gazette* when it was
established to defend the
Constitution of 1864. He was
appointed minister of finance three
years later. He was an intimate friend
of both KALAKAUA and
LILIUOKALANI and was sent to
Washington, D.C., to advance the
interests of the kingdom. He
returned to the islands in 1891 to
become minister of finance under
Liliuokalani, and upon the death of
H. A. P. CARTER became minister
plenipotentiary to Washington until
succeeded in 1893 by Lorrin A.
THURSTON. Dr. Mott-Smith in
1859 married Ellen Dominis Paty
and they had seven children,
some of whose descendants still
reside in Hawaii.

MUNRO, GEORGE CAMPBELL
(1866–1963)
Born in Auckland, New
Zealand, Munro came to Hawaii
with an expedition to collect birds. He
spent some years as a ranch manager.
From 1935 to 1958 he planted many
Norfolk pines on Kauai ridges as an
experiment in water conservation,
and thousands more trees at what
became the Na Laau Hawaii
Arboretum in Diamond Head State
Park on Oahu. Munro was dedicated
to the preservation of Hawaiian flora
and the study of Hawaiian birds.

MURPHY, COLUMBA. See
MAIGRET.

NAEOLE

A chief of Kohala, Hawaii, fearful of threats to the life of the infant KAMEHAMEHA I and wishing the honor of rearing the child, Naeole stole away the baby and placed it under the care of a woman named Keaka. For five years Naeole thus acted as kahu, or tutor, of the future conqueror.

NAHAOLELUA, PAUL (1806–1875)

Born at Kawaihae, Hawaii, Nahaolelua studied at Lahainaluna Seminary and then served as district and circuit judge on the island of Maui. He acted as deputy to the governor, James Young KANEHOA, and succeeded him in 1852, serving until 1874. During the election of 1874, Nahaolelua became president of the legislative assembly that voted for KALAKAUA rather than EMMA. He was soon appointed minister of finance but retired from the cabinet in October.

NAHIENAENA (HARRIET KEOPUOLANI) (1815–1836)

Daughter of KAMEHAMEHA I and his kapu wife KEOPUOLANI, and sister of KAMEHAMEHA II and KAMEHAMEHA III, Princess

Nahienaena was the darling of the court and was educated by the American missionaries. In 1824, the year following the departure of her brother Kamehameha II for England, she reverted to the belief in the ancient deities, and the conflict between two clashing doctrines disturbed her throughout her short life. She was excommunicated by the Protestants in May, 1835. Many of the chiefs felt that she should marry her brother, Kamehameha III, to concentrate the royal blood, but this Hawaiian custom was opposed by the Christians. In November, 1835, she married the high chief LELEIOHOKU and in September of the following year gave birth to a stillborn son. Nahienaena died a few months later at the age of twenty-one. See Marjorie Sinclair, *Nahienaena, Sacred Daughter of Hawaii* (Honolulu: University Press of Hawaii, 1976).

NAIHE (–1831)

A high chief of Kealakekua, orator for the first three Kamehamehas, Naihe was the husband of the KAPIOLANI who defied the volcano goddess PELE. He was acting governor of the island of Hawaii in 1831. He and his wife accompanied KAMEHAMEHA II from Oahu to Kauai in 1821 in a small sailing vessel that was nearly swamped in a storm, but the king refused to turn back and reached Kauai for meetings with KAUMUALII.

NAHIOLEA

A brother and supporter of KAIANA, Nahiolea was the father of KEKUANAOA, who accompanied the royal party to London in 1823.

NAKAHAMA, MANJIRO (1827–1898)

As a youth, Nakahama was rescued from a wrecked fishing vessel and taken to Honolulu. From there he went to Fairhaven, Massachusetts, and was given an American education and learned navigation. He was the first Japanese to come to the United States to be educated there. He later rose to leadership in Japanese diplomacy and naval affairs. See Emily V. Warriner, *Voyage to Destiny* (Indianapolis, Ind.: Bobbs-Merrill, 1956.).

NAKUINA, EMMA

See BECKLEY, Emma.

NAMAHANA

A chiefess of Maui, Namahana was a wife of KAMEHAMEHA I and later of KEEAUMOKU I, by whom she was the mother of KAAHUMANU, KALAKUA, KEEAUMOKU II (COX), and LYDIA PIIA NAMAHANA.

NAMAHANA, LYDIA PIIA

See NAMAHANA.

NAMAKEHA

See KAIANA.

NEAL, MARIE CATHERINE (STIMES) (1899–1965)

Born in Southington, Connecticut, Marie earned a bachelor's degree at Smith College. She came to Hawaii in 1920 as assistant malacologist at the Bernice P. Bishop Museum under Herbert E. GREGORY, for whom she had worked for three years at Yale University. In 1923 she joined an expedition to the summits of Mauna Loa and Mauna Kea. She received a master's degree from Yale in 1925 for a thesis on Hawaiian marine algae. She was a botanist in charge of the Bishop Museum herbarium from 1930 to 1965 and visited botanical gardens and herbaria in Asia and Europe in 1935. She is author of many articles and the valuable volume *In Gardens of Hawaii* (Honolulu: Bishop Museum Press, 1948); a 1965 edition contains almost a thousand pages of information for gardeners and botanists.

NEILSON, HENRY A.
See KAMEHAMEHA IV.

NEWELL, CHARLES MARTIN (1823–1900)
Newell was a whaling captain and physician who visited Hawaii often. He published a novel about a young chief, Kalanikupule, in *Kalani of Oahu* (Boston: published by the author, 1881). Under the pen name of "Captain Bill Barnacle," Newell published *Pehe Nu-e, the Tiger Whale of the Pacific* (Boston: D. Lothrop, 1877), a novel in which appears a whale called "Mocha Dick" (see MELVILLE), and a fictional biography, *Kamehameha, the Conquering King* (New York and London: Putnam, 1885).

NICOL, JOHN
Cooper on the *King George*, flagship of Nathaniel PORTLOCK, Nicol visited Hawaii several times in 1786–1788. He was kept busy cutting lengths of iron hoops which were ground sharp by the carpenter; these were the most valuable article of trade with the Hawaiians. Nicol's early account of the islands is found in his book, *The Life and Adventures of John Nicol, Mariner* (Edinburgh; William Blackwood, 1822; London: T. Cadell, 1822). The editor of a 1936 edition called this work "prose surpassed in its kind by none but that of Herman MELVILLE."

NIMITZ, CHESTER WILLIAM (1885–1966)
Born in Fredericksburg, Texas, Nimitz graduated from the United States Naval Academy in 1905 and was chief of staff to the commander of the submarine force of the Atlantic Fleet in World War I. He succeeded Admiral Husband E. KIMMEL on December 17, 1941, as commander of the Pacific Fleet in World War II and headed the victorious fighting forces throughout that war. He was made a five-star admiral in December, 1944. He retired in December, 1947. Nimitz Highway connecting Pearl Harbor and downtown Honolulu recalls his name.

NOBLE, JOHN AVERY (JOHNNY) (1892–1944)
Born in Honolulu, the future song writer attended the local public schools and in 1911 became associated with the Mutual Telephone Co., where he was head of the collection department at his death. He began his musical career at the age of fourteen, traveling as a soloist "whistling newsboy" with a group through the islands. He was a pianist and drummer with the Consolidated Amusement Co. from 1910 to 1922. From 1920 he was head of the orchestra at the Moana Hotel and changed the repertoire from its original native rhythms to modern dance music by adding the jazz tempo. He became director of entertainment for the Territorial Hotels Co. until his death.

Noble was music director of the Hawaiian opera "Pele and Lohiau" in Los Angeles in 1925, and broadcast programs over radio in 1927. He was musical director of the first company to make recordings of Hawaiian music in Hawaii, and during World War II worked on USO programs as performer, director, and arranger of shows. Among some three hundred of his songs, many of them appealing to visitors, are "My Little Grass Shack," "Hawaiian War Chant," "For

You a Lei," "Little Brown Girl," and "I Want to Learn to Speak Hawaiian." Noble married Emilie Kualii Dunn in 1921. See Gurre P. Noble, *Hula Blues* (Honolulu: E. D. Noble, 1948).

NORDHOFF, CHARLES
Bluejacket in the United States Navy, newspaper editor and correspondent, travel writer, Nordhoff visited Hawaii in 1873 and toured Oahu, Kauai, and the Big Island. See his *Northern California, Oregon, and the Sandwich Islands* (New York: Harper, 1874).

OBOOKIAH
See OPUKAHAIA.

OGDEN, MARIA (1792–1874)
Born in Philadelphia, Miss Ogden arrived in Honolulu in 1828 at the age of thirty-six as a member of the Third Company of American missionaries, and was stationed at Waimea, Kauai, for a year. From 1829 to 1838 she served at Lahaina, Maui, teaching a school for girls in the forenoon as well as a Sabbath school every Sunday. She then went to Wailuku Female Seminary and taught for twenty years before going to Punahou School from 1858 to 1859. She was the first principal of the Makiki Female Seminary from 1859 until 1868, when she retired and the school closed. She was beloved by about a thousand girls, two of whom she adopted, and also cared for the two children of Joseph KEKELA when this missionary was away in the Marquesas Group.

OKUMURA, TAKIE (1865–1951)
Born at Katamachi, Kochi
City, Kochi Prefecture, Japan,
Okumura was imprisoned for taking
part in a democratic movement. He
was baptized as a Christian in 1889
and graduated from Doshisha
Divinity School in 1894. In the same
year he came to Hawaii to succeed
Pastor Jiro Okabe when the latter
toured the world. He had married
Katsuko Ogawa in 1887 and in 1896
brought his family to the islands.

Okumura began missionary work
in Honolulu in 1902 and in 1903
organized the Aiyu Kai, the nucleus
of the Makiki Christian Church; he
retired as active pastor in 1937.
Okumura established the first
Japanese language school in Hawaii,
the Honolulu Shogakko, and was an
adviser to several other such schools.
He was one of the founders of the
YMCA in Honolulu, and his
Okumura Home trained more than
fifteen hundred young people. He
fought anti-Japanese sentiment and
his Americanization program, it is
believed, influenced many of the
young men who volunteered for
service during World War II. He
visited Japan and the mainland
several times, and made a world
tour and a visit to the Holy Land.

OLMSTED, FRANCIS ALLYN (1819–1844)
Born the son of a professor at
the University of North Carolina,
Olmsted graduated from Yale
University and went on a sailing ship
in search of improved health.
Although he spent only ten weeks in
Hawaii in the summer of 1840,
Olmsted filled six chapters of his
travel book with many observations
on the town of Honolulu, surfing
exploits, mission life, and the royal
family. A chapter is devoted to his
excursion to the Big Island and the
life of the bullock hunters that were
the predecessors of the Hawaiian
paniolos, or cowboys. See his book,
Incidents of a Whaling Voyage (New
York: D. Appleton, 1841; London:
John Neale, 1844), illustrated by
engravings from his own drawings.
The preface by W. Storrs Lee of a
1969 reprint considers Olmsted's
account of his stay in the islands
"one of the wittiest pictures of
Hawaii created prior to the visit
of Mark Twain."

OPAI
This young native of Kauai was
the first Hawaiian to visit the United
States. He sailed with Robert GRAY
on his round-the-world voyage in the
Columbia Rediviva, and returned to
the islands in 1791 on the *Hope*, commanded by Joseph INGRAHAM. In
true Polynesian fashion, Opai
swapped names with the captain and
thereafter called himself "Joseph
Ingraham." In 1792 Opai the
circumnavigator joined the flagship
of George VANCOUVER for a round
trip to the Northwest
Coast of America.

OPUKAHAIA, HENRY (OBOOKIAH) (1792–1818)
Born on the island of Hawaii,
the child saw his parents and small
brother slain in a tribal war when
he was ten years old. Reared at
Napoopoo on the shore of
Kealakekua Bay by an uncle who was
a kahuna or priest, Opukahaia (the
name means "stomach cut open") left
in 1809 and sailed in the ship *Triumph*
to New England. Befriended by the
students of Yale College and Andover
Seminary and other church people, he
became a Christian under the name
of Henry Obookiah, the first
Hawaiian convert. He was sent to the
foreign mission school at Cornwall,
Connecticut, and went into training
as a future field worker. He started to
translate the Bible into Hawaiian and
planned to join the First Company of
missionaries, but died of typhus fever
on February 17, 1818, aged twenty-
six. A funeral sermon preached by
the Rev. Lyman Beecher and the
publication of Obookiah's *Memoirs*
(New Haven, Conn.: Religious
Intelligencer, 1818), edited by Edwin
Dwight, aroused a wave of interest
that culminated a year after his death
in the departure of the bark *Thaddeus*
with the First Company of
Congregationalists to Hawaii. Thus
the wandering convert was the
inspiration for the first Christian
mission to the Sandwich Islands.

OSBOURNE, LLOYD (1868–1947)
Born in San Francisco, son of
Fanny Osbourne, who later married
Robert Louis STEVENSON,
Osbourne accompanied the author
during his Pacific years and
collaborated with him on two novels,
The Wrecker and *The Ebb-Tide*.
Following Stevenson's death in 1894,
Osbourne served as American vice
consul at Samoa for three years and
later went to New York to become
fairly successful as an author of
plays and fiction.

**PACHECO, MANUEL
(1874–1951)**
Born in the Azores, Pacheco
came to Hawaii with his family in
1883. He was trained as a bookbinder
in 1889 and worked for some years
for the Honolulu *Star-Bulletin*. He
married Julia Freitas in 1895.
Pacheco was one of the founders of
the Portuguese Political Club in
1900. He was a member of the Oahu
Board of Supervisors in 1912; court
clerk in 1914; chairman of the
Honolulu Charter Convention;
senator of the territorial legislature
from 1916 to 1918; and supervisor
from 1918 to 1934 and 1940 to 1951,
often in controversy over fiscal
matters. He was president of
the San Antonio Society.

PAKI, ABNER (1808–1855)
Paki was born on Molokai, a
descendant of the Kamehameha and
Kiwalao families of Maui and
Hawaii. He was the great-grandson
of KEKAULIKE. His father was
Kalanihelemaiiluna and his mother
was Kuhooheiheipahu. He was
captain of the fort at Honolulu in
1840 and a member of the national
council. In the early 1840s he joined
the Christian church. He was at
various times a Supreme Court judge,
member of the House of Nobles,
acting governor of Oahu, privy
councillor, and chamberlain to
Kamehameha III. He was the
husband of KONIA and father of
Bernice Pauahi BISHOP, for whom
in 1847 he built a large house in the
center of Honolulu.

**PALEA, KULUWAIMAKA
PAPIHENUI (1837?–1937)**
Born at Naalehu in the Ka'u
district of the Big Island, Palea came
to Honolulu and devoted his life to
the art of Hawaiian chanting. For
many years he was the chief chanter
at the court of Kalakaua. He was
famed for his powerful memory
—often for the beauty of his
chanting. He became chief instructor
at the Hawaiian language school of
George P. Mossman, who chanted
with the old man as he died, at nearly
one hundred years of age.

**PARIS, ELLA HUDSON
(1852–1938)**
Daughter of the Rev. John D.
PARIS, Ella for many years held
English lessons at her home in Kona,
and for eight years assisted in the
Sunday school of Lanakila Church.
She was later superintendent of the
Kahikola Trinity Church Sunday
School at Kealakekua for more than
thirty years. After the death of her
parents she transcribed more than
one hundred church songs into
Hawaiian under the pen name
of "Hualalai."

PARIS, JOHN DAVIS (1809–1892)
Born in Staunton, Virginia,
Paris attended Hanover College,
Indiana, for two years and graduated
from Bangor Theological Seminary,
Maine, in 1839. He married Mary
Grant in October, 1840, and the
couple sailed in November with the
Ninth Company of American
missionaries. They were stationed at
Waiohinu, Hawaii, in 1841, where
Mrs. Paris, having borne two
daughters, died six years later. On
a visit to the United States, Paris
married Mary Carpenter in 1851 and
returned with her to the islands. He
was stationed at Kealakekua from
1852 until his death forty years later.
He and his second wife were the
parents of two children, including
Ella Hudson PARIS.

**PARKE, WILLIAM COOPER
(1822–1889)**
The future marshal of the
kingdom, who served under five
rulers, was born in Portsmouth, New
Hampshire. He attended the schools
of Boston but ran away to sea at the
age of nineteen. He landed in
Honolulu in 1843 and worked as a
cabinetmaker. He was one of the first
men to locate a claim in California,
and brought back to Honolulu some
gold obtained near the mill of
General John Sutter.
Upon his return, Parke was named
marshal by Kamehameha III and

served until asked by Kalakaua to resign for political reasons in 1884. Parke organized an efficient police system which was especially effective during the smallpox epidemic of 1853. Previously, in 1851, he had warned off two dozen filibusters, led by Sam Brannan, who arrived from San Francisco in the hope of having the kingdom fall into their hands during a time of turmoil.

PARKER, BENJAMIN WYMAN (1803–1877)
Born in Reading, Massachusetts, Parker graduated from Amherst College in 1829 and Andover Theological Seminary in 1832. He married Mary Elizabeth Barker in September of that year and the couple sailed with the Sixth Company of American missionaries in November. After an attempt with the William Patterson ALEXANDERS and the Richard ARMSTRONGS to set up a mission in the Marquesas Islands in 1833–1834, the Parkers were stationed at Kaneohe, Oahu, in 1834 and served for more than thirty years. The Parkers had four children, including Henry Hodges PARKER.

PARKER, HENRY HODGES (1834–1927)
Born at Nukuhiva, Marquesas Islands, son of the Rev. Benjamin Wyman PARKER, Henry was a member of the first class at Punahou School. He studied theology under the Rev. Ephraim Weston CLARK, pastor of Kawaiahao Church; he was ordained in 1863, appointed assistant pastor, and served as pastor for more than fifty years. Parker was a friend and counselor of kings and chiefs, and was a delegate to the Constitutional Convention of 1864. His first language was Hawaiian, in which he always preached. He undertook the revision in 1914 of the Hawaiian dictionary of Lorrin ANDREWS which was published in 1922.

PARKER, JOHN PALMER (1790–1864)
The future founder of one of the great cattle ranches now under the American flag, Parker was born in Newton, Massachusetts, and sailed at the age of nineteen on a ship trading in furs. He saw Hawaii in 1811 and signed on a ship taking sandalwood to Canton, where it was blockaded for two years. Parker arrived again in 1815 and KAMEHAMEHA I hired him first as a supervisor of fishponds and then as a hunter of wild cattle in the forests of Waimea, where a kapu had allowed the animals brought by George VANCOUVER to propagate and overrun the countryside. The hides were prepared for shipment and the beef was salted for sale to visiting ships. In 1853 Parker showed George Washington BATES a rifle with which he had shot twelve hundred head of wild cattle.

Parker in 1818 married Rachel Kelii-kipikane-o-koolakala, a chiefess of an old Kohala family and a cousin of KANEKAPOLEI. The Parkers set up a small homestead at Mana on Mauna Kea and began collecting a herd of tame cattle. He worked for the William French Co. at Waimea in the 1830s, taking his pay in cattle. Parker acquired thousands of acres of grazing land on the uplands, built a sawmill, and bred a large herd. His son, John Palmer Parker II, did much to extend and consolidate the ranch, which was inherited by a third of the name, adopted by his grandfather after his own father died. See Joseph Brennan, *The Parker Ranch of Hawaii* (New York: John Day, 1974).

PATY, JOHN (1807–1868)
Paty, from Massachusetts, was commissioned by Kamehameha III in 1846 as his "consul and naval commander for the California coast with the rank of commodore." He was master of various vessels plying between Hawaii and California from 1850 to 1868.

PAUAHI. See BISHOP, Bernice Pauahi.

PAULDING, HIRAM. See PERCIVAL, John.

PAULET, LORD GEORGE (1803–1879)
Complaints against the Hawaiian crown by Richard CHARLTON in Mexico caused Rear Admiral Richard THOMAS to send the frigate *Carysfort* to Honolulu under the command of Lord George Paulet, who had entered the Royal Navy in 1817. Arriving on February 10, 1843, Captain Paulet listened to the angry words of Alexander SIMPSON. King Kamehameha III, summoned at once from Lahaina, was ordered to acknowledge the pro-British position of Simpson within eight hours or the town would be bombarded by cannons of the ship. Paulet made further demands, such as the payment of more than $100,000. The Hawaiian flag was replaced by the British flag on February 25, and three of the king's schooners were taken over.

The Union Jack flew over the islands for five months. Dr. G. P.

JUDD resigned when naval officers began to interfere with Hawaiian internal affairs. The arrival of Commodore Lawrence Kearney in his flagship, U.S.S. *Constellation*, caused it to be rumored that the Americans had recognized the independence of the islands. An open break between two nations was prevented by the timely arrival of Admiral Thomas in the *Dublin*, and the forced cession of Hawaii to Great Britain was ended.

PEIRCE, HENRY AUGUSTUS (1808–1885)

A successful merchant in Honolulu in the 1830s, Peirce returned to Boston but stopped in Hawaii in 1849 on a trading voyage to China. Seeing the possibilities of growing sugar cane, he organized the firm of H. A. Peirce & Co. in partnership with Judge William I. LEE and Charles R. BISHOP; from this beginning grew the present Lihue Plantation. In 1850 Peirce, James HUNNEWELL, and Charles BREWER, then all three residing in or near Boston, formed a partnership to conduct a freighting business between Boston and the leading ports of the Pacific; the Honolulu agent for this group was the firm of C. Brewer & Co. In 1853 Peirce supported the efforts of David M. WESTON in founding the Honolulu Iron Works.

In the summer of 1869 Peirce, who had kept in touch with Hawaiian interests in Washington, D.C., replaced General Edward M. McCook as American minister to Hawaii and served until 1878. He was a strong supporter of the idea of annexation of the islands by the United States, especially during the final years of Kamehameha V, last of the line of the conqueror. Peirce saw the need for a strong reciprocity treaty with the United States, and during the brief reign of LUNALILO advocated the inclusion of a clause that would cede the Pearl River lagoon as an American naval base; however, the signing of such a treaty did not come until the reign of KALAKAUA, whose election Peirce strongly supported and immediately recognized officially. Peirce was invited to accompany Kalakaua on his tour of the United States in 1874 and went with the party as far as Washington, D.C. After his replacement as American minister, Peirce acted as Hawaiian minister of foreign affairs for a few months in 1878 but was replaced by John M. KAPENA at the instigation of Walter Murray GIBSON.

PEMBERTON, CYRIL EUGENE (1886–1975)

Born in Los Angeles, Pemberton graduated from Mission High School in San Francisco and from Stanford University in 1911. He was associate entomologist at the United States Bureau of Entomology from that year until 1918, when he joined the Hawaiian Sugar Planters' Association Experiment Station and served until 1953. He visited many countries in search of insects beneficial to Hawaiian agriculture. Pemberton was author of more than a hundred papers on entomological subjects and a member of various commissions and professional societies.

PERCIVAL, JOHN (1779–1862)

Percival, who went to sea at the age of thirteen, was pressed into the Royal Navy and later fought as an American against this force during the War of 1812. He served as first lieutenant of Commodore Isaac Hull's flagship, U.S.S. *United States*, as part of the Pacific Exploring Squadron. He had achieved the nickname of "Mad Jack" or "Roaring Jack," and his temper matched his reputation. In command of the armed schooner *Dolphin*, he and his crew rounded up surviving mutineers of the whale ship *Globe* in the Marshall Islands and then headed north through the Hawaiian Chain.

The *Dolphin*, first American warship to visit Hawaii, arrived in Honolulu on January 16, 1826. The crew spent four months at the capital, refitting and carrying on business ashore. One result was the acknowledgement by the chiefs that they had run up a debt to American merchants of more than $300,000; this was the origin of the national debt of the Hawaiian kingdom. As a result of a missionary-inspired ban on the visiting of ships by Hawaiian women, a large group of sailors from the *Dolphin* and other ships broke into the house of Prime Minister KALANIMOKU on Sunday, February 26, and attacked the Rev. Hiram BINGHAM. Percival finally broke up the riot but the ban was revoked. When the captain returned to the United States he faced a court-martial for his behavior but was acquitted because he had helped to quell the mischief of his men. The cruise of the *Dolphin* is related by the first officer, Hiram Paulding (1797–1878) in *Journal of a Cruise of the United States Schooner "Dolphin"* (New York: G. & C. & H. Carvill, 1831; reprinted Honolulu: University of Hawaii Press, 1970, with an introduction by A. Grove Day).

PERKINS, EDWARD T.

Perkins sailed to Hawaii in 1848 and spent twenty months in the group before leaving for the Society Islands. He reveals in his book, in confidential style, many aspects of the life of Hawaii in mid-century. *See Na Motu; or Reef-Rovings in the South Seas* (New York: Pudney & Russell, 1854).

PERON, PIERRE FRANÇOIS (1769–1830?)

Perón was a French trading captain who owned his ship until it was captured by the British. He served as first officer under Captain Ebenezer Dorr of the Boston ship *Otter*. After cruising the Northwest Coast of America and California (the *Otter* was the first American ship to enter a California port), Dorr's ship reached Hawaii on December 2, 1796, and departed on New Year's Day for China. In his book, *Mémoires du Capitaine Perón sur ses voyages*, printed in two volumes in Paris in 1824, Perón reports that in 1796 about twenty-seven foreigners were residing in the islands, most of them quite happily. He gives a favorable description of KAMEHAMEHA I and stresses the power of the royal kapu. Perón settled in his native country and served as mayor of the town of Saumur, an office he gave up in 1830; his death date is unknown.

PÉROUSE. See LA PÉROUSE.

PERRIN, LOUIS EMILE (1810–1862)

The future French consul and commissioner first came to Hawaii in 1846 to sign a treaty on behalf of the French government. He succeeded Guillaume Patrice Dillon in 1851, arriving aboard the French warship *Sérieuse* on February 1 and repeating the famous ten demands of Legoarant de TROMELIN. When Perrin found that King KAMEHAMEHA III had signed a secret proclamation putting the islands under American protection, he modified his demands and returned to France. This ended the efforts of the French to annex Hawaii as they had annexed the Society and Marquesas Islands in the South Pacific.

PERRY, JASON (1826–1883)

Born on the island of Fayal in the Azores, Perry left home at seventeen on a whale ship and sailed around the Americas until he arrived in Honolulu in 1852 to live with his uncle. After a few years, Perry established himself in a drygoods store. He was appointed first consul for Portugal in Honolulu and served until he resigned because of poor health shortly before his death. His son, Antonio Perry, became a justice of the Hawaii Supreme Court.

PETIT-THOUARS, ABEL DU

Captain of the French warship *Vénus*, Petit-Thouars arrived off Honolulu in July, 1837, at the same time as Captain Edward Belcher of the British ship *Sulphur*. The two captains gave written pledges that the Catholic priests Bachelot and Short (see MAIGRET) would leave the islands at the first opportunity. Although Petit-Thouars had no authority to make a treaty, he signed a document on July 24 giving French subjects the same rights in Hawaii as those of the most favored other nation. The captain also appointed Jules DUDOIT as French consul. Petit-Thouars later took over the Society and Marquesas Islands as French protectorates.

PETRIE, LESTER (1878–1956)

Petrie was born in San Francisco but was brought to Hawaii as an infant. He attended Fort Street School and for fifty years was employed by the Oahu Railway & Land Co., retiring as general shop superintendent. He was a member of the Honolulu Board of Supervisors from 1913 to 1930, a territorial senator for four years, and mayor of the city for six years, 1941 to 1947. He served on various commissions and helped to establish the Shriner's Hospital for Crippled Children.

PIIKOI, DAVID KAHALEPOULI

Piikoi was the husband of Kinoiki Kekaulike (1843–1884) and the father of David KAWANANAKOA, Edward Keliiahonui (1869–1887), and Jonah Kuhio KALANIANAOLE.

PINKERTON, FORREST JAY (1892–1974)

Born in Lowell, Indiana, Pinkerton earned a degree at the Chicago College of Medicine and Surgery. He first came to Hawaii during World War I to serve at Schofield Barracks and Tripler Hospital in the Army Medical Corps. In 1920 he joined the staff of Queen's Hospital in Honolulu and served for twenty-six years. He was widely known as an ophthalmologist and was active in a number of medical and civic efforts. After the attack on Pearl Harbor in December, 1941, he helped to establish the Hawaii Blood Bank and was president and director for many years; the Blood Bank is still an important institution in Honolulu.

PINKHAM, LUCIUS EUGENE
(1850–1922)

Pinkham came to Hawaii from the mainland in 1891 and spent three years. He returned in 1898 and engaged in business until his retirement in 1903. He was president of the territorial Board of Health for two terms, and was concerned with the betterment of lepers at the Molokai colony. He also was in charge of methods to control bubonic plague and cholera epidemics. He was named fourth governor of Hawaii by President Woodrow Wilson in November, 1913, and served until June 22, 1918.

Since World War I broke out only a few months after he was appointed, Pinkham's administration was concerned with "preparedness" and Hawaii's participation in the war. One successful effort was the building up of a strong National Guard in the territory. Pinkham was also interested in the development of a civic center in Honolulu and in beginning the reclamation of Waikiki areas by draining and filling a large section of swamp land back from the beach. After his term ended, Pinkham continued world travels by touring Asia, Europe, and America.

PITT, BILLY
See KALANIMOKU.

POGUE, JOHN FAWCETT
(1814–1877)

Born in Wilmington, Delaware, Pogue graduated from Marietta College, Ohio, in 1840 and from Lane Theological Seminary, Ohio, in 1843. He was an unmarried member of the Eleventh Company of American missionaries that arrived in Hawaii in 1844. He was stationed at Koloa, Kauai, and in 1848 was transferred to Kaawaloa, Hawaii, and married Maria Kapule Whitney. Offspring of Samuel WHITNEY of the First Company, she was the first missionary daughter born in the islands, who after sixteen years in the United States had come back to Hawaii on the same ship as Pogue. The Pogues remained on the Big Island until 1850 and then were stationed at Lahainaluna from 1851 to 1866. They were then assigned to Waiohinu, Hawaii, from 1866 to 1868, and after a visit to Micronesia went to Honolulu, where Pogue was secretary of the Hawaiian Board from 1870 until he resigned from the Hawaiian Evangelical Association in 1877. The Pogues had four children.

POINDEXTER, JOSEPH
(1869–1951)

Born in Canyon City, Oregon, Poindexter was educated at Ohio Wesleyan University and earned a law degree from Washington University, St. Louis, in 1892. He won distinction at the Montana bar and was attorney general of that state when named a judge of the United States District Court in Hawaii in 1917. In 1924 he began a private law practice for a decade. He was named governor of the territory by President Franklin D. Roosevelt in 1934 and reappointed in 1938. Poindexter's first term fell during the depression years and the policy of frugality was continued. However, he helped to develop Keehi Lagoon as a seaplane base and greatly enlarged the Honolulu airport.

Realization that the territory was not free of adverse Congressional action further encouraged the statehood idea. The threat was enforced by the enactment in the spring of 1934 of the Jones-Costigan sugar control bill. The statehood movement was halted by the attack on Pearl Harbor on December 7, 1941, when Hawaii was immediately put on a war footing. In October of that year the Hawaii Defense Act, commonly called the M-Day Bill, giving the governor extended emergency powers, had been passed. At 11:30 a.m. on December 7, Poindexter proclaimed the existence of a defense period, and at 3:30 that afternoon, having talked with the president, he invoked martial law and requested Walter C. SHORT to take over all powers normally exercised by the governor. Thereafter for four years, civil government ceased to exist in Hawaii. Poindexter's second term expired in March, 1942, but he was not replaced until the inauguration on August 24 of Ingram M. STAINBACK. Poindexter returned to private practice until his death in 1951; he became a trustee of the Bernice P. Bishop Estate in 1943.

POKI
See BOKI.

POOMAIKELANI
See KAPIOLANI, QUEEN.

PORTEUS, STANLEY DAVID
(1883–1972)

Born in Victoria, Australia, Porteus married Frances Mainwaring Evans in 1909 and attended the University of Melbourne from 1912 to 1916. After teaching and administrative work in Melbourne he came to the United States and was naturalized in 1932. He became director of research at the Psychological Laboratory Training School at Vineland, New Jersey, from 1919 to 1925. He came to Hawaii as professor of clinical psychology and director of the Psychological and Psychopathic Clinic at the University of Hawaii in 1922 and served until 1948, when he retired.

Porteus was noted for his maze test of mental differences and his studies of primitive intelligence and environment. He led an expedition to northwestern Australia in 1929 and explored the Kalahari Desert of South Africa in 1934. He was author of a number of professional papers and some twenty volumes, including two novels (see CAMPBELL, Archibald). Non-fiction works about Hawaii include *Calabashes and Kings: An Introduction to Hawaii* (Palo Alto, Calif.: Pacific Books, 1954) and *And Blow Not the Trumpet* (Palo Alto, Calif.: Pacific Books, 1947), an account of the contributions of the sugar industry during World War II. Porteus edited *A Century of Social Thinking in Hawaii* (Palo Alto, Calif.: Pacific Books, 1962), a collection of essays presented before the Social Science Association of Honolulu. Porteus Hall on the Manoa campus of the University of Hawaii is named for the psychologist.

PORTLOCK, NATHANIEL (1748?–1817)
Born in the American Colonies, Portlock, like his fellow captain George DIXON, sailed on the third Pacific voyage of James COOK. Both captains returned to the islands in 1786 as masters of vessels making trading voyages between the Northwest Coast of America and China.

Portlock, in command of the *King George*, and Dixon, in command of the *Queen Charlotte*, were sent out by a group of English gentlemen who, under the name of the King George's Sound Company, had been given exclusive trading privileges on the Northwest Coast to avoid conflict with the South Sea Company and the East India Company. Later British ships on that coast thus had to sail under foreign flags. The two vessels left England in September, 1785, and

touched at the islands the following spring. The *King George* arrived May 24 and departed June 13; on another visit it arrived November 16 and wintered in the islands, departing on March 3, 1787. On a third visit it arrived September 27, 1787, and departed October 7.

Portlock and Dixon were the first foreign captains to visit the islands after the death of Cook seven years earlier. The frigates of LA PÉROUSE arrived off the island of Maui a few days after Portlock touched at the Big Island. The crews of Portlock and Dixon were the first to describe the life of the Hawaiians of the southern coast of Oahu. After returning from this voyage Portlock served in 1791 in command of the brig *Assistant* on the second breadfruit voyage of William BLIGH in the *Providence*. For the Hawaii visits, see Nathaniel Portlock, *A Voyage Round the World* (London: John Stockdale & George Goulding, 1789); this account was actually written by William Beresford, supercargo of the *Queen Charlotte*.

PRINCE OF HAWAII
See ALBERT.

PUAAIKI
See BARTIMEUS.

PUGET, PETER
Puget at the age of twelve enlisted in the Royal Navy in 1778 as a midshipman. As a lieutenant, he commanded the armed tender *Chatham* on the expedition of George VANCOUVER that visited Hawaii in 1792, 1793, and 1794. Puget first raised the British flag over Hawaii. After more than forty years of service he was promoted and commissioned Rear Admiral of the Blue. Puget Sound in the state of Washington, explored by Puget commanding sixteen men in two small boats in May, 1792, was named for him. See Robert Wing with Gordon Newell, *Peter Puget*, (Seattle: Gray Beard, 1979).

PURDY, IKUA (1873–1945)
Born at Mana on the Big Island's Parker Ranch, the outstanding paniolo, or Hawaiian cowboy, learned to ride before he could walk. He worked on this ranch and later on the Ulupalakua Ranch on Maui. He won the world steer-roping championship at the Cheyenne Frontier Days celebration in 1908 by roping, busting, and hog-tying his animal in fifty-six seconds.

QUIMPER, MANUEL
See COLNETT, James.

RESTARICK, HENRY BOND (1854–1933)
Born in Holcomb, England, the future Episcopal bishop of Honolulu was educated at King James School, Bridgewater. He became a naturalized citizen of the United States in 1879 and after attending Griswold College at Davenport, Iowa, was ordained as a priest in 1882. In the same year he married May L. Baker and they had three children. Restarick was given charge of the parish of San Diego, California, which at the time was larger than the State of Massachusetts. He was granted a divinity degree from King's College, Nova Scotia, in 1903.

After annexation of Hawaii, it was decided that the American Episcopal Church should have charge of the formerly autonomous Anglican Church in the islands, and on April 16, 1902, Restarick was elected the first American bishop of Honolulu. He was a friend of Queen LILIUOKALANI and conducted her funeral services. Membership in his church quadrupled under his eighteen years as bishop; he retired from active work in 1920. His best known work is *Hawaii, 1778–1920, From the Viewpoint of a Bishop* (Honolulu: Paradise of the Pacific, 1924, 1925). See his *My Personal Recollections* (Honolulu: Paradise of the Pacific, 1938), edited by Constance Restarick Withington.

REYNOLDS, STEPHEN
(1782–1857)

Born in Massachusetts, Reynolds made three visits to Hawaii on his ship *New Hazard* in 1811 and 1812, during the war between the United States and Great Britain. During a fourth visit in 1813 he arrived on the *Isabella* and returned on the *New Hazard*. In 1822 he returned to reside in Honolulu as merchant, lawyer, and harbor master. He was fond of sports and games and collided with missionaries who ruled against such pleasures. His first wife was Hawaiian; after her death in 1829 he married Susan Jackson. In August, 1845, he was declared a lunatic; his business was put in the hands of trustees, and he was sent back to Boston in May, 1856.

RICE, WILLIAM HARRISON
(1813–1862)

Born in Oswego, New York, Rice married Mary Sophia Hyde in October, 1840, and six weeks later the couple sailed from Boston with the Ninth Company of American missionaries. Arriving in Honolulu in 1841, they declined assignment to the Oregon Mission and were stationed at Hana, Maui, from that year until 1844. Rice was then a teacher at Punahou School until 1854, when he completed his term with the mission and moved his growing family to the island of Kauai. There he took over management of the Lihue Sugar Plantation, originally owned by H. A. PEIRCE & Co. Like his son, William Hyde RICE, the father was a student of Hawaiian legends, especially the myth of Pele. His eldest daughter married Paul ISENBERG. For an account of the Rice family on Kauai, see Ethel M. Damon, *Koamalu* (Honolulu: privately printed, 1931).

RICE, WILLIAM HYDE
(1846–1924)

Eldest son of William Harrison RICE, the future governor of Kauai was born in Honolulu. He attended a boarding school at Koloa, Kauai, Punahou School, and Braton's College in Oakland, California. He married Mary Waterhouse in 1872, and they reared eight children. For two years Rice was manager of the ranch at Lihue Plantation under Paul ISENBERG, his brother-in-law, and later was president of William Hyde Rice & Co., which owned Kipu Plantation and Lihue Ranch. He bred cattle and fine horses. Rice was for eight years a member of the House of Representatives under the monarchy. He was appointed governor of Kauai by Queen LILIUOKALANI and later helped to draw up the Constitution of the Republic of Hawaii. Rice spoke Hawaiian fluently and is known today as author of a valuable collection, *Hawaiian Legends* (Honolulu: Bishop Museum Bulletin No. 3, 1933).

RICHARDS, ATHERTON
(1895–1974)

Born of a missionary family, Richards was president of the Hawaiian Pineapple Co. from 1932 until 1941, when he was replaced for promoting a law forbidding the export of pineapple plants to foreign growers. During World War II he worked for the Office of Strategic Services. He then pursued a business career in New York and Washington, D.C. He was appointed a trustee of the Bishop Estate in 1952. He earned a reputation as a fighter and dissenter, sometimes taking out full-page newspaper advertisements to argue his views. In 1957 he tried to have Diamond Head Crater converted into a spectacular auditorium. In 1961 he supported the opening of Pearl Harbor for commercial use. In 1967 he opposed the Land Reform Bill, as well as the proposed location of the State Capitol. Richards took his fellow trustees of the Bishop Estate to court over land sales and developments that he opposed. He owned the 36,000-acre Kahua Ranch on the Big Island.

RICHARDS, WILLIAM
(1793–1847)

Born in Plainfield, Massachusetts, Richards was educated at Williams College and was ordained in 1822 after studying at Andover Theological Seminary. He married Clarissa Lyman in 1822 and the couple sailed for Hawaii the same year as members of the Second Company of American missionaries. Richards and C. S. STEWART were the pioneer ministers at the port of Lahaina, Maui. Their efforts were not appreciated by visiting seamen; in 1825 a mob from the whale ship *Daniel* besieged the Richards house but was driven away by friendly Hawaiians. Three years later Richards performed no fewer than six hundred wedding ceremonies within a few months; the grooms of the port often loudly responded "Aye, aye!" in place of "I do."

The need of the chiefs for tutelage in foreign customs was recognized in 1838 when Richards resigned from the mission to serve as "translator and recorder." As a result of his instruction, the chiefs began working

on a document that resulted in the Constitution of 1840, the first written embodiment of the government's functions. Richards and Timoteo HAALILIO left the islands on July 18, 1842, on a mission to join Sir George SIMPSON to obtain recognition. American recognition was reaffirmed to Richards and when the three signed a declaration in London in November 28, 1843, granting British and French recognition, American recognition was reaffirmed to Richards and Haalilio in Washington in the summer of 1844.

Richards was appointed the first minister of public instruction for the kingdom in 1846, and was succeeded at his death the following year by Richard ARMSTRONG. Richards translated about one third of the entire Hawaiian Bible. The couple had eight children; one descendant was Atherton RICHARDS. See Samuel Williston, *William Richards* (Cambridge, Mass.: privately printed, 1938).

RICHARDSON, ROBERT CHARLWOOD Jr. (1882–1954)

Born in South Carolina, Richardson graduated from the United States Military Academy in 1904 and devoted his career to the American army. He served in the Philippines and Europe, and was commandant of cadets at West Point from 1928 to 1933.

Lieutenant General Richardson was named commander of the Hawaiian Department and military governor of Hawaii in June, 1943, and commanding general of the United States Army forces in the Central Pacific in August. The following August he was head of all Army forces in the Pacific Ocean region. He carried out his duties as head of martial law in Hawaii until his retirement in 1946. He issued the notorious General Order No. 31 which threatened federal judges, lawyers, and others with fines and imprisonment if they attempted to file applications for the constitutional writ of habeas corpus. During the following proceedings, the general was fined $5,000 for contempt of court (later reduced to $100) but was pardoned by President Roosevelt. Richardson was decorated by five countries and was awarded the Distinguished Service Medal and the Legion of Merit.

RICORD, JOHN (1812–1861)

Born in Belville, New Jersey, Ricord was trained in New York as a lawyer and briefly served as secretary of state of the newly formed Republic of Texas in 1836. He arrived in Hawaii in February, 1844, at a time when it was clear that the government had to be put on a better organized footing, and he was at once appointed attorney general of the kingdom—a post he held for exactly three years. During this time, "the father of statute law in Hawaii" settled most of the outstanding government cases, usually to its advantage. Although of a disputatious nature that stirred up some hostility, Ricord had strong qualities of industry, honesty, and loyalty. His report of May 21, 1845, resulted in the passing of the organic acts of 1845–1847 that gave the kingdom an administrative and judicial system on Anglo-Saxon principles. In drafting these acts, Ricord, along with William L. LEE, took a leading part.

Ricord fell into debt and resigned in the spring of 1847 to face charges against him, of which he was acquitted in June. He departed from the islands in the autumn, and in 1854 the legislature passed an act releasing him of his debts.

RIVES, JEAN-BAPTISTE JASSONT LAFAYETTE (JOHN) (1793–1833)

Born in Bordeaux, France, Rives arrived in the islands in 1810, became a close friend of the future KAMEHAMEHA II, and gave medical advice to the chiefs. Rives was almost a dwarf in stature; KAAHUMANU gave him the name of "Luahine" (old woman) and protected him from harm. He married her niece, the chiefess Kaheikeimalie Holau, and held extensive lands on Oahu, Molokai, Maui, and the Big Island. He was chosen to accompany Kamehameha II and his party to England in 1823 as royal secretary. In France, he proposed the founding of a Catholic colony in the Hawaiian Islands; his plan resulted in the introduction of this religion (see MAIGRET) and various attempts by French warships to take over the group. Rives never returned to Hawaii but died in Mexico.

ROBINSON, AUBREY (1853–1936)

Robinson was born in Canterbury, New Zealand, son of Charles Barrington and Helen Sinclair Robinson, and came to Hawaii in 1863 with the family of Eliza McHutcheson SINCLAIR. He attended Boston University Law School and for several years traveled extensively in Europe and the Orient. On returning to Hawaii he began the cultivation of sugar cane and the breeding of Devon cattle on the family lands at Makaweli, Kauai, in partnership with Francis Gay, his cousin, under the name of Gay & Robinson.

Irrigation water was brought to the plantation in ditches from the Olokele and Koula Valleys through one of the greatest engineering feats in Hawaii at the time. The family also owned the small neighboring island of Niihau, which became a ranch devoted to the raising of purebred merino sheep and shorthorn cattle from the United States, Australia, and New Zealand. The first purebred Arabian horses in Hawaii were imported by Robinson from Arabia in 1884. About this time he also brought in a number of game birds and released them on the western side of Kauai, and stocked the streams of the island with trout and bass. He also introduced various improved varieties of tropical fruit trees to the region. Robinson married Alice Gay in 1885, and their five children left a number of descendants in the islands. One son was Aylmer Francis ROBINSON, rancher on the island of Maui.

ROBINSON, AYLMER FRANCIS (1888–1967)

Born at Makaweli, Kauai, son of Aubrey ROBINSON, Aylmer studied at St. Matthew's Military Academy and earned a bachelor's degree at Harvard in 1910. He became manager of the family's Makaweli Ranch in 1912 and held this post for ten years. In 1916 he became a partner in the Gay & Robinson sugar and cattle company and in 1920 business manager of the concern. In 1922 he resigned and took over management of the family island of Niihau, which is less than a hundred square miles in area. He tried to maintain the traditional Hawaiian culture among the Niihau residents and introduced honey and charcoal production to the economy in addition to rearing sheep and cattle.

ROBINSON, JAMES

Born in London, Robinson was carpenter on the brig *Hermes* that arrived in Honolulu in 1820 shortly before the first missionary ship, *Thaddeus*. In April, 1822, heading for Japan, the *Hermes* was wrecked on what was named Pearl and Hermes Reef in the leeward Hawaiian archipelago. Robinson built a small schooner from the wreckage and the survivors sailed back to Honolulu to remain permanently. With Robert Lawrence, a friend and fellow seafarer from England, Robinson established the firm of James Robinson & Co. in 1823; their shipyard was a landmark on the waterfront and the partnership lasted until 1868, when Lawrence died. Robinson married Rebecca Prever and founded a pioneer family. Among their eight children were Mary E. FOSTER, Victoria WARD, and Mark Prever Robinson, born in 1852, who was active in a lumber and shipping business as well as associated with a firm that operated inter-island sailing vessels with names like *Malolo*, *Haleakala*, and *Leahi*.

ROCK, JOSEPH FRANCIS CHARLES (1884–1962)

Born and educated in Austria, Rock came to Hawaii in 1907 as botanist for the Territorial Board of Agriculture and Forestry, and was a professor at the College of Hawaii from 1911 to 1919. He spent more than twenty years in remote southwestern China and was considered one of the world's leading botanists and linguists, as well as a ranking ornithologist, anthropologist, cartographer, and author. He wrote *Indigenous Trees of the Hawaiian Islands* (Honolulu: privately printed, 1913). He introduced blight-resistant chestnut trees into America from China, along with more than two hundred species of rhododendrons.

Rock was the first honorary member of the Board of Trustees of the Friends of Foster Gardens. See Stephanne Barry Sutton, *In China's Border Provinces: The Turbulent Career of Joseph Rock, Botanist-Explorer* (New York: Hastings House, 1974).

ROGERS, EDMUND HORTON (1807–1853)

Born in Newton, Massachusetts, and trained as a printer, Rogers was unmarried when he came to Hawaii with the Fifth Company of American missionaries in 1832. He was stationed in Honolulu in sole charge of the mission printing office, and in 1833 married Mary Ward. She died in 1834 and in 1836 he married Elizabeth Hitchcock, who bore him four children. Rogers worked at Lahainaluna Seminary from 1835 to 1840 and then returned to the Honolulu printing office, where he remained until his death.

ROOKE, T. C. B.

See EMMA.

ROWELL, GEORGE BERKELEY (1815–1884)

Born in Cornish, New Hampshire, Rowell graduated from Amherst College in 1837 and Andover Theological Seminary in 1841. He married Malvina Jerusha Chapin in April, 1842, and the couple sailed in May with the Tenth Company of American missionaries. The Rowells were stationed at Waioli, Kauai, from 1843 to 1846, and at Waimea, Kauai, from 1846 to 1853. He broke his connection with the Boston commissioners in that year and led a brotherhood of independent churches. Rowell built the great stone church at Waimea and later built a small wooden one nearby. The Rowells had seven children.

RUGGLES, SAMUEL (1795–1871)

Born in Brookfield, Connecticut, Ruggles studied at the mission school at Cornwall before sailing with the First Company of American missionaries in 1819. He and his wife, Nancy Wells Ruggles (1791–1873), future mother of six children, helped to establish two mission stations in the islands: one at Waimea, Kauai, with the Samuel WHITNEYS, and another, at Hilo, with the Joseph GOODRICHES. Ruggles, who was so beloved by the Hawaiians that they called him "Keiki" (child), struggled with ill health and finally returned to the United States with his family in 1834. Ruggles was a brother of Mrs. Thomas HOLMAN.

RUTH KEELIKOLANI (LUKA) (1826–1883)

Princess Ruth Keeuolani Kauanahoahoa Keelikolani was the daughter of Mataio KEKUANAOA and Pauahi. She was thus a half-sister of KAMEHAMEHA IV, KAMEHAMEHA V, and VICTORIA KAMAMALU. Soon after the death of her mother in childbirth the infant was placed under the care of KAAHUMANU. Ruth was too old to attend the Chief's Children's School when it was started, but was able to make herself understood in English. Ruth married twice. Her first husband was LELEIOHOKU, son of KALANIMOKU; one child died in infancy and the other, William Pitt Kinau (1842–1859), at the age of seventeen. Ruth's second husband was Isaac Young Davis, a grandson of Isaac DAVIS the sailor. A child of this couple died in infancy, but Ruth adopted a young brother of David KALAKAUA and named him William Pitt LELEIOHOKU. When this heir died in 1877, Ruth, who

owned large estates and houses, left most of her great wealth to Bernice PAUAHI. Ruth was "the largest and richest woman on the islands," according to Isabel Bird BISHOP, who saw her in 1874. "Her size and appearance are most unfortunate, but she is said to be good and kind." See Kristin Zambucka, *The High Chiefess Ruth Keelikolani* (Honolulu: Mana Publishing Co., 1977).

SAMWELL, DAVID (1751–1798)

Samwell, a Welsh physician, wrote the foremost account of the death of Captain James COOK. Samwell had a good education and qualified for medical service in the Royal Navy in 1775. The next year he was appointed surgeon's mate on Cook's *Resolution* during the third Pacific voyage, and later was promoted to surgeon on the *Discovery*. He kept a valuable log during the voyage, and his opinions on the introduction of venereal disease into Hawaii at this time are usually quoted to show that he held Cook's sailors to be not guilty of this act. His little book, *A Narrative of the Death of Captain James Cook* (London: Robinson, 1786), is a touching memorial. Samwell continued to serve on Navy ships until 1796. In his later years he was a member of the Welsh literary circle in London and produced much prose and verse in English and Welsh.

SCHEFFER, GEORG ANTON (EGOR NIKOLAEVICH SCHEFFER) (1779–1836)

Born in Bavaria, son of a miller, the future leader of the Russian filibustering forces in Hawaii gained a medical degree in Göttingen, Germany. He became a surgeon in the Russian army and in 1812 was building balloons in Moscow from which to observe the movements of Napoleon's troops. Dr. Scheffer was physician on the Russian-American Company's ship

Suvorov in 1813, but left it in Alaska. With orders from Aleksander BARANOV, Scheffer arrived in Hawaii toward the end of 1815, posing as a visiting botanist. He cured Kamehameha I of a feverish cold and as a reward was given lands on Oahu. He and his men began building a blockhouse on the Honolulu waterfront, an act that aroused John YOUNG to obtain an order from the king to halt the work. The blockhouse was completed by the Hawaiians in 1816 and gave its name to downtown Fort Street.

Reinforced by three Russian ships and their crews, Scheffer withdrew to the island of Kauai. There King KAUMUALII—who had promised Kamehameha in 1810 that after his death his realm would become a part of the kingdom of the conqueror—on May 21, 1816, signed a treasonous document putting Kauai under the protection of Czar Alexander Pavlovich of Russia. The Czar's flag flew over part of the Hawaiian Islands for the following year. Scheffer built a stronghold, Fort Elizabeth, at Waimea and breastworks in the valley of Hanalei. He had, however, aroused the fears of Kamehameha, as well as the antagonism of American ship captains, who feared that Russia would monopolize the profitable sandalwood trade. In May, 1817, Kaumualii renounced the filibusters, the Russian ships were sent away empty, and on July 7 Scheffer left for Macao on an American vessel. The acts of Scheffer were disowned by Otto von KOTZEBUE during his 1816 visit to the islands. The Czar ignored the benefits of a protectorate over Kauai and in June, 1819, authorized only normal trade relations; thereafter the shadow of a possible Russian colony in the Northern Pacific was removed.

Scheffer went to Brazil in 1821 and was made a nobleman by Emperor

Dom Pedro I under the title of Count von Frankenthal; he imported colonists to his estates and died far from his native Europe. See A. Grove Day, *Adventurers of the Pacific* (New York: Meredith Press, 1969), Chapter 1, with bibliography.

SCHENCK, EDGAR CRAIG (1909–1959)

Born in North Carolina, Schenck earned a bachelor's degree from Princeton University in 1931 and a master's degree in 1934. He was a member of archaeological expeditions to Angers, France, in 1931; to Minturno, Italy, in 1932; and to Syria in 1933. He married Belle Lupton Pike in 1934 and became acting director of the Honolulu Academy of Arts and an instructor at the University of Hawaii. Schenck was director of the Academy from 1936 to 1947 and did much to build its collections. Later he directed other museums: Smith College, 1946–1949; Albright in Buffalo, New York, 1949–1954; and Brooklyn, New York, 1954–1959. Schenck died in Istanbul, Turkey, while on a world speaking tour sponsored by the State Department.

SCHOFIELD, JOHN McALLISTER (1831–1906)

A West Point graduate of 1853, Schofield won the Congressional Medal of Honor in the American Civil War and was one of Sherman's leaders in the march through Georgia. He served from 1868 to 1869 as secretary of war under President Andrew Johnson. He was headquartered in San Francisco in command of the Military Division of the Pacific in 1872 with the rank of major general when he was ordered to go to Hawaii "for the purpose of ascertaining the defensive

capabilities of the different ports and their commercial facilities, and . . . to collect all information that would be of service to the country in the event of war with a powerful maritime nation."

Schofield arrived on the U.S.S. *California* in company with Brevet Brigadier General B. S. Alexander of the Corps of Engineers, ostensibly on a vacation. The pair spent about two months visiting the islands of Oahu, Kauai, and Hawaii, and discussed the possibility of a reciprocity treaty with the newly elected King LUNALILO. Schofield made a secret report stating that he was much impressed with Pearl Harbor as the only feasible port in the North Pacific, and prophesied that annexation of Hawaii by the United States would arrive by a process of evolution. Schofield retired in 1895 with the rank of lieutenant general. Schofield Barracks, the military installation on the Leilehua plain in central Oahu, started in 1908, bears the general's name.

SCOTT, MARION MacCARRELL (1843–1920)

Born in Fauquier, Kentucky, Scott attended Urania College and the University of Virginia. In 1874, after teaching in San Francisco, he became a member of the faculty of the Imperial University in Japan; he organized the first normal school in that country and founded a system of public schools. He came to Hawaii in 1881 and established the first public high school, Honolulu High School (later renamed McKinley) on King Street. He was principal from 1885 to 1919, and helped to provide secondary education to many young people of varied ethnic backgrounds. His daughter, Gertrude Scott Ivers Straub, established a two-million-dollar trust fund in her father's name to provide scholarships for Hawaii public-school graduates attending mainland colleges and universities.

SHALER, WILLIAM (1773?–1833)

Shaler, American trader, was the partner of Richard CLEVELAND when the *Lelia Byrd* brought the first horses to Hawaii in 1803. On Shaler's second visit, in 1805, the *Lelia Byrd* leaked so badly that he exchanged her for the *Tamana*, a schooner being built for Kamehameha I. The *Lelia Byrd* became the flagship of the king's growing fleet.

SHEPARD, STEPHEN (1800–1834)

Shepard was employed as a printer in New York when he decided to become a member of the mission to Hawaii. He married Margaret Caroline Slow in October, 1827, and the couple sailed with the Third Company in November. They were stationed at Honolulu, where Shepard worked in the printing office from 1828 to 1831; in the latter year he spent some time at Lahainaluna Seminary before returning to Honolulu to serve until his death three years later. The Shepards had three children.

SHINGLE, ROBERT WITT (1876–1935)

Born in Cheyenne, Wyoming, Shingle was a cub reporter on the local newspaper published by his father, and for three years worked on the Denver *Republican*. From 1896 to 1898 he was city editor of the *Hawaiian Star* in Honolulu and then worked for a year on the Honolulu *Advertiser* before joining the real-estate firm of Henry Waterhouse & Co. Shingle was associated with this firm from 1899 until 1931, when it merged with the Bishop Trust Co. Later he was officer or director of half a dozen other concerns.

Shingle married Muriel Campbell, daughter of James CAMPBELL, in 1909 and their eight children were among the heirs of the Campbell Estate. In the same year he was elected to the territorial legislature, and from 1911 to 1913 he was treasurer of the City and County of Honolulu. He was elected to the senate in 1916 and 1922. Shingle was chairman of the central committee of the Republican Party, participated in every political campaign for many years after annexation, and was a close advisor of Prince Jonah Kuhio KALANIANAOLE. With the prince and others, Shingle succeeded in having the Republican National Convention adopt a pledge to give home rule to Hawaii; he helped in 1921 to have Congress enact a bill permitting only residents to hold judgeships and important federal positions in the islands. He built the Robert W. Shingle Jr. Memorial Hospital at Hoolehua, Molokai, in 1931, at the time the only hospital on that island.

SHIPMAN, WILLIAM CORNELIUS (1824–1861)
Born in Wethersfield, Connecticut, Shipman graduated from the Mission Institute, Quincy, Illinois, in 1850, and the New Haven Theological Seminary, Connecticut, in 1853. He married Jane Stobie in that year and the couple arrived in the ship *Chaska* at Lahaina in 1854. They were stationed at Waiohinu, Hawaii, where Shipman labored until his death six years later. The Shipmans had three children. The wife continued with her family school, and later married William H. Reed of Hilo.

SHORT, PATRICK
See MAIGRET.

SHORT, WALTER CAMPBELL (1880–1949)
Born in Fillmore, Illinois, Short graduated from the University of Illinois in 1901 and was appointed second lieutenant in the United States Army the following year. He served in the Philippines and Alaska and on the Mexican border in 1916 before acting as assistant chief of staff of the

Third Army after the outbreak of World War II. Lieutenant General Short came to Hawaii in February, 1941, in command of the Hawaiian Department of the United States Army, which on December 7 suffered the attack of Japanese warplanes. On December 8, at the request of Governor Joseph B. POINDEXTER, he assumed the post of governor of Hawaii under martial law. Short was replaced by Delos C. EMMONS on December 17, returned to the mainland in February, 1942, and retired from the Army during the next month. Two years later, he was exonerated by a court of inquiry for his actions during the attack, but a Congressional investigation in 1945–1946 found that responsibility for the defeat lay with Short and Admiral Husband E. KIMMEL.

SIMPSON, ALEXANDER
Nephew of Sir George SIMPSON, Alexander left the employ of the Hudson's Bay Co. in Canada and between 1839 and 1842 made four visits to Hawaii. Unlike his peacemaking uncle, Alexander allied himself with Richard CHARLTON and other anti-American residents who hoped to make Hawaii a colony of the British Empire. Simpson was made acting consul of Great Britain by Charlton when Charlton left for London in 1842. On the arrival of Lord George PAULET, Simpson pursued his efforts to annex Hawaii. He journeyed to London to carry Paulet's report to the Foreign Office and continued to argue British claims in opposition to those of the American courier, J. F. B. MARSHALL, both of whom arrived in London in June, 1843. After Great Britain decided to acknowledge Hawaiian independence, Simpson, embittered, retired to private life.

SIMPSON, SIR GEORGE (1792–1860)
Simpson entered the service of the Hudson's Bay Co. in 1820, and became governor of the company's Canadian interests in 1821. He was knighted twenty years later. He came to Hawaii in February, 1842, to explore commercial possibilities. In August Captain S. MALLET threatened the chiefs, and British expansionists led by Richard CHARLTON and Simpson's nephew, Alexander SIMPSON, were seeking annexation by the British Empire.

Sir George, anticipating the eventual London decision in favor of independence, granted £10,000 of his company's funds to finance the mission of William RICHARDS and Timoteo HAALILIO. In February, 1843, the three envoys began negotiations in London, and on November 28 in that city a document was signed giving British and French recognition of Hawaiian independence; American recognition was to follow. Thus, despite the complication of the PAULET episode, the "grand ultimate object" of the proposal of Sir George was attained. His account of travels, *Narrative of a Journey Round the World during the Years 1841 and 1842* (Philadelphia: Lea & Blanchard, 1847; London: H. Colburn, 1847), is of interest to the history of British Columbia as well as of Hawaii.

SINCLAIR, ARCHIBALD NEIL (1871–1930)
Born in New York, Sinclair was brought to Hawaii as a boy by his father, who was associated with the construction of Iolani Palace. The young man attended Punahou School

and studied medicine in Glasgow, Scotland, and Yaxley, England. He first practised in Waianae, Oahu, and in 1900, the year he married Flora Margaret Perry, he began serving for nine years as physician of the city of Honolulu. He was also made a director of Leahi Home in that year, and later devoted all his time to Leahi Hospital as medical director; one of the buildings at that facility is named for him. Dr. Sinclair was physician in charge of the tuberculosis bureau and bacteriological department of the Territorial Board of Health from 1911 to 1916, and was made a fellow of the American College of Physicians in recognition of his work on tuberculosis. He was a strong advocate of preventive measures and made studies of several other diseases.

SINCLAIR, ELIZA McHUTCHESON (1803–1895)

Born in Scotland, Eliza McHutcheson married Captain Francis S. Sinclair, who had commanded the British man-of-war on which the Duke of Wellington made his triumphant return to England after the battle of Waterloo. The couple emigrated to New Zealand in 1840. She was widowed when her husband was lost at sea off Christchurch, New Zealand. She sold her property in 1863 and left with her family on the *Corsair*, a vessel owned and sailed by her son-in-law. It was laden with household goods, farming tools, and valuable sheep.

The family first went to British Columbia by way of Tahiti and Hawaii. When Canada did not suit Mrs. Sinclair, she brought the clan back to Hawaii. Soon after their arrival, KAMEHAMEHA V put the island of Niihau up for sale in 1864. Mrs. Sinclair bought the land in 1864 in the names of her two sons for $10,000. She also bought tracts of land at Makaweli and other regions on the island of Kauai. This was the origin of the landholding dynasty of the Sinclair-Robinsons. The matriarch lived until the age of ninety-two. The island of Niihau is still private property, and few persons have been given permission to visit there. See Aubrey ROBINSON and Aylmer Francis ROBINSON.

SINCLAIR, GREGG MANNERS (1890–1976)

Born in St. Mary's, Ontario, Canada, Sinclair earned a bachelor's degree from the University of Minnesota in 1912 and a master's degree from Columbia University in 1919. He taught English in Japan from 1912 to 1915 and then engaged in business in Minneapolis until he joined the Department of English at the University of Hawaii in 1928. Thereafter he was associated with the University; he was president from 1942 to 1955, when he became president emeritus. He married Marjorie Putnam in 1939. Sinclair was director of the Oriental Institute of the University from 1935 to 1945, and early recognized the possible role of Hawaii in cultural exchange that led to the founding of the East-West Center on that campus. Under his guidance the University made many advances before and after World War II; Sinclair was co-founder with Charles A. Moore of the first East-West Philosophers' Conference in 1939. For many years Sinclair was chairman of the Citizens' Advisory Committee on Statehood for Hawaii and he was an influential member of the Democratic Party. Sinclair Library on the Manoa campus of the University bears his name.

SMITH, ASA BOWEN (1809–1886)

Born in Williamstown, Vermont, Smith graduated from Middlebury College, Vermont, in 1834 and from Andover Theological Seminary in 1837. He married Sarah Gilbert White in March, 1838, and in the same month they left overland for the mission field in Oregon. At Lapwai in what is now Idaho, he helped to prepare material in the language of the Nez Percé Indians such as seen in the primer printed by E. O. HALL. The Smiths were sent to Honolulu, arriving in January, 1842, and were stationed from 1843 to 1845 at Waialua, Oahu. They returned to the United States in 1845.

SMITH, JAMES WILLIAM (1810–1887)

Born in Stamford, Connecticut, Smith was educated at the New York College of Physicians and Surgeons. He practised medicine in that city for five years before sailing with his wife, Melicent Knapp Smith, with the Tenth Company of American missionaries. The couple arrived in 1842 and were stationed at Koloa, Kauai, for the remainder of their lives. In 1844 Smith was the only physician on the island, but was helped from that year until 1848 by the Rev. John POGUE. He was also assisted by Samuel Kahookui, a graduate of the second class at Lahainaluna Seminary. Dr. Smith fell ill during an 1845 influenza epidemic and took a whaling cruise to correct a lung ailment. In 1851 he asked to be released from the Mission Board and in 1854 was ordained and installed as pastor of Koloa Church, although he continued his medical practice. Mrs. Smith established the Koloa Boarding School for Girls in 1861 and maintained it for ten years. The couple reared nine children.

SMITH, LOWELL (1802–1891)

Born in Heath, Massachusetts, Smith graduated from Williams College in 1829 and from Auburn Theological Seminary in 1832. He married Abigail Willis Tenney in October, 1832, and the couple sailed with the Sixth Company of American missionaries in November. They were stationed at Kaluaaha, Molokai, in 1833 and at Ewa, Oahu, in 1834. Smith was assigned to Honolulu in 1836, first as superintendent of the Kawaiahao schools and then for thirty years as pastor of the Second Church (Kaumakapili). He retired from the pastorate in 1869 but still worked for the Hawaiian people for the rest of his life.

Mrs. Smith began a day school for Hawaiian children in Nuuanu Valley, to which from time to time came English, Chinese, Negro, and Pacific Island students. In 1856 this became a government school, the first English-teaching common school in Hawaii. Only two of her children survived infancy; Emma Louisa (1844–1920) married Benjamin Franklin DILLINGHAM in 1869. See *Lowell and Abigail: A Realistic Idyll* (New Haven, Conn.: privately printed, 1934) by Mary Dillingham Frear, a granddaughter of the Smiths.

SMITH, MARCIA MARIA (1806–1896)

Born in Burlington, New York, Miss Smith arrived in Hawaii in 1837 with the Eighth Company of American missionaries. She was first stationed at Kaneohe, Oahu, as a teacher, and later opened a forerunner of Punahou School in Honolulu with twenty pupils, children of missionaries. She conducted classes in the backyard of Dr. Gerrit P. JUDD. Later she taught children of missionaries at Koloa, Kauai. After Punahou School was organized in 1842 she was associated with the Daniel DOLE family as matron and teacher for eleven years. She returned to the United States in 1852 but kept up her interest in Punahou during the remaining forty-four years of her life. She was a sister of the second wife of Lorenzo LYONS.

SMYTH, MABEL LEILANI (1892–1936)

Mabel Smyth, who was part Hawaiian, graduated from Simmons College, Boston, and completed studies at the Springfield Hospital School of Nursing, Massachusetts. She returned to Honolulu to become a director of the Palama Settlement's public health nursing service. In 1927 this work was joined with that of the Territorial Board of Health, and she directed the combined service until her death. A nationally recognized figure in public health nursing, she was honored by having a building near Queen's Hospital named for her in 1941.

SOARES, ANTONIO V. (1860–1930)

Born at St. Jorge in the Azores, Soares was one of the many Protestants persecuted in his native land who became refugees in the United States. He and his wife, Rachel Fernandez Soares, came to Hawaii in 1890. He was asked by the Hawaiian Board of Missions to care for the Portuguese Protestants. He was ordained at Central Union Church in 1891, and after five years of meetings in temporary quarters, the cornerstone of his church was laid in July, 1896. Soares assisted in the development of Portuguese churches on Maui and at Hilo, and for forty years helped his minority group to establish themselves in the larger community. The son, Oliver P. Soares, became a well-known lawyer in Honolulu.

SOGA, YASUTARO (1873–1957)

Born in Tokyo, Soga attended the Tokyo Pharmacy School and the English Law Institute. He arrived in Hawaii in 1896 and after four years as a clerk in stores became assistant editor of the *Hawaii Shimpo*; he was editor by 1906. As a result of the strike by Japanese laborers on the sugar plantations of Oahu in 1909 and 1910, Soga was imprisoned with three other Japanese leaders on March 10, 1910, but was pardoned by Governor Walter F. FREAR on July 4. Soga attended the coronation of Emperor Taisho in 1915 and the Washington Conference on Limitation of Naval Armaments in 1921, and was the only Japanese from Hawaii to be invited to the Imperial Chrysanthemum Party in Tokyo in 1934. In 1919 Soga became editor, president, and publisher of the *Nippu Jiji* and began a section in English, the first published by any Japanese newspaper. The name was changed to *Hawaii Times* in 1942, during World War II.

SOPER, JOHN HARRIS (1846–1944)

Born in Plymouth, England, Soper was brought by his parents to New York and then to Illinois, where he attended normal school. He went to California in 1861 and was active in mining and engineering until he came to Hawaii in 1877. He began a career in raising sugar cane by becoming manager of the Pioneer Mill at Lahaina, Maui. He was first appointed marshal of the kingdom in 1884 to succeed William C. PARKE; after two years he resigned to re-enter business, but King KALAKAUA again called him to the post in 1888.

Soper was head of the force that suppressed the Robert W. WILCOX rebellion of 1889, but resigned once more in 1890. When the critical year of 1893 arrived, Soper was called upon by the Provisional Government to head their forces, and under his command the monarchy was bloodlessly overthrown. He was commissioned in January, 1894, as general in the National Guard, and suppressed the counter-revolution of 1895. He continued in this office until 1907, when he was retired with the rank of brigadier general by authorization of the War Department in Washington. During all these years, Soper's business interests prospered. He married Mary Wundenberg of Vallejo, California, in 1871, and the couple had five children. Soper lived for almost a century, and spent two thirds of his career in Hawaii.

SPALDING, ZEPHANIAH SWIFT

With the Civil War rank of a lieutenant colonel, Spalding, son of a United States Congressman, arrived in Honolulu in December, 1867, to secretly sound out opinion concerning a reciprocity treaty then being studied in Washington. He was in favor of outright annexation and felt that it would be hastened by rejection of the proposed treaty. He became acting United States vice consul in Honolulu in 1868 and received a regular commission the following year. However, Spalding joined a group to develop sugar growing on the island of Maui and by 1870 he had been converted into a strong supporter of reciprocity. He built a two-story house on a ninety-acre estate, but eventually went to live in Europe, where his three daughters married Italian noblemen. His wife was a Makee of Ulupalakua, Maui.

SPAULDING, EPHRAIM
(1802–1840)

Born in Ludlow, Vermont, Spaulding graduated from Middlebury College, Vermont, in 1828 and from Andover Theological Seminary, Massachusetts, in 1831. He married Julia Brooks in November of that year, shortly before the couple sailed with the Fifth Company of American missionaries. They were stationed in 1832 at Lahaina, Maui, where he worked among the schools and churches and was chaplain for the many sailors that thronged the port during the whaling season. Ill health compelled him to return to the United States in 1837. The Spauldings had four children.

SPRECKELS, CLAUS
(1828–1908)

Born in Lamstedt, Hanover, Germany, Spreckels became a financier in California and was associated with the California Sugar Refinery in San Francisco before arriving in Hawaii in 1876. He had fought the proposed reciprocity treaty that would give favorable terms to Hawaiian exporters to the United States, but when it became a reality he invested heavily in sugar land, sugar mills, railway lines, and irrigation systems such as the one he built below the Hamakua Ditch of

Alexander & Baldwin on the island of Maui. By 1878 this project had reclaimed some seventeen thousand acres of leased crown lands and led to the establishment of the Hawaiian Commercial & Sugar Co., operators of the finest plantation in all the islands. His son, John D. Spreckels, founded the Oceanic Steamship Co., which ran between the islands and San Francisco for many years and later extended its operations to Australia and New Zeàland. Claus Spreckels also established a banking and agency house in Honolulu, later operated by his partner, William G. IRWIN, under Irwin's name; in 1882 Irwin claimed that the firm had a complete monopoly of the Hawaiian sugar crop.

In 1878 King KALAKAUA, poker-playing crony of Spreckels, began a dangerous course of dismissing cabinets that did not agree with his habit of raising money by dubious means. Spreckels applied for an extensive water privilege on his Maui sugar lands. When it was rejected, he made a personal loan to the king and a new cabinet promptly granted the requested rights for thirty years at $500 a year. Along with men like Celso Caesar MORENO and Walter Murray GIBSON, Spreckels encouraged corruption. In 1882 the legislature conveyed to him some twenty-four-thousand acres of crown lands at Wailuku, Maui, to settle a claim that he had purchased from Princess RUTH for $10,000. As the result of another bill, one million dollars in silver coins bearing the head of Kalakaua was minted in San Francisco and circulated; Spreckels made a profit of from $100,000 to $200,000 from this coinage deal.

Spreckels became known as "the power behind the throne" and "the uncrowned king of Hawaii"; even after his political influence waned he remained "the sugar king of Hawaii." When friction arose between the king and the "Spreckels party," the financier returned to San Francisco in

1886, but sometimes came back to survey his Hawaii properties. He supported Queen LILIUOKALANI after she was deposed and gradually withdrew his money from the islands, finally selling the H. C. & S. Co. to Alexander & Baldwin. His last visit to Hawaii came in 1905. See Jacob Adler, *Claus Spreckels, the Sugar King in Hawaii* (Honolulu: University of Hawaii Press, 1966).

STAINBACK, INGRAM MACKLIN (1883–1961)

Born in Tennessee, Stainback graduated with highest honors from both Princeton University (1907) and the University of Chicago Law School (1912). In the latter year he arrived in Hawaii and practised law for two years before being appointed attorney general of the territory. He served as an officer in World War I for a year, and from 1918 to 1934 was a partner in a leading law firm. From 1934 to 1940 he was United States attorney in the islands, and was made a federal judge in 1940. After the 1941 attack on Pearl Harbor, Stainback was made adviser to the "military governor's office," under martial law, and in August, 1942, President Roosevelt appointed him governor of the territory.

Stainback and his attorney general went to Washington in December to urge prompt restoration of civil rights, and with the approval of General Delos C. EMMONS a proclamation of March 10, 1943, restored civil authority for many operations of the territorial and county governments. Martial law continued in other areas, however, until February, 1946. Stainback was re-appointed as governor by President Truman and served until 1951. From that year until 1959 he was an associate justice of the Territorial Supreme Court, and thereafter was a consultant for various law firms.

STALEY, THOMAS NETTLESHIP (1823–1898)

Staley, born in Yorkshire, England, became a fellow of Cambridge University. He was selected in 1861 by Archbishop Sumner to act as the first Anglican bishop of Honolulu. He and his wife, Catherine W. Shirley Staley, arrived in Honolulu in October, 1862, a few weeks after the death of ALBERT, Prince of Hawaii. The bishop was appointed to the privy council and to the Board of Education, and began two church-operated boarding schools. He retired from this post in 1870. His own account of his labors appears in his book, *Five Years' Church Work in the Kingdom of Hawaii* (London: Rivington, 1868).

STANGENWALD, HUGO (1829–1899)

Born in Germany, the young man left with a group of exiles led by Carl Schurz. After living in various parts of the mainland he arrived in Hawaii in 1851. He practised medicine successfully; the Hawaiians called him "the instantaneous healer." His office was first set up on Merchant Street near Fort, where was later erected the Stangenwald Building, a six-story structure called Hawaii's first skyscraper. Dr. Stangenwald experimented with photography and was the first to make daguerreotypes in the islands. In 1854 he married Mary Catherine Dimond, daughter of the merchant Henry DIMOND.

STEVENS, JOHN LEAVITT (1820–1895)

Born in Mount Vernon, Maine, Stevens studied at the Waterville Liberal Institute and the Maine Wesleyan Seminary. He discontinued his studies for the ministry and began a career in journalism in 1855 as owner of the Kennebec *Journal.* After a career in politics he was appointed minister to Uruguay and Paraguay from 1870 to 1874; from 1877 to 1883 he was minister to Norway and Sweden.

Stevens arrived in Hawaii in 1889, first as minister, then as envoy extraordinary and minister plenipotentiary. On January 16, 1893, the day before the Provisional Government took over the rule in the islands, Minister Stevens caused American troops to be landed in Honolulu for the protection of American lives and property. He was, in fact, friendly with the annexationist cause and quickly recognized the new government. He was replaced by President Grover Cleveland's appointment of Albert S. WILLIS, and left the islands in 1893.

STEVENSON, ROBERT LOUIS (1850–1894)

The world-famed Scottish author first arrived in Hawaii with his family on his chartered yacht *Casco* in 1889 and spent five months exploring the islands and writing some of his best fiction and essays. Stevenson's step-daughter, Isobel Osbourne Strong, wife of King Kalakaua's court painter Joseph

Strong, had arrived earlier, and Stevenson and his wife Fanny were immediately accepted as a part of the royal circle. He chatted with the half-Scottish, half-Hawaiian Princess KAIULANI under her father's banyan tree in Waikiki and wrote for her a poem still treasured, "Forth from her land to mine she goes." He sailed to the Kona Coast, rode around the City of Refuge, and then spent a week in the guest house of the leper colony on the island of Molokai soon after the death of Father DAMIEN. Stevenson made a five-week return visit to Hawaii in 1893, a year before his death in Samoa, and found his royal friend LILIUOKALANI deposed and a pro-American Provisional Government in power.

Two of Stevenson's best short stories—"The Bottle Imp" and "The Isle of Voices"—have settings in Hawaii, and the inspiration for his Pacific novel of adventure, *The Wrecker,* written in collaboration with his stepson Lloyed OSBOURNE, came from an incident reported in the Honolulu newspapers during his residence at Waikiki. The most notorious of Stevenson's writings about Hawaii, however, was his attack upon the Rev. Charles McEwen HYDE of Honolulu, who had written a letter defaming Damien. The best account of the activities of "R.L.S." during his two visits is *Stevenson in Hawaii* by Sister Martha Mary McGaw (Honolulu: University of Hawaii Press, 1950). A collection of Stevenson's prose and verse edited and with an introduction by A. Grove Day is *Travels in Hawaii* (Honolulu: University Press of Hawaii, 1973).

STEWART, CHARLES SAMUEL (1795–1870)

Born in Flemington, New Jersey, Stewart studied law, graduated from Princeton College in 1815, and attended Princeton Theological Seminary, where he was ordained in 1821. He married Harriet Bradford Tiffany (1798–1830) and the couple arrive in Hawaii with the Second Company in 1823. Stewart was a pioneer preacher at Lahaina, Maui, along with William RICHARDS. The illness of his wife compelled their return to the United States in 1825, where he lectured as a missionary. He revisited the islands in 1829 as chaplain of the U.S. Sloop *Vincennes,* the first American naval vessel to tour the world, and remained in the employ of the mission until 1830. Stewart had three children by Harriet and one daughter by a second wife, Sarah Ann Stewart Skillman Stewart, who died in 1854.

Stewart is the entertaining author of *Private Journal of a Voyage to the Pacific Ocean* (New York: J. P. Haven, 1828); *Journal of a Residence in the Sandwich Islands* (London: H. Fisher, Son & Jackson, 1828); *A Visit to the South Seas, in the U.S. Ship "Vincennes"* (London: Fisher, Son & Jackson, 1832); and *A Residence in the Sandwich Islands* (Boston: Weeks, Jordan, 1839).

STOCKTON, BETSEY (1798?–1865)

Born a black slave, Betsey lived for many years as a servant in the family of President Green of Princeton College in New Jersey. She still found time for wide reading and was qualified to teach school. She was accepted by the American mission and arrived with the Second Company at Honolulu in 1823. She was stationed at Lahaina, where she assisted the family of the Rev. C. S. STEWART and conducted a school for working Hawaiians and their families. She returned to the United States with the Stewarts in 1825 and continued to labor in the mission field.

STODDARD, CHARLES WARREN (1843–1909)

Born in Rochester, New York, Stoddard became one of the well-known San Francisco group of writers and extended his travels into the Pacific. He spent several years in Hawaii and celebrated the languorous life of the islands. *South-Sea Idylls* (Boston: James R. Osgood, 1873) contains several sketches and an account of a ride through the crater of Haleakala. Other books by Stoddard that deal with the Hawaiian scene are *The Lepers of Molokai* (Notre Dame, Ind.: Ave Maria Press, 1885); *Hawaiian Life* (Chicago and New York: F. T. Neely, 1894); and *The Island of Tranquil Delights* (Boston: H. B. Turner), 1904.

STOKES, JOHN FRANCIS GRAY (1875–1960)

Born in Newcastle, New South Wales, Australia, Stokes came to Hawaii in 1899 and was connected with the Bernice P. Bishop Museum until he retired in 1928. He served as librarian, curator of Polynesian ethnology, curator of collections, and ethnologist. He was also assistant to Dr. W. T. BRIGHAM, and was acting director in 1912 and in 1918. Stokes was a founder and officer of the Hawaii Anthropological Society and an officer of the Hawaiian Historical Society, in whose publications he printed a dozen articles. He made special studies of the City of Refuge on the island of Hawaii and of claims that Spaniards had preceded James COOK in revealing the existence of the islands to the rest of the world.

STRAUB, GEORGE F. (1879–1966)

Born in Germany, Straub took his preliminary training in Wuerzburg and his clinical training in Heidelberg. His father was surgeon general to King Ludwig III of Bavaria. Dr. Straub came to Hawaii in 1906 and after many years of private practice founded in Honolulu, in 1921, The Clinic (later called The Straub Clinic), in which medical needs were met by a group of specialists. The busy Straub Hospital on King Street is a memorial to him today.

The doctor retired from medicine in 1933 but was briefly called back to practice during World War II. He was a cellist with the Honolulu Symphony and after his retirement he turned his attention to the construction of many fine violins, a cello, and a viola.

SWANZY, JULIA JUDD (1860–1941)

Julia Judd was born in Hawaii, daughter of Col. Charles Hastings Judd and granddaughter of Dr. G. P. JUDD. She was educated at Punahou School and Mills College in Oakland, California. She married Francis Mills Swanzy in 1887 and for half a century thereafter was a leading civic and social figure in Honolulu. Her husband, born in Ireland, was for many years managing director of Theo. H. Davies & Co. and president for two terms of the Hawaii Sugar Planters' Association. She is best remembered for her work in education; she established and directed the activities of the Free Kindergarten and Children's Aid Association. She was also chairman of the recreation

commission of the City and County of Honolulu; Swanzy Beach Park at Kaaawa on Oahu's North Shore, on land donated by her in 1921, was named in her memory. Among other projects in historical restoration, Mrs. Swanzy, in her twelfth year as regent of the Daughters of Hawaii, dedicated in 1927 the restored Hulihee Palace at Kailua, Hawaii, built in 1837. The Swanzys had two daughters.

TAGGARD, GENEVIEVE (1894–1948)

Born in Waitsburg, Washington, the future poet was two years old when her parents came to Hawaii to teach in the public schools. Up until the time she entered Punahou School, her playmates were almost entirely children of the various races that predominated in the islands in the early part of the century. She taught for a year at a rural school near Pearl Harbor and then in 1914 left to study at the University of California. After graduation she went east and became an editor, a poet, and a teacher of literature and writing in several women's colleges. Five of her twelve volumes of poems contain verses about Hawaii. A number of these pieces have been collected in *Origin: Hawaii* (Honolulu: privately printed, 1947), edited by Donald Angus. She also wrote two classic short stories of the islands, "The Plague" and "Hiawatha in Hawaii."

TAMOREE
See KAUMUALII.

TAVERNIER, JULES (1844–1889)

Born in Paris, Tavernier spent his childhood in England but began his art career in France. He became an illustrator in London, New York, and San Francisco, where he became well known as a painter, especially of American Indian subjects. The Taverniers followed the family of Joseph Strong, stepson-in-law of Robert Louis STEVENSON, when they came to Hawaii in 1884. During his five years of painting in Hawaii previous to his death. Tavernier found the Kilauea Volcano to be an actively co-operative subject, along with other island scenery. At least three of his paintings are to be found in the collections of the Honolulu Academy of Arts.

TAYLOR, TOWNSEND ELIJAH (1818–1883)

Born in La Grange, New York, Taylor graduated from Middlebury College, Vermont, in 1844 and Union Theological Seminary in New York City in 1847. In that year he married Persis Goodale Thurston, daughter of the pioneer missionary Asa THURSTON; she had gone to the United States to gain an education and later had taught at Mount Holyoke Seminary. The Taylors arrived at Lahaina in 1848 and he preached there until assigned to Honolulu in 1851. After serving at the Honolulu Bethel for a year, he became pastor of the Second Foreign Church (afterward Fort Street Church) from 1852 to 1854. He later moved to California for his health. The Taylors had six children.

TEMPSKI, ARMINE VON (1899–1943)

Born on a Maui ranch, Armine was the granddaughter of a Polish political exile, Major Gustavus Ferdinand von Tempsky, who was killed in the Maori wars in New Zealand. Her father, Louis von Tempsky, came to Hawaii at the age of eighteen and became manager of the 60,000-acre Haleakala Ranch. Armine spent her childhood, along with her younger sister Gwen, on the slopes of the titanic crater of "The House of the Sun." Her account of growing up in the saddle, *Born in Paradise* (New York: Duell, Sloan & Pearce, 1940), tells of wide mountain pastures, volcanoes and tidal waves, viewing a cattle drive, rodeos and festivities, roping wild cattle, driving herds into the surf and loading them on an offshore steamer, and sharing the life of a ranching family. Armine and her sister accompanied Jack LONDON and his wife Charmian on a pack trip through Haleakala Crater in 1908 and he encouraged Armine in her efforts to become a published writer.

Novels of Hawaii by Armine von Tempski include *Hula* (New York: Stokes, 1927); *Dust* (same, 1928); *Fire* (same, 1929); *Lava* (same, 1930); *Hawaiian Harvest* (same, 1935); *Ripe Breadfruit* (New York: Dodd, Mead, 1935); and *Thunder in Heaven* (New York: Duell, Sloan & Pearce, 1942). A posthumous sequel to the autobiography is *Aloha, My Love to You* (New York: Duell, Sloan & Pearce, 1946).

TEN EYCK, ANTHONY (1810–1867)

Born in Watertown, New York, Ten Eyck studied law and opened an office in Detroit in 1835. Ten years later he was appointed commissioner to Hawaii by President Polk, replacing the obdurate George Brown, and was empowered to make a treaty with the kingdom. In Honolulu, Ten Eyck rented the home of Captain John DOMINIS as the United States Legation and gave it the name of Washington Place; it is at present the official residence of the governors of the State of Hawaii.

Ten Eyck argued unsuccessfully to have the government permit foreigners to hold land titles in fee simple and to give American consuls the right to nominate jurors in civil and criminal cases. Negotiations reached an impasse in December, 1848, and Ten Eyck was replaced by Charles Eames. Ten Eyck served during the Civil War as paymaster of volunteers and was mustered out with the rank of major.

TENNENT, MADELINE GRACE COOK (MADGE) (1889?–1972)

Born in Dulwich, England, Madeline went with her family to South Africa but later they moved to Paris so that the daughter could study art with Adolphe William Bouguereau. She married Hugh Tennent, a New Zealand soldier, in Cape Town in 1915, and the couple went to New Zealand in 1917. Madge began working with Polynesian subjects in British Samoa, where her husband was treasurer of the colony from 1919 to 1923.

During a visit to Hawaii the couple was persuaded to settle in Honolulu, where Hugh ran an accounting firm. Madge opened a studio on Liliha Street and concentrated first on portraits of multiracial and Hawaiian children. In 1930 and 1931 her Polynesian and Oriental portraits were shown in New York, Chicago, Oakland, and San Francisco; thereafter she held other exhibits of her work. A portfolio, *Hawaiian People* (Honolulu: Advertiser, 1936), is representative of her style at the time. The couple opened the Tennent Art Foundation on the grounds of their Prospect Street home in 1954 as a showplace for the work of island artists. Madge stopped painting at the age of seventy-six. Her drawings, etchings, and paintings are treasured by collectors in Hawaii and elsewhere. See Arthur Tennent, *The Art and Writing of Madge Tennent* (Norfolk Island, Australia: Island Heritage, 1977).

THOMAS, RICHARD DARTON (1777–1851)

Rear Admiral Thomas, R.N., led in the restoration of the monarchy after the rule of Lord George PAULET. The admiral arrived in his ship *Dublin* on July 26, 1843. During a colorful ceremony on July 31, the Hawaiian flag was once more raised over the islands. At a thanksgiving service at Kawaiahao Church, KAMEHAMEHA III is said to have uttered the words that are still the motto of the State of Hawaii: "The life of the land is preserved in righteousness." Thomas remained in the islands for the following six months, until the arrival of consul general William MILLER. Thomas was greatly liked by the people, and the site of the restoration in Honolulu still bears the name of Thomas Square.

THOUARS
See PETIT-THOUARS.

THRUM, THOMAS GEORGE (1842–1932)

Born in Newcastle, New South Wales, Australia, Thrum was brought by his parents to Hawaii at the age of eleven. He clerked in stores and worked on the Koloa Plantation. He took over the stationery and news firm of Black & Auld in Honolulu in 1870. He began a publishing career in 1875 by issuing the first *Hawaiian Almanac and Annual,* a standard reference work that appeared under his editorship for the rest of his life. With James J. WILLIAMS he founded in 1888 a monthly magazine, *Paradise of the Pacific,* which was incorporated in 1966 into the present *Honolulu Magazine.* Thrum was a leading writer on Hawaiian archeology and folklore. He located and listed more than five hundred heiaus on the islands. His publications include *Hawaiian Folk Tales: A Collection of Native Legends* (Chicago: A. C. McClurg, 1907); *Stories of the Menehunes* (Chicago: same, 1910); and *More Hawaiian Folk Tales* (same, 1923). On the death of William De Witt ALEXANDER, who was editing the *Collection of Hawaiian Antiquities and Folklore* of Abraham FORNANDER, Thrum completed and published what has been called the greatest single

repository of Hawaiian lore. Thrum was made an associate in Hawaiian folklore at the Bernice P. Bishop Museum in 1921. He married Anna Laura Brown and the couple had four children.

THURSTON, ASA (1787–1868)

Born in Fitchburg, Massachusetts, Thurston graduated from Yale College in 1816 and Andover Theological Seminary in 1819. He and Hiram BINGHAM, with whom he was ordained, were leaders of the First Company selected by the American mission to work in Hawaii. A few weeks before sailing, since the men of the group had to be wedded, Asa married Lucy Goodale, a cousin of a classmate. The Thurstons, unlike most missionary couples, were fated to spend the rest of their lives in the islands.

The Thurstons went first to Kailua, Hawaii, then to Maui, then to Oahu, and finally back to Kailua in 1823. He was one of the leading translators of the Bible into Hawaiian. He worked as a missionary for forty years, returning to New England only for the period 1840 to 1842, and built schools, churches, and a following among the people. His wife Lucy (1795–1876), daughter of a deacon of the Congregational Church, compiled in her old age (she lived until the centennial of the Declaration of Independence) one of

the most vivid accounts of the early mission days in Hawaii, *The Life and Times of Lucy G. Thurston* (Ann Arbor, Mich.: S. C. Andrews, 1882). The Thurstons with five children began a family prominent in the history of the islands up to the present.

THURSTON, LORRIN ANDREWS (1858–1931)

Born in Honolulu, grandson of Asa THURSTON and son of Asa Goodale Tyerman Thurston and Sarah Andrews Thurston, Lorrin was educated at Punahou School and studied law at Columbia University. He was admitted to the Honolulu bar in 1878. He was elected to the House of Representatives in 1886 and to the House of Nobles in 1892. Thurston was named minister of the interior in 1887 and began a lifelong interest in developing parks in the islands. He built the first road to the Volcano House on Hawaii, later put up the first modern hotel on that site, fostered the Kilauea Observatory, and helped to set aside Haleakala and Kilauea as federal reserves.

Thurston was a leader in the Revolution of 1893, and on January 18 left for Washington, D.C., to serve the Provisional Government as envoy extraordinary and minister pleni-potentiary. He stayed for two years, assisting to a large extent in paving the way for annexation of Hawaii by the United States. He was again appointed as annexation commissioner in 1898. He wrote of his experiences in *Memoirs of the Hawaiian Revolution* (Honolulu: Advertiser, 1936). From 1899 until 1915 Thurston engaged in plantation and railway development; with B. F. DILLINGHAM he promoted the Kihei, Maui, and Olaa, Hawaii, Plantations. He organized and served as vice president of the Honolulu Rapid Transit Co., which brought the first electric streetcars to the city. In 1900 he became publisher of the Honolulu *Advertiser,* a daily paper that is still under the management of a descendant.

Thurston married twice: first to Margaret Clara Shipman of Hilo, by whom he had a son, Robert Simpson Thurston; and then to Harriet Potter, by whom he had a son, Lorrin Potter Thurston, who carried on the publishing tradition, and a daughter, Margaret Carter Thurston, who married William Twigg-Smith.

THURSTON, LUCY GOODALE
See THURSTON, Asa.

TINKER, REUBEN (1799–1854)
Born in Chester, Massachusetts, Tinker graduated from Amherst College in 1827 and from Auburn Theological Seminary in 1830. He married Mary Throop Wood in November of that year and the couple sailed with the Fourth Company of American missionaries in December. Tinker was stationed at Lahaina as seaman's chaplain for a few months and after visiting the Marquesas Islands in 1832 was assigned to Wailuku, Maui, until 1834. From 1834 to 1838 he was in Honolulu as editor of the Hawaiian-language publications *Kumu Hawaii* and *Kumu Kamalii,* and was editor of the *Hawaiian Spectator,* a 100-page literary quarterly which began publication in January, 1838, "conducted by an association of gentlemen." The Tinkers left for the United States in October, 1840, and were released from the Boston mission soon after arrival. The family had seven children.

TROMELIN, LEGOARANT DE
As rear admiral in the French Navy, Tromelin arrived off Honolulu in April, 1848, in command of two vessels, *La Poursuivante* and the steam-corvette *Gassendi.* The admiral sent KAMEHAMEHA III ten demands that included everything from equality of worship to the punishment of impious schoolboys. To enforce these, he landed troops that took over government buildings, smashed everything in the fort, and seized the king's yacht. The ships departed after ten days, taking along the French consul, Guillaume Patrice Dillon, whose complaints had brought the demonstration.

TROUSSEAU, GEORGE P. (1833–1894)
Born in Paris, son of a famed physician, Trousseau graduated from the Ecole de Médicine in that city, served in the French Army, and arrived in Honolulu in 1872 by way of Australia. He was appointed to the new Board of Health by King LUNALILO and, given control of measures against the recent smallpox epidemic, managed to limit the number of deaths to seventeen. On his advice, in 1873 the first effort was made to segregate lepers. Trousseau acted as the physician of Lunalilo and was the confidant of two later monarchs. He not only practised medicine at the Oahu Insane Asylum, Queen's Hospital, Oahu Prison, and the port of Honolulu but was interested in rearing sheep at Kona, sugar at Hamakua, and ostriches at Waikiki. He helped to organize a yachting revival in the islands in 1889.

TSUKIYAMA, WILFRED CHOMATSU (1897–1966)
Born in Honolulu, the young man graduated from Kaahumanu School in 1914, Japanese language school in 1915, McKinley High School in 1918, and Coe College in 1921. After obtaining a law degree from the University of Chicago he was an attorney for the City of Honolulu from 1929 to 1940, when he became senior partner in a law firm. He served in the territorial senate from 1946 to 1959 before becoming chief justice of the Supreme Court after statehood was granted, and acted until his retirement in 1965. Tsukiyama was the first American of Oriental ancestry to serve as chief justice of any state. In 1965 he was awarded the Order of the Sacred Treasure, second class, by Premier Ikeda of Japan, the highest decoration ever given to an American of Japanese ancestry. Tsukiyama married Marian Misao Matsusaka in 1946 and the couple had six children.

TURNER, FARRANT LEWIS (1895–1959)
Born at Hilo, Turner graduated from Punahou School and obtained a bachelor's degree at Wesleyan University, Connecticut, in 1917. After working at Waialua Plantation from 1919 to 1922 he joined Lewers & Cooke, eventually becoming vice

president. Turner served in France in World War I, was discharged with the rank of captain, and from 1924 was an officer in the 298th Infantry, Hawaii National Guard, U.S.A. In World War II he was executive officer of the 298th Infantry, from October 15, 1940, through 1942. In June, 1942, Turner organized the 100th Infantry Battalion consisting of Americans of Japanese ancestry, which fought in Europe from September, 1943. Turner was discharged in August, 1944, with the rank of colonel, and decorated with the Legion of Merit. He rejoined Lewers & Cooke the same year.

Turner was secretary of the territory in 1953. He ran for delegate to Congress in 1956 but was defeated by John A. BURNS. At the time of his death, Turner was head of Hawaii's Small Business Administration Agency. He married Helen Van Inwegen in 1921 and the couple had one son.

TWAIN, MARK
See CLEMENS, S. L.

ULUMAHEIHEI
See HOAPILI.

UMI
Umi, son of LILOA, was probably the most famous of the early chiefs. His story has been called "one of the most popular of all Hawaiian prose sagas of heroes, embellished as it is with many stock episodes but still preserving the thread of historical accuracy." He was conceived by Liloa on his travels, who left with the child several recognition tokens that the young man later brought to his father. The oppressive older brother HAKAU was stoned to death, and Umi left his poverty and became a ruling chief of the island of Hawaii. He was famed as a farmer and fisherman. He kept up the worship of the gods and increased the practice of human sacrifice. He was succeeded by his son, Keliiokaloa.

VANCOUVER, GEORGE (1758–1798)
Vancouver entered the Royal Navy at the age of thirteen. He served as an able seaman during the second Pacific voyage of Captain James COOK and was a midshipman during Cook's fateful third voyage. In September, 1789, he was appointed to head an exploring expedition to the South Seas, to repossess the fur-rich Nootka Sound region and to seek, as Cook had done, the fabled Northwest Passage. His ships were the sloop *Discovery* (not the same vessel in which he had sailed with Cook), and the *Chatham*, commanded at first by Lieutenant William Robert Broughton and later by Lieutenant Peter PUGET. A supply vessel, the *Daedalus*, met the squadron twice.

While spending two years charting and naming the coasts north of San Francisco, Vancouver and his crews passed three winters in Hawaii between 1792 and 1794. Vancouver was the most important visitor to the islands during the reign of KAMEHAMEHA I and gave a number of valuable descriptions of the life at this period. On his second visit his ships brought in cattle and sheep, as well as goats and geese. The following year he learned that the king had separated from his favorite wife, KAAHUMANU, who was suspected of dalliance with KAIANA, and arranged to reunite the pair. He helped the king's

carpenter to finish building a sailing ship, but spoke out strongly against the trade in defective arms and ammunition that foreigners were carrying on among the chiefs. Vancouver obtained from Kamehameha what the Englishman called a "cession" of the Big Island to Great Britain. This agreement was never ratified; nevertheless, English influence was foremost in the islands in the early years.

Vancouver returned to London in October, 1795, and in ill health spent the remaining months of his life preparing his journals for publication. The result, *Voyage of Discovery to the North Pacific Ocean* (London: C. J. and J. Robinson, J. Edwards, 1798), appeared in three volumes. A biography of this Pacific explorer is *Surveyor of the Sea* by Bern Anderson (Seattle: University of Washington Press, 1960).

VARIGNY, CHARLES-VICTOR CROSNIER DE (1829–1899)
Born in Versailles, France, and educated at the Lycée Bourbon, Varigny left his country as one of three agents in charge of a party of emigrants bound for California after the Revolution of 1848. On arrival in San Francisco he married a fellow passenger, Louise Constantin (1828–1894), and for two years was editor of a California newspaper. The couple arrived in Honolulu in 1855 on their way back to France and he decided to remain as interpreter, secretary, and finally acting French consul.

Varigny resigned his post when he was appointed by KAMEHAMEHA V as minister of finance in 1863; he replaced R. C. WYLLIE as minister of foreign affairs in 1865. He took an active part in drafting the Constitution of 1864 and endorsed the king's intention to sign a reciprocity treaty with the United States. In 1868 the Varigny family, including a son and two daughters born in Honolulu, returned to France.

When negotiations for trade treaties with various European nations came to nothing, he resigned his post as foreign minister and returned to journalism. His first significant book, *Quatorze Ans aux Iles Sandwich* (Paris: Hachette, 1874), a mixture of travel narrative, Hawaiian history, and political memoir, remains the only substantial account of Hawaii's development up to the 1870s from the point of view of such a shrewd participant and observer. Down to the close of the century, and especially during the time of the Revolution of 1893, Varigny continued to write numerous accounts of life in Oceania. See his *Fourteen Years in the Sandwich Islands, 1855–1868* (Honolulu: University of Honolulu Press, 1981), translated by Alfons L. Korn.

VICTORIA KAAHUMANU KAMAMALU. See KAMAMALU.

VON CHAMISSO, ADELBERT See KOTZEBUE.

VON HAMM, CONRAD CARL (1870–1965) Born in Bremen, Germany, Von Hamm attended the Realschule in that city and went to work in the Deutschen Bank in 1885. As the result of correspondence with his cousin William Maertens, senior partner in the importing firm of Hoffschlaeger & Co. of Honolulu, about their mutual interest in collecting stamps, Von Hamm came to Honolulu in 1891 to work in his cousin's firm. He was offered a

partnership after ten years, but instead Von Hamm launched his own business in 1899 with Archibald A. Young and Alexander YOUNG under the name of Von Hamm-Young Co., Ltd. The company lost extensively in the Chinatown fire in 1900 but carried on. They imported automobiles and gasoline, and in 1907 opened a garage. The business thrived, and branches were opened in Hilo and on Maui and Kauai. Von Hamm became president of the company in 1925 and chairman of the board in 1942, and retired in 1958. He estimated his personal wealth at twenty million dollars in 1964. In 1898 he married Ida Bernice Young, daughter of Alexander Young, and the marriage lasted sixty-five years, until her death in 1963. The couple had two daughters.

VON HOLT, HERMANN J. F. (1830–1867) Born in Hamburg, the founder of the Hawaii branch of the family came to Honolulu in 1851 with a cargo of merchandise and stayed to open a successful store. He married Alice Brown and the couple had one son and two daughters.

VON KOTZEBUE, OTTO See KOTZEBUE.

VON KRUSENSTERN, A. J. See KRUSENSTERN.

VON TEMPSKI, ARMINE See TEMPSKI.

WALDEN, LIONEL (1861–1933) Born in Norwich, Connecticut, Walden attended school in Boston and was an art student of Carolus Duran in Paris. He first exhibited his work at the Paris Salon of 1877 and later became internationally known, especially for unusual seascapes and nudes. He was made a Chevalier of

the Legion of Honor of France in 1910. He came to Hawaii in 1911, enamoured of the landscapes and seascapes of the islands, and painted until his death. His works received numerous honors. Several of his pictures were bought by the British and French governments for national museums and galleries, including his Hawaiian canvas, "Sea Breaking over the Reef."

WALSH, ARSENIUS See MAIGRET.

WARD, CURTIS PERRY A Southerner who came to the islands in the 1860s, Ward married Victoria Robinson. Their home and estate, named Old Plantation, was on King Street at the site now occupied by the Neal F. BLAISDELL Center. The Ward Estate possesses much of the area near the waterfront called Kakaako.

WATANABE, KENICHI (1910–1969) Born in Honolulu, Watanabe earned a bachelor's degree from the California Institute of Technology in 1936 and a doctorate in 1940. He taught mathematics at the University of Hawaii from 1940 to 1947 before teaching physics at Wabash College for a year. In 1949 Watanabe began three years as physicist at the United States Naval Research Laboratory and then three more as head of the atmospheric composition section at the United States Air Force Cambridge Research Center. He was especially concerned with the composition of the atmosphere at the highest levels. He returned to the University of Hawaii in 1954 as professor of physics and was senior professor from 1961 to 1969; he served as chairman of the department from 1956 to 1958. A physics building on the Manoa campus is nàmed Watanabe Hall. He married Betty Keiko in 1945 and they had three daughters.

WATERHOUSE, JOHN THOMAS Jr. (1845–1904)

Born in Tasmania, grandson of a Methodist missionary, the boy came to Hawaii in 1851 with his father, John Thomas Waterhouse Sr. The father engaged in various enterprises, such as the Waterhouse Investment Co., the W. W. Dimond firm, and H. May & Co. The son entered business and established the commercial and financial firm of Waterhouse Trust Co., with interests in insurance, brokerage, real estate, and investment. He inherited his father's annexationist views and promoted them while serving in the legislature under the monarchy, the Provisional Government, and the Republic.

More comfortable in Hawaiian than in English, Waterhouse preached regularly for ten years to the Kaumakapili congregation and from 1899 until his death was superintendent of the Kawaiahao Sunday School. He was an officer of Central Union Church from its inception, a founder and trustee of the First Methodist Church, and a trustee of the Sailor's Home, the Lunalilo Home, and Queen's Hospital, of which he was also treasurer. John Thomas Waterhouse Jr. married Elizabeth B. Pinder and their sons, George S. and John Waterhouse, became prominent in the business scene in the islands.

WEBBER, JOHN (1752–1793)

Webber, son of a Swiss sculptor living in England, was engaged by the British Admiralty to accompany Captain James COOK on his third Pacific voyage, "in order to make drawings and paintings . . . to give a more perfect idea thereof than can be formed by written descriptions only." His many sketches and paintings were the first visual records of Hawaii, and his skill was applauded by Sir Joshua Reynolds. After returning to England in October, 1780, Webber was employed by the Admiralty to supervise the engraving of the sixty-one views appearing in the *Atlas* of the four-year voyage, published in 1784. Later Webber published privately a series of more interesting colored views. He was elected to the prestigious Royal Academy and is remembered for having provided the most prolific illustration of any sea voyage previous to the invention of photography.

WENTWORTH, CHESTER K. (1891–1969)

Born in Aspen, Colorado, Wentworth earned a bachelor's degree from the University of Chicago in 1918 and master's and doctor's degrees in 1921 and 1923 from the University of Iowa. He taught at Washington University in St. Louis and at the University of Iowa before coming to the Hilo campus of the University of Hawaii, where the physical science building was later named for him. Wentworth served for seventeen years as head geologist for the Honolulu Board of Water Supply and retired to become a part-time member of the Volcano Observatory staff at Kilauea Volcano for thirteen years, retiring in 1963. The author of some 150 scientific papers, mostly dealing with volcanology, he devised the Wentworth Scale, a set of standards for classifying sedimentary rock.

WESTERVELT, WILLIAM DRAKE (1849–1939)

Born in Oberlin, Ohio, Westervelt received both an A.B. and a B.D. degree from Oberlin College. After serving as pastor of various churches on the mainland he came to Hawaii in 1889 for two years to study mission achievements, and returned to stay in 1899. In 1905 he married Caroline Dickinson Castle of the missionary family. By daily study with a native Hawaiian and diligent research, Westervelt made himself an authority on the ancient customs, beliefs, history, and legends of Hawaii. He was also a pioneer stamp collector. Between 1900 and 1925 he published more than a hundred articles in Honolulu periodicals and annuals, and from these he selected and edited enough material for half a dozen books on Hawaiian legends, published between 1910 and 1923. Among these are *Legends of Ma-ui* (Honolulu: Gazette, 1910); *Legends of Old Honolulu* (Boston: Ellis, 1915); *Legends of Gods and Ghosts* (same, 1915); *Hawaiian Legends of Volcanoes* (same, 1916); and *Hawaiian Historical Legends* (New York: Revell, 1923).

WESTON, DAVID M.

In 1851 Weston devised a centrifugal machine for separating sugar from molasses, which shortened the time of this process from weeks to minutes. Moreover, the superior grade of sugar thus produced sold for a better price. With the support of Henry A. PEIRCE in 1853, Weston opened a prosperous machine shop in downtown Honolulu and founded the Honolulu Iron Works.

WETMORE, CHARLES HINCKLEY (1820–1898)

Born in Lebanon, Connecticut, Wetmore graduated in 1846 from the Berkshire Medical Institute, Massachusetts. He married Lucy Sheldon Taylor in September, 1848, and the couple sailed a month later for Hawaii. They were stationed in 1849 at Hilo, where Wetmore served for six years as a missionary and government physician. Wetmore became Hilo's first druggist, after his wife had helped him concoct simple home remedies in great demand among Hawaiians, foreign residents, and seamen. In 1855 Dr. Wetmore took his first patient in his Seaman's Hospital in Hilo, which he directed for ten years. Mrs. Wetmore, who bore five children, in 1850 started an important school for part-Hawaiian children. The doctor and his wife were students of natural science. He invested in early sugar plantations near Hilo and in the first carbonated beverage plant in Hilo. In 1881 the Mauna Loa lava flow came within one mile of his home, and stopped only when Princess RUTH threw a white chicken into the flow with a prayer.

The last medical missionary to Hawaii died May 13, 1898, ninety days before the annexation of the islands by the United States.

WHITNEY, HENRY MARTYN (1824–1904)

Born at Waimea, Kauai, a son of Samuel WHITNEY, Henry went to Rochester, New York, for schooling in 1831 but suffered a hearing loss and gave up thoughts of college. This pioneer commercial printer and publisher in Hawaii learned the printer's trade and worked in New York City with Harper & Brothers. He married Catharine Olivia March in June, 1849, and in November the couple arrived in Hawaii.

Whitney set up the first post office in Hawaii in 1850 and was postmaster until 1886. He put out stamps with values of two, five, and thirteen cents; these are the "Missionaries" that are among the rarest collectors' items today. When the mission press closed down in 1858, Whitney, who had recently set up his own printing and publishing company, was employed to do all the future mission work on a commercial basis. Presses, type, and furniture were sold to him for $1,000, which he was to pay for in future printed matter. He put out half a dozen important volumes, and in 1856 founded the weekly *Pacific Commercial Advertiser*, forerunner of the current daily Honolulu *Advertiser*, but in 1870 sold it to Black & Auld. He also established a weekly Hawaiian-language newspaper, *Ka Nupepa Kuokoa*, in 1860, which ran until 1927. In 1873 he acquired the *Hawaiian Gazette*, which replaced the old *Polynesian*, and was editor of the *Planters' Monthly* from 1886 to 1903. In 1888 the *Pacific Commercial Advertiser*, by then a daily, was reacquired from Black & Auld by Whitney's Hawaiian Gazette Co. He managed this firm and its publications until his retirement in 1894. Whitney served on the privy council of the kingdom from 1873 to 1891.

WHITNEY, SAMUEL (1793–1845)

Whitney, born in Branford, Connecticut, was educated at Yale College and with his wife, Mercy Partridge Whitney (1795–1872), were members of the First Company of American missionaries arriving in Hawaii in 1820. The Whitneys established the mission station at Waimea, Kauai, with the Samuel RUGGLES family. With the exception of a journey to the South Pacific in 1832, Whitney remained on Kauai until he died while seeking health at Lahaina, Maui. Four children were born of the couple. His wife remained on Kauai, where she died after a residence of fifty-two years, having made only one visit back to the United States. Whitney translated a number of books into Hawaiian between 1832 and 1836.

WHITTLESEY, ELIPHALET (1816–1889)

Born in Salisbury, Connecticut, Whittlesey graduated from Williams College, Massachusetts, and from Union Theological Seminary, New York City, in 1843. He married Elizabeth Keene Baldwin in November of that year and the couple sailed in December with the Eleventh Company of American missionaries. They were stationed at Hana, Maui, from 1844 to 1846 and after a year at Kaupo returned to Hana from 1847 to 1854. They returned to the United States in the latter year and were released from the Boston mission after serving for a decade in mainland churches.

126

WILCOX, ABNER (1808–1869)

Born in Harwinton, Connecticut, Wilcox, a teacher, married Lucy Elizabeth Hart in 1836, shortly before sailing with the Eighth Company of American missionaries. The couple was stationed at Hilo from 1837 until 1844, where both taught school. They were transferred in 1844 to Waialua, Oahu, where Wilcox was put in charge of the Manual Labor Boarding School. Two years later they were stationed at Waioli, Kauai, where he taught a select school for Hawaiian boys for more than twenty years and preached on Sundays. The couple made a trip back to Connecticut in 1869 and died there within a week of each other. The eight Wilcox children founded an enduring clan especially associated with Kauai. See Albert Spencer WILCOX and George Norton WILCOX. See also Ethel M. Damon, ed., *Letters from the Life of Abner and Lucy Wilcox, 1836–1869* (Honolulu; privately printed, 1950).

WILCOX, ALBERT SPENCER (1844–1919)

Born in Hilo, son of Abner WILCOX, Albert attended Punahou School and joined his elder brother George Norton WILCOX in a cane-planting venture at Hanalei, Kauai. Albert then became manager of Hanamaulu Plantation; later he was associated with the Princeville Plantation. In 1898 he settled at his stock ranch at Kilohana, Lihue, Kauai. Wilcox held a number of other business interests, and was a member of the House of Representatives of the kingdom from 1891 to 1892. He founded the Sam Mahelona Hospital at Kapaa, Kauai, as a memorial to a stepson, and also established the Kauikeolani Children's Hospital in Honolulu. In 1898 Wilcox married Emma Kauikeolani Napoleon Mahelona, a widow.

WILCOX, GEORGE NORTON (1839–1933)

Born in Hilo, son of Abner WILCOX, George as a young man spent several months at Jarvis Island with the American Guano Co., a pioneer attempt by Honolulu businessmen to develop the export of fertilizer from Pacific Islands. Later in life, as a result of his efforts, Wilcox became president of the Pacific Guano & Fertilizer Co., which supplied many Hawaii plantations. After a year at Yale, Wilcox became a prominent planter on Kauai. In 1864 he leased Grove Farm from H. A. Wiedemann; he developed irrigation water, enlarged the holdings from 7,000 to 12,000 acres, and eventually became sole owner of the property. His scientific training made him a leader in various projects for better living conditions on Kauai.

Wilcox held other business interests but also found time for public service. He was a member of every legislative body from 1888 until 1898; he was prime minister of the Kalakaua cabinet of 1892. He was also a noted philanthropist, especially in promoting religious and educational efforts. He never married. See Bob Krauss with W. P. Alexander, *Grove Farm Plantation* (Palo Alto, Calif.: Pacific Books, 1963).

WILCOX, ROBERT WILLIAM (1855–1903)

The future firebrand of the islands was born at Honuaula, Maui, son of Captain William Wilcox and Kalua Makoleokalani, a descendant of Maui royalty. He went to school at Wailuku at the age of eight and two years later attended an English school on a ranch. He was one of the first pupils of the Haleakala School in 1869 and graduated in 1875. He taught school at Ulupalakua and was elected to the legislature in 1880.

Wilcox was one of the three students sent by KALAKAUA to Italy under the guardianship of Celso Caesar MORENO. Wilcox graduated from the Royal Military Academy at Turin and began two years at the Royal Application School for Engineer and Artillery Officers. He married the Baroness Gina Sobrero in 1887 and returned to Hawaii. In July, 1889, rebelling against the Constitution of 1887, Wilcox, resplendent in his Italian cadet uniform, and about a hundred and fifty followers surrounded the government buildings and barricaded a bungalow on the palace grounds. Seven revolutionaries were killed and a dozen wounded. Wilcox surrendered the next day and was

Wilcox, Samuel Whitney

tried for treason, but was acquitted when he pleaded that he had acted with the king's sanction.

Wilcox represented Honolulu in the legislature in 1890 and Koolauloa in 1892 as head of the Liberal Party. After LILIUOKALANI was deposed, Wilcox led an abortive counter-revolution in 1895 and was condemned to death, but the United States Congress intervened. President Sanford B. DOLE of the Republic of Hawaii commuted the sentence to thirty-five years' imprisonment at hard labor and a fine of $10,000, but the firebrand and all the rebels were pardoned within a few months. While Wilcox was in prison, his Italian wife obtained an annulment of the marriage and in 1896 Wilcox married Princess Theresa Owana Kaohelelani, a direct descendant of KEOUA KALANI, father of Kamehameha I. Wilcox was elected the first delegate to Congress in 1900 under the Home Rule Party with the slogan "Hawaii for the Hawaiians," but was defeated in 1902 by a Hawaiian, Prince Jonah Kuhio KALANIANAOLE.

WILCOX, SAMUEL WHITNEY (1847–1929)

Like his elder brothers, Albert and George WILCOX, sons of Abner WILCOX, Samuel, born at Waioli, Kauai, attended Punahou School and became a sugar planter. For many years he was manager of the cattle-raising branch of Grove Farm Plantation in association with George. He became sheriff of the island of Kauai in 1872 and held that office for twenty-five years. He was a member of the House of Representatives from 1901 to 1902 and a senator from 1903 to 1907. He married Emma Washburn Lyman of Hilo, of the missionary family, in 1874 and the couple had six children. The parents were the donors of the Lihue Parish House as a memorial to their deceased sons Ralph and Charles.

WILDER, GERRIT PARMELE (1863–1935)

Born in Honolulu, son of Samuel Gardner WILDER, Gerrit attended Atkinson Valley School and Punahou. He worked for the Kahului Railroad Co. on the island of Maui in 1884 and became president in 1896. Two years later he became president of the estate of S. G. Wilder, Ltd., and retired from active business to devote his time to horticulture. In 1924, after earning a master's degree at the University of Hawaii, he became an associate in botany at the Bernice P. Bishop Museum. He made expeditions to the South Pacific, the West Indies, Ceylon, and other areas and introduced many plants and trees into Hawaii. He hybridized and created many new varieties of hibiscus. Among other volumes he published *Fruits of the Hawaiian Islands* (Honolulu: Gazette, 1907).

WILDER, JAMES AUSTIN (KIMO) (1868–1934)

Born in Honolulu, son of Samuel Gardner WILDER, James graduated from Punahou School and, planning a career in law, attended Harvard from 1893 to 1895. He became interested in art, however, and later studied under prominent painters in Paris. Returning to Honolulu in 1895, he was not interested in the family shipping business and made a trip to Japan; a year later he joined an expedition to Okinawa and Borneo. During the Spanish-American War, when Wilder was on a six-month stay in Guam, he was condemned to death as an American spy, but survived to supply a full report on conditions in Guam that led to the seizure of that island by the United States. After his Paris studies Wilder had lived in New York City and had become a leader in the Boy Scout movement, being granted at length the title of Chief Sea Scout. He served in World War I and then he and his family toured Spain and other European countries. In 1922 they returned to settle in Honolulu, where Wilder opened a studio as a portrait painter. In 1899 he married Sara Harnden in California and they had two children.

WILDER, SAMUEL GARDNER (1831–1888)

Born in Leominster, Massachusetts, Wilder lived in the western states and for a time was one of the daring riders for the Pony Express. He was with the Adams Express Co. in California until he made his first visit to Hawaii in 1856. A year later he married Elizabeth Kinau Judd, daughter of Dr. G. P. JUDD, and thereafter was prominent in business affairs in Hawaii. He was a pioneer in the shipping of guano from the South Pacific to New York to be used as fertilizer. He also was associated with his father-in-law in starting a sugar plantation at Kualoa, Oahu.

128

In 1871, when Wilder was in charge of the firm of James Isaac DOWSETT and was agent for the government steamer *Kilauea*, he saw the opportunity of setting up a private shipping line. In 1872, with the aid of Christopher H. LEWERS, he purchased the Dowsett interests and established Wilder & Co., which later took over the government steamers and began operations that merged in 1905 with the Inter-Island Steam Navigation Co., founded in 1882. Wilder went on to develop railways on the island of Hawaii in 1881 and on Maui in 1884, and conceived the idea of building a marine railway in Honolulu which was completed in 1883, the first in Hawaii.

Wilder was appointed to the House of Nobles by King Lunalilo in 1873 and continued as a member when the office became elective in 1887. King Kalakaua made Wilder minister of the interior from 1878 to 1880. Wilder also served for years on the Board of Health and visited the leper colony on the island of Molokai every three months. The five children of the Wilders, including Gerrit Parmele WILDER and James Austin WILDER, formed a clan prominent in the history of the islands. See Kinau Wilder, *The Wilders of Waikiki* (Honolulu: Topgallant, 1978).

WILKES, CHARLES (1798–1877)
Born in New York, Wilkes entered the United States Navy as a midshipman and became an authority on oceanography. While still a lieutenant he was appointed to command an expedition to survey the Northwest Coast of America and the Pacific region. The most ambitious scientific expedition hitherto sent out by any nation, it consisted of the flagship *Vincennes* and five other vessels, which sailed in 1838 and spent four years on the work. The ships arrived in Honolulu in the autumn of 1841 and teams of scientists explored Oahu, Maui, and the Big Island; Dr. G. P. JUDD led a party that spent three weeks on Mauna Loa volcano. Many social and cultural observations are found in the eleven large volumes of the report, *Narrative of the United States Exploring Expedition during the Years 1838, 1839, 1840, 1841, 1843* (Philadelphia: Lea & Blanchard, 1845). Two biographies of Wilkes have been published: *The Hidden Coasts* (New York: William Sloane Associates, 1953) by Daniel M. Henderson and *Stormy Voyager: The Story of Charles Wilkes* (Philadelphia: Lippincott, 1968) by Robert Silverberg.

WILKINSON, JOHN (–1826)
A middle-aged English gardener who was brought to Hawaii on the *Blonde* in 1825 by Chief BOKI was a pioneer sugar planter. Wilkinson had lived in the West Indies and had been a captain in the Peninsular War against Napoleon. He laid out an area in Manoa Valley, Oahu, and despite poor health and a lack of tools and laborers he put one hundred acres under cultivation in eighteen months. He also began the growing of coffee trees and the distilling of rum. The strain of the enterprise was too much for him and he died in November, 1826; the plantation was abandoned in 1829. Wilkinson's work antedated by a decade the first serious cultivation of sugar cane at Koloa on Kauai.

WILLIAMS, JAMES J. (1853–1926)
Born in England, Williams came to Honolulu from Cleveland around 1879 to work for Dixon Brothers. He bought the firm and changed the name to J. J. Williams Studio. He was the leading photographer in Honolulu for forty-five years, acquired hundreds of thousands of rare plates, and possessed one of the greatest collections of photographs of Hawaiian royalty and oldtime Honolulu, as well as views of volcano eruptions and historic events. He was the first person to operate a travel agency in the territory, and with Thomas G. THRUM established in 1888 the monthly *Paradise of the Pacific*, designed to attract visitors to Hawaii. Williams died in a streetcar accident at the age of seventy-two.

WILLIS, ALBERT S.
Appointed as United States minister to Hawaii by President Grover Cleveland to replace John L. STEVENS, Willis arrived on November 4, 1893, with instructions to try to restore the former queen, LILIUOKALANI, to the throne. When his efforts failed to get her to allow clemency for those who had accomplished the bloodless revolution, Willis was notified in January, 1894, that his mission was ended and that matters were henceforth in the hands of Congress.

WILSON, JENNIE (1873–1962)
Born as Ana Kini Kapahuhula-o-Kamamalu Kuulalani, she was a dancer at the court of King Kalakaua, who taught her the hula and playing the ukulele. She joined a theatrical troupe in 1892 and toured the mainland and Europe, where she performed for royalty and chiefs of state. She married John Henry WILSON in 1908 and moved to Pelekunu Valley, Molokai, to engage in the growing of taro. She was a leader in the Ahahui Kaahumanu and when her husband was mayor of Honolulu she was "honorary first lady."

WILSON, JOHN HENRY
(1861–1956)

Descended on both sides from early settlers in Hawaii and Tahiti (his mother was a granddaughter of Captain Blanchard, who brought the *Thaddeus* to Hawaii in 1820 with the first American missionaries), Wilson was reared with the royal family at the Waikiki residence of LILIUOKALANI and spoke fluent Hawaiian. He was educated in the schools of Honolulu and graduated with the first class from Stanford University in 1895.

Wilson began his engineering career with the Oahu Railway and Land Co. the following year. In 1897 he was with the Department of Public Works under the Republic and became a partner with L. M. Whitehouse in a private firm. Wilson and Whitehouse were engineers for the construction of the Pali Road over the Koolau Range above Honolulu. Whitehouse left the firm in 1900 but Wilson continued contracting work until 1919. He supervised the construction of the Oahu Railway grade around Kaena Point and built the Honolulu outfall sewer, the Lahaina waterworks system, and the first macadam roads on Maui and Kauai. Wilson was made city engineer of Honolulu in 1919 and in 1920 was appointed mayor to succeed Joseph James FERN. Wilson served in that office 1920–1926, 1929–1930, and 1947–1954. He was a prominent member of the Democrat Party in the islands. He married Jennie Kapahu WILSON in 1908. The Wilson Tunnel on Likelike Highway bears his name.

WINNE, JANE LATHROP
(1884–1976)

Born in Alameda, California, Jane Winne attended Punahou School, studied music in various mainland institutions, and returned to teach that subject in several Honolulu schools. She obtained a bachelor's degree from the Columbia School of Music in Chicago in 1916, and in that year began teaching at Punahou, serving until her retirement in 1943. During World War II she aided the Musicians Center in providing concerts for the armed forces. She gave her talents to a number of local groups. The Bernice P. Bishop Museum in 1925 published her paper on "Music in the Marquesas Islands," and she was an outstanding researcher on the music of Hawaii.

WINSHIP, JONATHAN

Jonathan and his brother Nathan are considered, along with Captain William Heath DAVIS, as pioneers in the sandalwood trade. Jonathan made his first trading voyage from New England to the Northwest Coast and China in the ship *O'Cain* in 1803, and in 1805 commanded this ship on the Northwest Coast. With his brother as chief mate, Jonathan arrived at Oahu in the spring of 1806 to trade with the Hawaiians, and returned there in October. Nathan returned to Oahu as captain of the *Albatross* in the spring of 1810 and brought King KAUMUALII from Kauai to Honolulu to cede his island to KAMEHAMEHA I after his death.

The brothers visited Oahu again in the winter of 1811, with Nathan commanding the *Albatross* and Jonathan commanding the *O'Cain*. Along with a cargo of furs they took a load of sandalwood, part of which was for the account of King Kamehameha. The ruler was pleased with his share of the returns and on July 12, 1812, granted the Winships, along with Captain Davis, an exclusive ten-year sales contract for all the sandalwood cut in the islands, except for Kauai. Various chiefs on whose lands the wood was to be cut were not included in the contract. Five shiploads sold at Canton in 1813 brought a high price.

At home in Honolulu, the Winships were neighbors of the Spanish settler Francisco de Paula MARÍN. The War of 1812 between the United States and Britain interfered with development of the sandalwood trade, and after the 1813 voyage the king cancelled the contract. However, sandalwood was the main source of island income for the next fifteen years. The brothers returned to Boston in 1816 and retired from the sea.

WINSHIP, NATHAN

See WINSHIP, Jonathan.

WISE, JOHN HENRY
(1869–1937)

Wise was born at Kohala, Hawaii, son of Julius A. Wise, a native of Germany, and Rebecca Nawaa. He graduated from Hilo Boarding School in 1886 and in 1887 entered the first class in the Kamehameha School for Boys. He graduated from theological seminary in Oberlin, Ohio, in 1893. In 1895 he joined the counter-revolution led by monarchy forces and served a year in prison for his acts. He was appointed interpreter of the House of Representatives in 1901 and thereafter was associated with political efforts on behalf of native Hawaiians. Wise was considered an authority on the Hawaiian language and lore and was a consultant concerning landholdings, water rights, and customs. He was appointed director of prohibition enforcement for Hawaii in 1923. Wise served for many years on the faculty of the Kamehameha Schools and was co-author of a textbook on the Hawaiian language. He married Lois Kawai in 1897 and the couple had ten children.

WISE, WILLIAM SPENCER Sr. (1903–1964)

Born at Kamuela, Hawaii, Wise played football for McKinley High School and the University of Hawaii. Regarded as the best forward-passer and all-round backfield player ever developed in Hawaii, Wise was signal caller for his team when McKinley won its first Interscholastic League championship in 1921. Wise graduated from McKinley in 1922 and played football for four years under the University coach Otto Klum; he also played basketball and threw the javelin. He coached at the Kamehameha School for Boys (1926–1937), Punahou School (1938–1940), and McKinley High School (1941–1954). Wise retired in 1954 but remained as advisory coach at McKinley.

WIST, BENJAMIN OTHELLO (1889–1951)

Born in St. Paul, Minnesota, Wist earned a bachelor's degree from Spokane College and a doctorate from Yale University. He came to Hawaii in 1911 and taught for ten years at schools in Kawiki, Pahala, and Honokaa on the island of Hawaii and at the Kamehameha III Elementary School on Maui. He was made president of the Territorial Normal School in 1921 and later was dean of Teachers College at the University of Hawaii, where he developed the five-year training program later adopted by many mainland colleges. In 1932 he was named chairman of an educational survey commission in American Samoa, where he reorganized public schools and served as educational adviser to the governor. He also established the Teachers College laboratory schools and did the early planning for the University High School.

A friend and adviser to Oren E. LONG, Wist was head of the committee on style of the Hawaii Constitutional Convention of 1950; after his retirement from the University, he was vice chairman of the Hawaii Statehood Commission, for which he campaigned strenuously on the mainland. Wist married Blanche Canario in 1912 and the couple had three daughters. Wist was author of *A Century of Public Education in Hawaii, October 15, 1840 to October 15, 1940* (Honolulu: Hawaii Educational Review, 1940).

WOOD, HART (1880–1957)

Born in Philadelphia, Wood worked for architectural firms in San Francisco before coming to Hawaii in 1919 as chief designer for C. W. DICKEY and later became a partner in the firm. Still later he founded his own concern, Wood, Weed & Associates.

Wood designed the Alexander & Baldwin Building; other designs include those of the Christian Science Church on Punahou Street, the Chinese Christian Church on King Street, the Gump Building at Lewers and Kalakaua in Waikiki, and the Honolulu Board of Water Supply pumping stations. He also designed a number of prominent residences. His independent nature allowed him to experiment with forms unique to the islands. He was influenced at various times by Spanish Mission, Chinese, Italian Classic, and American eclectic styles, and adapted these to the natural landscape, climate, and rich cultural background of Hawaii. He married Jessie F. Spangler in 1906 and they had four children.

WOOD, ROBERT W. (–1892)

Wood was born, it is believed, in Augusta, Maine. He graduated from Waterville College and obtained a medical degree from Bowdoin College in 1832. He arrived in Honolulu in 1839 and for a decade was head of the American Seamen's Hospital in that city. He was also doing a profitable business in selling drugs and medical and surgical supplies to visiting ships.

Wood was the principal creditor of Ladd & Co., pioneer planters on the island of Kauai. When the mission of Peter H. BRINSMADE failed, Wood took over the management of the Koloa Plantation in 1844 and placed it on a firmer foundation. He also financed the East Maui Plantation in partnership with A. H. Spencer in 1849; there he hired a young mechanic, David M. WESTON, whose invention in 1851 of a centrifugal method of separating sugar from molasses revolutionized the industry. Wood opened Honolulu's first public pharmacy in 1848. He also owned ships and a mercantile business. He was the only financier to succeed in the sugar industry previous to the signing of the reciprocity treaty with the United States in 1876. After heading the Koloa Plantation for twenty-seven years he sold it to a consortium in 1872, and it was incorporated in 1878 as the Koloa Sugar Co. The very wealthy Dr. Wood left Hawaii in 1866 and settled in Massachusetts, where he retired in 1878 and died in 1892.

WOOLLEY, SAMUEL EDWIN (1859–1925)

Born in Salt Lake City of pioneer Mormon ancestors, Woolley worked on his father's Utah ranch until he was sent to Hawaii in 1880 and spent four years at the colony at Laie, Oahu. He returned in 1895 to take charge of Laie Plantation and to serve as president of the Latter Day Saints' Hawaiian Mission in its work throughout the territory. He was a skillful organizer whose efforts were markedly successful in a back-to-the-soil movement among native Hawaiians and mainlanders. Woolley established credit for the church among the businessmen of the islands, and during his presidency the landmark Mormon Temple at Laie was planned and erected; his son Ralph E. Woolley supervised the construction, which was completed in 1919. The senior Woolley was succeeded as president in that year by E. Wesley Smith, son of Joseph F. Smith, but he retained managership of Laie Plantation and became president of the Koolau Agricultural Co., which had been purchased in that year by the Mormon Church. Woolley retired to his Salt Lake home in 1921. He married Alice Rowberry in Utah in 1885 and the couple had five children, several of whom carried on careers in Hawaii.

WRIGHT, GEORGE FRED (1881–1938)

Born in Honolulu, Wright was the son of a carriagemaker who had come there to set up a business the previous year. Wright graduated from Honolulu High School in 1898 and entered the government survey department in June. He continued there until in 1909 he went into business for himself as a land surveyor. He married Martha Lycett in 1905. He was a surveyor for the Territorial Land Court and a member of the licensing board for engineers, architects, and surveyors. Wright was elected to the Board of Supervisors in 1926 and elected mayor of Honolulu for four two-year terms beginning in 1930. He supported city beautification, as well as using public-works programs for unemployment relief during the depression. He died while in office, on a cruise from Auckland, New Zealand, taken for his health; his unexpired term was filled by Charles S. CRANE. Mayor Wright Housing in Honolulu is named in honor of the four-term office holder.

WYLLIE, ROBERT CRICHTON (1798–1865)

Wyllie was born at Hazelbank, Ayrshire, Scotland, and at the age of twelve entered the University of Glasgow. He early went to sea as a ship's doctor, and later was a successful merchant in South America and Mexico, and then a prominent businessman in London. When General William MILLER was appointed British consul general in Honolulu, he invited his friend Wyllie to go there with him. Not long after Wyllie arrived, in March, 1844, he replaced Miller for a year during Miller's travels. Wyllie's business talent qualified him to serve in the cabinet of KAMEHAMEHA III, and he was minister of foreign affairs from 1845 until his death.

Wyllie was one of the foremost men in the kingdom for almost twenty years, but he always kept his Scottish appearance and speech. He was a busy writer of letters. In 1862 he left his Presbyterian faith to join the newly founded Episcopal Church of Hawaii. For ten years he took the lead in seeking to make treaties that would make clear the relations of the kingdom with other nations of the world. He was owner of the large Princeville Plantation on the north shore of Kauai, a ranch named for the little Prince ALBERT.

YOUNG, ALEXANDER (1832–1910)

Born in Blackburn, Scotland, Young became a machinist and mechanical engineer. He married Ruth Pearce in 1860 and the couple sailed around Cape Horn to Vancouver Island, where he was to spend five years building and operating a sawmill. They arrived in Hawaii in 1865, and Young formed a partnership with William Lidgate to operate a foundry and machine shop at Hilo. He then moved to Honolulu and bought an interest in the Honolulu Iron Works, continuing in this business for thirty-two years. He also invested in sugar plantations; he was president of the Waiakea Mill Co. and had an interest in Kahuku Plantation. During the monarchy he was a member of the House of Nobles in 1889, and after the Revolution of 1893 he was minister of the interior in the cabinet of President Sanford B. DOLE.

In 1900, when Hawaii became part of the United States, Young began construction of the Alexander Young Building, mainly for use as a hotel; it was completed in 1903. In 1905 he bought the Moana Hotel on Waikiki Beach and later the Hawaiian Hotel, located at Richards and Hotel Streets. At about the same time he branched into the automobile business, and along with his son-in-law Conrad Carl VON HAMM and others formed the Von Hamm-Young Co. The Alexander Youngs had nine children, including Archibald Alfred Young, who followed in his father's business footsteps.

YOUNG, JOHN (OLOHANA) (1749?–1835)

Young was the English boatswain of a small American fur-trading vessel, *Eleanora*, in 1790. Off the coast of Maui, the ship was attacked and the captain, Simon METCALFE, punished the Hawaiians severely. Later off the Big Island at Kawaihae, Young —whose boatswain's call of "All hands!" gave him the nickname of "Olohana"—was ashore when the *Fair American*, commanded by Metcalf's eighteen-year-old son Thomas, was captured and only one of the six members of the crew, Isaac DAVIS, was saved.

Young was detained ashore and thereafter KAMEHAMEHA I trusted both Young and Davis to advise him on the ways of people from overseas, and both took important roles in history. Both manned large guns mounted on canoes when the chief invaded the northern side of the island of Hawaii, and later were in charge of the cannons during the attack on Oahu.

Young married Kaonaeha (Melie Kuamoo), a niece of Kamehameha, and held landed estates on five islands. He served as governor of several of the islands, and helped to repel the Russian filibusters under Dr. George Anton SCHEFFER. Young took part in all the major changes in the islands as an elder statesman, joining in the overthrow of the ancient tabus in 1819. He did not object to the landing of the American missionaries in 1820 but feared the rivalry might grow between the United States and Great Britain, which at the time was supposed to hold a protectorate over the kingdom. Young also foresaw the decline of the native population through wars and disease. He died in 1835 and in 1865 his body was placed in the Royal Mausoleum. His granddaughter reigned as Queen EMMA.

YOUNG, JOHN II (KEONI ANA) (1810–1857).

Son of John YOUNG and the chiefess Kaonaeha, Keoni Ana, as he was called, was born at Kawaihae, Hawaii. He married Alapai and succeeded KEKAULUOKI as kuhina nui, or prime minister, from 1845 to 1854. He also served as governor of Maui, minister of the interior, chamberlain of the king's household, and Supreme Court justice. He aided in communication between native and foreign elements in the community.

ZEPHYRIN
See KEPELINO.

The Government Post Office was a prominent building on Merchant Street when it opened in 1871 during the reign of the last Kamehameha.

LEGENDARY FIGURES OF HAWAII NEI

AIAI. A god of fishermen, son of KUULAKAI and HINAPUKUIA. He traveled around the islands setting up fishing bases and altars.

AILAAU. A fire god working before the arrival of PELE.

AIWOHIKUPUA. The Kauai hero who vainly wooed LAIEIKAWAI in the legendary land of Paliuli on the island of Hawaii.

ANIANAKA. 1. An older cousin of KAWELO. On becoming chief of Kauai he banished Kawelo's parents and started an invasion. He was grandfather of KALAKAUA and LILIUOKALANI. 2. A chief of Oahu who sent men to bring the beautiful wife of HALEMANO to him, thus causing the couple to flee their island. 3. A Maui chief who married HINAHANAIAKAMA-LAMA. He tried to prevent her from leaping to the moon, where she dwells today.

AUHEA. See KEKAULUOHI.

AUKELENUIAIKU. A hero, a son of Iku, bearing a strong resemblance to the Joseph of the Bible, this character was probably an invention by a Christian informant.

HAINAKOLO. 1. A forest-dwelling goddess of kapa makers and bird catchers; also called HAIWAHINE or HAI. 2. A legendary woman who, crazed by the desertion of her husband, ran away to Waipio.

HAKAU. See UMI and LILOA.

HALELEHUA. A sea goddess who lived in the waters between Oahu and Kauai.

HALEMANO. This Oahu hero wooed the Puna princess KAMALA-LAWALU.

HALOA. Youngest son of WAKEA, the first man, by his daughter HOOHOKUKALANI. Haloa was born a shapeless mass and buried beside Wakea's house. A taro plant grew at the spot, and the symbol for Haloa is a calabash of taro. According to David MALO, Haloa was "the progenitor of all the peoples of the earth."

HALOANAKALAUKAPALILI. Oldest son of WAKEA and HOOHO-KUKALANI. See HALOA.

HALULUIKEKIHIOKAMOKU. 1. A bird god said to have been born from the shoulder of his mother, HAUMEA. 2. A man-eating bird killed by AUKELE.

HALULUKOAKOA. A wind god living in the low-spreading rainbow; he made the winds roar.

HANAIAKAMALAMA. A benevolent goddess, wife of Haka-lanileo and mother of KANA.

HANAKAHI. An ancient chief, symbol of the Hilo district.

HAULANI. A plant goddess, daughter of HINA and sister of HAUNUU and KAMAPUAA.

HAULILI. A Kauai god of speech.

HAUMAKAPUU. A god who watches over fish ponds.

HAUMEA. An earth-mother goddess with many husbands and children. She presided over child-birth. She is equated with PAPA and KAMEHAIKANA. She married WAKEA and later married HALOA. She is considered the mother of PELE and Pele's brothers and sisters, who were born from her mouth or armpits. See KAULU and PU-NAAIKOAE.

HAUNUU. A plant goddess, daughter of HINA and sister of HAULANI and KAMAPUAA.

HAUWAHINE. A good mo'o goddess living in ponds at Kailua, Oahu. She brought an abundance of fish, warded off sickness, and punished oppressive owners of ponds.

HAWAIILOA. Hawaiiloa was the legendary discoverer of the Hawaiian Islands.

IOULI. A bird god.

A Chief and Chiefess of the Sandwich Islands

IWA. The master thief who stole the magic cowry squid lure of UMI and other treasures.

KAAHUPAHAU. She was chiefess of the shark gods of Puuloa (Pearl Harbor). She and her brother, KAHIUKA, were born human but were changed into sharks that vowed to protect Oahu from other sharks. See KAEHUIKIMANO-O-PUULOA and KUHAIMOANA.

KAALAENUIAHINA. A goddess associated with MAUI; her name means "the great mudhen of Hina," and Maui learned the art of fire-making from a mudhen.

KAEHUIKIMANO-O-PUULOA. A shark god of Puna, named for KAAHUPAHAU.

KAHAI. A hero, born on Maui, who went to Kahiki to find his father, MEHA. He brought the breadfruit plant from Upolu, Samoa, to Oahu. See NAMAKA-O-KUHAI.

KAHALA-O-MAPUANA. Young-est and most important of the MAILE sisters.

KAHALA-O-PUNA. A lovely girl of Manoa Valley, wife of HAUHI. He beat her to death for being unfaithful and buried her under an ohia tree, but she was restored to life by passers-by.

KAHANAIAKEAKUA. See POLIAHU.

KAHIUKA. See KAAHUPAHAU.

KAHOALII. A god, said to belong to the family of PELE, associated with the underworld and the worship of KU.

KAHOLIAKANE. A shark god who lived in a cave at Puhi, Kauai, and was the guardian of KALANIOPUU. See KUA.

KAHOLOKALANI. See KOALAUKANI.

KAHUHIHEWA. Perhaps Oahu's most famous chief, he appears in many legends. He supplied KA-WELO with a canoe as he prepared to invade Kauai.

KAHUILAOKALANI. See KALAIPAHOA.

KAIKAPU. 1. A cannibalistic mo'o who lived in a cave at Ninole, Ka'u. In another account she lived at Punaluu, Ka'u, and was killed by KALA and his helpers. In another account she was blind; she was restored to sight by AUKELE-NUIAKIKI and guided him to the water of life of KANE.

KAIPALAOA. A boy expert in riddling and punning.

KALAIPAHOA. This sorcery god was represented by images made of wood of three trees at Maunaloa, Molokai. Chips from these trees were used in sorcery.

KAMAIKAAHUI. See PALILA.

KAMAKANUIAHAILONO. The god who introduced the art of healing to Hawaii, he caused the foot of LONOPUHA to swell and then taught him to cure such wonders.

KAMALALAWALU. 1. A Maui chief whose large army, through a series of stupid actions, was annihi-lated by the forces of LONOIKAMA-KAHIKI. 2. The Puna princess wooed by HALEMANO.

KAMAPUAA. Many legends are told of this hog demigod, whose rootings created valleys and springs. He had many affairs and was a symbol of lechery. He could stretch his body to great lengths and assume many other forms. He taunted PELE and finally mated with her, dividing the lands of the island of Hawaii between them. He fought and killed the dog KUILIOLOA. See HINA 2, MAKALII, and OLOPANA.

KAMAUNUANIHO. See HINA 2.

KAMEHAIKANA. Another name for HAUMEA, when associated with breadfruit trees.

KAMOHOALII. The older and favorite brother of PELE, who could assume the form of a shark or a fish.

KANA. The stretching demigod born as a rope on Maui. He could stretch from Molokai to Hawaii and wade in the deep sea. He restored the sun and, with his brother NIHEU, rescued his mother, HINA, from a chief of Molokai.

KANALOA. One of the four great gods of Hawaii, along with KANE, KU, and LONO. He was a companion of Kane and together they drank awa and found water in many places. He was considered by some to be a god of the ocean. A Christian storyteller identified Kanaloa as Satan in the conflict with the trinity of the other three great gods.

KANE. He was worshiped by many as the leading god among the four great ones, along with KANALOA, KU, and LONO. He was a god of creation and the ancestor of chiefs and commoners. He was a god of sunlight, fresh water, and forests. Prayers to Kane mention him in more than seventy forms.

KANEAPUA. A trickster in many stories, he is variously described as a brother of PELE, a bird brother of NAMAKAOKAHAI, as a younger shark brother of KANE and KANA-LOA, and as a fish god of Lanai.

KANEHEKILI. God of thunder.

KANEHOALANI. A ruler of the heavens, and father or ancestor of PELE.

KANEHUNAMOKU. He was a family god who carried away the bodies of worshipers when they died. KANE and KANALOA were supposed to live on a lovely island, visible on the distant horizon at sunrise and sunset, ruled by Kane-hunamoku.

KANEPUNIU. A demigod who assumed the form of a coconut.

KAONOHIOKALA. 1. A sky-dwelling god who conducted the souls of dead chiefs; see KUWA-HAILO. 2. A supernatural being who lived in the eyeball of the sun. He lived in the sun with LAIEIKA-WAI, but on a later journey to the earth he was unfaithful and she banished him to become the first wandering spirit or ghost.

KAPOULAKINAU. She was an older sister of PELE and a daughter of HAUMEA. She had a dual nature—as a benevolent hula goddess associated with LAKA, and as a fierce sorceress. See PUEOKAHI.

KAPUAIAIA. See MANAKIKEOE.

KAPUOALAKAI. A forest goddess who presided over the lines by which new canoes were guided as they were pulled from the mountains to the sea.

KAUHI. 1. A demigod chained to a cliff by PELE near Kahana, Oahu. He asked HIIAKA to free him, but when she regretfully refused he tried to tear himself loose and rose to a crouching position. Today he is pointed out as the "crouching lion" statue. 2. The murderous husband of KAHALAOPUNA.

KAULU. A trickster demigod who performed many feats. He was born in the form of a rope, but as a human being with strong hands he created surf by breaking waves. He created small dogs by breaking KUILIO-LOA, the long dog, into pieces. He made the sea salty by swallowing and spitting it out. MAKALII gave him his nets and he entangled and killed HAUMEA. He defeated LONO-KAEHO and gained control of Koolau, Oahu.

KAUMAILIULA. Brother and husband of KEAOMELEMELE.

KAWELOLEIMAKUA. The hero of a story of battle between invaders of Kauai and this staunch defender; see AIKANAKA 1.

KAWELOMAHAMAHAIA. An older brother of KAWELOLEIMA-KUA, he was turned into a shark.

KAWELU. Daughter of OLOPANA and wife of HIKUIKANAHELE; see MILU.

KEALIIKAUOKAU. A shark god who protected the Ka'u region from other sharks. He was a cousin of PELE and a son of KUA.

KEAOMELEMELE. A daughter of KU and HINA. She was reared at the mythical land of Kealohilani by MO'OINANEA, chiefess of all the mo'o, and guarded by horizon clouds. She finally married her brother, KAUMAILIULA. She visited all the islands and excelled in chanting, hula, and surfing. She was worshiped by soothsayers and readers of omens.

KEAWENUIAUMI. See PAKAA.

KIHANUILULUMOKU. The fierce mo'o guardian of Pali-uli, the mythical paradise on the island of Hawaii and home of LAIEIKAWAI.

KIHAWAHINE. She was a Maui chiefess who at death became the most famous of the mo'o tribe and a goddess worshiped on Maui and Hawaii. She could take the form of a dog, chicken, mullet, or spider. The famous chief PIILANI was descended from her, and his son KIHAA-PIILANI was named for her.

KILA. Son of MOIKEHA, who went to Kahiki to fetch the adopted son of Moikeha, LAAMAIKAHIKI.

KOU. 1. An officer under chief Kakehihewa of Oahu, after whom old Honolulu (Kou) was named. 2. A second wife of the hero KAWELO.

KU. One of the four leading gods of Hawaii. In some accounts, Ku (representing the male principle) and HINA (the female principle) were the first gods to reach these islands, followed next by KANE and KANA-LOA, and last by LONO. Ku also refers to the rising sun, and Hina to the setting sun; hence their realm includes the whole earth and the heavens and all generations of man born and unborn. Ku is found also in dozens of other aspects. He was appealed to for rain and growth, fishing, and sorcery, but was best known as the fierce god of war. He sometimes assumed the form of the ohia tree or the io hawk.

KUA. A shark god called the king shark of Ka'u. With KAHO-LIAKANE he raised a storm between Kauai and Oahu to prevent the marriage of their divine relative, PELE, and LOHIAU, a mortal.

KUAPAKAA. See PAKAA.

KUHAIMOANA. A shark god, brother of PELE. He was said to be thirty fathoms long and to be the husband of KAAHUPAHAU.

KUHOONEENUU. An Oahu war god similar to KUKEOLOEWA.

KUIALUA. The god of trainees in lua fighting. After finishing training, the student ate the eyeball of a victim.

KUILIOLOA. A giant man-dog who was killed by KAMAPUAA. The hero KAULU tore the giant dog to pieces; therefore dogs are small today.

KUKAILIMOKU. The most famous of the KU images, it was possessed by KAMEHAMEHA I. These fearsome battle standards were believed to utter cries during the fighting. The original image was named Kaili and was inherited by UMI from his father, LILOA. It was housed at Puukohola.

KUKAOO. A god of farmers, named for their o'o or digging stick.

KUKAUAKAHI. An important owl aumakua or family totem. He saved a relative from drowning, and opened a jail door for another relative.

KUKEOLOEWA. A war god of Maui chiefs. His image was made from a supernatural tree which was first used as a shelf (oloewa); it was later made into an image linked with sorcery. This was kept by KAMEHA-MEHA I as a guide for the souls of the dead. It was also associated with healing and rain, and was considered a visible symbol of KUNUIAKEA.

KUKEOLOWALU. See KUKAOO.

KULEONUI. A loud-voiced menehune god.

KUMOKUHALII. A god of forests and canoe makers, married to LEA.

KUMUHEA. A god of cutworms, able to take the form of a caterpillar or a sea cucumber. A son of KU, he married a girl from Puuenuhe (Caterpillar Hill), Ka'u, but she wasted away on his diet, sweet-potato leaves.

KUMUHONUA. A mythical ancestor twenty generations before WAKEA; also called HULIHONUA.

KUMUKAHI. 1. The aumakua of plovers. On his way back from Kahiki he stopped at the easternmost point of the island of Hawaii, which now bears his name. 2. The favorite younger brother of KAMALALA-WALU.

KUNUIAKEA. The head of all the KU gods. Heiaus were erected to him in times of crisis, especially war. He was an unseen god living in the highest heaven. His visible symbols were KUKAILIMOKU, KUHOO-NEENUU, and KUKEOLOEWA. He was represented on heiaus by blocks of freshly cut ohia wood.

KUOHIALAKA. Father of HI-KUIKANAHELE. See LAKA 2.

KUPAAIKEE. A god of canoe makers, worshiped as the inventor of the adz.

KUPULUPULU. A god of the forest and canoe makers.

KUULAKAI. God of fishermen, husband of HINAPUKUIA and father of AIAI. He built the first fishpond. He gave magic objects to Aiai and told him to set up fishing bases and shrines. All fishermen's stone images and altars bear his name. Red was kapu to Kuula and persons wearing red might not approach a fishing shrine.

KUWAHAILO. A man-eating god, who introduced human sacrifice. It was believed that he ate the souls of men when KAONOHIOKALA conducted them to him. He was the husband of HAUMEA and father of PELE. He could assume many forms, such as a mo'o or a caterpillar. Other names for him are MILU and Kahanuoawa (the breath of sourness). He once ate a man infested with maggots.

LAAHANA. Patron goddess of kapa makers and a daughter of MAIKOHA.

LAAMAIKAHIKI. An early settler brought from Kahiki by KILA. He introduced image worship in the form of a figure called LO-NOIKAOUALII.

LAAMAOMAO. A goddess of winds and the mother of PAKAA. She gave him a calabash containing the bones of her mother. He could thus control the winds by chanting their various names.

LAENIHI. A sister of HALE-MANO, she often assumed the form of the laenihi fish. She found Halemano's sweetheart for him, and twice brought him back to life after he had died of love sickness.

LAIEIKAWAI. Heroine of a lengthy story by S. N. HALEOLE, called "the masterpiece of Hawaiian romantic fiction." She was hidden at birth in a pool at Laie, Oahu, and later reared in a sacred house of yellow feathers at Pali-uli, a mythical paradise on the island of Hawaii. AIWOHIKUPUA wooed her in vain. She married KAONOHIOKALA and they lived in the sun, but he was unfaithful. Laie was worshiped as the lady of the twilight. See MAILE and WAKA.

LAKA. 1. Goddess of the hula and various forest plants, she was often identified with KAPOULAKINAU; see MAILE. 2. A hero whose log, which was felled for a canoe, was found growing upright the following morning. 3. A god worshiped by canoe makers; also known as KUOHIALAKA.

LANIKAULA. A mo'o-slaying prophet who lived at a kukui grove in East Molokai.

LAUKAPALII. See MAKANI-KEOE.

LEA. Goddess of canoe makers, she was the wife of KUMOKUHALII and sister of HINAPUKUAI. Both sisters took the form of an elepaio bird to help canoe makers choose proper logs. She was also called HINAKUWAA.

LIHIAU. The dream sweetheart of PELE, he was brought by HIIAKA from Kauai. See PAOA.

LILINOE. A goddess of the mists and younger sister of POLIAHU.

LIMALOA. A god of mirages on Kauai and guardian of the sea. As a human being he asked KAMAPUAA to help him court some pretty sisters; instead, Kamapuaa got them for himself.

LOLUPE. A Maui demigod in the form of a stingray or kite (lupe), he was invoked to bring a person back to life. He consigned to death those speaking ill of a chief and led the souls of the righteous persons in safety. At the death of a ruling chief, priests of Lolupe detected the sorcerer who had caused the death. Kites could not be flown about houses but only in certain open fields, or famine would result.

LONO. Along with KANE, KU, and KANALOA, Lono was one of the four principal gods of ancient Hawaii. He presided over agriculture, rain, clouds, winds, the harvest, sports, the arts of peace, and medicine. The legend ran that Lono was a king who had killed his wife in a fit of anger. He had gone mad with grief, and had wandered through all the islands, boxing and wrestling with anyone he met. Then he had set out, "in a singularly shaped canoe," for foreign lands, promising to return. The annual procession around the islands during the makahiki season was led by priests of LONOMAKUA who carried a banner that looked like sails on the yard of a ship. When Captain James COOK sailed around the island of Hawaii during the makahiki season in 1778, the people decided that he was their god Lono, coming to celebrate the season of peace. During the festivities, thousands of persons would gather to watch bouts of boxing, wrestling, bowling, and spear-throwing, and gamble heavily on the outcome. Lono also could take the form of KAMAPUAA. Some fifty Lono gods were worshiped in the islands; see below.

LONOIKAMAKAHIKI. 1. The god of the makahiki festival, whose priests circled the islands when taxes were collected. 2. A younger son of KEAWENUIAUMI who became chief of the island of Hawaii and defeated the invading forces of KAMALALAWALU of Maui. He was also famous as a debater and as a boxer and wrestler.

LONOIKAOUALII. This was an image taken by LAAMAIKAHIKI from Raiatea in the Society Islands to Wailua, Kauai. At the request of MAUI, this Lono lengthened the night so that Maui might kill Peapea.

LONOIKEAWEAWEALOHA. A god of mercy and lovemaking, he miraculously taught MAKALII all the name chants of KAMAPUAA in order to appease his wrath. This Lono was an uncle of PELE and was also known as LONOAWEAWEKI-KALOHA.

LONOKAEHO. This was an eight-headed chief from Kahiki who pierced the cliff at Kanehoalani, Kualoa, Oahu, and severed Kahuku from Kahipa. He was killed by KAMAPUAA, who called on his plant bodies to entangle the eight stone foreheads of Lonokaeho.

LONOMAKAIHE. A god of spear throwers.

LONOMAKUA. An uncle of PELE, who brought fire at her command. He kept the sacred fire of the under-world beneath his armpit.

LONOPUHA. A god of healing; see KAMAKANUIAHAILONO.

MAIKOHA. A deified hairy man who became a god of kapa makers. From his grave at Kaupo, Maui, grew the first wauke plant, whose inner bark is used for making kapa.

MAILE. Four sweet-scented sisters with human and plant forms. They were MAILE HAIWALE (brittle maile), MAILEKALUHEA (fragrant maile), MAILELAULII (small-leaved maile), and MAILEPAHAKA. They appear in many legends, most notably as guardians of LAIEIKAWAI and her house thatched with bird feathers in legendary Paliuli. Fragrance was associated with gods, royalty, and religion, especially for worshipers of LAKA. See KAHALAOMA-PUANA.

MAIOLA. A god of healing who was said to occupy certain trees. The wood of these trees would counteract the poison of certain other trees.

MAKAKUKOAE. A god who induced palsy and insanity. The insane jumped over cliffs where tropic birds flew. He was invoked by sorcerers who desired the death of an enemy.

MAKALII. A chief of Waimea, Kauai, father-in-law of MANOKA-LANIPO, and famous as a grower of plants. During the makahiki festivals, food plants were symbolically dropped from his net. Several times KAMAKUAA killed all the men of OLOPANA except Makalii. Later, he placated KAMAPUAA by reciting all the name songs honoring the man-hog. Still later, Makalii gave his nets to KAULU so that he might entangle and kill HAUMEA. The name of Makalii is given to the cluster of stars called the Pleiades. By some he was considered a navigator.

MAKANIKEOE. A wind god who could make plants grow and could take the form of a tree. A variant name was KAPUAIAIA.

MAKUAAIHUE. A god worshiped by thieves.

MALEI. A fishing goddess. Fishermen placed seaweed on her altars with prayers for success.

MANOKALANIPO. A Kauai chief, husband of Naekapulani, daughter of MAKALII, and an ancestor of KAWELO.

MAUI. The demigod Maui was the most famed trickster of ancient times, known even better in the South Pacific than in Hawaii, where an island bears his name. According to most stories, his birth was mysterious. His many adventures include pushing up the sky; getting fire from a mudhen (see KAALAENUI-AHINA); fishing up the islands; and snaring the sun at Haleakala, Maui, in order to lengthen the day and thus permit his mother, HINA, to dry her kapa. He attempted vainly to draw the islands together near Kaena Point (see MOANAONUIKALEHUA). Although associated with the island of Maui, the demigod's name is marked by a long *a*. See HINAOPU-HALAKOA, LONOIKAOUALII, and PIMOE.

MAULIOLA. A god of health.

MEHA. See KAHAI.

MILU. A thief who was banished to the underworld, Milu became the ruler of this region, which took his name. "Going to Milu" was a popular term for dying. In a story comparable to the Greek myth of Orpheus, HIKU went to Milu to bring back his wife, KAWELU, who had strangled herself in the belief that she was unloved. See KUWAHAILO.

MOANONUIKALEHUA. A goddess who came with PELE from Kahiki and lived in the channel between Kauai and Oahu. She had two forms: one of a woman as beautiful as a lehua tree laden with blossoms, the other of a red goatfish. When MAUI tried to draw the islands together, Moano and others snagged his hook into a rock, which was then pulled to Kaena Point. Maui caught Moano's fish body and laid it on a shrine.

MOIKEHA. The son of a settler from Kahiki and the father of KILA.

MOOINANEA. She was the matriarch of all the mo'o gods and goddesses. She brought countless bands of them from a mythical land to Oahu. She lived for a time in a clay pit at Puunui, Honolulu, and is said to have made a mythical pool in the sky land. She was also known as KAMOOINANEA. See AUKELE-NUIAIKU and KEAOMELEMELE.

NAMAKAOKAHAI. She was an older sister of PELE, said to have been born from the breasts of MAUMEA. Because of a quarrel with her, Pele migrated with her family to Hawaii. Namaka came also and brought certain plants to the islands. She is said to have married AUKE-LENUIAIKU. Namaka fought with Pele on Maui; Pele escaped with her life, but left some of her bones at Naiwi-o-Pele near Hana.

NANAHOA. A man of Molokai who abused his wife; both he and she were turned into upright rocks.

NIHEU. A trickster demigod, mischievous younger brother of KANA.

NIOLOPUA. God of sleep.

NIULOAHIKI. He was a kupua who could take three forms: man, eel, and coconut. In his tree form, he was the pathway to a mythical island of the same name (niu or coconut) to which persons keeping the kapu might go after death.

NUAKEA. A goddess called on to help nursing mothers and to wean infants. She was called the wife of Keoloewa, a ruling chief of Molokai.

OLOHANA. 1. An Oahu giant; see PALILA. 2. Nickname of John YOUNG.

OLOPANA. 1. An Oahu chief and uncle of KAMAPUAA. When his nephew stole his chickens, the chief repeatedly sent hundreds of men to catch him; but each time Kamapuaa's grandmother, KAMAUNAANIHO, sang the man-pig's name songs and the men carrying him were killed. See MAKALII.

OPELUNUIKAUHAALILO. A god of thieves and medical practitioners; he was a son of PELE by KAMAPUAA.

PAAO. A legendary priest and navigator supposed to have sailed from Tahiti around 1000 A. D. and landed at Puna, Hawaii. He and his companions were welcomed by earlier settlers and built the heiau of Mookini at Hawaii. He is said to have introduced human sacrifice, walled heiaus, red-feather girdles as a sign of rank, kapu songs, the prostrating kapu, and the feather god Kaili. Finding no resident suited to be ruler of the island, Paao returned to Tahiti and brought back a chief named Pilikaaiea, whose line extended to the Kamehamehas.

PAHULU. 1.A Lanai goddess whose family of ghosts was killed off by LANIKAULA or by the mischievous KAULU. 2 A god whose soul enchanted certain fish, especially weke, causing nightmares to those who ate the fish.

PAKAA. The son of the head steward of KEAWENUIAUMI and LAAMAOMAO. Because of jealousy, Pakaa was banished to Molokai, where he taught his young son, KUAPAKAA, the names of more than a hundred wind chants.

PALILA. A kupua hero of Kauai born as a cord, thrown out, and rescued by his grandmother, HINA. He felled a forest with a single stroke, forming a hole at Waihohonu, Kauai. He vaulted with his club from Kauai to the shoulder of an Oahu giant, OLOMANA, and cut him in two; the peak of Olomana remains today. He killed a terrorist, KAMAIKAAHUI, at Waipahu, Oahu. Later he killed warriors of the Hamakua Coast and became the ruling chief of Hilo.

PAOA. The great friend of LOHIAU, lover of PELE. After Lohiau was killed by Pele, his spirit summoned Paoa to Kilauea, where he met Pele and her sisters, succumbed to their charms, and spent three days with the goddess.

PAPA. Probably the same as HAUMEA, and symbolic of the female principle. She is usually considered the wife of WAKEA.

PEAPEA. See LONOIKAOUALII.

PELE. The powerful volcano goddess was born as a flame in the mouth of HAUMEA. Innumerable stories claim various rocks and land forms resulted from the wrath of Pele. She appeared at different times as fire, as a wrinkled hag, as a child, and as a beautiful girl. She is sometimes considered to have come to Hawaii from Tahiti. See HIIAKAIKAPOLI-O-PELE, KAMAPUAA, and KANE-HOALANI.

PIIKEA. See PIILANI.

PIILANI. A Maui chief celebrated for ruling six bays. He also ruled the parts of Molokai, Lanai, and Kahoolawe seen from these bays. His daughter PIIKEA married UMI.

PIKOIKAALALA. Pikoi was a demigod born at Wailua, Kauai, of a crow. His sisters were a rat and a bat. He was carried out to sea and to Kou (Honolulu), where he won contests in rat-shooting and riddling. He sometimes appeared as a rat.

PIMOE. Pimoe was a demigoddess in the form of an ulua fish that was hooked by MAUI in his efforts to unite the islands. He warned his older brothers not to look back. They disobeyed and saw a canoe bailer which they placed in their vessel. It changed into a beautiful woman, HINAIKEKA. When they tried to embrace her, the fish-woman slipped away.

PINEA. See KUAII.

POLIAHU. The beautiful snow goddess of Mauna Kea, who sometimes quenched the fires of PELE. She married AIHOHIKAPUA. He was won in a game of konane by HINA of Hana, Maui, who went to Kauai and seized him. Poliahu enveloped the two in alternate waves of heat and cold until they separated, and then retired to her mountaintop home. In another version she stole for a time KAHANAIAKEAKUA, a son of the god KANE, from his sister-wife, but eventually lost him.

PUA. A Molokai sorcery goddess with human and mudhen forms. It was believed that if a mudhen flew over a house crying at night, trouble would follow.

PUEOKAHI. An owl god of Hana, Maui, he married KAPOULAKI-NAU, older sister of PELE, after appearing to her in a dream for seven nights in a row. Later she married his younger brother, PUANUI, and lived with him at Wailua Iki, Maui.

PUNAAIKOAE. A supernatural man in the form of a tropic bird, Punaaikoae lived at Puna, Hawaii. He often flew to the sacred cliff of KAMOHOALII at Kilauea Crater and hovered there; this is the reason why so many such birds are seen there today. While surfing as a man near Laie, Oahu, he was enticed on to the surfboard of a beautiful mo'o woman, then taken to Kaena Point and finally over the mountains to a cave. He was killed in his sleep in upper Kalihi, Oahu, but a new wife, HAUMEA, took his body, and the two disappeared into a breadfruit tree. Later he was a lover of PELE.

PUNIA. A clever son of HINA at Kohala, Hawaii, he tricked sharks guarding a lobster cave by throwing stones into the ocean. When the sharks quarreled, they killed each other until only the chief shark was left. He swallowed Punia whole, and the lad lived inside for ten days until he was thrown ashore, baldheaded. A retelling of the tale is found in "The Water Baby," a story by Jack LONDON.

ULI. Called "the arch-goddess of sorcery," she was supposed to have come from Tahiti. She was invoked by HIIAKA in her prayers to bring LOHIAU back to life.

WAHINEEOMAO. A green woman, companion of HIIAKA on her journey to Kauai to bring LOHIAU to PELE.

WAIA. A son of HALOA noted for corruption and sin.

WAKA. A mo'o woman, Waka appears in many stories in human, spider, or eel form. As guardian of LAIEIKAWAI she prepared for her a house thatched with feathers. In the form of HINAKEKA she floated as a gourd bailer in the sea and was taken into the canoe of WAKEA.

WAKEA. Ancestor of all those of Hawaiian blood, Wakea was, according to tradition, a man rather than a god. See HAUMEA, HOOHOKU-KALANI, PAPA, and WAKA.

Hawaiian Chief

CHRONOLOGY OF HAWAIIAN AND UNITED STATES HISTORY

Some outstanding contemporary events in the history of the United States after 1776 appear in paragraphs following the annals of Hawaii.

750 A. D.? The first settlers in Hawaii arrive from Polynesia, perhaps by way of the Marquesas Islands.

1100? A two-century period of canoe voyages between Hawaii and Tahiti begins.

1713? KAHEKILI is born.

1728. James COOK is born in a farm cottage in Yorkshire, England.

1736? KEEAUMOKU is born.

1748. KAEOKULANI is born.

1756? KAIANA is born.

1758? *November.* KAMEHAMEHA I is born in Kohala, northern part of the island of Hawaii.

1760. KALANIKUPULE is born.

1765. KAIKIOEWA is born.

1768. KALANIMOKU (BILLY PITT) is born. KAAHUMANU is born at Hana on the island of Maui.

1774. Francisco de Paula MARIN is born in Andalusia, Spain.

1776. HOAPILI KANE is born.
U.S. *July 4.* The Declaration of Independence is proclaimed in Philadelphia. Battles between British and American forces conclude with George Washington's victory at Trenton at Christmas.

1778. KEOPUOLANI, sacred wife of KAMEHAMEHA I and mother of two kings and a princess, is born. *January 18.* Captain James COOK and crews of ships *Resolution* and *Discovery* sight northwestern islands of Hawaiian group and he names them the Sandwich Islands; he first goes ashore at Waimea, Kauai, on the 21st. *November 26.* Cook's expedition, returning from the Arctic, sights the island of Maui and begins charting the coasts of the island of Hawaii.
U. S. Surviving a terrible winter in camp at Valley Forge, the American army fights at Monmouth and Newport.

1779. *January 17.* The English ships arrive at Kealakekua Bay on the Kona coast of the Big Island, to be greeted by ten thousand Hawaiians offshore. *February 14.* Skirmish ashore at Kealakekua results in death of COOK, four marines, and many Hawaiians; Cook's bones are buried in the bay on the 21st.
U. S. Spain joins France in an alliance supporting the revolutionary efforts of the fledgling United States.

1780? KAUMUALII, future king of the island of Kauai, is born.

1781. KAPIOLANI, who will defy the volcano goddess PELE in 1824, is born.
U. S. The Articles of Confederation are signed by "The United States in Congress Assembled."

1782. KALANIOPUU dies and a decade of war among leading Hawaiian chiefs begins. KAMEHAMEHA defeats and kills KIWALAO at Mokuohai.
U. S. Preliminary Articles of Peace are signed between Great Britain and the United States and allies.

1785. The first trading ship, an unnamed fur-trading brig under Captain James Hanna, stops in the islands on its return to China.

1786. *May 24.* Two British trading ships, the *King George* under Nathaniel PORTLOCK and the *Queen Charlotte* under George DIXON, visit Hawaii on voyage from the Northwest Coast of America to China. *May 29.* The French naval frigates *Boussole* and *Astrolabe*, under the command of Count de la PEROUSE, spend a day off the island of Maui.
U. S. The Virginia Statute for Religious Freedom, model for the First Amendment of the Constitution, is adopted by the Congress.

1787. *May 20.* The British ship *Imperial Eagle*, flying Austrian colors, arrives in the islands under Charles William BARKLEY. *August 2.* The British ship *Nootka*, under John MEARES, arrives. On its departure for China, KAIANA sails as a passenger and returns with William DOUGLAS in 1788.
U. S. "The Contrast," by Royall Tyler, first American comedy produced by a professional theater company, is performed in New York. *May 25.* The Constitutional Convention opens in Philadelphia.

1788. *January 2.* The British ship *Prince of Wales*, under James COLNETT, arrives in company with *Princess Royal* under Charles Duncan.

1789. *August.* The Boston ship *Columbia Rediviva*, under Robert GRAY, first American vessel to circumnavigate the globe, arrives in the islands. KAMEHAMEHA I invades Maui.
U. S. America holds its first presidential election and Washington is inaugurated in New York.

1790. An explosive eruption of Kilauea Volcano destroys part of the forces of KEOUA KUAHUULA, an opponent of KAMEHAMEHA I. Simon METCALFE, master of the

American snow *Eleanora*, commits "Olowalu Massacre"; in retaliation, Chief KAMEEIAMOKU attacks consort *Fair American*, and John YOUNG (OLOHANA) and Isaac DAVIS remain in the islands as advisers to Kamehameha.

U. S. Ninety-two newspapers are published in the nation: eight dailies, seventy weeklies, and fourteen semiweekly or at other intervals.

1791. KUAKINI (John Adams), future governor of the Big Island, is born. *Spring*. In a battle of canoe fleets off the north coast of Hawaii, cannon fire directed by YOUNG and DAVIS is used to effect. *March 20*. The *Princess Royal*, captured by Spanish in 1789 and now under Spanish colors, arrives off the Big Island under Manuel Quimper; COLNETT, former captain of the vessel, almost comes to blows with Quimper. *May 20*. The American brigantine *Hope*, under Joseph INGRAHAM, arrives in islands. *Summer*. KEOUA KUAHUULA meets his death at the heiau of Kawaihai under the orders of KAMEHAMEHA I. *October*. The American brigantine *Lady Washington* arrives under John KENDRICK. *October 4*. The first French trading ship, *Solide*, under Etienne Marchand, passes through the islands.

U. S. Washington signs a bill to charter the Bank of the United States. The opposing views of Thomas Jefferson and Alexander Hamilton presage a growing tendency to form national political parties.

1792. Oliver HOLMES arrives on American ship *Margaret*. *March 5*. The ships of George VANCOUVER arrive at Kealakekua Bay on first of three annual visits to islands.

1793. *February*. The British trading ship *Butterworth* arrives in the islands under William BROWN, who may be the first captain to enter Honolulu Harbor. *February 14*. VANCOUVER makes second visit and on the Big Island lands the first cattle seen in Hawaii.

U. S. In the international turmoil aroused by the French Revolution, President Washington proclaims America's neutrality. The invention of the cotton gin by Eli Whitney greatly advances the agriculture of the southern states.

1794. Mataio KEKUANAOA, father of two kings and two princesses of the realm, is born. Probable birth of Miriam Auhea KEKAULUOHI. *January 9*. Vancouver ships make third visit; an informal cession of the islands to Great Britain is made on February 25. *February*. The first vessel of foreign design is built in the islands, the 36-foot *Britannia*, constructed by Vancouver's carpenters for the fleet of KAMEHAMEHA I. *Summer*. The death of KAHEKILI, who divides his kingdom between his brother KAEO and his son KALANIKUPULE, leads to fatal strife between the two heirs. *December 12*. KALANIKUPULE wins a battle against KAEO near Pearl Harbor with the aid of Captains William BROWN and John KENDRICK; Kendrick is killed by accidental firing of a loaded cannon.

1795. *May*. A victory in battle at Nuuanu Pali on Oahu enables the invading forces of KAMEHAMEHA to unite all the islands, except Kauai, under his rule.

U. S. A treaty with Spain defines United States boundaries and gives Americans free navigation of the Mississippi River to New Orleans.

1796. *January 1*. The British sloop of war *Providence*, under William Robert Broughton, brings the first grapes to the islands. *April*. KAMEHAMEHA I attempts the conquest of Kauai but his fleet is shattered by a storm. *October 31*. The snow *Arthur* from Bengal under Henry BARBER is wrecked on what is known thereafter as Barbers Point. *December 2*. The Boston trading ship *Otter* arrives under Ebenezer Dorr; the first officer is Pierre François PERON.

U. S. Washington publishes his Farewell Address when retiring from the presidency.

1797. Liholiho, the future KAMEHAMEHA II, is born at Hilo.

1798. George P. KAUMUALII, son of the king of Kauai, is born. Deborah KAPULE, future queen of KAUMUALII, is born.

U. S. *December 14*. Washington dies at Mount Vernon estate.

1801. Amasa DELANO makes first visit to Hawaii.

1803. The first horses brought to Hawaii are landed on the Big Island by the American brig *Lelia Byrd* under William Shaler; Richard CLEVELAND is supercargo.

U. S. Negotiating the Louisiana Purchase from France for $15,000,000, the nation doubles its domain.

1804. A great plague, probably bubonic, ravages the islands, kills KAMEEIAMOKU and other chiefs, and prevents the invasion of Kauai by the peleliu fleet of KAMEHAMEHA I. *June 7*. The first ships of the exploring Imperial Russian service arrive in the islands: *Nadeshda* under Adam Johann von KRUSENSTERN and *Neva* under Urey Lisiansky.

1805. KINAU, mother of KAMEHAMEHA IV and KAMEHAMEHA V and Victoria KAMAMALU, is born.

1806. *September*? The Boston trading ship *O'Cain*, under Jonathan WINSHIP, arrives.

U. S. Noah Webster publishes his influential American dictionary.

1809. *January 27*. The Russian ship *Neva* under L. A. HAGEMEISTER returns with Archibald CAMPBELL as a passenger.

1810. *April*. KAUMUALII makes a forced cession of his island of Kauai to KAMEHAMEHA I. Isaac DAVIS dies, probably poisoned for giving a warning to Kaumualii.

1811. *February 13*. The trading ship *Tonquin* arrives under Jonathan Thorn, first of three supply ships sent out by John Jacob Astor to his settlement at the mouth of the Columbia River. Twelve Hawaiians join the ship to work in Oregon Territory.

1812. Three Boston sea captains—Jonathan WINSHIP, Nathan Winship, and William Heath DAVIS—sign a contract with KAMEHAMEHA I giving them a monopoly in the export of valuable sandalwood.

U. S. The Congress declares war against Great Britain to defend freedom of the seas for American vessels, and the U. S. S. *Constitution* sinks a British frigate.

1814. *March 17*. Kauikeaouli, the future KAMEHAMEHA III, is born. *May 23*. The British privateer *Sir Andrew Hammond*, captured by Americans during the war, enters Honolulu Harbor; at sea, it is retaken by the British ship *Cherub* on June 13 and returned to Honolulu. The captured *Hammond* is the first war vessel flying the American flag to enter this harbor.

1815. NAHIENAENA, sister of two kings, is born. John Palmer PARKER settles at Waimea, Hawaii, under contract with KAMEHAMEHA I to shoot wild cattle for hides and meat; this is the origin of the thriving Parker Ranch of modern times.

1816. *January 1*. A resident musical group, the King's Oahu Band, first performs for some foreigners. *May 21*. KAUMUALII on Kauai, at the urging of Dr. Georg Anton SCHEFFER, signs a treasonous document putting the island under the protection of the Czar of Russia. *November 21*. The Russian Navy brig *Rurik*, under Otto von KOTZEBUE, arrives off the island of Hawaii and crew—including Louis CHORIS, Adelbert von Chamisso, and Johan Friedrich Eschscholtz—are entertained by KAMEHAMEHA I.

1817. KALAMA, future queen, is born. The Hawaiian flag is first flown in a foreign port by Alexander ADAMS at Macao. *May*. KAUMUALII renounces Russian sovereignty over the island of Kauai, and SCHEFFER leaves for Macao on July 7. *August 12*. James HUNNE-WELL makes first visit to Hawaii when *Bordeaux Packet* arrives under Andrew Blanchard.

1818. *February 17*. OPUKAHAIA (HENRY OBOOKIAH) dies at Cornwall, Connecticut, inspiring the origin of the first American mission to the Sandwich Islands. *May*. *Santa Rosa*, a pirate ship, reaches Hawaii; it is recovered by Hypolite BOU-CHARD, who arrives in September in command of frigate *Argentina*. The *Santa Rosa* departs under the command of Peter CORNEY. *October 20*. The Russian sloop of war *Kamchatka*, under V. M. GOLOVNIN, arrives in islands.

U. S. Transatlantic packet ship lines are established by New York merchants.

1819. Sugar is manufactured by Francisco de Paula MARIN. *May 8*. KAMEHAMEHA I dies at Kailua, Hawaii; his son Liholiho is proclaimed KAMEHAMEHA II on May 20. *August 8*. The French corvette *Uranie* arrives in the islands under Louis de FREYCINET, with Jacques ARAGO as draftsman. *September 29*. The first whale ships arrive in the islands—the *Balena* of New Bedford under Edmund Gardner and the *Equator* of Newburyport under Elisha Folger; at anchor in Kealakekua Bay in the autumn the *Balena* catches a whale that yields 110 barrels of oil. *October 23*. The brig *Thaddeus*, under Andrew Blanchard, sails from Boston with the First Company of American missionaries to the Sandwich Islands. *November*. KAMEHAMEHA II and advisers openly overthrow the old pagan system of religion; a rebellion of conservatives under KE-KUAOKALANI on the Big Island is put down by KALANIMOKU.

1820. The Nantucket ship *Maro*, under Joseph Allen, is the first whale ship to enter Honolulu Harbor; Allen later discovers the rich "on Japan" whaling grounds. *March 31*. The First Company of American missionaries arrives off the island of Hawaii, along with four Hawaiian youths, to begin Congregational mission work in the islands. *July 16*. Levi Sartwell Loomis, son of Elisha LOOMIS, is first white child born in the Sandwich Islands.

U. S. The "Missouri Compromise" allows Missouri to be admitted as a slave-owning state but bars further admission of such states north of 36°30'.

1821. *July 21.* KAMEHAMEHA II sails for Kauai to bring back KAUMUALII to pledge renewed loyalty; the ruler of Kauai comes to Honolulu as a virtual hostage and is married to KAAHUMANU. *September 15.* The first Christian meetinghouse is dedicated in Honolulu on the site of the present Kawaiahao Church.

1822. *January 7.* The first printing in the North Pacific region is struck off by Elisha LOOMIS. *March 29.* The British sloop *Mermaid* arrives with William ELLIS, Daniel Tyerman, and George Bennet of the London Missionary Society aboard, in company with the *Prince Regent*, a 70-ton schooner built at Port Jackson, New South Wales, which is presented to the king to fulfill a promise made by VANCOUVER to KAMEHA-MEHA I. *April.* The brig *Hermes* is wrecked on what is later called Pearl and Hermes Reef; James ROBINSON sails to Honolulu to seek aid and remains in Honolulu. *August 11.* The first Christian marriage in the islands unites Thomas HOPU, missionary youth, and bride Delia. The first chiefs to marry are HOAPILI KANE and KALAKUA, on October 19, 1823.

1823. *April 27.* The ship *Thames* under Reuben Clasby arrives with the Second Company of American missionaries. *May 1.* The Nantucket whale ship *Globe* first arrives in Honolulu under Thomas Worth; the worst mutiny in whaling history erupts at midnight, January 25–26, 1824, near Fanning Island, led by Samuel Comstock. *September 16.* The queen mother KEOPUOLANI is baptized on her deathbed, first Hawaiian to receive this Protestant rite. *November 27.* KAMEHAMEHA II and party depart on the whale ship *L'Aigle* to visit England.

U. S. The Monroe Doctrine warns European nations not to interfere with affairs in Western Hemisphere.

1824. James KEKELA, first ordained Protestant minister of Hawaiian blood, is born. *May.* The death of KAUMUALII leaves the island of Kauai under the crown, thus uniting all major islands as a kingdom. The son, George P. KAUMUALII, leads a brief revolt in August against KAAHUMANU and spends the remainder of his life as a prisoner. *July 8.* Queen KAMAMALU dies in London, and KAMEHAMEHA II dies on the 14th. *December.* Queen KAPIOLANI defies the goddess PELE at Kilauea Crater. *December 13.* The Russian Imperial Navy frigate *Predpiyatie*, under Otto von KOTZEBUE, arrives in the islands; the vessel returns on September 12, 1825.

1825. Sugar, rum, and coffee are produced on the plantation of Chief BOKI in Manoa Valley by John WILKINSON. *May 3.* The British Navy frigate *Blonde*, with George Anson Lord BYRON in command, arrives bearing the bodies of KAME-HAMEHA II and KAMAMALU; Robert DAMPIER, artist and draftsman, and Andrew BLOXAM, naturalist, are on the staff. *June 6.* Kauikeaouli is proclaimed king as KAMEHAMEHA III, with KAAHU-MANU as kuhina nui. *July 10.* The first Hawaiian commoner, BARTI-MEUS, is baptized by the Congrega-tionalist missionaries. *October.* The crew of the British whale ship *Daniel*, under Captain Buckle, attacks the home of William RICH-ARDS at Lahaina, Maui.

U. S. Robert Owen, British social reformer, sets up at New Harmony, Indiana, a short-lived collectivist colony.

1826. Princess RUTH is born. Mosquitoes are deliberately intro-duced into the islands at Lahaina by crew of the ship *Wellington* from San Blas, Mexico. *January 16.* The United States schooner *Dolphin* arrives, under John PERCIVAL, with William Lay and Cyrus Hussey, survivors of the *Globe* mutiny, aboard. Sailors from the ship on February 26 attack the house of Prime Minister KALANIMOKU and assault Hiram BINGHAM. The *Dolphin* is the first American warship to visit the Hawaiian Islands. However, in October the United States sloop of war *Peacock*, under Thomas ap Catesby JONES, arrives in Honolulu. *October 21.* James HUNNEWELL arrives as master of the *Missionary Packet*. *December 27.* The first general tax law is enacted, to provide revenue for shipbuilding and other developments.

1827. *July 7.* The *Comète* arrives under Captain Plassard with three Catholic missionaries aboard: Alexis Bachelot, Abraham Armand, and Patrick Short. The first baptism, of a child of MARIN the Spaniard, is performed on November 30; the first Catholic chapel is opened in Honolulu in January, 1828. *October.* Sailors from the British whale ship *John Palmer*, under Elisha Clarke, fire cannon at the missionary house at Lahaina, Maui. *December.* The chiefs agree on five laws, prohibiting murder, theft, rum-selling, prostitution, and gambling.

U.S. Joseph Henry of New York begins experiments in electricity that contribute much to advances in this branch of science. The first volume of *The Birds of America* is published by John James Audubon.

1828. *March 30.* The Third Company of American missionaries arrives in the *Parthian*, under Richard D. Blinn.

1829. *October 2.* The United States Navy corvette *Vincennes* arrives under William Finch; Charles S. STEWART is the chaplain. *December 2.* BOKI and about five hundred followers depart to seek sandalwood in the South Pacific in the *Kamehameha* and the *Becket*; the *Kamehameha* is lost at sea and the *Becket* returns August 3, 1830, with news of disasters.

1830. Cowboys from Mexican California arrive to teach the Hawaiians of the Big Island to manage cattle; this is the origin of commercial stock raising in the islands. *December 11.* Lot Kamehameha, the future KAMEHAMEHA V, is born.

1831. *June 7.* The Fourth Company of American missionaries arrives in ship *New England* under Avery F. Parker. *September.* Lahainaluna Seminary is established on the island of Maui to train young Hawaiian men to become preachers.
   U. S. *January 1.* The first number of *The Liberator*, published by William Lloyd Garrison, serves as the organ of the militant movement to abolish black slavery in the nation.

1832. The American missionaries estimate the island population at 130,313. The *Denmark Hill*, the first whale ship under the Hawaiian flag, is fitted out by Henry A. PEIRCE and Captain G. W. Cole. *May 17.* The Fifth Company of American missionaries arrives in the whale ship *Averick* under Captain Swain. *June 5.* KAAHUMANU, kuhina nui, dies. *July 23.* The United States Navy frigate *Potomac* arrives under Commodore John Downes.

1833. The Seamen's Bethel is opened in Honolulu by John DIELL. *May 1.* The Sixth Company of American missionaries arrives in the ship *Mentor* under Captain Rice.

1834. KAPIOLANI, future queen of KALAKAUA, is born. David DOUGLAS, naturalist, is killed in a bullock pit on the Big Island. *February 9.* Alexander Liholiho, the future KAMEHAMEHA IV, is born. *February 14.* The first issue of *Ka Lama Hawaii*, first periodical to appear in the North Pacific region, is printed at Lahainaluna Seminary press, a four-page weekly in the Hawaiian language. *March 5.* The first production of the Oahu Amateur Theatre, later described as "Honolulu's first community theater," is given at the royal palace by some young Americans. *December 5.* The Seventh Company of American missionaries arrives in the ship *Hellespont*, under Captain Henry.

1835. Lydia BROWN conducts classes in spinning and weaving cloth from locally grown cotton at Wailuku, Maui; the largest cotton export crop, 22,000 pounds, is produced in 1866. *January 31.* Future King LUNALILO is born. *July 29.* A fifty-year lease on land at Koloa, Kauai, is given to an American firm, Ladd & Co., to establish commercial sugar planting. The company struggles until Dr. R. W. WOOD obtains control in 1848 and gives it strong management. *December 16.* Death of old John YOUNG.

1836. A boarding school for boys opens at Hilo under David B. Lyman. The first Hawaiian-English dictionary, by Lorrin ANDREWS, is published and contains about 5,700 words. Experiments are conducted in silk production at Koloa and Hanalei, Kauai; this effort never succeeds as an industry. *July 30.* The first English-language newspaper, the *Sandwich Island Gazette*, is published in Honolulu by two Americans, Nelson Hall and S. D. MacIntosh. *September 28.* The French Navy corvette *Bonite* under August Nicolas Vaillant arrives; the captain obtains permission for the Irish Catholic priest Arsenius Walsh, who arrives September 30 on the American brig *Garafilia*, to remain in Hawaii provided he does not teach Hawaiians. *October 23.* The British sloop of war *Acteon* under Lord Edward Russell arrives; on November 16 Lord Russell negotiates a treaty between Great Britain and the Sandwich Islands.
   U. S. The entire garrison of The Alamo is wiped out but the Texans win independence from Mexico after the battle of San Jacinto. The American Temperance Union, devoted to moderation in the use of alcohol, observes its first national convention.

1837. The Oahu Bethel Church in Honolulu is opened for worship in charge of the Rev. John DIELL. The Central Female Boarding Seminary starts at Wailuku, Maui, to train suitable wives for graduates of Lahainaluna Seminary. *April 9.* The Eighth Company of American missionaries arrives on the barque *Mary Frazier* under Charles Sumner. *April 17.* The British brig *Clementine* under Captain Handley, chartered by Jules DUDOIT, arrives with Catholic missionaries Alexis Bachelot and Patrick Short aboard. *July 8.* The Royal Navy ship *Sulphur*, under Sir Edward Belcher, arrives in

Honolulu. The French naval vessel *Venus*, under Abel du PETIT-THOUARS, arrives in Honolulu and with Belcher becomes involved in the trouble over the future of the Catholic priests on the *Clementine*; Petit-Thouars signs a treaty with the crown assuring to French residents equal treatment with other foreigners.

1838. The "Great Revival," an evangelical crusade led by Titus COAN and other preachers, begins and in a few years results in converting more than twenty thousand Hawaiians to membership in the Congregational Church. *January*. The *Hawaiian Spectator*, the first literary journal in the North Pacific region, begins publication at the American mission, "conducted by an association of gentlemen." *July 3*. William RICHARDS is engaged to leave the mission and conduct meetings on political science with the chiefs. *September 2*. Future queen Lydia LILIUOKALANI is born.

1839. The first printing in the Pacific Northwest is run off by Edwin Oscar HALL on a small press brought from Honolulu. The Chiefs' Children's School is opened in Honolulu under Mr. and Mrs. Amos Starr COOKE; by an act of 1846 it is designated as the "Royal School" and placed under the ministry of public instruction. *May 10*. A complete translation of the Holy Bible is available in Hawaiian. *June 7*. A declaration of rights and duties, predecessor of a formal constitution, is drafted under the direction of William RICHARDS. *June 17*. A virtual edict of toleration of religious differences is issued by KAMEHAMEHA III. *July 9*. The French Navy frigate *Artémise* under C. P. T. LAPLACE arrives, and the captain forces the Hawaiian government under duress to sign a treaty favorable to France and to pay $20,000 in reparations.

1840. *May 15*. The *Clementine* returns with Catholic missionaries Louis MAIGRET, Bishop Rouchouze, and two other priests, who are allowed to stay and work in Hawaii. *June*. The *Polynesian*, a newspaper, is reestablished by James J. JARVES as the official government journal. *Summer*. Frederick A. Olmsted, future author of *Incidents of a Whaling Voyage* (1841), visits the islands. *September 23*. The United States sloop of war *Vincennes* arrives under Commodore John Wilkes, head of the United States Exploring Expedition. *October 8*. The first constitution of the kingdom is proclaimed by KAMEHAMEHA III.

1841. *May 21*. The Ninth Company of American missionaries arrives in ship *Gloucester* under Captain Easterbrook.

U. S. Ralph Waldo Emerson, New England sage, begins publishing his *Essays*, which establish his international reputation.

1842. *July 11*. A school for children of Protestant missionaries is opened under the Rev. and Mrs. Daniel DOLE; in 1853 it is chartered as "Punahou School and Oahu College." It is still operating as "the oldest high school west of the Rockies." *July 18*. William RICHARDS and Timoteo HAALILIO set out on an attempt to win recognition of Hawaiian independence in Great Britain, France, and the United States. *August 24*. The French corvette *Embuscade*, under Captain S. MALLET, arrives in Honolulu but leaves without enforcing previous demands. *September 21*. The Tenth Company of American missionaries arrives in brig *Sarah Abigail* under Captain Doane.

1843. *History of the Sandwich Islands* by the Rev. Sheldon DIBBLE is published at the Lahainaluna Seminary Press. A monthly journal, *The Friend*, is established by the Rev. S. C. DAMON and runs for more than a century. *January*. George Brown is appointed "commissioner of the United States for the Sandwich Islands"; he proves unsatisfactory and is replaced by Anthony TEN EYCK, who arrives in Honolulu on June 9, 1846. *February 10*. Lord George PAULET arrives in the islands in the British frigate *Carysfort* to demand "provisional cession" of the kingdom to Great Britain. *May 2*. Herman MELVILLE is discharged from the whale ship *Charles and Henry* at Lahaina, Maui; he comes to Honolulu and departs August 20 as an enlisted seaman on the frigate *United States* under James Armstrong. *July 26*. Admiral Richard THOMAS arrives in H. M. S. flagship *Dublin* with instructions to rescind cession under Paulet and conclude a favorable trade treaty. On July 31 the Hawaiian flag is again raised and the kingdom is restored to KAMEHAMEHA III. *November 28*. A joint Anglo-French declaration is signed in London formally recognizing the independence of the Sandwich Islands; in the summer of 1844, Secretary of State John C. Calhoun in Washington reaffirms American recognition.

1844. *February 3*. General William MILLER and Robert Crichton WYLLIE arrive in Honolulu on ship *Hazard*; Wyllie is to serve in the cabinet of the kingdom for twenty years. *April 23*. Sanford Ballard DOLE, future president of the Republic of Hawaii and first governor of the territory, is born. *July 15*. Eleventh Company of American missionaries arrives in brig *Globe* under Captain Doane.

U. S. Samuel Finley Breese Morse receives a patent on his invention of a practical electrical-telegraph system.

1845. The first English-Hawaiian dictionary is published by the Lahainaluna Seminary Press, prepared by Joseph S. EMERSON and Artemas BISHOP. The first crop of island coffee is exported, only 248 pounds. *May 17.* Daguerrotype photographs are being taken at the rooms of Theophilus Metcalf, Hawaii's first commercial photographer. *May 21.* The report of Attorney General John RICORD to the legislative session recommends drafting of Organic Acts to organize the government under modern principles; this report eventuates in the Organic Acts of 1845–1847.

1846. This is a banner year for the arrival of whale ships in the islands; no fewer than 596 vessels visit, of which 429 touch at Lahaina and the rest at Honolulu. *February 11.* The Land Commission is organized. *March.* The First Organic Act goes into effect, setting up the executive branch of the government and the privy council. *March 22.* The French naval frigate *Virginie*, under Rear Admiral Hamelin, arrives and the captain restores the $20,000 taken by LAPLACE in 1839. *April 27.* The Second Organic Act goes into effect during the year under the name of the "Great Mahele," dividing the lands among the king, his chiefs, Hawaiian commoners, and foreigners. *May 22.* The British sidewheel steamer *Cormorant*, under Sir George W. Gordon, arrives, first steam vessel to visit Hawaii under power. *June.* A group of Mormons headed by Sam Brannan arrives in *Brooklyn* on their way to California. *October 5.* The Danish Navy corvette *Galathea* under Steen Bille arrives; on the 16th Bille negotiates a Danish treaty with Hawaii.
    U. S. Elias Howe obtains a patent on his sewing machine. *May.* The Congress declares war against the Republic of Mexico; at its successful termination, the territory of the United States is greatly enlarged to the westward.

1847. The first fire engine arrives in Honolulu, a hand pump that is filled from buckets; the first volunteer fire company is organized on November 6, 1850. *September 11.* The Thespian Theatre, the "first regular theater in Honolulu," opens with a melodrama and a farce; it closes in January, 1848, and is succeeded by the Royal Hawaiian Theatre, on June 15. *November 1.* The ministry of the interior issues an exclusive charter to James Hough to hunt whales off the coast of the island of Maui.

1848. An epidemic of measles begins that causes the deaths of some ten thousand people, mostly native Hawaiians. *January 10.* The third Organic Act goes into effect, improving the island's judicial system. *January 27–March 7.* The Great Mahele, or division of lands, is conducted. *February 26.* The Twelfth (and last) Company of American missionaries arrives in bark *Samoset* under Captain Hollis. *August.* The first party from Hawaii leaves to search for gold in California.
    U. S. *January 24.* James W. Marshall, working for Johann Augustus Sutter in the lower Sacramento River Valley, discovers gold. The subsequent rush to California swells the population and advances the "manifest destiny" of the nation.

1849. The H. Hackfeld Department Store is opened in Honolulu, predecessor of the present-day Liberty House. *May 1.* A newspaper in Lowville, New York, publishes a two-column editorial advocating annexation and statehood for the Hawaiian Islands. *August 12.* The French Navy frigate *Poursuivante* arrives under Rear Admiral Legoarant de TROMELIN, who conducts a series of reprisals after presenting ten demands drawn up by Guillaume Patrice DILLON; the *Poursuivante* is accompanied by the steam-corvette *Gassendi*. *September 11.* Dr. G. P. JUDD, accompanied by the royal brothers Alexander Liholiho and Lot Kamehameha, depart for the United States and Europe on a mission to improve international relations.

1850. A post office is set up in Honolulu with Henry M. WHITNEY as postmaster; in 1855 mail arrives from New York in the record time of thirty-five days. *January 22.* The privy council approves the opening of the first public park in the islands, Thomas Square, named in honor of Admiral Richard THOMAS. *June 21.* The legislature authorizes the establishment of a contract labor system to bring badly needed workers to island fields. *August 13.* The Royal Hawaiian Agricultural Society is founded. *August 30.* Honolulu is officially declared a city. *December 12.* The first Mormon missionaries arrive, ten young men from the California gold camps; among them is George Q. CANNON, who becomes celebrated as a preacher and a leader in translating the Book of Mormon into Hawaiian. *December 13.* The French Navy corvette *Serieuse*, under Captain Cosnier, arrives with Emile PERRIN, commissioner, aboard; Perrin again presents the demands of TROMELIN.

1851. The Honolulu Fire Department is organized by A. J. CARTRIGHT. The courthouse of coral blocks cut by prisoners is built in downtown Honolulu. The partnership of S. N. CASTLE and A. S. COOKE forms a company later to become one of the "Big Five." The invention by David M. WESTON at the East Maui Plantation of a centrifugal machine for separating sugar from molasses greatly increases the speed of drying. *February 1.* KAMEHAMEHA III signs a secret agreement placing the kingdom under the protection of the United States if French imperialism continues.

U. S. Herman Melville publishes *Moby Dick* and Harriet Beecher Stowe publishes *Uncle Tom's Cabin.*

1852. At one time Honolulu Harbor holds 131 whale ships and 18 merchant ships. The Second Foreign Church (later called Fort Street Church) opens; it ultimately combines with rival Oahu Bethel Church to form Central Union Church of Honolulu. *January.* The *Thetis* brings from China the first contingent of contract laborers from that country, some two hundred men and boys. *June 14.* To replace the relatively simple Constitution of 1840, a new Constitution of 1852 is promulgated by KAMEHAMEHA III. *November 8.* The death of an imprisoned whaleman, Henry Burns, triggers a riot in Honolulu by several thousand sailors who set fire to the police station and threaten the lives of citizens.

U.S. The National Typographical Union leads other groups in country-wide labor unionization.

1853. The first general census of Hawaii lists 73,138 population; a steady diminishing of native Hawaiians indicates a trend that will continue for a generation. A small-pox epidemic reaps a toll of 2,485 persons in eight months; the same disease recurs in 1881. The Amateur Musical Society is formed and meets monthly for a number of years. Lihue Plantation installs the first steam-operated sugar mill. *January 15.* The famed American clipper ship *Sovereign of the Seas* arrives under Lauchlan McKay, with passenger G. W. BATES; on its return voyage to New York this fast sailing vessel is the first to chalk up more than four hundred sea miles in one day. *November 14.* The *S. B. Wheeler,* American sidewheel steamer, arrives under Gus Ellis; renamed *Akamai,* the first ship owned by the Hawaiian Steam Navigation Co., it is used in inter-island trade.

1854. A law is passed "for the encouragement and support of English schools for Hawaiian youth," and ten such schools open; previously, common education had been given only in the Hawaiian language. High-yield "Lahaina cane" is introduced to sugar plantations from Tahiti. *December 15.* KAMEHAMEHA III dies after longest reign on the throne of Hawaii, and is succeeded by Alexander Liholiho as KAMEHAMEHA IV.

U.S. An expedition under Commodore Matthew C. Perry persuades Japan to sign a treaty opening ports for American trade with this Asian nation that had been virtually isolated from the western world. Horace Greeley founds the New York *Tribune,* highly influential in shaping American opinion.

1855. Scheduled sailing packet service between Hawaii and the mainland is introduced by Regular Dispatch Line. Charles VARIGNY and his family arrive in Honolulu, where he is to reside for fourteen years. A three-man Board of Education headed by Prince Lot Kamehameha replaces the jurisdiction of the ministry of public education. The Methodist Episcopal Church is organized in Hawaii, with the Rev. W. S. Turner of the California Conference as its first pastor. *August 11.* A great eruption of Mauna Loa begins, with a lava flow threatening destruction of Hilo.

U.S. Walt Whitman publishes first version of *Leaves of Grass.*

1856. A ten-mile ditch is dug to supply Lihue Plantation, Kauai, with irrigation water. Hiram Bingham II sails *Morning Star,* first missionary vessel of that name, to Honolulu. The *Pacific Commercial Advertiser,* weekly newspaper, is established; it becomes a daily on May 1, 1882. *June 19.* KAMEHAMEHA IV is married to EMMA at Kawaiahao Church; their child, Prince ALBERT, is born May 20, 1858.

1857. *June 12.* A marine telegraph, a semaphore system erected at Diamond Head, sends signals to downtown post office when a ship is sighted.

U.S. The Supreme Court decision in the Dred Scott case arouses denunciation by the anti-slavery forces in the northern states.

1858. The firm of Aldrich and BISHOP opens the first bank in the islands; later it becomes the Bank of Bishop and today is the First Hawaiian Bank. All Mormon missionaries withdraw to Utah as a result of the "Mormon War."

U.S. Frederick Law Olmsted is named chief architect of Central Park in New York City and begins a career as the leading designer of American landscapes.

1859. Gas lighting is introduced to the streets of Honolulu. Ten South Pacific islanders are imported to work on Koloa Plantation; but in all, only some 2,500 Pacific islanders are recruited for field labor, and other sources must be found.

U.S. Petroleum is successfully drilled by Edwin L. Drake near Titusville, Pennsylvania; increased production threatens use of whale oil for lighting. *October*. A band led by John Brown attacks Harper's Ferry, Virginia, in a demonstration against the institution of slavery.

1860. A new census shows total population of 69,800 persons in islands. Trial planting of rice seed from South Carolina begins a craze for rice raising, resulting by the end of the 1870s in a crop of about two million pounds annually. *March 5*. The American Navy steam frigate *Powhatan*, under George F. Pearson, visits Hawaii, bringing from Japan members of the first Japanese embassy to the United States. *July 17*. The cornerstone of Queen's Hospital is laid in Honolulu under royal auspices. *July 18*. The steamer *Kilauea* makes its first regular inter-island run.

U.S. Abraham Lincoln, Republican candidate, is elected president, the first of two terms he is to serve.

1861. The American Civil War boosts demand for sugar at higher prices. The Pioneer Mill Co. at Lahaina is founded by James CAMPBELL. The invention of a vacuum pan enables boiling of sugar at lower temperatures and without scorching. *March 8*. The first operatic performance in Honolulu is given at the Royal Hawaiian Theatre by a local amateur group. *July 4*. Walter Murray GIBSON arrives in the islands; he will play a leading role in politics under King KALAKAUA. *Summer*. Lady Jane Franklin and Sophia CRACROFT visit the islands.

1862. *April 4*. The first professional operatic performance is given at the Royal Hawaiian Theatre by a troupe en route from Sydney to San Francisco. *May*. Paul ISENBERG becomes manager of Lihue Plantation on Kauai. *October 11*. Thomas N. STALEY, Episcopal Bishop of Hawaii, arrives from England too late to baptize Prince ALBERT, who had died August 27.

1863. Hawaii is declared a "home mission" and the American Board of Commissioners for Foreign Missions in Boston withdraws from the field, leaving it to the Hawaii Evangelical Association. The firm of C. BREWER & CO., going back to the 1826 company of James HUNNEWELL, becomes the agency for three sugar plantations; this is the beginning of the factor system that enables Brewer to become one of the "Big Five." *November 30*. KAMEHAMEHA IV dies and is succeeded by his elder brother, Lot Kamehameha, as KAMEHAMEHA V.

1864. Kamehameha V sells the island of Niihau to the Sinclair-Robinson family for $10,000. *August 20*. The king promulgates a new Constitution of 1864 to strengthen his royal powers.

U.S. The Bessemer steel industry is established at Wyandotte, Michigan, mainly to meet growing demand for railroad rails.

1865. Reorganization of the Board of Education results in a Bureau of Public Instruction; the first inspector general of schools is Abraham FORNANDER. Ejected from their stronghold on Lanai by GIBSON, the Mormon community gathers at Laie, Oahu. The first inn building is erected at the edge of Kilauea Crater, later the site of the Volcano House Hotel managed by George LYCURGUS.

U.S. *April*. Robert E. Lee surrenders to Ulysses S. Grant, ending Civil War. President Lincoln is fatally shot at Ford's Theater by John Wilkes Booth, and Andrew Johnson is sworn in as his successor.

1866. Articles on Hawaiiana by John Papa II begin appearing in the newspaper *Kuokoa*. *January 6*. The first patients arrive on the peninsula on Kalawao, Molokai, set up for the isolation of victims of the imported disease of leprosy. By 1873, some eight hundred patients are settled at the colony. Father DAMIEN is sent there in that year at his request, and dies there of the disease in 1889. *March 18*. Samuel L. CLEMENS (Mark Twain), roving correspondent for a California newspaper, arrives in the islands to prepare a series of travel letters. *September 4*. The first daily newspaper begins publication in the islands, the *Hawaiian Herald*.

1867. *March 5*. The cornerstone of the Anglican cathedral is laid in Honolulu. *May 21*. A Hawaiian-American reciprocity treaty, giving special consideration to imports of sugar from the islands, is negotiated by American minister E. M. McCook and Hawaiian minister of finance C. C. HARRIS; ratification by the Senate in Washington is delayed until 1870 by opposition of the mainland sugar lobby.

1868. The Spring Pioneer Omnibus Line, using horse-drawn vehicles in Honolulu, begins public transit service. Theo. H. DAVIES & Co. agency is formed from R. C. Janion Co. founded in 1845; the new concern will become one of the "Big Five." *April 2.* Mauna Loa erupts violently, with accompanying earthquakes. *June 24.* A band of 148 laborers arrives from Japan, but thereafter no more come until 1885, when the *City of Tokyo* brings the first of a wave of imported workers from that country.

1870. S. T. ALEXANDER and H. P. BALDWIN set up an informal partnership; the firm that will become a member of the "Big Five" is not formally organized until 1895. *April 19.* The *Wonga Wonga*, first steamer on the Australian route, arrives in Honolulu. *June.* The fiftieth anniversary of the arrival of the First Company of American missionaries is celebrated as a jubilee.

1871. *July 22.* Roller skating is introduced to the islands when Williams & Wallace open their Honolulu Skating Rink in Buffum's Hall on Hotel Street. *August.* More than thirty whale ships (seven of them Hawaii-owned) are caught in the ice north of Bering Strait and lost. In a similar Arctic disaster in 1876, fifty lives are lost and thirteen ships (two Hawaiian) are abandoned. *October.* Madame Agatha States' Italian Opera presents several professional operas, but the accompaniment is limited to a single piano.

U.S. A great fire in Chicago causes 250 deaths and damage amounting to $196,000,000.

1872. The average annual island production of sugar is 9,586 tons. *February 19.* The cornerstone is laid of Aliiolani Hale, a large government building constructed in Honolulu of concrete blocks. *June 11.* Henry BERGER, brought from Germany to conduct the Royal Hawaiian Band, gives his first concert; he holds this post for forty-three years. *October 19.* An electric telegraph is in operation in downtown Honolulu. *December 11.* KAMEHAMEHA V dies and under the constitution a special session of the legislature is called to elect a new monarch.

1873. *January 8.* William C. LUNA-LILO is elected king by the legislature. *January 25.* Isabella Bird BISHOP, Scottish traveler, arrives for a visit to the islands. *September 7.* The Household Troops mutiny in their barracks; this "useless and expensive army" is disbanded on the 12th by LUNALILO.

U.S. The Congress establishes gold as the sole monetary standard.

1874. *February 3.* King LUNALILO dies. *February 12.* The election in Honolulu by the legislature of David KALAKAUA results in a riot at Courthouse led by disappointed supporters of the candidacy of dowager queen EMMA; order is restored by armed marines from British and American warships in the harbor. *November 17.* King KALA-KAUA and a royal party leave on steamer *Benicia* for San Francisco on a goodwill tour of the United States, returning on the U.S.S. *Pensacola* on February 15, 1875.

1875. *January 30.* A reciprocity treaty is signed in Washington, to be put into effect eighteen months later. Fifteen years later, sugar tonnage has increased tenfold, and thereafter sugar shipments double every ten years. *October 16.* Princess KAIULANI is born, daughter of A. S. CLEGHORN and Princess Miriam LIKELIKE; she dies, heiress apparent to the vanished throne, in 1899.

U.S. The first Kentucky Derby race meetings are held.

1876. S. T. ALEXANDER and H. P. BALDWIN begin construction of the Hamakua-Haiku Ditch to irrigate Maui sugar lands. Claus SPRECK-ELS first arrives in the islands, scene of his coming financial exploits. *August 15.* Ratification of reciprocity treaty by the United States Senate.

U.S. General George A. Custer and 264 troopers are killed by Sioux Indians at the Little Big Horn River. Alexander Graham Bell patents the telephone. America celebrates centennial of independence.

Royal Hawaiian Band

1877. E. H. ALLEN becomes the first Hawaiian minister to the United States. *April 9.* Prince William Pitt LELEIOHOKU, heir to KALA-KAUA, dies on the mainland. *June 11.* Kapiolani Park, the first with extensive recreational facilities, is opened at Waikiki under charter to a private group. *September 1.* C. H. Dickey operates the earliest commercial telegraph system, connecting his store in Haiku with his store in Makawao, Maui. Dickey and C. H. Wallace are granted a charter on January 12, 1878, as the Hawaiian Telegraph Co.

U.S. A period of labor violence begins with a general railroad strike, and Federal troops are sent to restore order after violence erupts.

1878. Scottish author Constance F. GORDON-CUMMING visits the islands. *May or June.* Only two years after Alexander Graham Bell patents the telephone, C. H. Dickey puts into operation the first line, between Kahului and Wailuku, Maui, under the name of the East Maui Telegraph Co. The Hawaiian Bell Telephone Co. is incorporated on December 30, 1880. *September 30.* The first contingent of Portuguese workers from the Madeira Islands arrives to labor in the fields; by end of the century some eighteen thousand have settled in Hawaii.

1879. *February.* A demonstration of the first recorded sound is given by a Mr. Kohler, who arrives in Honolulu with an Edison phonograph. *July 1.* The first artesian wells are bored by James CAMPBELL at Ewa, Oahu, enabling the irrigation of thousands of acres of fields. *July 20.* The Kahului & Wailuku Railroad is opened on Maui, the first rail common carrier in the islands. *December 31.* The cornerstone of Iolani Palace is laid in Honolulu.

1880. The firm of Lewers & Cooke is founded by Robert LEWERS and C. M. COOKE, Sr. St. Louis College, Catholic high school for boys, is set up in Honolulu; later it is supplemented by Chaminade College. Henry ADAMS and John LA FARGE visit islands. *August 14.* C. C. MORENO becomes prime minister after KALAKAUA prorogues legislature for failing to grant ten-million-dollar loan to a steamship company; a popular uprising forces the resignation of Moreno five days later. *November.* An eruption of Mauna Loa causes a lava flow to approach the outskirts of Hilo; rites by Princess RUTH, a granddaughter of KAMEHAMEHA I, halt the torrent at the edge of town.

U.S. *November 3.* A treaty allows the United States to restrict immigration from China.

1881. *January.* KALAKAUA sets out to become the first monarch to circle the globe; he returns to Honolulu at the end of October. The Music Hall Theatre opens across from the palace on King Street; it is soon closed by a smallpox epidemic but re-opens in 1883 as the Royal Opera House.

U.S. President James A. Garfield is fatally shot by an assassin and is succeeded by Chester A. Arthur. Booker T. Washington heads a normal and industrial institute in Tuskegee, Alabama, and becomes the foremost advocate of black education.

1882. The legislature conveys to Claus SPRECKELS a large tract of crown lands at Wailuku, Maui, to settle a claim purchased by him from Princess RUTH for $10,000. The Inter-Island Steam Navigation Co. is organized; it merges in 1905 with the WILDER Steamship Co. Captain William MATSON acquires the first vessel of his fleet of sailing ships running between Hawaii and the mainland. *December.* Iolani Palace is completed.

1883. H. A. P. CARTER becomes the second Hawaiian minister to the United States. Mother Marianne (Barbara KOPP) and six nuns arrive in Hawaii, hoping to serve at the leper colony on Molokai. The mongoose is imported from the East Indies by way of Jamaica to attack rats in the canefields, with mixed results. The first YMCA building in Honolulu is dedicated. *February 12.* KALAKAUA and KAPIOLANI hold coronation ceremony in front of Iolani Palace on the ninth anniversary of his accession to the throne. *February 14.* The statue of KAMEHAMEHA I in front of Aliiolani Hale is unveiled to commemorate the centennial of the arrival of Captain James COOK.

U.S. Brooklyn Bridge and the Metropolitan Opera House, both imposing structures, are completed.

1884. A census reports 80,578 inhabitants, an increase of 24,000 in twelve years. The circulation of silver coins showing a bust of KALA-KAUA, minted in San Francisco, brings Claus SPRECKELS a profit of $150,000. *June 13.* Smooth Cayenne pineapple plants are introduced from Madeira.

U.S. Mark Twain publishes *The Adventures of Huckleberry Finn.*

1885. *April 25.* Dowager Queen EMMA dies.

1886. Japan relaxes its laws against emigration, and a great wave of laborers from that country begins to arrive; in 1896 Japanese comprise no less than one-fourth of the population. *July 21.* Iolani Palace Square is illuminated by electric bulbs; two years later, electric street lighting replaces gasoline lamps in Honolulu.

U.S. The Statue of Liberty, a gift from the French people, is dedicated in New York Harbor by President Grover Cleveland. *December 8.* The American Federation of Labor is formed at Columbus, Ohio, with Samuel Gompers as first president.

1887. The Kamehameha School for Boys, under terms of the will of Bernice P. BISHOP, opens in Honolulu; the girls' division opens in 1894. *January.* A mission headed by John E. Bush arrives in Samoa to begin implementing the program of KALAKAUA to assert Hawaii's "primacy in the family of Polynesian states." *January 20.* The Senate in Washington inserts an amendment in the renewal of the reciprocity treaty with Hawaii, giving the United States the exclusive right to set up a coaling station in Pearl Harbor; this right is never exercised during the period of Hawaiian independence. *June.* The armed vessel *Kaimiloa*, sent by KALAKAUA to implement his policy of primacy in the Pacific, arrives in Samoan waters, but the mission is aborted. *July 6.* KALAKAUA is forced by the Hawaiian League, formed to fight for a more liberal constitution, to sign the "Bayonet Constitution"; W. M. GIBSON is allowed to leave for the mainland on July 5 to avoid being lynched. *November 9.* The reciprocity treaty is renewed for seven years.

1888. *December 28.* Hawaiian Tramways, Ltd., starts a mule-car service in Honolulu; the company is taken over in November, 1900, by the Honolulu Rapid Transit & Land Co. (HRT).

U. S. George Eastman patents a box camera that becomes the popular Kodak.

1889. The first section of an inter-island undersea cable is laid between Maui and Molokai. A parcel-post system is set up in co-operation with the United States mail. W. D. WESTERVELT, author of books on Hawaiian legends, first comes to Hawaii. *January.* The chartered yacht *Casco* arrives with Robert Louis STEVENSON and his family aboard; the noted Scottish author spends six months in the islands and writes some of his best stories about this region. Stevenson is to return briefly

Robert Louis Stevenson and the future Queen Liliuokalani converse at a Waikiki party in 1889

in 1893, after the downfall of his royal friend LILIUOKALANI. *July 30.* A brief revolt against the new Constitution, headed by Robert W. WILCOX, is put down by John Harris SOPER; it results in seven deaths and a dozen wounded among the rebels. *September 4.* The first train runs on the Oahu Railroad.

U. S. The Indian Territory of Oklahoma is opened for settlement.

1890. The McKinley Tariff wipes out the advantages formerly held by Hawaiian sugar producers over other foreign growers.

U. S. Chief Sitting Bull is killed during the suppression of a Sioux uprising.

1891. *January 20.* KALAKAUA dies in San Francisco, where he had gone in search of improved health. His body is brought back to the islands on the U. S. S. *Charleston*, and on January 29 his sister. LILIUOKA-LANI, is proclaimed queen.

1892. The Bernice P. BISHOP Museum, founded in 1889, opens its doors in Honolulu, devoted to the natural history and ethnology of the Pacific region.

1893. *January 17.* A bloodless revolution deposes LILIUOKALANI and sets up a Provisional Government under Sanford B. DOLE, abrogating the monarchy until annexation by the United States can be arranged. The American minister, John B. STEVENS, lands marines from the U. S. S. *Boston* in Honolulu Harbor. *March 4.* Inauguration of President Grover Cleveland, a Democrat, replaces Republican administration in Washington friendly to annexation of Hawaii. *March 29.* James H. BLOUNT arrives in Hawaii with "paramount" authority from President Cleveland to investigate circumstances of the revolution. *July.* The National Guard Auxiliary of the Provisional Government attempts to subdue a band of lepers in Kalalau Valley, Kauai, led by KOOLAU. *November 4.* Albert S. WILLIS arrives in Honolulu to replace John L. STEVENS as American minister.

1894. Takie OKUMURA, Christian missionary, comes to Hawaii from Japan. *July 3.* The Constitution of the Republic of Hawaii is adopted. *July 4.* Sanford B. DOLE becomes president of the Republic; he is to

Squad No. 4 of the Citizen's Guard reports for duty in the Counter-revolution of 1895.

head the government of the islands for the next decade.

U. S. Jacob S. Coxey of Ohio leads "Coxey's Army" of unemployed on Washington, D. C.

1895. A cholera epidemic hits the islands. The first island tennis championship match takes place under the newly created Hawaiian Lawn Tennis Association. The Hawaiian Sugar Planters' Association is founded; its Experiment Station does much to handle problems and improve efficiency. *January 6.* A counter-revolution, designed to restore the monarchy, breaks out, headed by Robert W. WILCOX; it is put down and as a result LILIUOKA-LANI agrees on January 24 to abdicate and takes the oath of allegiance to the Republic.

1896. The population before annexation is estimated to total 109,020: Hawaiian and part-Hawaiian, 39,504; born in Hawaii of non-Hawaiian ancestors, 12,844; foreign-born, 56,672. The Honolulu Normal and Training School is set up to educate skilled teachers.

U. S. William Jennings Bryan delivers "Cross of Gold" speech at Democratic Convention in Chicago.

George Washington Carver becomes director of agricultural research at Tuskegee Institute in Alabama and begins work on utilization of common crops, including the peanut, sweet potato, and soy bean.

1897. Another annexation treaty is signed in Washington by President William McKinley. *February 5.* The first motion pictures to be shown in Hawaii are seven brief scenes screened by Edison's Veriscope.

1898. *April 24.* Spain declares war on the United States, and Congress retorts on the 25th, retroactive to the 21st. As a result, the Hawaiian Islands assume strategic importance and troops use Oahu as a base. The first federal garrison troops, an infantry regiment and a battalion of engineers, set up a temporary post, Camp McKinley, near Diamond Head. *May 10.* The first motion pictures filmed in Hawaii are several scenes taken by two Edison photographers on their way through Honolulu. *July 7.* President McKinley signs a joint Congressional resolution annexing Hawaii to the United States. *August 12.* Sovereignty of Hawaii is formally transferred at ceremonies in Honolulu attended by crew of the

U. S. S. *Philadelphia.* However, the machinery of the Republic is to function until 1900.

U. S. *February 15.* U. S. S. *Maine,* American battleship, explodes in Havana Harbor; *April 24,* Spain declares war on the United States; *May 1,* Commodore George Dewey wins a seven-hour battle at Manila Bay; *July 3,* Spanish fleet is destroyed off Santiago, Cuba.

1899. The Oahu Steam Railway is constructed under B. F. DILLINGHAM and connects Honolulu and Ewa. *October 8.* The first automobiles operate on the streets of Honolulu; newly arrived cars belong to Henry P. BALDWIN and Edward D. Tenney. *December 12.* Five persons die of bubonic plague at the outbreak of an epidemic in Honolulu.

1900. The 1900 census reports a total population of 154,001: Japanese comprise two-fifths; Hawaiians and part-Hawaiians one-fourth; Chinese about one-sixth; Portuguese about one-eighth; fewer than half are citizens and fewer than five percent are of Anglo-Saxon blood. The American-Hawaiian Steamship Co. begins construction of twenty-two steel cargo vessels suitable for shipping bulk sugar to the mainland around South America. The firm of Alexander & Baldwin, member of the "Big Five," is incorporated in San Francisco. Lorrin A. THURSTON becomes publisher of the *Honolulu Advertiser,* still a daily newspaper. *January 20.* A fire to purge premises of plague gets out of control and burns thirty-eight acres of houses in Chinatown, Honolulu; more than four thousand residents are left homeless. *April 30.* President McKinley signs the Organic Act that sets up territorial government in Hawaii. *June 14.* The incorporated Territory of Hawaii is inaugurated with Sanford B. DOLE as first governor. *November.* Robert W. WILCOX is elected first territorial delegate to Congress under the Home

Rule Party. *November 12*. The first inter-island message by Marconi wireless is sent from Kaimuki, Honolulu, to Molokai.

U. S. A hurricane ravages Galveston, Texas, and some 6,000 persons drown.

1901. A territorial income-tax law is passed. The first golf course constructed in Honolulu, at Moanalua, is shortened from eighteen to nine holes. The earliest known recordings of Hawaiian music are listed in a Columbia Records catalog: "Aloha Oe" (30200) and "Pua i Kaoakalani" (30201), labeled "vocal solos in Hawaiian." *February 20*. The first territorial legislature convenes in Honolulu. *March 1*. The first radio communication among the islands is established. *August 31*. Electric streetcars replace horse-drawn trams in Honolulu. *December 4*. James D. DOLE organizes the Hawaiian Pineapple Co., whose first crop is packed in 1903 to begin rapid growth in the canning industry.

U. S. As President William McKinley begins his second term, he is fatally shot by anarchist Leon Czolgosz and Theodore Roosevelt is sworn in as successor.

1902. Henry Bond RESTARICK, an Anglican priest, is elected first American bishop of Honolulu. *March 28*. In the earliest recorded basketball game played in the islands, Oahu College girls defeat the YWCA team 19–17. *November*. Prince Jonah Kuhio KALANIANAOLE is elected second territorial delegate to Congress as a Republican, and serves until his death in 1922. *December 28*. A Pacific cable linking Hawaii with the American mainland is landed at Honolulu.

1903. A system of county government is established. A Board of Immigration is organized to encourage settlement from the mainland United States. The legislature petitions Congress for admission of Hawaii as a state. *January 1*. The first message by commercial cable is sent from San Francisco to Waikiki; the westward extension of this cable, connecting Oahu with Midway, Guam, and the Philippines, is completed on July 4. *January 13*. The S. S. *Gaelic* brings one hundred workers from Korea; by April, 1905, almost eight thousand have come to Hawaii from this country. *May 2*. The first public performance of the Honolulu Symphony Society is given at the Hawaiian Opera House. *November*. George R. CARTER is appointed second governor of the territory.

U. S. *December 17*. Aviation is born when Orville and Wilbur Wright achieve first successful heavier-than-air machine flight at Kitty Hawk, North Carolina.

1904. The Volcano House Hotel at Kilauea is acquired by George LYCURGUS. *March 19*. The Waikiki Aquarium is opened, initially built and operated by the Honolulu Rapid Transit & Land Co.; the City and County of Honolulu assumes control July 1, 1919.

U. S. President Roosevelt mediates the Treaty of Portsmouth, New Hampshire at the end of the Russo-Japanese War.

1906. A few workers from the Philippines arrive in the *Doric*, beginning a wave of imported labor from these islands; after the founding of the Philippine Republic in 1946, the largest number of applicants for naturalization in Hawaii are Filipino. The Iwilei cannery of the Hawaiian Pineapple Co. is erected. The first

regular motion-picture theater in the islands is Joel C. Cohen's Orpheum on Fort Street.

U. S. An earthquake and three-day fire in San Francisco leave five hundred dead and cause great destruction.

1907. The legislature passes a law creating municipal administration for the City and County of Honolulu, which replaces Oahu County government at the opening of 1909. Fort Shafter, Army headquarters in the territory, is the first permanent post of federal troops. The College of Agriculture and Mechanic Arts is organized under the Land Grant Act and opens in the autumn with five students and a faculty of twelve; the name is changed in 1911 to College of Hawaii, which becomes the University of Hawaii in 1920. The "Gentleman's Agreement" attempts to check the flow of Japanese labor into the United States and its territories. *May 21*. Jack LONDON and wife Charmian LONDON arrive in ketch *Snark* to begin a four-month tour of the islands; the Londons return in 1915 and 1916, and both write much about Hawaii. *May 31*. Mid-Pacific Institute, combining Kawaiahao Girls' Seminary and the institution started by Francis W. DAMON and Mary DAMON, opens its doors in Manoa Valley. *August*. Walter Francis FREAR is appointed third governor of the territory.

U. S. A financial panic results in national suffering.

1908. Congress authorizes construction of Naval Station, Honolulu, at Pearl Harbor. The Hawaiian Pineapple Growers Association is founded to begin a successful campaign to popularize the use of this fruit. *September*. The Great White Fleet of President Theodore Roosevelt visits the islands en route around the world to show the flag. *November*. The City and County of Honolulu is formed, with Joseph James FERN as first mayor.

1909. Schofield Barracks, named for J. M. SCHOFIELD, is established near Wahiawa, Oahu, and grows to be the largest permanent Army post under the American flag. *September.* Sacred Hearts Academy, Catholic girls' school, opens in Honolulu. *October 23.* The first football game by the College is played at Alexander Field on Punahou School campus, defeating McKinley High School, 6–5.

U. S. The North Pole is reached overland by American explorers Robert E. Peary and Matthew Henson. Ford Motor Co. begins reorganizing assembly process to set up a continuous flow of automobile production.

1910. The census of 1910 reports a population of 191,909. The steamer *Wilhelmina* begins its run as a Matson Line passenger ship between Honolulu and the Pacific Coast. Ray Jerome BAKER, early photographer, opens a shop in Honolulu. *August 28.* Honolulu telephones are converted to dial operation, but the last manual phones in the islands are not phased out until 1957. *December 31.* The first airplane flights in the islands are given by J. C. "Bud" Mars in a Curtiss P-18 biplane from Moanalua Polo Field.

U. S. The Boy Scouts of America is incorporated.

1911. The Hawaii Volcano Research Association is founded by Dr. T. A. JAGGAR. *September 25.* The first Pan-Pacific Conference, organized by Alexander Hume FORD, is held in Honolulu on Balboa Day.

U. S. Irving Berlin publishes popular song, "Alexander's Ragtime Band."

1912. *July 6.* Duke KAHANA-MOKU is proclaimed world champion swimmer at the Olympic Games in Stockholm, Sweden.

1913. The *Hawaiian Star* is merged with the Honolulu *Bulletin* to form the present evening *Star-Bulletin*, with Wallace R. FARRINGTON as vice president and general manager. The Library of Hawaii (later the State Library of Hawaii), the first true public library, opens in Honolulu. The "Ginaca machine" is invented to speedily remove the shell and core of pineapples in canneries. *February.* The foundation of the naval drydock at Pearl Harbor collapses; the renewed project is not completed until the summer of 1919. The first of many Hollywood productions made on location in the islands are two single-reel, hand-colored films, "Hawaiian Love" and "The Shark God." *June 13.* The earliest military aircraft—two Curtiss seaplanes— arrive by ship with aviation person- nel. *October.* The Underwood Tariff leaves sugar production unprotected, and the price drops to 2.28 cents a pound. *November.* Lucius Eugene PINKHAM is appointed fourth governor of the territory.

U.S. The Sixteenth Amendment is passed by Congress, instituting a graduated income tax. A bill creating a Federal Reserve System becomes law.

1914. The Honolulu Zoo has a small beginning in Waikiki, a modest collection of birds and animals. The first airmail flight takes place when Tom Gunn carries souvenir postcards and letters from Koloa to Lihue on Kauai. *May 8.* The first cargo to pass through the newly constructed Panama Canal is a bargeload of sugar from Hawaii.

U.S. Americans attempt to remain neutral after outbreak of World War I in Europe.

1915. Bus service is inaugurated by Honolulu Rapid Transit Co.; trolley buses operate on a number of routes from January, 1938, to the spring of 1958, and electric streetcars, first used in 1901, are withdrawn early on the morning of July 1, 1941. *March 25.* The Navy submarine F-4, one of four based in the islands, sinks in Honolulu Harbor with loss of the entire crew of twenty-one men. *April 28.* The Footlights Club gives its first public performance, at the Hawaiian Opera House; it is the predecessor of the Honolulu Community Theatre, organized in December, 1934.

U.S. The United States protests German submarine actions and British blockade of Germany in World War I. During Mexican Revolution, President Woodrow Wilson proclaims a policy of "watch- ful waiting" on the border. D. W. Griffith produces notable early motion picture, "The Birth of a Nation."

1916. *February 4.* The German cruiser *Geier* and half a dozen other steamships interned during World War I are set on fire by their crews in Honolulu Harbor, although the United States is not yet at war. *August 1.* The Hawaii National Park is established under federal auspices on both Maui and the Big Island. *November 20.* The United States Army Hawaiian Air Office is activated.

U.S. The government purchases the Virgin Islands from Denmark for $25,000,000.

1917. The Hawaii National Guard is mobilized for service in World War I. *November 11*. Former Queen LILUOKALANI dies.

U.S. *April 6*. President Wilson declares war on Germany and the first American combat troops land in France.

1918. The earliest inter-island flight is made by Major Harold M. Clark from Honolulu to Molokai and back. *June*. Charles J. McCARTHY is appointed fifth governor of the territory. *August*. The Pearl Harbor drydock is formally opened by Secretary of the Navy Josephus Daniels.

U.S. American and allied troops intervene in Russia during civil war following the October Revolution of the previous autumn.

1919. The Mormon Temple is dedicated at Laie, Oahu. Yasutaro SOGA becomes editor of *Nippu Jiji*, Japanese newspaper (later *Hawaii Times*). Governor McCARTHY recommends to the legislature the adoption of a memorial to Congress pressing for statehood, and on February 11, Delegate KALANI-ANAOLE introduces the first of a long succession of bills to grant statehood to Hawaii. *April 29*. Luke Field on Ford Island, Pearl Harbor, is developed as a joint Army and Navy air facility. *July 3*. The first inter-island airmail flight takes place; two Army seaplanes leave Luke Field and arrive in Hilo with a bag of mail.

U.S. At Versailles, a treaty is signed by the allies and Germany, incorporating Wilson's draft Covenant of the League of Nations. The Eighteenth Amendment, promoting national temperance, is adopted by Congress.

1920. The 1920 census reports a population of 255,912; the Japanese group comprises 42.7 percent of total, but the percentage declines thereafter. The centenary of the arrival of the first American missionaries is observed. Removal of wartime price controls on sugar results in wholesale price of 23.5 cents a pound. The College of Hawaii is reorganized as the University of Hawaii. *October*. The earliest broadcast of music and speech is transmitted from the Electric Shop in downtown Honolulu to the Pacific Heights home of a local family. *November*. John Henry WILSON, engineer, is elected second mayor of the City and County of Honolulu, to succeed Joseph J. FERN.

U.S. The Nineteenth Amendment, granting suffrage to women, is adopted.

1921. Congress amends the Organic Act to make a three-year residence in the territory a qualification for appointment to most territorial and federal posts. The STRAUB Clinic begins medical service in Honolulu. *July*. Wallace Rider FARRINGTON is appointed sixth governor of the territory.

U.S. Nicola Sacco and Bartolomeo Vanzetti, Italian-born anarchists, are convicted of armed robbery and murder in a case that stirs worldwide concern.

1922. The Hawaiian Pineapple Co. purchases the entire island of Lanai and develops it to supply fruit to its Honolulu cannery. The Federal Building in Honolulu is opened. *January 7*. Prince KALANIANA-OLE, delegate to Congress since 1902, dies in office, and Harry A. Baldwin completes his term. *April 20*. Washington Place, former home of Queen LILUOKALANI, is opened as the executive mansion of territorial governors. *May 11*. Two Honolulu commercial radio stations, KGU and KDYX, begin scheduled broadcasts. *July 9*. Congress enacts the Hawaiian

Homes Commission Act, providing for homesteading by people of Hawaiian ancestry. *November*. William P. JARRETT is elected delegate to Congress.

1923. The legislature enacts "Hawaii's Bill of Rights," to obtain for the territory the same treatment from Congress as that received by the individual states.

U.S. Widespread Ku Klux Klan violence occurs in the nation.

1924. Congress passes the Hawaiian Bill of Rights. An eight-month plantation strike on Kauai led by Pablo MANLAPIT results in the deaths of four policemen and seventeen strikers. Use of tarred mulching paper in the pineapple fields, borrowed from the sugar industry, protects and fosters young plants. *November*. Delegate JAR-RETT is re-elected to Congress.

U.S. Interior Secretary Albert B. Fall and oil tycoons Harry Sinclair and Edward L. Doheny are charged with conspiracy and bribery in the Teapot Dome scandal, involving fraudulent leases of naval oil reserves.

1925. The United States battle fleet conducts extensive maneuvers in Hawaiian waters. The Fronk-Wynn Clinic (later the Fronk Clinic) is founded in Honolulu by Dr. Clarence E. FRONK. *April 16*. The earliest locally written operetta, *Pele and Lohiau*, by Fred Beckley, is performed at the Hawaii Theater; another, *Prince of Hawaii*, by Charles E. KING, is performed at the Liberty Theater on May 4. *July 5*. Wallace R. FARRINGTON is the first territorial governor to be appointed to a second term. *August 31*. The first flight between the mainland and Hawaii begins near San Francisco with departure of a two-engine PN-9 Navy seaplane under John Rodgers and crew of four; running out of fuel about three hundred miles from the islands, the plane is rescued on

September 10 off Nawiliwili, Kauai, by Submarine R-4.

U.S. Nellie Tayloe Ross is the first woman to be elected governor of a state (Wyoming).

1926. *June 9*. Death of Sanford B. DOLE.

U.S. Gertrude Ederle of the United States is the first woman to swim the English Channel.

1927. *April 8*. The Honolulu Academy of Arts, incorporated in 1922 under the sponsorship of Anna Charlotte Rice COOKE, opens as a gallery and museum. *June 28–29*. Lieutenants Lester Maitland and Albert Hegenberger, United States Army, make first fully successful non-stop flight from mainland to Hawaii in Fokker C-2–3 Wright trimotor plane *Bird of Paradise*. *July 15*. The first civilian flight from the mainland ends in a crash landing when Ernest L. Smith and Emory B. Bronte, who flew their Travelair monoplane for twenty-five hours, run out of fuel and land unhurt after crashing into a keawe tree on Molokai. *August 16*. The Dole air derby from Oakland, California, to Hawaii is won by Art Goebel in monoplane *Woolaroc* with William Davis as navigator; Martin Jensen of Honolulu is second, with navigator Paul Schluter in *Aloha*. (Two prizes, one of $25,000 and one of $10,000, were offered by James D. DOLE.) Out of eight planes starting at Oakland, two smash in taking off, two are forced to turn back, and two others disappear over the ocean; altogether this "first trans-oceanic flight race in history" costs ten lives.

U.S. Charles Augustus Lindbergh in monoplane *Spirit of St. Louis* achieves the first solo transatlantic flight and lands near Paris.

1928. The first complete crossing of the Pacific by air is achieved when Charles Kingsford-Smith and a crew of three fly their Fokker trimotor plane *Southern Cross* from Oakland, California, to Australia by way of Hawaii and Fiji. *March 21*. John Rodgers Airport (later renamed Honolulu International Airport) is dedicated, thus becoming the first formally designated civilian airfield in Hawaii.

U.S. Richard E. Byrd begins his two-year expedition to Antarctica.

1929. *July*. Lawrence M. JUDD is appointed seventh governor of the territory. *July 13*. First regular showing of sound films begins at Hawaii Theater. *November 11*. Scheduled operations begin of Inter-Island Airways, Ltd. (now Hawaiian Airlines), using two Sikorsky S-38-C seven-passenger amphibians and a Bellanca monoplane.

U.S. Stock-market prices collapse in autumn and American securities decline by twenty-six billion dollars; beginning of great worldwide depression and economic suffering.

1930. The fourth federal census shows the island population to be 368,336. The growing depression loosens dominance of big corporations in the islands and encourages challenges by labor organizers. First visit of Henry J. KAISER to Hawaii, the future scene of his many activities. *November*. George Fred Wright is elected mayor of the City and County of Honolulu and serves four two-year terms. *November 22*. The first direct transmission of sports events from the mainland is brought when KGU experimentally broadcasts the first quarter of the California-Stanford football game, carried by shortwave to Honolulu.

U.S. Cyclotron is developed by Ernest O. Lawrence, American physicist.

1931. The claim by Thalia MASSIE of assault by five "local boys" puts Hawaii in national headlines and leads to investigations of crime in the islands; the threat arises that Hawaii will be governed by a commission in which the Army and Navy would have a voice. *November 2*. The Mutual Telephone Co. inaugurates inter-island radio telephone service; the company extends this service to the mainland on November 20.

U.S. Al Capone, Chicago gangster, sentenced to eleven years in prison for tax evasion.

1932. The first commercial radio telephone service connects Honolulu and London; later the service is extended to principal European and South American countries. The Pineapple Research Institute is formed to carry on scientific programs to aid the industry. *Bufo marinus*, a large insect-eating toad, is imported from Puerto Rico to help control centipedes, scorpions, and other pests.

U.S. In November elections, Franklin Delano Roosevelt is overwhelmingly elected president. Amelia Earhart is the first woman to fly the Atlantic Ocean solo.

1933. U.S. Roosevelt launches the New Deal to fight for economic recovery. The prohibition amendment to the Constitution is repealed. The government of Soviet Russia is recognized by the United States. Thomas Hunt Morgan receives the Nobel prize for his work in physiology and medicine. *July 15–22*. Wiley Post pilots the first round-the-world solo flight.

1934. Passage by Congress of the Jones-Costigan Act protects mainland cane and beet production at the expense of foreign sugar growers and those of island possessions like Hawaii. Franklin D. Roosevelt visits Hawaii, first president to do so. Sir Charles Kingsford-Smith and Patrick Gordon Taylor fly a single-engine Lockheed Altair, *Lady Southern Cross*, leaving Brisbane, Australia, in mid-October and after stops in Fiji and Honolulu land in Oakland, California, having achieved the first eastbound flight from Hawaii to the mainland. The first mass flight from the mainland to Hawaii is made by United States Navy seaplanes. *March*. Joseph B. POINDEXTER is appointed eighth governor of Hawaii; he is re-appointed in April, 1938. *October 8*. Regular inter-island airmail service is inaugurated.

1935. The United States battle fleet conducts extensive maneuvers in Hawaiian waters. The first pay telephones are installed in public places. *January 11–12*. Amelia Earhart makes the first solo flight between Hawaii and the mainland, flying a single-engine Lockheed Vega monoplane from Wheeler Field, Oahu, to Oakland, California, airport. *April 16–17*. Pan American Airways Clipper makes first flight from Alameda, California, to Honolulu. *October*. A subcommittee of the House of Representatives Committee on Territories holds hearings in the islands and finds the territory "to be a modern unit of the American Commonwealth, with a political, social, and economic structure of the highest type," and recommends further study of qualifications for statehood. *November*. Mauna Loa erupts, producing a spectacular lava flow. *November 22–*

23. The first airmail flight linking the Pacific Coast and Hawaii takes place when Pan American Airways Martin M-130 four-engine flying boat, *China Clipper*, flies from Alameda, California, to Pearl Harbor; the next day it continues westward to Midway, Wake, Guam, and Manila.

U.S. Huey Long, United States senator from Louisiana, is assassinated.

1936. A party goes skiing on Mauna Kea at an elevation of 9,500 feet near Halepohaku.

1937. The passage of a favorable sugar act grants a quota to Hawaii as a domestic producer.

U.S. American gunboat *Panay* is sunk by invading Japanese forces on the Yangtze River in China. *May 6*. The German zeppelin *Hindenburg* crashes and is destroyed by fire at Lakehurst, New Jersey.

1938. Sporadic strikes in two previous years culminate in a shutdown of docks of the Inter-Island Steamship Company; more than twenty persons are hospitalized when violence breaks out on August 1.

1939. U.S. On outbreak of World War II, Roosevelt declares a limited emergency, submits a $1,319-million defense budget, and proclaims American neutrality. The New York World's Fair opens.

1940. The fifth federal census shows the island population to be 423,330. *Born in Paradise*, autobiography of Armine von TEMPSKI, is first published. *November*. A plebiscite at the general election results in a two-to-one vote favoring statehood.

U.S. The Selective Service Act is signed by President Roosevelt.

1941. Mabel SMYTH Building is opened near Queen's Hospital in Honolulu. *May 14*. Build-up of American air strength is marked by a flight of twenty-one Flying Fortresses from California to Hawaii. *November*. Lester PETRIE is elected mayor of the City and County of Honolulu and will serve for six years. *December 7*. An attack by Japanese planes on Pearl Harbor and other military installations in the islands plunges the United States into World War II; Army and Navy casualties reach 3,435, with 2,323 killed; civilian casualties reach about three hundred wounded and sixty killed. Governor POINDEXTER proclaims martial law and requests General Walter D. SHORT to take over all normal powers of the governor. The only combat against an armed enemy in the islands during World War II begins on the island of Niihau with the landing of a Japanese flyer who is later killed by unarmed Benehakaka KANAHELE. *December 17*. Chester W. NIMITZ succeeds Husband E. KIMMEL in command of the Pacific Fleet. *December 30*. Japanese submarines shell the ports of Hilo, Nawiliwili, and Kahului.

U. S. *December 8*. With only one dissenting vote, the Congress declares war on Japan. *December 11*. Germany and Italy declare war on the United States, which then recognizes a state of war with these Axis nations.

1942. *January 28*. The Army transport *Royal T. Frank* is torpedoed by a Japanese submarine in Hawaiian waters, with the loss of twenty-one lives. *March 2*. A single Japanese plane bombs Honolulu, increasing fears of invasion of the islands. *May 10*. A major eruption of Mauna Loa threatens defense facilities in Hilo, and Army planes seek to divert the lava flow by aerial bombing. *June 5*. Admiral NIMITZ announces a major defeat of the Japanese fleet at Battle of Midway. *Summer*. About thirteen hundred volunteer Americans of Japanese ancestry leave Hawaii for Camp McCoy, Wisconsin, to train as 100th Infantry Battalion for service in the war; nine months later this "Purple Heart Battalion" is incorporated into the 442nd Regimental Combat Team. *July 23*. Ingram M. STAINBACK is named ninth governor of the territory; he is reappointed on August 24, 1946.

U. S. The Declaration of the United Nations is signed in Washington, D. C.

1943. U. S. President Roosevelt freezes prices, salaries, and wages to prevent wartime inflation.

1944. *July 19*. The Democratic National Convention endorses statehood for Hawaii. *July 29*. President Roosevelt completes a five-day wartime visit to the islands. *October 24*. Martial law is terminated by presidential order.

U. S. Bretton Woods Conference creates International Monetary Fund and World Bank.

1945. *August 14*. News of atom bombing of Hiroshima and Nagasaki and imminent collapse of Japan's military forces arouses a spontaneous celebration of "V-J Day."

U. S. *May 7*. German forces surrender. San Francisco Conference in spring establishes United Nations. *September 2*. Japanese forces surrender.

1946. *January 7*. Another subcommittee of the House Committee on Territories, headed by Henry D. Larcade, Jr., holds hearings and recommends immediate consideration of legislation to admit Hawaii as a state; however, for the next decade the movement encounters opposition in the Senate. *February 25*. The Supreme Court of the United States

declares the reign of martial law in the territory to have been unconstitutional. *April 1*. A tsunami (seismic sea wave series) strikes early in the morning, and is the most destructive such disaster in island history, as well as one of the most violent. More than 150 persons are killed, principally by drowning, and at least 161 others are injured; property damage reaches about $25,000,000.

U. S. Winston Churchill, on a visit to the United States, gives "Iron Curtain" speech at Fulton, Missouri, warning of Soviet expansion.

1947. On the opening day of the Eightieth Congress, Delegate Joseph R. FARRINGTON introduces H. R. 49, designed to admit Hawaii as the Forty-ninth State. The Senate Committee on Interior and Insular Affairs investigation headed by Guy Cordon concludes that "Hawaii has met the requirements for statehood," but votes for further study. *June 30*. The House of Representatives votes out the statehood bill by a majority of 196 to 193, but the bill dies in the Senate.

U. S. The Marshall Plan is proposed, a co-ordinated program to help European nations recover from the ravages of World War II. *June*. The Taft-Hartley Act is passed by Congress over President Harry Truman's veto, giving greatly enlarged powers to the union labor movement.

1948. *February 2*. President Harry Truman endorses a Hawaiian statehood bill in his annual message to Congress.

U. S. The charter of the Organization of American States is signed.

1949. The legislature authorizes holding a constitutional convention in an effort to obtain statehood; the convention convenes on April 4, 1950, and the resulting constitution is ratified by voters by better than a three-to-one vote. *May 1*. A six-month strike by the International Longshoremen's and Warehousemen's Union led by Jack HALL begins and causes much hardship for island businessmen and consumers.

U. S. *April 4*. A pact setting up the North Atlantic Treaty Organization (NATO) is signed by twelve nations.

1950. The sixth federal census shows the island population to number 499,769. *March*. The House of Representatives passes a statehood enabling act by a majority of 262 to 110. On June 29 the Senate Committee on Interior and Insular Affairs reports favorably; however, the Korean conflict breaks out four days later and advocates of statehood must start from the beginning. *April 19*. The House Un-American Activities Committee concludes extended hearings in Honolulu on Communist domination of the labor movement; of sixty-eight witnesses called by the committee, thirty-nine refuse to testify on constitutional grounds.

U. S. North Korean Communists invade South Korea and President Truman orders American forces to the country under a United Nations call for a cease-fire. General Douglas MacArthur is designated commander of unified U. N. forces.

1951. Wartime novel, *From Here to Eternity*, by James JONES, is published.

U. S. Color-television reception is introduced in the nation.

1952. Both Republican and Democrat parties and their presidential candidates endorse statehood for Hawaii. Eligibility for citizenship is extended to Japanese, Koreans, and Samoans. *December 1*. Scheduled television broadcasting is inaugurated by KGMB-TV.

U. S. The Atomic Energy Commission announces "satisfactory" experiments in hydrogen-weapons research after explosions at Pacific island of Eniwetok.

1953. Jack HALL and six other defendants are convicted under the anti-Communist Smith Act. First frequency modulation radio stations KVOK and KAIM-FM, are licensed to broadcast.

U. S. General Dwight D. Eisenhower is inaugurated as president.

1954. *January 27*. The Senate Committee on Interior and Insular Affairs approves a statehood bill even though former Governor STAINBACK testifies that labor unions in the islands are infiltrated with Communists.

1955. *February 16*. A Hawaii-Alaska joint statehood bill passes the House Committee on Interior and Insular Affairs by a vote of 19 to 6; however, in May the House votes 218 to 170 to send the bill back to committee.

U. S. First atomic submarine, *Nautilus*, is launched. The Supreme Court unanimously bans racial segregation in public schools. A mass testing of the value of a vaccine for the prevention of polio shows that the research by Jonas Salk of New York was safe and highly effective.

1955. U. S. Two great labor unions, AFL and CIO, become one massive single organization.

1956. *December 7*. The Senate Internal Security Committee concludes a week of hearings in Honolulu with a statement that "conspiratorial forces" appear to control labor movement.

U. S. The first aerial hydrogen bomb is tested on Bikini Atoll, with an explosive equivalent of ten million tons of TNT.

1957. The Pacific armed forces of the United States are reorganized under centralized command of CINCPAC on Oahu, creating the largest single unified military command in the world, covering forty percent of the earth's surface. A statehood bill fails to pass Congress for the twenty-second time since 1903; in the closing weeks of the Eighty-fifth Congress, Alaska is voted into the union as a state, but action on Hawaii is delayed unti the following session. *May 5*. The first commercial color television broadcast, of color slides and films, is offered by KHVH-TV. *October 8*. The first submarine telephone cable connecting Hawaii and mainland is used to send a message to New York.

U. S. The Eisenhower Doctrine calls for aid to Mideast countries that resist armed aggression from Communist-controlled nations.

1958. *August*. Containerized cargo shipments begin on altered C-3 Matson freighters.

U. S. The Army's Jupiter-C rocket fires the first American earth satellite, *Explorer I*, into orbit.

1959. *STATEHOOD. March 11*. An enabling act granting statehood to Hawaii is passed by the Senate by a vote of 76 to 15 and by the House of Representatives on the 12th by a vote of 323 to 89. The act is made law when President Dwight D. Eisenhower signs it on March 18, provided a plebiscite of residents approves; approval comes on June 27 with a majority of seventeen to one. *July 28*. At the first general election, in which ninety-three percent of the registered voters cast ballots, a slate of officials is chosen to set up the Fiftieth State of the Union. Territorial governor William F. Quinn, Republican, is elected governor; Democrat Oren E. LONG and Republican Hiram L. Fong become the first senators, and the first Congressman is Daniel K. Inouye, Democrat. *July 29*. Commercial jet aircraft service is introduced to Hawaii when Qantas Empire Airways begins a route connecting Sydney, Nadi, Honolulu, and San Francisco, using Boeing 707 aircraft; on September 5, Pan American begins 707 service between the Pacific Coast and Tokyo via Honolulu and Wake island. *August 21*. President Eisenhower proclaims Admission Day and Governor Quinn takes the oath of office; a later law designated Admission Day as the third Friday in August. *August 31*. The first state legislature convenes in special session; it adjourns on October 22. *November 9*. The second special legistlative session convenes; it adjourns November 14.

U. S. The St. Lawrence Seaway is opened, allowed oceangoing ships to reach ports in the Midwest.

1960. The seventh federal census shows the island population as 609,096. Congress authorizes the creation of the Center for Cultural and Technical Interchange between East and West (East-West Center) at the University of Hawaii; grantees come from all fifty states of the Union and from twenty-six countries of Asia and the Pacific to obtain advanced education in Hawaii and travel on the mainland. *February 18.* The state legislature convenes in its first regular session; it adjourns May 2. *May 23.* Devastating tsunami waves strike the islands and kill fifty-seven persons; earthquakes rock the Puna district and an eruption pours lava on Kula subdivision. *July 4.* Hawaii's state flag becomes official and a fiftieth star is added to the American flag. *November.* The people of Hawaii have their first chance to vote for president of the United States; John F. Kennedy wins over Richard Nixon by a margin of 115 votes out of 184,705. All three Congressional incumbents are re-elected.

1961. *January 12.* Honolulu obtains a minor league professional baseball franchise from the Pacific Coast League; the first game under the franchise is played at Honolulu Stadium between the Hawaii Islanders and the Vancouver Mounties on April 20, and won by the Islanders, 4–3. *April 20.* The first cable television service is offered by Kaiser-Teleprompter. *June 25.* The Conference of State Governors holds its annual meeting in Honolulu. *July 1.* The two sections of Hawaii National Park become separate entitites, Hawaii Volcanoes National Park and Haleakala National Park; on the same day the National Park Service creates the City of Refuge National Historical Park at Kona.

U. S. The United States breaks diplomatic relations with the Communist government of Castro's Cuba. John F. Kennedy is inaugurated as president. The first American spaceman, Navy Commander Alan B. Shepard, Jr., is rocketed in 302-mile trip.

1962. *October 6.* Astronaut Walter M. Schirra, after circling the earth six times in Sigma 7 spacecraft, drops into the ocean 1,300 miles northwest of Honolulu; he is picked up by carrier *Kearsarge* and flown to Hickam Air Force Base before going on to the mainland. *November.* Governor Quinn is defeated by John A. BURNS. Daniel K. Inouye joins Hiram L. Fong as the first Senate members of Oriental ancestry. Reapportionment brings two seats in the House, which are filled by two Democrats, Thomas P. Gill and Spark M. Matsunaga. For the first time in history, Democrats control both houses of the legislature.

U. S. Lieutenant Colonel John H. Glenn, Jr. is the first American to orbit the earth.

1963. *June 9.* President John F. Kennedy addresses the National Conference of Mayors in Honolulu.

U. S. *November 22.* President Kennedy is shot and killed by a sniper in Dallas, Texas, and Vice President Lyndon B. Johnson is sworn in as his successor the same day.

1964. An undersea cable costing $84,000,000 begins operation between Hawaii and Tokyo. *November.* Senator Fong is elected to a full six-year term; Congressman Matsunaga is re-elected, and Patsy T. Mink becomes a member of the House.

U. S. The Supreme Court rules that Congressional districts should be roughly equal in population.

1965. The Vietnam conflict calls the 25th Division and the Marines to the Asian area. A proposed Kauai National Park arouses a mass of controversy.

U. S. Medicare, a government-sponsored medical assistance program for senior citizens, begins operations.

1966. *April 25.* The United States Supreme Court upholds Hawaii's reapportionment plan based on registered voters rather than population. *November 19.* Live television to and from the mainland is inaugurated when KHVH-TV uses the Lani Bird satellite to bring a football game to Hawaii.

1967. This becomes the first year during which one million tourists visit the islands.

U. S. Thurgood Marshall is sworn in as first black Supreme Court justice.

1968. Frank F. Fasi becomes mayor of the City and County of Honolulu for the first time, and the neighbor islands elect their first mayors. The legistature meets for the first time in the new Capitol building. *November 5.* A few changes in the Constitution of 1950 are ratified by the voters as a result of the second constitutional convention.

U. S. Senator Robert F. Kennedy is assassinated in a Los Angeles hotel after winning the California primary.

1969. *July 22.* The Civil Aeronautics Board awards domestic Pacific routes to seven airlines from Hawaii to thirty-five mainland cities. *July 26.* The first human beings returning from the moon, astronauts Neil A. Armstrong, Edwin E. Aldrin, Jr., and Michael Collins, arrive at Pearl Harbor aboard carrier *Hornet*, which had picked them up after splashdown of their Apollo 11 craft, *Columbia 3.*

U. S. Richard M. Nixon is inaugurated as the thirty-seventh president.

1970. Eighth federal census records island population to be 769,913.

U. S. Four students at Kent State University in Ohio are slain by National Guardsmen at a campus demonstration.

1971. Honolulu Rapid Transit, because of a labor dispute, is taken over by the City and County of Honolulu and operated as MTL, Inc.

U. S. Twenty-sixth Amendment to Constitution lowers voting age to eighteen years.

1972. Direct distance dialing permits callers to bypass long-distance operators on calls from Oahu to the rest of the world.

U. S. President Nixon makes an unprecedented visit to Communist China. Bobby Fischer becomes the first American world chess champion, defeating Boris Spassky of the U.S.S.R.

1973. *April 2*. Hawaii's teachers begin the nation's first statewide school strike in a dispute over pay and working conditions. *April 26*. Hilo suffers an earthquake causing $1,000,000 in damage. *September*. "Roll-on, roll-off" trailership service is introduced by Matson Navigation Co. with two ships, *Lurline* and *Matsonia*.

U. S. American bombing ends in Southeast Asia, marking the end of twelve years of combat against Vietnamese forces.

1974. The forty-year-old sugar act expires and prices soar from 11 cents a pound to 65.5 cents. Hawaii becomes the first state to impose limits on the sale of gasoline during a world shortage; the ban is ended on April 30. *August 12–16*. The American Bar Association holds its 97th annual convention in Honolulu.

November. George Ariyoshi is elected governor of Hawaii as a Democrat.

U. S. Under threat of impeachment by the House of Representatives, Nixon resigns as president, the first American to do so. Vice President Gerald R. Ford is sworn in as successor.

1975. *July 6*. The Civil Aeronautics Board and the Ford Administration approve the transfer of mainland-Hawaii flights from Trans-World Airlines to Pan-American. *June 15*. Sea Flite makes its first scheduled inter-island passenger trip by hydrofoil with the 45-knot *Kamehameha*, but service is discontinued on January 15, 1978.

U. S. *Apollo* and *Soyuz* spacecraft achieve first international link-up beyond earth's atmosphere.

1976. Hawaii takes part in the national American Bicentennial celebrations and carries out numerous projects to commemorate the signing of the Declaration of Independence. The sailing craft *Hokulea* makes a voyage to Tahiti and return to recall the days of Polynesian canoe travel. Hawaiian activists begin efforts to obtain release of the island of Kahoolawe from Navy use. *November*. Senators from Hawaii are Daniel K. Inouye and Spark M. Matsunaga and representatives are Cecil Heftel and Daniel K. Akaka, first Congressman of Hawaiian ancestry.

U. S. America celebrates widely the bicentennial of independence. In autumn elections, Jimmy Carter is named president.

1977. *September 13*. Kilauea, the world's most active volcano, begins to erupt and continues intermittent outbursts until September 28.

U. S. A nuclear-proliferation pact to curb spread of atomic weapons is signed by fifteen countries, including the United States and Soviet Russia.

1978. Hawaii celebrates the bicentennial of the arrival of Captain James COOK and two British ships. *July 5*. The third constitutional convention since the first in 1950 is convened; a ninety-day session produces numerous proposals, all of which are ratified by voters in the November elections. *November*. George Ariyoshi wins a second term as governor and state senator Jean Sadako King becomes the first woman lieutenant governor in the history of the state.

U. S. The Senate approves a Panama Canal neutrality treaty and votes to turn over the canal to the Republic of Panama by the year 2000.

1979. Hawaii celebrates its twentieth anniversary of statehood twenty years before the last year of the twentieth century. Despite a strike against United Airlines and grounding of DC-10 planes because of safety problems, almost four million visitors come to Hawaii. *October*. Many international dignitaries attend the dedication of one of the largest infrared telescopes in the world, joining other observatories atop Mauna Kea on the Big Island, where clear skies advance astronomical research. *October 21*. A forty-one-day strike by the lowest-paid unit of the United Public Workers begins and lasts until December 3. *November*. The fiftieth anniversary of inauguration of the first inter-island air service is celebrated.

U. S. Carter and Leonid Brezhnev sign a SALT II agreement to limit the superpower arms race. Spacecraft *Pioneer II* gets the first close photographs of the planet Saturn.

1980. A new decade opens as residents of the Hawaiian Islands look toward their third century of challenges in the circle of nations.

U.S. The Federal government creates a forty-million-acre wildlife refuge in Alaska. In autumn elections, Ronald Reagan gains the presidency in a Republican sweep.

HEADS OF GOVERNMENT IN THE HAWAIIAN ISLANDS 1795–1980

1. Native Monarchs

NAME	BIRTH	ACCESSION	DEATH
Kamehameha I	c. 1758	1795	May 8, 1819
Kamehameha II (Liholiho)	1797	May 20, 1819	July 14, 1824
Kamehameha III (Kauikeaouli)	March 17, 1814	June 6, 1825	Dec. 15, 1854
Kamehameha IV (Alexander Liholiho)	Feb. 9, 1834	Dec. 15, 1854	Nov. 30, 1863
Kamehameha V (Lot Kamehameha)	Dec. 11, 1830	Nov. 30, 1863	Dec. 11, 1872
William C. Lunalilo	Jan. 31, 1835	Jan. 8, 1873	Feb. 3, 1874
David Kalakaua	Nov. 16, 1836	Feb. 13, 1874	Jan. 20, 1891
Liliuokalani	Sept. 2, 1838	Jan. 29, 1891	Nov. 11, 1917

Liliuokalani was deposed and the Hawaiian Kingdom came to an end on January 17, 1893.

Officers and retainers of the Royal Court.

2. *President of Provisional Government*

NAME	TERM BEGAN	TERM ENDED
Sanford B. Dole	Jan. 17, 1893	July 4, 1894

3. *President of Republic of Hawaii*

Sanford B. Dole	July 4, 1894	June 14, 1900

Hawaii was annexed to the United States on August 12, 1898, but the territorial government was not established until June 14, 1900.

4. *Governors of Territory of Hawaii*

NAME	APPOINTED BY PRESIDENT	TERM ENDED
Sanford B. Dole	McKinley	Nov. 23, 1903
George R. Carter	T. Roosevelt	Aug. 15, 1907
Walter F. Frear	T. Roosevelt	Nov. 29, 1913
Lucius E. Pinkham	Wilson	June 22, 1918
Charles J. McCarthy	Wilson	July 5, 1921
Wallace R. Farrington	Harding	July 5, 1925
(second term)	Coolidge	July 5, 1929
Lawrence M. Judd	Hoover	March 1, 1934
Joseph B. Poindexter	F. D. Roosevelt	April 2, 1938
(second term)	F. D. Roosevelt	Aug. 24, 1942
Ingram M. Stainback	F. D. Roosevelt	Aug. 24, 1946
(second term)	Truman	April 30, 1951
Oren E. Long	Truman	Feb. 28, 1953
Samuel Wilder King	Eisenhower	Sept. 2, 1957
William F. Quinn	Eisenhower	Aug. 21, 1959

5. *Governors of State of Hawaii*

NAME	TERM BEGAN	TERM ENDED
William F. Q	August, 1959	December, 1962
John A. Burns	December, 1962	November, 1974
George Ariyoshi	November, 1974	

APPENDIX IV

TERRITORIAL DELEGATES TO CONGRESS

1900–1902	Robert W. Wilcox, Home Rule
1902–1922	Jonah Kuhio Kalanianaole, Republican
1922–1923	Henry A. Baldwin, Republican (unexpired term)
1923–1927	William P. Jarrett, Democrat
1927–1933	Victor S. K. Houston, Republican
1933–1935	Lincoln Loy McCandless, Democrat
1935–1943	Samuel Wilder King, Republican
1943–1954	Joseph R. Farrington, Republican
1954	Elizabeth P. Farrington, Republican (unexpired term)
1954–1957	Elizabeth P. Farrington
1957–1959	John A. Burns, Democrat (to coming of statehood)

APPENDIX V

CONGRESSIONAL SENATORS AND REPRESENTATIVES, 1960–1980

SENATE

Oren E. Long	1960–1962
Hiram L. Fong	1960–1976
Daniel K. Inouye	1962–
Spark M. Matsunaga	1976–

HOUSE OF REPRESENTATIVES

Daniel K. Inouye	1960–1962
Spark M. Matsunaga	1962–1976
Thomas P. Gill	1962–1964
Patsy T. Mink	1964–1976
Daniel K. Akaka	1976–
Cecil Heftel	1976–

Officers of the Provisional Government of Hawaii after the overthrow of the Monarchy and shortly before the establishment of the short-lived Republic which was followed by U.S. Annexation. Shown here are (l. to r.), James A. King, Sanford B. Dole (president of the Republic and first Territorial governor), William O. Smith and Peter C. Jones.

STATIONS AND MISSIONARIES

Names listed approximately in order of their first arrival at the station, based on lists in the American Board annual reports, minutes of the General Meetings and manuscript letters in the Hawaiian Mission Children's Society.

KAUAI *Waimea—Established 1820*
Samuel Whitney
Samuel Ruggles
Artemas Bishop
Peter J. Gulick
Maria Ogden
Maria K. Whitney

OAHU *Honolulu—Established 1820*
Hiram Bingham
Elisha Loomis
Daniel Chamberlain
Asa Thurston
Abraham Blatchely
Levi Chamberlain
Joseph Goodrich
Ephraim W. Clark
Gerrit P. Judd
Stephen Shepard
Mary Ward
Reuben Tinker
Andrew Johnston
Edmund Rogers
Lemuel Fuller
John Diell
Henry Dimond
Edwin O. Hall

MOLOKAI *Kaluaaha—Established 1832*
Harvey R. Hitchcock
Richard Armstrong
Lowell Smith

MAUI *Lahaina—Established 1823*
William Richards
Charles S. Stewart
Betsey Stockton
Lorrin Andrews
Maria Patton
Maria Ogden
Jonathan Green
Reuben Tinker
Stephen Shepard
Mary Ward
Ephraim W. Spaulding
Alonzo Chapin
Dwight Baldwin
Charles McDonald
Cochran Forbes
Townsend E. Taylor
Sereno E. Bishop

George B. Rowell
Koloa—Established 1834
Peter J. Gulick
Thomas Lafon
Reuben Tinker
Marcia Smith
James W. Smith

Lowell Smith
Samuel N. Castle
Amos S. Cooke
Horton O. Knapp
Richard Armstrong
Peter J. Gulick
Samuel C. Damon
William H. Rice
Timothy D. Hunt
Townsend E. Taylor
Artemas Bishop
Henry H. Parker
John F. Pogue
Anderson O. Forbes
Oliver P. Emerson
John Leadingham
Punahou School—
Established 1841
Daniel Dole

Elizabeth Hitchcock
Bethuel Munn
Lydia Brown
Peter J. Gulick

Lahainaluna School—
Established 1831
Lorrin Andrews
Mary Ward
Ephraim W. Clark
Edmund H. Rogers
Sheldon Dibble
Lucia G. Smith
Horton O. Knapp
Edward Bailey
John S. Emerson
William P. Alexander
Timothy D. Hunt
Claudius B. Andrews
John F. Pogue
Henry H. Parker
Sereno E. Bishop
Anderson O. Forbes

John F. Pogue
Daniel Dole
Waioli—Established 1834
William P. Alexander
Edward Johnson
George B. Rowell
Abner Wilcox

Marcia Smith
William H. Rice
Maria Ogden
Waialua—Established 1832
John S. Emerson
Ephraim W. Clark
Edwin Locke
George B. Rowell
Asa B. Smith
Abner Wilcox
Peter J. Gulick
Kaneohe—Established 1834
Benjamin W. Parker
Marcia M. Smith
Ewa—Established 1834
Lowell Smith
Artemas Bishop
William S. Van Duzee

Claudius B. Andrews
Samuel G. Dwight
Anderson O. Forbes

Wailuku—Established 1832
Jonathan S. Green
Reuben Tinker
Richard Armstrong
Lydia Brown
Maria Ogden
Edward Bailey
Ephraim W. Clark
Daniel T. Conde
William P. Alexander
John F. Pogue
Hana—Established 1837
Daniel T. Conde
Mark Ives
William H. Rice
Eliphalet W. Whittlesey
William O. Baldwin
Sereno E. Bishop

HAWAII   *Kailua—Established 1820*
        Asa Thurston
        Thomas Holman
        Artemas Bishop
        James Ely
        Delia Stone
        Seth L. Andrews
    Hilo—Established 1824
        Joseph Goodrich
        Samuel Ruggles
        Sheldon Dibble
        Jonathan S. Green
        David B. Lyman

    Titus Coan
    Abner Wilcox
    Charles H. Wetmore
Kaawaloa—Established 1824
    James Ely
    Samuel Ruggles
    Cochran Forbes
    William S. Van Duzee
    Mark Ives
    John F. Pogue
    John D. Paris
Waimea—Established 1832
    Dwight Baldwin

    Lorenzo Lyons
    Horton O. Knapp
Kohala—Established 1837
    Edward Bailey
    Isaac Bliss
    Elias Bond
Waiohino—Established 1841
    John D. Paris
    Timothy D. Hunt
    Henry Kinney
    William C. Shipman
    Orramel H. Gulick
    John F. Pogue

Source: *Missionary Album: Sesquicentennial Edition* (Honolulu: Hawaiian Mission Children's Society, 1969), p. 16.
Reprinted by permission.

Queen Kaahumanu listens to a sermon by Hiram Bingham at Waimea, Oahu, in 1826.

MAYORS OF COUNTIES, STATE OF HAWAII

City and County of Honolulu	Term Begins
Joseph James Fern	January 4, 1909
John Carey Lane	January 4, 1915
Joseph James Fern	July 2, 1917
John Henry Wilson	February 25, 1920
Charles N. Arnold	January 2, 1927
John Henry Wilson	January 2, 1929
George Fred Wright	January 2, 1931
Charles Spencer Crane	July 15, 1938
Lester Petrie	January 2, 1941
John Henry Wilson	January 2, 1947
Neal Shaw Blaisdell	January 2, 1955
Frank Francis Fasi	January 2, 1969
Eileen Anderson	January 2, 1982

Hawaii County

Shunichi Kimura	1969
Herbert Tatsuo Matayoshi	1974

Kauai County

Antone K. Vidinha	1969
Francis M. F. Ching	1972
Eduardo E. Malapit	1974
Tony Kunimura	1982

Maui County

Elmer Franklin Cravalho	1969
Hannibal Tavares	1979

APPENDIX VIII

PRESIDENTS OF THE UNIVERSITY OF HAWAII, 1907–1984

The College of Hawaii became the University of Hawaii in 1920.

Willis T. Pope, 1907–1908 (acting)
John W. Gilmore, 1908–1913
John S. Donaghho, 1913–1914 (acting)
Arthur L. Dean, 1914–1927
David L. Crawford, 1927–1941
Arthur R. Keller, 1941–1942 (acting)
Gregg M. Sinclair, 1942–1955
Paul S. Bachman, 1955–1957
Willard Wilson, 1957–1958 (acting)
Laurence H. Snyder, 1958–1963
Thomas H. Hamilton, 1963–1968
Robert W. Hiatt, 1968–1969 (acting)
Richard S. Takasaki, 1969 (acting)
Harlan Cleveland, 1969–1974
Fujio Matsuda, 1974–1984

SELECTED GENERAL REFERENCES

ALEXANDER, WILLIAM D. *History of the Later Years of the Hawaiian Monarchy and the Revolution of 1893*. Honolulu: Gazette, 1896.

ABRAMSON, JOAN. *Photographers of Old Hawaii*. Norfolk Island, Australia: Island Heritage, 1976.

Artists of Hawaii. Vol. I. Photographs by Francis Haar; interviews by Prithwish Neogy; introduction by Jean Charlot. Honolulu: University Press of Hawaii with the State Foundation of Culture and the Arts, 1974. Vol. II. Photographs and interviews by Francis Haar; edited by Murray Turnbull. Same, 1977.

BAILEY, PAUL. *Those Kings and Queens of Old Hawaii: A Mele to Their Memory*. Los Angeles: Westernlore Books, 1975.

BARRÈRE, DOROTHY B. *Kamehameha in Kona: Two Documentary Studies*. Pacific Anthropological Records No. 23. Honolulu: Bernice P. Bishop Museum, 1975.

BECKWITH, MARTHA. *Hawaiian Mythology*. New Haven, Conn.: Yale University Press, 1940; Honolulu: University of Hawaii Press, 1970.

_____ . *The Kumulipo: A Hawaiian Creation Chant*. Chicago: University of Chicago Press, 1951; Honolulu: University Press of Hawaii, 1972.

BINGHAM, HIRAM. *A Residence of Twenty-one Years in the Sandwich Islands*. New York: Sherman Converse, 1847.

BRADLEY, HAROLD W. *The American Frontier in Hawaii: The Pioneers, 1789–1843*. Palo Alto, Calif.: Stanford University Press, 1942.

CONROY, HILARY. *The Japanese Frontier in Hawaii*. Berkeley: University of California Press, 1953.

CURTIS, CAROLINE. *Builders of Hawaii*. Honolulu: Kamehameha Schools Press, 1966.

DAWS, GAVAN. *Shoal of Time: A History of the Hawaiian Islands*. New York: Macmillan, 1968; Honolulu: University Press of Hawaii, 1974.

DAY, A. GROVE. *Hawaii and Its People*. New York: Duell, Sloan &Pearce, 1955, 1960, 1969.

DIBBLE, SHELDON, *A History and General Views of the Sandwich Islands Mission*. New York: Taylor & Dodd, 1839.

EMERSON, NATHANIEL B. *Pele and Hiiaka*. Honolulu: Star-Bulletin, 1915.

FEHER, JOSEPH. *Hawaii: A Pictorial History*. Honolulu: Bishop Museum Press, 1969. Text by O. A. Bushnell and Edward Joesting.

FORNANDER, ABRAHAM. *Collection of Hawaiian Antiquities and Folklore*. Translation revised and illustrated with notes by T. G. Thrum. Honolulu: Bernice P. Bishop Museum, Memoirs, 1916–1920.

GALLAGHER, CHARLES F. *Hawaii and Its Gods*. Foreword by O. A. Bushnell. New York: Weatherhill/Kapa, 1975.

GIBBS, JIM. *Shipwrecks in Paradise*. Seattle, Wash.: Superior, 1977.

HALEOLE, S. N. *The Hawaiian Romance of Laieikawai*. Translated by Martha Beckwith. Washington, D.C.: 33rd Annual Report, Bureau of American Ethnology, 1911–1912, 1918.

Hawaiian Journal of History. Honolulu: Hawaiian Historical Society, 1967—. See also

Hawaiian Historical Review: Selected Readings, ed. Richard A. Greer, Honolulu: Hawaiian Historical Society, 1969.

II, JOHN PAPA. *Fragments of Hawaiian History*. Honolulu: Bishop Museum Press, 1959.

Index to the Honolulu Advertiser and Honolulu Star-Bulletin, 1929—. Honolulu: Hawaiian and Pacific Section, Hawaii State Library.

JARVES, JAMES. J. *The History of the Hawaiian or Sandwich Islands*. Boston: Tappan & Dennet, 1843; London: E. Moxon, 1843.

JENNINGS, HELEN. *Chronology and Documentary Handbook of the State of Hawaii*. Dobbs Ferry, N.Y.: Oceana Publications, 1978.

JOESTING, EDWARD. *Hawaii, an Uncommon History*. New York: W. W. Norton, 1972.

JUDD, BERNICE. *Voyages to Hawaii before 1860*. Honolulu: Hawaiian Mission Children's Society, 1929; rev. ed. (with Helen Y. Lind), Honolulu: University Press of Hawaii, 1973.

JUDD, GERRIT P. IV. *Hawaii: an Informal History*. New York: Crowell-Collier, 1961.

KAMAKAU, SAMUEL M. *Ka Po'e Kahiko: The People of Old*. Translated by Mary K. Pukui; edited by Dorothy B. Barrère. Honolulu: Bernice P. Bishop Museum, Special Publication No. 51, 1964.

_____ . *Ruling Chiefs of Hawaii*. Honolulu: Kamehameha Schools Press, 1961.

_____ . *The Works of the People of Old: Na Hana a Ka Po'e Kahiko*. Translated by Mary K. Pukui; edited by Dorothy B. Barrère. Honolulu: Bernice P. Bishop Museum, Special

Publication No. 61, 1976. A sequel to *Ka Poʻe Kahiko: The People of Old.*

KANAHELE, GEORGE S. *Hawaiian Music and Musicians.* Honolulu: University Press of Hawaii, 1979.

KEPELINO KEAUOKALANI [ZEPHRYIN]. *Traditions of Hawaii.* Honolulu: Bishop Museum Press, 1932.

KORN, ALFONS L. *The Victorian Visitors.* Honolulu: University of Hawaii Press, 1958.

KUYKENDALL, RALPH S. *The Hawaiian Kingdom.* Vol. I: *Foundation and Transformation.* Honolulu: University of Hawaii Press, 1938, 1947. Vol. II: *Twenty Critical Years.* Honolulu: same, 1953. Vol. III. *The Kalakaua Dynasty.* Honolulu: same, 1967.

KUYKENDALL, RALPH S., and A. GROVE DAY. *Hawaii: A History.* New York: Prentice-Hall, 1948, 1961, 1976.

LEADERS OF HAWAII. Louisville, Ky.: Senecal, 1983.

LEE, W. STORRS. *The Islands.* New York: Holt, 1966.

LEIB, AMOS P. and A. GROVE DAY. *Hawaiian Legends in English: An Annotated Bibliography.* Honolulu: University of Hawaii Press, 1949; rev. ed., Honolulu: University Press of Hawaii, 1979.

LUOMALA, KATHARINE. *Voices on the Wind: Polynesian Myths and Chants.* Honolulu: Bishop Museum Press, 1955.

McKINZIE, EDITH, translator, and ISHMAEL W. STAGNER, editor. *Hawaiian Genealogies.* Vol. 1. Honolulu: University of Hawaii Press, 1983.

MALO, DAVID. *Hawaiian Antiquities.* Translated by Nathaniel B. Emerson. Honolulu: Gazette, 1903, 1951, 1971.

Men of Hawaii: A Biographical Reference Library. Honolulu: Star-Bulletin, 1917—. In 1954 the name was changed to *Men and Women of Hawaii.* Of special interest is *Builders of Hawaii,* which incorporates *Men of Modern Hawaii,* 1925.

Missionary Album. Honolulu: Hawaiian Mission Children's Society, 1901, 1937, 1969. The 1901 title was *Portraits of American Protestant Missionaries to Hawaii.*

MULHOLLAND, JOHN F. *Hawaii's Religions.* Honolulu: Kamehameha Schools, 1961; rev. ed., *Religion in Hawaii,* Rutland, Vt. and Tokyo: Tuttle, 1970.

MULLINS, JOSEPH G. *Hawaiian Journey.* Honolulu: Mutual, 1978.

PETERSON, BARBARA. *Notable Women of Hawaii.* Honolulu: University Press of Hawaii, 1984.

PIERCE, RICHARD A. *Russia's Hawaiian Adventure, 1815–1817.* Berkeley: University of California Press, 1965.

PUKUI, MARY K., and SAMUEL H. ELBERT. *Hawaiian Dictionary.* Honolulu: University Press of Hawaii, 1971.

PUKUI, MARY K., SAMUEL H. ELBERT, and ESTHER MOOKINI. *Place Names of Hawaii.* Honolulu: University Press of Hawaii, 1974.

RICE, WILLIAM HYDE. *Hawaiian Legends.* Honolulu: Bishop Museum Bulletin No. 3, 1923.

RICHARDS, MARY ATHERTON, ed. *The Chiefs' Children's School.* Honolulu: Star-Bulletin, 1937.

RUSS, WILLIAM A. *The Hawaiian Revolution, 1893–94.* Selinsgrove, Penna.: Susquehanna University Press, 1959.

SCHMITT, ROBERT C. "Some Firsts in Island Leisure." *Hawaiian Journal of History,* 12 (1978), 99–119.

—————. "Some Transportation and Communication Firsts in Hawaii." same, 13 (1979), 99–123.

SCOTT, EDWARD B. *The Saga of the Sandwich Islands.* Lake Tahoe, Nev.: Sierra-Tahoe, 1968.

SIMPICH, FREDERICK, Jr. *Anatomy of Hawaii.* New York: Coward, McCann & Geoghegan, 1971.

SMITH, BRADFORD. *Yankees in Paradise: The New England Impact on Hawaii.* Philadelphia and New York: Lippincott, 1956.

STEVENS, SYLVESTER K. *American Expansion in Hawaii, 1842–1898.* Harrisburg, Penna.: Archives, 1945; New York: Russell & Russell, 1968.

TAYLOR, FRANK J., EARL M. WELTY, and DAVID W. EYRE. *From Land and Sea: The Story of Castle & Cooke of Hawaii.* San Francisco: Chronicle Books, 1976.

THRUM, THOMAS G. *Hawaiian Folk Tales: A Collection of Native Legends.* Chicago: A. C. McClurg, 1907.

TODARO, TONY. *The Golden Years of Hawaiian Entertainment, 1874–1894.* Honolulu: the author, 1974.

WIST, BENJAMIN C. *A Century of Public Education in Hawaii.* Honolulu: Hawaii Educational Review, 1940.

WITHINGTON, ANTOINETTE. *The Golden Cloak.* Honolulu: Hawaiiana Press, 1953.

Women of Hawaii. Ed. George F. Nellist. Honolulu: Paradise of the Pacific, 1929.

YOUNG, NANCY FOON, and JUDY R. PARRISH. *Montage: An Ethnic History of Women in Hawaii.* Honolulu: University of Hawaii, College of Education, 1977.

YZENDOORN, REGINALD. *History of the Catholic Mission in the Hawaiian Islands.* Honolulu: Star-Bulletin, 1927.